W9-BZU-712

8TH EDITION • 2006-2010

THE BOOK OF
U.S. POSTAL
EXAMS

How to Score 95-100% on 473/473-C/460 Tests and Other Exams

VELTISEZAR B. BAUTISTA

BOOKHAUS PUBLISHERS

Publisher's Cataloging-in-Publication

(Provided by Quality Books, Inc.)

Bautista, Veltisezar B., 1933-

The book of U.S. postal exams : how to score 95-100%

on 473/473-C/460 tests and other exams / Veltisezar B.

Bautista. -- 8th ed., 2006-2010.

p. cm.

LCCN 2006900804

ISBN 0-931613-20-5

1. Postal service--United States--Examinations,

questions, etc. 2. Civil service--United States--

Examinations--Study guides. 3. Postal service--United

States--Employees. I. Title.

HE6499.B38 2006 383'.145'076

QBI06-600043

Printed in the United States of America

Bookhaus Publishers
P.O. Box 836
Warren, Michigan 48090-0836
U.S.A.

Dedication

I dedicate this book to the light of my life,
Genoveva Abes-Bautista;
to my beloved children,
Hubert, Lester, Melvin, Ronald, and Janet;
to my daughter-in-law,
Maria Cecilia Asi-Bautista;
and to all job seekers who will read this book.

A Special Reminder: You now have in your possession a complete guide to scoring 95-100% on Post Office exams. The book covers exams for clerk-carrier, rural carrier, rural carrier associate, mail handler, mail processor, clerk-typist, clerk-stenographer, mark-up clerk, distribution clerk, flat sorting machine, operator, stationary engineer, electronics technician, garageman, and many more, making it the only book of its kind in the world.

The book is written in simple, easy-to-understand English. It covers in detail all the Postal exams and goings-on in the U.S. Postal Service. The book gives straight-to-the-point instructions that you can easily follow.

You can use this book as a reference not only for postal exams but also for civil service exams, so let it be a useful tool for you in this land of the survival of the fittest.

With this book, you'll know my test-taking secrets. Keep the secrets to yourself, and you and your family will always have the edge in competing for high-paying Postal jobs.

Similarities between characters in this book and persons living or dead are intentional, and not coincidental, for they are Real People like you!

Good luck!—The Author

Table of Contents

Acknowledgment

About the Author

Foreword

Foreword

You Can Pass ANY Post Office Exam with Flying Colors—and Get a $35,000 Job!

I know the above is a **bold** statement.

But it's 100% true.

You can get that job with the Post Office and make $35,000 a year. But first you have to pass the required examination, and this is what stops most people.

Here's why:
Although 70% is a passing score you want to make 90 to 100% because the Post Office usually hires people who score in that range. To make a high score, you need to know certain tricks of the trade.

First, let me emphasize one point:

I'm not basing my knowledge on hearsay. I'm based it on my own practical experience in taking these exams. I don't brag, but I've been among the top scorers on postal exams. As a result of my hands-on-experience, I've put all the tricks of the trade, ins and outs, tips, strategies and secrets into one power-packed book called The Book of U.S. Postal Exams: How to Score 95-100% on 473/473-C/460 Tests and Other Exams, now on its 8th edition.

But before you read the book from cover to cover, let's see what life is like for a Postal Service employee.

One word describes it: tremendous! Did you know that postal jobs are recession-proof? As inflation rises, your cost-of-living allowance rises too. It's automatically added to your salary. (How many jobs in business give you this benefit?)

But that's not all--far from it.

The pay is high (the average postal employee makes $35,000 a year).

The fringe benefits are sensational. Retirement income is great. You have freedom from layoffs. In short, you've got *lifetime financial security.*

What's more, there's no age limit. As long as you're at least 18, you can take any exam and compete with people in their 40s and 50s. It's not your age or experience or education that counts. The only thing that matters is *the score you make on the exam. Period.*

Take education, for example.

I've known college-educated people who made low scores on the exam. Were they selected? No, indeed. The jobs went to high school graduates who managed a score between 90% and 100%. I can't emphasize enough how important that score is.

Making a good grade on the exam is as easy as falling off a log backwards -- *if you know how.*

Let me assure you that with my book, you'll go into any exam with all the confidence in the world. You'll already know beforehand what to expect. You'll know how to take the test. You'll know how to make that 95 to 100%.

Employment hinges on one thing and one thing only: *how well you do on the exam.*

This rule is strictly enforced with no ifs, ands, or buts. You could have a Ph.D. and still not be hired if you didn't come through on the exam. It doesn't matter whether you're a United States citizen or a permanent resident alien, man or woman, black or white, brown or yellow; you name it. *It's your exam score that counts.*

As I've said so many times, making a high score is essential.

This book is based on my success and on the systems I've worked out.

In fact, Susan L. Lindeman, Notary Public, Wayne County, Michigan, certifies that my scores on postal exams have been 78.5%, 88.5%, 95.8%, 99%, and 100's.

Notice how the scores have gone up and up--because I worked out sure-fire, can't fail systems; the very systems I want to share with you now. Use them and you can't fail!

Veltisezar B. Bautista
Author

The U.S. Postal Service   1
A Short History of the U.S. Postal System

More than three hundred years ago, in 1657 to be exact, the Post Office of England was established as a government entity. In the same year, the Colonial Court of Virginia required every tobacco planter to convey official mail dispatches to the next plantation. This action became the first move in the colonies to transport mail from one locality to another. This service, however, was intended only for official mail. Another four years passed before the Virginia assembly required planters to forward "all letters superscribed for the service of His Majesty or publique," or to pay a fine of 350 pounds of tobacco. This step opened the service to all people in the colony.

Today, the U.S. Postal Service, a semiprivate corporation but still considered a federal agency, remains the giant in US civilian employment. Compared to previous years' employment of more than 660,000, the USPS now employs more than 900,000. The number of employees rose to this number with the hiring of a variety of categories of temporary employees. These temporary workers, many of whom are considered as not temps, number more than 186,000. They include the part-time flexible, part-time regular, and transitional employees or workers. The new employees are replacements of those who die or retire or workers who fill new positions created by expansion.

Scheduled Postal Service

Way back in 1672, the first serious attempt was made to establish scheduled postal service between several of the northern colonies. Francis Lovelace, the governor of New York, directed a man to carry letters monthly on horseback between New York and Boston. Then in 1692 Great Britain established the first national postal system for the American colonies. In 1753, Britain appointed Benjamin Franklin, then postmaster of Philadelphia, as a deputy postmaster general for all the colonies. In 1774, however, Franklin was removed from his post because of his questionable allegiance to the Crown.

New U.S. Postal System

After the colonies severed their ties to England in 1775, the Continental Congress established its own postal system and appointed Franklin as its head. On February 20, 1792, the U.S. Congress authorized the Post Office as a permanent government agency. By 1794 Congress had authorized the hiring of letter carriers and paid them a two-cent fee for every letter delivered to a business firm.

Then in 1825 the name Post Office Department acquired official sanction. In that year, Congress also authorized the delivery of mail to private homes. The carriers, however, were paid not by the government but by the addressees.

Pony Express

The famous Pony Express was established on April 3, 1860. A private postal and express system, the service ran between St. Joseph, Missouri and San Francisco, via Sacramento. Horses, running in relays at 190 stations along the 2,000-mile route, took eight to ten days to complete the delivery route. The Pony Express met its demise when telegraph lines were established between the east and the west.

By 1861 President Abraham Lincoln's postmaster general, Montgomery Blair, had introduced free city delivery, postal money orders, and railway post offices. In 1862 the first railway post office began to operate in the United States. In the 1880's the government added more postal services and established more railroad post offices.

New Services

In 1953 air mail service was begun; in 1955 the certified mail service was established. On June 30, 1971 the name of U.S. Post Office Department was changed to U.S. Postal Service. The Service became independent and is no longer supervised by the Office of Personnel Management (OPM), formerly the Civil Service Commission. Its head is still called the Postmaster General, but he is not a member of the President's Cabinet. Over 25 percent of all federal employees are paid under the coordinated Federal Wage Board System, but postal workers are paid according to wage schedules set under the Postal Pay Act.

Pay Rates

At present, the Postal Service pay scale consists of several rate schedules. These schedules cover different types and levels of postal employees such as technical, clerical, production, supervisory, mail carriers, and executive management. Pay schedules provide periodic paid cost-of-living adjustments (COLA). When inflation rises, postal COLA rises, too.

When a man or woman is hired as a postal employee, he or she may join the American Postal Workers Union (APWU), the largest postal union in the world, the National Association of Letter Carriers, or one of other post office unions.

Who Can Apply for Exams?

Qualification and Physical Requirements

Age Requirements

"The general minimum age requirement for positions in the Postal Service," according to the United States Postal Service, "is 18 at the time of employment." For high school graduates or for persons certified by local authorities as having terminated formal education for adequate reasons, the minimum age is 16. Applicants who are less than 18 years of age, who are not high school graduates, and have not terminated formal education, may participate in the examination if they will reach 18 within two years from the date of examination. For carrier positions which require driving, applicants must be 18 years of age or over. There is no maximum age limit."

If you are 18 years old and if you're really ambitious, you might already be a supervisor when you reach 30 or 35.

Citizenship

"All applicants must be citizens of or owe allegiance to the United States of America, or have been granted permanent resident alien status in the United States."

Whether you are from the Philippines, Haiti, or Nicaragua, provided you are an immigrant with permanent resident alien status, you are eligible to take a postal exam and to be employed with the USPS.

Qualification Requirements

Many positions, such as clerk and carrier, require passing an entrance exam; but some do not. To be a plumber, a machinist, or a maintenance mechanic, you have to pass a written exam. Your rating will be based both on the written test and on your qualifications. But you don't need to pass a written exam, for example, if you're a physician, a nurse, a psychologist, or a computer programmer. Your rating on these jobs will be based on your education, training, and experience. On the written tests, the passing score is 70 (excluding the extra five or 10 points for applicants entitled to veteran preference.)

Educational Requirements

The U.S. Postal Service does not indicate that you must be a high school graduate to be eligible for any position. So unless it is stated specifically that you need a college degree to be qualified for a certain position, such as a doctor, a nurse, or an engineer, you will be considered for any position if you meet the requirements and win over other competitors.

Physical Requirements

Applicants must be physically able to perform efficiently the arduous duties of any position. For instance, the physical requirements for a carrier are different from those for a maintenance electrician. The carrier must be able to carry a load of 70 pounds and must be on the road in all conditions. The electrician must be able to perform the duties of the position, which may involve standing, walking, climbing, bending, reaching, and stooping for prolonged periods of time as well as intermittent lifting and carrying of heavy tools, tool boxes, and equipment on level surfaces and up ladders and stairways.

All applicants who will be called for employment must undergo a thorough physical examination, including eye and ear tests. The Post Offices does not care whether you're the size of Tinker Belle or Mr. T.

Like your car, you should always be in top condition. No matter how cold or how hot it is, your own engine must be on the go as soon as you turn the ignition key. Your body must be in good condition to withstand the conditions of the roads and the climate. Whether you are a carrier or clerk, you must be healthy enough to carry a load of mail weighing up to 70 pounds.

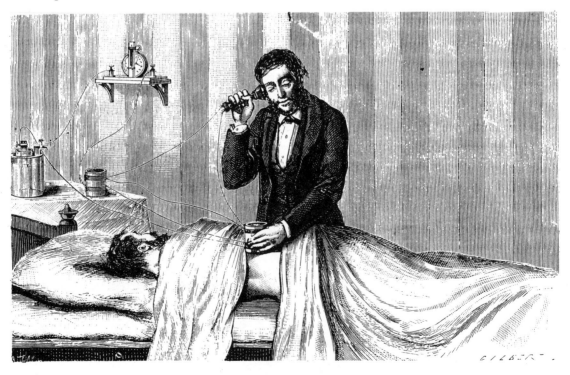

Thorough Physical Exam

It's a Test of Strength

As for the lifting or carrying a sack of mail up to seventy pounds, don't worry. Although, it's a test of strength, it's not for the championship of the world. You don't need the help of The Incredible Hulk, either. Even a thin woman can lift a seventy-pound sack of paper. If you lift weights, then you can lift it with one hand. (Look Ma, only one hand!)

Eye Examination. As regards the eye examination, the Post Office says that the requirement for distance vision is 20/40 (Snellen) in the better eye and at least 20/100 (Snellen) in the other eye. However, you are allowed to wear eyeglasses. Don't ask me what these figures mean; frankly, I don't know. I do know that during the eye test, you are asked to read some letters a few yards away, just as when you are taking eye examinations to be fitted for a new pair of glasses.

The person who gives your eye test will also determine whether you can read printing as small as a Jaeger's test, type No. 4 (whatever it is) at 14 inches with the better eye. I don't know how small this is, but as long as you can read letters and figures ordinarily written on envelopes, you'll pass the eye test.

Hearing Test. Like other applicants for any postal job, you must also have good hearing. For this reason, your ears will be tested;

you'll be wearing a headset and you'll be asked which ear hears a certain sound produced by a testing machine. Your ears must be keen enough to hear ordinary conversation; if you are an applicant for a letter carrier or a rural carrier position, you must be able to hear shouts from a distance, such as *"The dogs are coming, the dogs are coming!"*

According to USPS announcement sheets, Post Office jobs offer paid vacations, on-the-job training, liberal retirement, sick leave with pay, life insurance, low-cost health insurance, cash for suggestions, promotion opportunities, and paid holidays. Employees are paid ten percent extra for work performed between 6 p.m. and 6 a.m.

"The Dogs Are Coming! The Dogs Are Coming!"

Training Requirements

Applicants for some positions may be required to complete satisfactorily a prescribed training course or courses before assignment, reassignment, or promotion.

Operator's Permit

Some positions may require driving a government vehicle. Such positions include city carrier, rural carrier, garageman, and electronics technician.

Before you are hired for one of those jobs, you must hold a valid driver's license from the state in which the post office is located. After that you must obtain the appropriate government operator's permit.

Road Test

As an applicant for a carrier position or any other position requiring that you drive a government vehicle, you must demonstrate a safe driving record and pass a postal road test. If you fail the road test, the first time, you cannot be hired. But you may be given a second chance later. Some people who have taken this test complain that it is more difficult than the state road test. That's because safety is the name of the game in the Postal Service. To pass this road test, you must show that you follow traffic rules, drive safely, and deliver letters, magazines, and parcels to the addressees without damage.

Rates and Salaries

Under the APWU National Agreement, *(Schedule One - Salary and Rates* (Effective March 19, 2005) provided with automatic pay increases, the pay scales depending on grade levels are as follows:

Schedule One - Annual Salary & Rates (Effective 2005)

Grade 2 - (Steps D - H) $39,733 - $40,355
Grade 3 - (Steps D - H) $40,349 - $41,451
Grade 4 - (Steps D - H) $41,018 - $42,207
Grade 5 - (Steps D - H) $42,522 - $43,023
Grade 6 - (Steps D - H) $42,522 - $43,914
Grade 7 - (Steps D - H) $43,367 - $44,867

The above salaries are for regular postal employees. Part-time flexible employees at grade level receive from Grade 2 - $19.87 per hour to Grade 7 - $21.68 per hour. Part-time regular rates get from Grade 2 - $19.10 to Grade 7 - $20.85 per hour. (See the APWU Salary and Rates, *Schedule 1 and 2* on pages 412 - 415.

Schedule Two - Annual Salary & Rates (Effective (2005)

Grade 1 - (Steps BB - RC) $26,079 - $42,716
Grade 2 - (Steps BB - RC) $27,191 - $43,490
Grade 3 - (Steps BB - RC) $28,297 - $44,328
Grade 4 - (Steps A - RC) $31,871 - $45,176
Grade 5 - (Steps A- RC) $33,509 - $46,109
Grade 6 - (Steps A - RC) $35,252 - $47,132
Grade 7 - (Steps A - RC) $36,059 - $48,299
Grade 8 - (Steps A - RC) $42,033 - $49,976
Grade 9 - (Steps A - RC) $42,985 - $51,730
Grade 10 - (Steps A - RC) $43,988 - $52,906
Grade 11 - (Steps A - RC $45,047 - $54,485
Grade 12 - (Steps A - RC) $46,162 - $56,1857

For a complete schedule of salary and rates, see pages 412-415.

Postal examinations are held in testing centers throughout the United States (See Supplement B: National Directory of U.S. Postal Service Centers.) How often tests are held depends on the need for new or additional personnel. Examinations are not usually announced in the newspapers, over the radio, or on television.

Call the testing center in your area at least once a week so you won't miss any examination. The personnel department will not say whether there will be an exam any week in the future; an exam is usually announced only during the week when it accepts applications for tests. Postal exams are announced only by posting announcement sheets on postal bulletin boards; it is usually posted only for the week when it is announced. After that, the announcement is gone! If you wish to apply for any examinations in any location throughout the country, go to:

https://uspsapps.hr-services.org/

Eligibility Is Transferable

You must file an application for examinations, even if the test is for a city far from your home. In that way, you'll gain test experience. Furthermore, if you make a high score, you can request the transfer of your "eligibility" to the city where you live or to any city of your choice. The best time to transfer your eligibility is when there are "openings" in the city where you intend to move. In other words, you can take postal exams in any city of any state and if you make a high score, you can request the transfer of your eligibility to the city where you want to live and work. If your eligibility is transferred, you'll lose your eligibility in the city where you took the exam. When you are an *eligible,* you can postpone your employment in the Post Office for a certain period of time and still remain an eligible.

## 3

How to Get a US Postal Job

Eligibility and Employment Requirements

If doesn't matter whether you're an electrician, a professional person or just a high school graduate. It doesn't matter where you were born or where you grew up. If you're a U.S. citizen, or a permanent resident alien (immigrant), you can get a job with the U.S. Postal Service by one of two routes—either by getting high scores on postal entrance examinations or by getting a job without any examinations (if you're a doctor, nurse, or other professional).

Civil Service Eligibles

You cannot just apply for a job with the USPS without being a civil service eligible (except for technical positions). To be an eligible, you must pass the postal entrance exams. The Postal Service gives different exams for different positions, such as clerk, carrier, mail handler, mark-up clerk, distribution clerk, rural carrier, and other positions.

You can't apply for an exam if there is no opening. It's best if you have a friend or relative working in the Post Office who can tell you when an exam is forthcoming, but if you don't, you must call the personnel department of the local management sectional center. Or you may go to this website of the US Postal Service: https://uspsapps.hr-services.org/ and see where examinations are currently being held.

Post Offices throughout the country give exams to compile a *register of eligibles* from which they can take people, according to their ranking, to fill current and future vacancies. Tests are usually given by district Post Offices. For instance, the Pittsburgh (Pennsylvania) MSC gives examinations for its associate offices within the area covered by 150, 151, 153, 154, 156, and 200 (West Virginia) ZIP codes.

Although the Postal Service says that 70% is a passing score, your hair will turn grey while you wait to be called for employment if you score only in the 70's. The records show that only those who score from 90 to 100% are usually called by the Post Office, because hundreds and even thousands of people take and pass the exams and the Post Office can afford to be selective. Also, if you wish, you may request for the transfer of your eligibility to the city where you live or to any city of your choice. The best time to transfer your eligibility is when there are openings in the city where you intend to move. You can take postal exams in any city If you make a high score, request that your eligibility be transferred to the city where you want to live and work.

Route to Other Positions

When you are already employed by the Post Office, as a clerk, for instance, and you have gained enough seniority, you can submit bids for other positions. You may also take in-service examinations for other positions. The most qualified, of course, gets the job on the basis of seniority, rating, and experience. The opportunities for promotion are unlimited; it's up to you. You can be the master of your fate and the captain of your soul!

Flexible Employees

Before you obtain any of these positions, however, you start as a part-time flexible clerk or carrier. You are not yet a regular employee, but this doesn't mean that you are employed temporarily: your employment is permanent. You receive benefits similar to those given to regular employees.

"Part-time" does not mean you work only part-time. Usually you work five or six days a week. In many cases, you work six days as a part-time flexible. You are not guaranteed 40 hours' work a week, but you may sometimes work about 50 hours a week.   In other words, you may work less than 40 hours a week, and sometimes more. The major difference between a part-time flexible employee and a regular is that the former does not receive any holiday pay.

All employees of the U.S. Postal Service (except those who occupy technical positions) start as part-time flexibles. From that position one moves up to a regular position with a monthly salary after six months to one or two years' employment, depending on the Post Office where one is employed. Positions become available through promotion, retirement, death, transfer, employees' leaving, and expansion of postal facilities.

Hiring Through Interviews

You can get some positions in the Postal Service without taking written examinations; these include jobs as doctors, nurses, computer analysts, psychologists, and forensic chemists. However, these jobs have to be offered first to current postal employees. For instance, if there is a vacancy for a medical officer in a certain area, the job will be offered first to insiders. Would you expect a physician working as a clerk in the Post Office? Of course not. Then, if there is no qualified person in the service, the position will be offered to an outsider through an ad in a newspaper.

My son, Lester, a computer science graduate from Michigan State University, wrote a letter to the Postal Service headquarters in Washington, DC, to inquire about postal employment. He received the following letter, which is self-explanatory:

UNITED STATES POSTAL SERVICE
475 L'Enfant Plaza, SW
Washington, DC 20260

February 23, 1987

Mr. Lester A. Bartista
Post Office Box 299
East Detroit, Michigan   48021

Dear Mr. Bartista:

Thank you for your February 16 letter seeking information concerning Postal Service employment.

The majority of professional staff positions advertised are filled by qualified applicants from within the Postal Service. However, occasionally we will be unable to fill a position from within and will subsequently advertise outside the Service, usually through advertisements in the local newspapers. Headquarters ads usually appear in the Washington Post, New York Times and Wall Street Journal.

Usually, the positions which are advertised outside the Service fall in the technical fields (computer analyst, programmer, engineer, architect, etc.). I would urge you, if you are interested in Postal Service employment in the computer field, to watch for Postal Service ads in your local paper for local positions, or the Washington Post for Headquarters positions. Your public library probably has a subscription and should have the paper available on a regular basis. In addition, I would urge you to check with the personnel office at your local post office on a periodic basis.

I hope this information is of help to you. Best wishes as you graduate and begin your career.

Sincerely,

Roberta S. Kroggel
Administrative Coordinator
Marketing Department

As indicated in the letter, if you are interested in a technical position, such as computer analyst, programmer, or engineer, watch for postal ads in the local newspapers for local positions or in the *Washington Post* for headquarters positions. If you have a friend or a relative in the local management sectional center, let him or her advise you of any vacancies for those positions. Vacancy announcements are posted on the bulletin board. In that way you'll know where the vacancies are; you may contact the local office or the headquarters, when the Postal Service advertises in the local paper for local positions or in the *Washington Post* for headquarters positions.

It's a Good Idea, But Not in the Bag

If you're a computer programmer or an analyst and if you want to get a job in a large postal installation or at headquarters in Washington, you may take a Test 473 Exam, the test for entry-level jobs, such as mail processing clerks. When you are called for employment, accept a clerk position. When you have seniority, bid for a position as computer programmer or computer analyst or any other position. Because these jobs are offered first to insiders (like you), you have the edge in competing with outside programmers and analysts. Still, there's no guarantee that you'll get the job. Before you follow this strategy, it's best to talk with the personnel department of your local post office or the sectional center. Ask if it's really a good idea and what your chances are.

Know Where the Jobs Are

Postal Jobs for Veterans

Veteran Preference & Requirements

## 4

Veterans are given preference for employment in Federal jobs. If you are a veteran, a certain number of points will be added to your basic rating on the exam, so long as you make at least 70% on the exam. This is what the law dictates: if you have served in the Armed Forces of the United States, you deserve some kind of priority in government employment.

Whether you are a veteran who participated in World war II, Vietnam war, or Iraq war, you will receive this preference so long as you were honorably separated from the Armed Forces of the United States.

In the competitive tests for appointment to the positions in the Postal Service, these preference benefits are given to veterans under certain conditions.

If you are claiming the ten-point veteran disability preference, you are more fortunate than someone who is eligible for the ordinary five-point preference. Why? Because veteran eligibles who have service-connected disabilities and have extra ten points are placed first at the top of the register in the order of their scores.

That simply means that you're followed by all other eligibles, including the five-point preference veterans, who are listed according to their ratings. So if you're a ten-point preference veteran, you'll be on top of the list, even if your basic score is lower than the top scorers. You'll bump the other eligibles as if to say, "Move down, move down, move down!" The so-called *preference eligibles* who receive five points additional are listed with the other eligibles (civilians) according to scores. In other words, if you are a five-point preference veteran, it does not mean you will be ahead of those who make higher scores than yours. If you score 75, including your five points, you won't be listed above a nonpreference eligible who scores 76. However, if you are a preference eligible, you'll be listed ahead of the nonpreference eligibles who make the same scores as you.

Standard Form 15

If you're claiming veteran preference, you'll have to fill out and submit Standard Form 15 to prove that you really served in the Armed Forces.

Questions and complaints have come up because of the veteran preference. One woman who bought this book and scored 100% score on a Postal exam complained to the congressman of her district that she was discriminated against because people with lower scores than hers were appointed to positions while she was still on the waiting list. The postmaster had to explain that those who were appointed were veterans.

Because of veteran preference, many who have retired from the Army, Navy, Air Force and Marines have been appointed to postal positions after making the required scores on civil service exams.

In the competitive tests for appointment to the positions in the Postal Service, these preference benefits are given to veterans under certain conditions.

1. Five points are added to the basic rating of an examinee who scores at least 70 percent (the passing grade). If you make a score of 70, your final score will be 75; if you score 98 on the exam, your final score will be 103.
2. Ten points are added to the basic rating of an examinee who scores 70 percent or above and who is:
   a. a disabled veteran or a veteran who has received a Purple Heart award. Physical requirements are waived for persons who receive this preference, so long as they can do efficiently the duties of a postal worker.
   b. the wife of a disabled veteran if the veteran is physically disqualified by his service-connected disability for civil service appointment to positions along the line of his prewar or usual occupation.

c. the widow of a serviceman who died on active duty while serving in the Armed Forces, but only if she has not married again. (The law does not say whether she'll be disqualified if she falls in love again.)

d. The mother of a deceased or disabled veteran son or daughter, if she is either widowed, divorced, or separated, or if her present husband is permanently and totally disabled.

Veterans Preference Explained

With regard to the veterans preference, the *Postal Bulletin,* in its issue of May 30, 1985 stated:

"The following revises Handbook P-11, Personnel Operations. Section 241.31. The principal change is to incorporate the minimum 408 of *Public Law 87-300,* enacted October 14, 1982, which amended Title 38 *U.S. Code of Federal Regulations* Section 3103A. To obtain veterans preference in Federal employment, a person who enlists after September 7, 1980 (or begins active duty on or after October 14, 1982, and has not previously completed 24 months of continuous active duty), must perform active duty in the Armed Forces during a war or in a campaign or expedition for which is campaign badge has been authorized, and serve for 2 years or the full period called or ordered to active duty. The time limit does not affect eligibility for veterans preference based on peacetime service exceeding 180 days from 1955 to 1976. This change is effective immediately and will be included in a future transmittal letter."

"241.3 Kinds of Veterans Preference
.31 5-Point Preference. Five-point preference is given to honorably separated veterans (see 241.5) who served on active duty in the armed forces of the United States.

"a. During a war; or
"b. During the period April 28, 1952 to July 1, 1955; or
"c. In any campaign or expedition for which a campaign badge has been authorized (exception: a person who enlisted after September 7, 1980; or begins active duty on or after October 14, 1982, and has not previously completed 24 months of continuous active duty must perform active duty in the armed forces, during a war or in a campaign or expedition for which a campaign badge has been authorized, and serve for 2 years or the full period called or ordered for active duty. The law

excepts a person who is discharged or released from active duty (a) for a disability incurred or aggravated in the line of duty, or (b) under 10 U.S.C. 1171 or 1173 for hardship or other reasons or"

"d. For more than 180 consecutive days any part of which occurred after January 31, 1955, and before October 15, 1976. (An initial period of active duty for training under the 6-month Reserve or National Guard Program does not count.)"

City and Rural Carriers

Men and Women on the Road

## 5

City Carrier:

Grade 1

Salary Range: (Steps A to O) - $34,144 - $45,095 per year
Part-time Flexible: $17.07 - $22.55 per hour

Grade 2

Salary Range: (Steps A to O) - $35,865 - $48,166 per year
Part-time Flexible: $17.93 per hour

Rural Carrier:

For info, go to Internet website:
http://www.nrlca.org/PDF/25_05PAY.PDF
Part-time Flexible
Salary Range: (Grade A-C to 1 to 12): $17.58 - $23.07 per hour

Rural Carrier Associate/Rural Carrier Relief:

Salary Range: Schedule 1 - $16.45; Schedule 2 - $19.78 per hour

Persons Eligible to Apply: Open to the general public
Examination Requirement: Must pass the Postal Test 473-473-C, 460 RCA exam, and the driving test

As a carrier, (whether city or rural), you'll be required to sort, rack, and tie mail at the post office before you start making deliveries within your route or area of delivery. In sorting letters, you must arrange them in the same order as the streets occur on the route. Letters and magazines for occupants of an apartment complex must be tied together with a rubber band or a leather belt. If you make a mistake in reading an address, the letter may go into the wrong home mailbox, causing a delay in delivery. The next day, you may find a note that says, *"This is not ours. Opened by mistake."* The letter might be a "deadline" letter, an order from the court, or a warning from a creditor.

As a carrier, you'll also maintain required information, record changes of addresses, maintain other reports, and forward undeliverable-as-addressed mail.

As a carrier, you'll also maintain required information, record changes of addresses, maintain other reports, and forward undeliverable-as-addressed mail.

In some ways, a rural carrier's duty is different from that of a city carrier. If you are hired as a rural carrier or a rural carrier associate, you'll be a jack of all trades; you'll also be a "walking post office." You may carry stamps, scales, and other equipment and supplies to serve the people of the rural area you cover. For this reason, you must know how to compute the cost of a piece of mail or a package whether it's going to a neighboring city, Iraq, or the North Pole

Regular Route

Once you're a carrier, you'll have a regular route. Day in and day out, you'll walk on the same streets and open the same mailboxes. You won't get lost and you'll probably have time for a cup of coffee at McDonald's or Burger King after you've finished covering your route.

As a letter carrier you can become "the great observer." As you pound on the streets on your route, you'll notice unusual lawn ornaments, flagpoles, signs, and other out-of-the-ordinary things.

Once a letter carrier saw this sign nailed to a wooden fence: *"Dogs: Beware of Letter Carriers."*

***This is Not How
the Mail Room Looks Today***

If you're still a flexible city carrier or a rural carrier associate, that's a different story. Sometimes, as a flex, you'll cover different routes everyday. Before you go out, you'll have to look at the city map to see where you are going to   so that you'll finish delivering all your mail. You'll cover the routes of carriers who are off on a particular day or who have called in sick. Don't worry—once they were flexibles, and your time will come. Seniority is the rule in the post office.

Love Notes

If you are a carrier, you must remember names as well as you can. If you don't know, you'll receive many notes and envelopes saying: "How many times have we told you that this man moved five years ago! or "I've told you a dozen times that this man has long been dead!"

Once a friend of mine who is a letter carrier found some notes on an envelope returned to him: "Gone! Not back! Not coming back anymore!"

Road Adventures

I asked my friend whether he had ever been accosted by anyone on the streets while he was covering his route.

"Yes, many times," he said

"By thieves?" I asked

"No...by retirees!" He responded.

Sometimes in the spring or the fall you'll have to bring an umbrella or a raincoast. When it rains, it pours. You may also wish to put a sticker on the back bumper of your car or jeep that says, *"Warning—Give a Break to Animals."*

Undeliverable-as-Addressed (UAA) Mail

Underliverable-as-addressed mail is sent to the Computerized Forwarding System (CFS) unit in every sectional center, where the mail is processed by the mark-up clerks in every post office. Undeliverable-as-addressed mail goes to the CFS for forwarding. Changes of addresses are computerized, and every change of address (COA) is entered into the system, where it is stored on disks. When the letter, magazine, or package is keyed—that is, when the operator types in the first three letters of the last name and the last two numbers of the street address—the computer generates a corresponding change of address label.

No Record ("N") Mail

As a carrier, you will also send mail that has no change of addresses to the CFS. This mail (called "N" mail) will be returned to you for proper disposition. N mail has a "returned to sender, unde-liverable as addressed" label with the letter N, meaning that there's no record of the address in the CFS or that a change of address has not been submitted to the CFS. Maybe you didn't send in the Form 3575 (change of address card), filled in properly by the one whose family moved. At times like this you will exchange some kind of note with the people in the CFS.

Once when a carrier received an N mail letter, he was angry because he had already written the word "deceased" on the envelope, but it was returned to him anyway as N mail by the CFS. He wrote a note on the envelope and sent it back to the CFS. The note said: *"This man is already dead. Where shall I deliver the mail—to hell?*

Form 3575

He might have been right. But he should have filled out Form 3575, the change-of-address card, with the name and address of the dead person and the "diseased" under "new address." This information is entered into the computer, and the mail is returned to the sender. When a CFS mark-up clerk keys this address, the label that is produced will say, *"Return to Sender, Moved. Left No Address."*

Examination Requirements

As an applicant, you have to pass an entrance examination. The Test 473/473-C and the 460 Examination are the most important exams in the Postal Service. Why? Because 80 percent of employees hired by the USPS get high scores on these tests. The 473/473-C Test consists of four parts: Part A: Address-Checking Test; Part B: Forms Completion; Part C: Coding and Memory, and Part D: Inventory of Experiences and Characteristics.The rural carrier associate Exam 460 consists of Part A: Address Checking Test; Part B: Memory-for-Address Test; Part C: Number Series Test; and Part D: Following Oral Instructions

Clerk Position

The Key to Other Postal Jobs

## 6

Distribution Clerk (Manual)

Grade: L-5

Salary Range: See schedule of salary & rates on pages 9 - 10; 412-415.

Persons Eligible to Apply: Open to the public

Examination Requirements: Must pass the 473 Test

A clerk may be the jack-of-all-trades position in the U.S. Postal Service. If you score high on the Test 473 and land a job in the Postal Service, you can be a manual distribution clerk.

As a distribution clerk, you'll work indoors and will handle sacks of mail weighing as heavy as 70 pounds. You'll sort mail and distribute it by using a complicated scheme, which must be memorized. You'll place letters or flats (magazines and pieces of mail in big envelopes) into the correct boxes or pigeonholes. If you make a mistake in reading addresses or numbers, the letter will go to the wrong box, thus causing a delay in delivery. Letters from different boxes in a "case" go to different routes served by carriers, who will distribute the mail door to door.

As a distribution clerk, you'll also dump sacks of mail onto conveyors for culling and sorting; you'll load and unload sacks and trays of mail on and off mail transporters, such as APCs (All-Purpose Containers) and BMCs (Bulk Mail Containers). As a clerk, you may also be assigned to a public counter or window, doing such jobs as selling stamps and weighing parcels, and you'll be personally responsible for all money and stamps.

How Not to Unload Parcels

A friend of mine who works in a post office has told me this story:

While he was still a flexible employee at the post office in Mt. Clemens, Michigan, Post Office, he was assigned to unload parcels from a BMC. He had to work fast because there were several BMCs to be unloaded. While he was unloading a big parcel, the bottom of it suddenly gave way, and hundreds of nuts poured onto the floor! He was embarrassed and had a hard time picking up the nuts, and some of the other employees helped him, too. Then on one side of the carton that had contained the nuts, my red-faced friend read a note: *Glass—please handle with care.*

Clerk-Typist

Grade: L-4 to L-6

Salary Range: See schedule of salary & rates on pages 9 - 10; 412-415.

Persons Eligible to Apply: Open to the general public.

Examination Requirements: Must pass Examination 710 and a typing test.

Duties: Originates and maintains routine records, composes memoranda and letters; acts as receptionist, answering telephone calls, talking and relaying messages and furnishing information requested; relieves office clerks; and does all other related clerical jobs.

Qualifications: Ability to read and understand instructions, to perform basic arithmetic computations, to maintain accurate records, to prepare reports and correspondence, and to operate office machines, such as calculator, adding machine, and duplicator.

Experience Requirements:
A. For PS-Level 4 or PMS-Level, 1 year
B. For PS-Level 5 or PMS-Level, 2 years
C. PS-Level 6 or PMS-level, 3 years
  Substitution of Education for Experience. Successful completion of a full 4-year high school course, including credits in commercial or business subjects, such as general business education, business arithmetic, or office practice, may be substituted for 1 year of the required experience.

Study completed in a business or secretarial school or an academic institution above high school level may be substituted for a maximum of 1 year of experience on the basis of 36 weeks of study for 1 year of experience. Credit will be followed for full-time or part-time study at the rate of 20 class hours of instruction for one week of study in such subjects as business English, office machines, filing and indexing, office practice, business mathematics, and accounting or bookkeeping.

Typing Requirements: Ability to type 40 words per minute for 5 minutes with no more than two errors. This ability will be tested in the performance section of the examination.

Clerk-Stenographer

Grades: L - 5

Salary Range: See schedule of salary & rates on pages 9 - 10; 412-415.

Persons Eligible to Apply: Open to the general public

Examination Requirements: Applicants must pass Examination 710. They must also pass the Dictation test.

Duties: Same as the duties performed by a clerk-typist, except that he or she must take dictation.

Dictation Requirement: Ability to take dictation in shorthand or on a shorthand machine at 80 words per minute. This ability will be tested in the performance section of the examination.

Typing Requirement: Ability to type 40 words per minute for 5 minutes with no more than two errors. This ability will be tested in the performance section of the examination.

If There's No Opening Yet

If you're planning to take Examination 710, which is the exam for clerk-typist and clerk-stenographer, but there are no openings yet, there's an easier way to get one of those positions. Take the 473 Test and obtain a clerk position.

After you have gained enough seniority, submit your bid for a clerk-typist or clerk-stenographer position, if there are any vacancies. You won't take a written examination, but you'll have to take a typing test for a clerk-typist position, and a typing test and short-hand dictation for a clerk-stenographer position.

After you pass the test, you'll obtain the position if you win in the bidding on the basis of seniority, experience, and qualifications. Before such a position is offered to an eligible (who made a high score on an entrance exam), it is offered to an insider (like you).

Other Positions

From your clerk position, you can also transfer to any accounting technician position, if you love working with figures, or to any other available position in the Postal Service. Some positions may require you to pass "in-service" examinations or training; others do not. For instance, if you're a letter-sorting machine operator and are already tired of hitting machine keys, you can move to a manual distribution clerk position. As a distribution clerk or any other kind of clerk, you can move from one job to another (moving forward, not backward, of course) by submitting a bid and winning the job on the basis of your seniority, education, and other qualifications.

Mark-Up Clerk

The Mail Forwarder

## 7

Grade: L-4

Salary: See schedule of salary & rates on pages 9 - 10; 412-415.

Persons Eligible to Apply: Open to the general public

Examination Requirement: Applicants must pass the 473 Test and the typing test.

Mark-Up clerks process mail that is undeliverable as addressed. Previously they were just known as mark-up clerks, but now they are known as mark-up clerks, automated. Your duty as a mark-up clerk, automated, consists of keying on the machine, labeling, and other related jobs.

Mark-up clerks used to mark undeliverable-as-addressed mail with rubber stamps that said "Return to Sender, Address Unknown." They used to stick preprinted labels with new addresses on envelopes. These labels were inserted between change-of-addressed cards, arranged alphabetically in an index card tray.

Computerized Forwarding System Units

Today, CFS units have been installed in USPS sectional centers throughout the country. If a CFS unit is to be established by a post office, or if a CFS unit needs additional employees, postal officials will have to give a 473 Test. Those already in the service may get these jobs if they wish, by bidding for positions. But they must pass a special written exam and a typing test. Civilian employees in military headquarters or offices may also request transfer to mark-up clerks, as in other positions. But they must pass the written and typing test.

The first priority of the CFS in establishing a data bank for all changes of address in a sectional center is the conversion program (CP). All the changes of addresses in post offices under the jurisdiction of a certain sectional center is entered into the system. The change-of-address notice is contained on a card known as Form 3575.

Change-of-Address Input

On the basis of the information on the change-of-address card, the mark-up clerk enters the change of address (COA) into the system.

The operator goes to the data management (DM) program. The first words to appear on the computer screen are *Zone* and *Function*. *Zone* means the ZIP code and the function asks if you're entering a COA for the first time or if you are modifying the file that is already in the system.

For Instance:

Zone: 48336
Extract Code: Smit431 (In entering the extract code, you type the first four letters of the family name and the last three numbers of the address. If it's a business address change, then you have to type the first four numbers of the business name and the last three numbers of the address.)

Function: ( )

A - Add
M - Modify
E - EC

Usually you'll type the A or M.

When you select the A, this will appear:

Zone:
Extraction Code:
Address Selection
1. Street Address
2. P.O. Box
3. Rural Route
4. Hwy Contract
5. General Delivery
6. Foreign

For instance, if the original (or old) address is a street, then select 1, and this information will appear:

COA Information FP4

The FP4 indicates that this is a permanent (P) address for a family (F). If it's for an individual, it should be IP4. If the change is temporary, then it should be FT4 or IT4. The 4 indicates that the address is willing to pay for 4th class mail forwarded to the new address:

Start Date:
Last Name:
First Name:
Number:
Pre-Directional:
Apt/Suite No:
DNF Code:
Additional Extraction Code:

(Note: The Last Name and the First Name will be changed to Business, if it's a business moving.)
If you are to enter the new address, this information will appear on the screen:

Number:
Pre Directional:
Street Name:
Post Directional:
Apt/Suite No.
City:
State:
ZIP:

If the person is moving from a P.O. Box and you check the selection P.O. Box, this will appear on the screen.

COA Info:
Start Date:
Last Name:
First Name:
P.O. Box
DNF Code:
Additional Extract Code:

After this, as in the street address, you must select whether the person or the business is moving to a street, a P.O. Box, a rural route, etc.

In generating labels, the mark-up clerk then goes to the Label Generation (LG) Program and the zone and extraction code questions appear. (The machinable letters pass in front of the operator (through a revolving mini-conveyor, as if asking "Where am I going?") The operator then keys the extract code (as if answering, "I Don't know") for each piece of mail passing by, typing the first four letters of the last name or first four letters of the business name and the last three numbers of the address. Then bingo! The computer automatically generates the yellow label (installed in a built-in case on the machine). This machine is different from the computer wherein COAs (changes of addresses) are entered. The letters are directed to different bins: some to the "local bin," others to the "out-of-town bin," some others to the "return-to-sender" bin, etc.

Why Do People Move?

Why do many people move so often? Because they want a change of environment or atmosphere: they seek new jobs, find new friends, and, if they are already in good financial shape, they want to live where the rich or the retirees live. Sometimes people can no longer bear the bitter cold and blizzards in northern states, so they move temporarily to places like Florida, California, or Arizona. People are like birds: they fly to certain places, depending on the season. Some of the changes are not for families, but for individuals when members of a family move to different places. For instance, two people find they no longer care for each other, so they move to different locations to try to forget each other and to find new playmates.

Extraction Codes

Why does a mark-up clerk enter additional extraction codes? The reason for this is that we think differently. An operator must type the first four letters of the family name and last three numbers of the old address to produce the label for a new address. But sometimes he or she doesn't know which is which. Hence, new additional extra codes.

Different Shifts

Mark-up clerks work in shifts: one may come at 6 a.m., another at 8 a.m., and another at 3:30 p.m.

Other Major Postal Jobs 8

5 Entry-Level Jobs

Distribution Clerk, Machine

Grade: L-5

Salary Range: See schedule of salary & rates on pages 9 - 10; 412-415.

Persons Eligible to Apply: Open to the general public

Examination Requirements: Must pass Test 473

The distribution clerk, machine, known as a Letter Sorting Machine (LSM) operator, is a clerk who operates a machine (called a console) that is attached to a giant letter-sorting machine. The console has a keyboard similar to that of a piano. Some people say that if you're a pianist or know how to play the piano, you'll be a good LSM operator.

There are two kinds of LSM operators. One is assigned to learn one or more distribution schemes; the other is assigned to key ZIP codes.

Every post office has its schemes, based on its ZIP codes. For example, Warren, Michigan has four ZIP codes: 48089, 48091, 48092, and 48093. The scheme involves the routes to which letter carriers are assigned. For instance, a carrier may be assigned to Route 38, which covers certain streets. Sometimes a street is divided into several routes. Also, letters must be diverted to their proper routes. This is the job of an LSM operator (distribution clerk, machine). A manual distribution clerk sorts letters according to their routes by putting letters into pigeonholes on a case.

If you're assigned to key schemes, you must hit the right keys (two) on the machine (all numbers) as you read the addresses on envelopes that are moving from right to left at the speed of 50 letters per minute. Your vision must not move back and forth as if you're watching a smiling John McEnroe and a frowning basketball star Magic Johnson in a tennis exhibition game. Your sight must be focused in front of you. Your eyes must be on red alert for the letters passing by, and you must hit the proper keys as soon as each letter passes. Sometimes, while you're deciding what route a letter is destined for, it's already going, going—gone! If that happens, go on to the next letter. All letters keyed wrong or unkeyed go to the nixies. You must not make many mistakes because you are allowed only a certain percentage of errors.

If you're assigned to key ZIP codes, you have to key only the first three numbers in the ZIP code. Your speed must be 60 letters per minute.

Do you think you can handle the job? Why not? They're doing it. As the saying goes, if they can do it, you can do it, too. (You must undergo training, of course, and must pass that training.)

Mail Handler

Grade: Level 4
(Full-Time Regular Employees)
Salary Range: (Steps A to O) $29,980 - $44,181) per year
Grade: Level 5
Salary Range: (Steps A to O) $31,412 - $45,120) per year
Also, go to the Internet website:
http://www.local300npmhu.org/rsc-m-09-04-04-Excel-wp.htm

Part-Time Regular Employees
Salary: (Steps A to O) - $14.41 - $21.24 per hour
Flexible Employees
Salary: (Steps A to O) - $14.99 per hour

Persons Eligible to Apply: Open to the general public

Examination Requirement: Must pass the Test 473.

If you get a job as a mail handler, you'll work mostly in the dock area, the canceling section, and the operation area. As the title indicates, you'll load and unload mail onto and off trucks and perform duties incidental to the movement and processing of mail.

As a mail handler, your duties include separating mail sacks to go to different routes or cities; canceling parcel post stamps; rewrapping parcels; and operating canceling machines, addressographs, mimeographs, and fork-lifts.

Mail Processor

Grade: L-4

Salary Range: See schedule of salary & rates on pages 9 - 10; 412-415.

Persons Eligible to Apply: Open to the general public. Occasionally, positions are open only to current employees.

Examination Requirement: Muss pass the 473 Test

If you're appointed as a mail processor, you'll process mail using a variety of automated mail processing equipment. You'll work at the optical character reader (OCR) mail processing equipment area.

Flat Sorting
Machine Operator

Grade: L-5

Salary Range: See schedule of salary & rates on pages 9 - 10; 412-415.

Persons Eligible to Apply: Open to the general public

Examination Requirement: Must pass the 473 Test

As a flat-sorting machine operator, your major duty is to operate a single- or multi-position operator-faced electronic-mechanical machine in the distribution of flats. (Flats are mailed material mostly contained in manila envelopes and other self-sealed mail, and are fed to the machine by an operator to go to different cities or routes.) You may also be assigned to work in other areas as needed.

As an applicant you must have skills in operating an electromechanical machine and in the application of approved machine distribution. Heavy lifting is also required.

Data Conversion Operator

Grade: L-4

Salary Range: See schedule of salary & rates on pages 9 - 10; 412-415.

Persons Eligible to Apply: Open to the general public

Examination Requirements: Must pass Examination 710, the Computer-Based Test 714, and a keyboard qualification test.

If you get high score on Examination 710 and pass the computer test and a keyboard qualification test, you may be hired as a data conversion operator in a Remote Encoding Center.

As a data conversion operator, you'll use a computer terminal to prepare mail for automated sorting equipment.

You'll key the essential information needed so that an address bar code can be applied to each letter.

How to Mark Circles On Answer Sheet

The Secret Way to Marking It Effectively

Your answer sheet is separate from the question sheet. This answer sheet is corrected by computer in California. The USPS furnishes lead pencils to be used during the examination; you may not use your own. You must make the pencil point broad enough to mark or darken the circle in one or two strokes.

Don't Sharpen the Point or Tip of Your Pencil.

The USPS Way

The sample below is included in a booklet published by the USPS, but it is not sent out. It is used only by organized groups that are participating in the Postal Service's affirmative action program by preparing applicants for the tests. The sample shows how an answer sheet is to be marked.

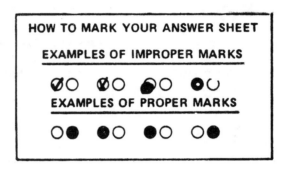

Some reviewers advise that you make this kind of mark. Others do not even discuss how a circle is to be marked.

A book on postal tests says that the instructions you receive at the time of the official test will include instructions on how to blacken the circles on the answer sheet. It reminds you to follow the instructions strictly and not to misinterpret the directions.

According to that book you are to darken completely the circle you have selected as the correct answer like this:

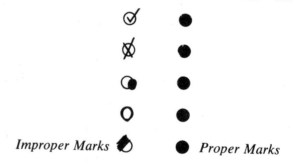

The Bautista Version

When I took an exam for the Warren (Michigan) Post Office, I tried to blacken the circles almost completely. I tried to be a Picassso; my final score was 78.5%. Then I decided to change my stroke in marking the circles after I had devised some other tests systems. I made the mark smaller; the smaller it became, the higher score I made.

Pablo R. Abesamis of Glendale, California, marked the circles better than I did (much smaller marks), and this is what he wrote to me:

"It's unbelievable! Just imagine, using your method I got five scores of 100% on postal entrance examinations. I also acquired 98.80% and 97% on two other exams. Your systems really work..."

I received flood of letters from readers, congratulating me for my efforts for showing them my own way of marking the circles. I included illustrations of how Abesamis and many others marked the circles and made high scores.

In **Booklist,** a publication of the American Library Association, a reviewer writes:

"Bautista provides valuable advice for passing the civil service exams necessary to obtain several U.S. Postal jobs...the text supplies practical background on eligibility for post office jobs, on the veteran preference system, on the actual contents of the exams, and on techniques for studying and memorization."

Here's how I made the markings.

●   ●   ●   ●   ●   ●   ●   ●   ●

Your exam score may be higher when you don't completely mark the whole circles on the answer sheet. It's simply common sense that when you compare addresses and mark the circle on a six-minute, 95-questions test, you have to work fast. To compare 95 sets of addressess in six minutes, you must take less than four seconds to answer each question, including marking the circles on the answer sheet. If you blacken the circles completely, (as advised by other postal books), you won't be able to answer all the 95 questions, but only about one-half of the items. The smaller you mark the circle, the more questions you'll answer because of the time limit.

On the basis of my experience in taking exams, the marking depends on what type of test you're taking. If you're taking the 473/473-C Test or the RCA 460 test, you can make a smaller mark; if you're taking the arithmetic and reading comprehension portions of another exam, you can make the mark bigger simply because you've the time to do it.

You can chat with your local carrier or any other current postal employee and ask him or her how he or she made the markings on the answer sheet when he or she took the exam. Maybe he or she did the right thing.

Many other people who bought my book and did what I did also made high scores on tests. When Bautista talks, people listen.

From all over the United States, readers have written to tell me that they made high marks after they had followed my step-by-step instructions on taking exams.

If You Followed My Instructions,
This Would Not Have Happened to You.

473/473-C Battery Test 10

Test for Major Entry-Level Jobs

The Postal 473/473-C Test is an exam for major entry-Level Jobs: **City Carriers, Mail Processing Clerks, Mail Handlers,** and **Sales, Services, and Distribution Associates.** It replaced the old 470 Battery Test that was first introduced in 1994.

Actually, Test 473 and Test 473-C Test are the same. However, when Test 473-C is given, it is exclusively for applicants for city carriers. Of course, a job applicant for a Test 473 who score high on the test can also be hired as a city carrier.

The duties involved in the work for these major entry-level jobs are as follows:

City Carriers: These carriers sort, rack, and tie mail at the post office before they start making deliveries within their route or area of delivery. They also maintain required information, record changes of address. maintain other reports, and forward undeliverable-as-addressed mail.

Mail Processing Clerks: These clerks operate and maintain automated mail processing equipment or do manual sorting of mail. They collate, bundle, and move processed mail from one location to another.

Mail Handlers: They load and unload mail onto and off trucks and perform duties incidental to the movement and processing of mail. Duties include separating mail sacks to go to different routes or cities; cancel parcel post stamps and operate canceling machines, addressoggraphs, and fork-lifts.

Sales, Services, and Distribution Associates: They do direct sales and customer support services and distribution of mail. The associates must pass an on-the-job training program.

The 473/473-C Battery Test consists of the following Parts:

Part A: Address Checking
Part B: Forms Completion
Part C: Coding and Memory
Part D: Inventory of Personal Characteristics and Experience

When you pass the test, you'll be listed in the **Register of Eligibles.** But **although 70 is the passing score, you need to score 95-100% on the exams,** to have a better chance of being called for employment. Remember, the first to be called for employment are the ones on the top of the list.

The Test 473 requires memorizing numbers, streets, states, and ZIP codes. What you need to do is to know how to memorize these things in a very short time. Remember, this is a timed test. For example, for the Address Checking part, you need to answer 60 questions in 11 minutes; for the Coding section of the test, you are to answer 36 questions in 6 minutes. On the actual Memory section test, you have to answer 36 questions in 7 minutes. Our strategies for memorizing codes and street names and addresses will be useful to you.

Beat the Competition!

Parts of Test 473/473-C:

The test covers the following parts:

Test Unit	No. of Questions	Time Allowed	Subjects Covered
Part A Address Checking	60	11 minutes	Identify if 2 compared addresses have errors or no errors.
Part B Forms Completion	30	15 minutes	Determine if completion of form is correct.
Part C Section 1 - Coding	36	6 minutes	Create address codes to remember address range assigned to routes.
Section 2 - Memory	36	7 minutes	Use address codes to remember address range assigned to routes.
Part D Identify Job-Related Experiences & Characteristics.	236	90 minutes	Identify job-related experiences and characteristics.

Part A: Address-Checking Test

Part A of Postal Exam 473 involves 60 questions to be finished in 11 minutes, comparing two rows of addresses as quickly as possible. You have to match the *Correct List* (left column) of addresses containing numbers, names of streets, city, and state and zip codes, and the *List to Be Checked* containing the same items. You must compare the left and right rows of addresses and ZIP codes. Determine if there are **No Errors**, if there are **Errors in the Address Only**, **Errors in the ZIP Code only**, or **Errors in Both** the address and the ZIP code.

Address-Checking Sample Items

A. No Errors	B. Address Only	C: ZIP Code Only	D: Both

Correct List

Address	ZIP Code
3540 Willow Ct Sedona, AZ	86351-0001
2163 Jones Dr Palm Desert, CA	92217-2306

List to Be Checked

Address	ZIP Code
3540 Willow Ct Sedona, AZ	86451-0001
2163 Jones St Palm Desert, CA	92211-2306

As mentioned before, you must determine if there are errors in the rows of addresses and ZIP codes being compared for correctness or incorrectness of addresses and zip codes. If there are no errors in both the addresses and the ZIP codes, meaning they are exactly the same, the answer should be **A (No Errors);** if there is an error in the address only, the answer should be **B (Address Only);** if there is an error in the ZIP code only, the answer should be **C (ZIP Code Only);** and if there are errors in both address and ZIP code, the answers should be **D (Both).**

Part B: Forms Completion.

Part B involves the identification of information required to fill out or complete a Postal form for customers and Postal employees.

Part C: Coding and Memory Sections.

Part C of the new Test 473 consists of two parts or sections: the Coding Section and the Memory Section.

Part D: Inventory of Personal Experiences and Characteristics.

Part D involves the inventory of personal experiences and characteristics containing 236 test items to be finished in 90 minutes.

11

Address-Checking Strategies

Techniques for Answering Questions Instantly

The Address-Checking Test for the **Postal 473/473-C Battery Test** and the **Address-Checking Test** for the **RCA 460 Examination** have similarities and differences.

In the Address-Checking test of the **RCA 460 Examination**, you have to determine if two addresses are *Alike* and *Different*. You have to answer the questions with an "A" for Alike and "D" for Different. In other words, there are only two choices; it's either "A" (for Alike) and "D" (for Different). However, in the Address-Checking Test of the **473/473-C Battery Test,** you have to answer the questions in different ways. What you have to do is to compare the addresses and zip codes in each row of the **List to Be Checked** with those of the **Correct List.** Decide if they are exactly alike or different (left column). You will select any of the A, B, C, or D choices; **A** for **No Errors; B** for an error in the **Address Only; C** for an error in the **ZIP Code Only;** and **D** for errors in **Both** address and ZIP code.

The Address-Checking test of the Postal 473/473-C Battery Test consists of 60 questions to be answered in 11 minutes only. So you have to compare the two addresses and zip codes quickly but accurately to score high on the exams. (On the other hand, the address-checking test of the RCA 460 examination involves 95 items to be answered in 6 minutes).

Here are some strategies needed to answer all the questions within the time allocated to the items or questions.

How to Use Your Fingers

In comparing addresses and zip codes (**Corrected List** and **List to Be Checked**), you can point at the numbers and streets with your fingers. Place the little finger of your nonwriting hand on one column of address and the index finger of the same hand on the other column. Move your hand downward as you make comparisons, while your writing hand marks the answers.

How to Do the Comparison

Compare the two addresses (left and right) by one or two eye sweeps of the line. The question sheet and the answer sheet should be lying side by side; the question sheet on your non-writing side, the answer sheet on your writing side. Don't jerk your neck from left to right as you read; just let your eyes do the sweeping. Then hold your pencil in your writing hand and don't move your non-writing hand from the question sheet. Then move it downward as you mark a circle with two or three strikes by your writing hand. Be sure that the line you are marking corresponds to the question you are answering.

Spellings: Note the spellings of street, city, state, and numbers in the ZIP code. There are times that the first address has a zip code such as 48012 and the second address has a ZIP code of 48021.

Differences: Most of the time, there are differences in abbreviations, such as Ave, St., or Rd. Sometimes the first address (left) is abbreviated as St and the second address (right) is Ave, or vice versa.

In a nutshell, here are the ways to compare the addresses and ZIP codes:

First Way: Compare the two addresses by moving your eyes from left to right. That is, compare the address on the left column to the one on the right. Make one or two "eye sweeps" of the address (number, street, city, and state). After that, compare the ZIP codes.

Example:

28091 Hickory Dr	48091	28097 Hickory Dr.	48091
Farmington Hills, MI		Farmington Hills, MA	

Since there's an error in the address, the answer should be **B** (Address Only).

Second Way: Compare only the street numbers and the abbreviations such as Ct, Rd, St, or Ave of both columns. If they are alike, compare the ZIP code on the left to the ZIP code on the right. Then compare the city and state, of both columns. If they are all alike, mark **A (No Errors)**. If there is an error in the address only, answer **B (Address Only)**.

Example:

3192 Aberdeen Ct.	34743	3192 Aberden Ct	34743
Kissimmee, FL		Kissimme, FL	

In the above example, the answer is **B (Address Only)**.

Third Way: First, compare only the street names and the abbreviations: St. Rd., or Ave of both columns. If they are alike, then compare the street numbers on the left column to the numbers on the right column. If they are all alike, then the answer is **A.**

Example:

> 2200 Martin Ave   23221   2200 Martin Ave   23221
> Richmond, VA   Richmond, VA

In the above example, the answer is A.

Fourth Way: You compare the numbers at the left to the numbers at the right, (including the street name, and abbreviation Rd, etc.) and the ZIP codes. If there are errors, then compare the city and state names of both columns. If there are also errors, answer **D** (Both).

Here's an example:

> 3812 Bourbon Ln   60565-2101   3813 Bourbon Ln   60566-2101
> Naperville, IL   Naperville, IL

In the above example, the answer is **D (Both)**. It's because there's an error in the address (numbers 12 and 13 of the address) and there's an error in the Zip codes (60565 and 60566).

Fifth Way: Compare the zip codes first; then compare the numbers in the address on the left and the numbers in the address on the right. Then compare the city and street names. If you see errors in the address (numbers, city, and state) and in the zip code, the answer is **D (Both)**. If there is an error in the **zip code only**, the answer is **C (Zip code only)**.

> 3590 Sonoma Ln   84770   3590 Sonoma Ln   84710
> Saint George, UT   Saint George, UT

In the above example, the answer is **C** (Zip code only)

Sixth Way: Compare the city, state and ZIP Code on the left to the city, state, and ZIP code on the right. Then compare the address (numbers and street names) on the left column to the ones on the right. if there are errors in both address and ZIP codes, then mark **D (Both)**.

If there is an error in the address only, the answer is **B (Address Only)**; if there are no errors in both address and ZIP codes, then mark **A (No Errors)**.

Example:

> 12478 Dorchester Ct   55124-0110   12478 Dorchester Ct   55124-0110
> Saint Paul MN   Saint Paul MN

In the above example, the answer is **A: (No Errors)**.

Seventh Way: Compare the address on the left column and the address on the right column. Granting that they are different, compare both ZIP codes (left and right column). If the ZIP codes have no errors, then the answer is **B: (Address Only)**.

Example:

23661 Pepper Tree Dr 48091		23671 Pepper Tree 48091	
Warren, MI		Warren, MI	

Remember, the address includes the numbers, street name (and abbreviation Rd (Road) or St (Street). and city and state names) and the ZIP codes which consist of five or more numbers, such as 20850 and 48091-1721.

Important:

In analyzing the numbers of streets, be sure to take note of numbers with similar shapes, such as 3 and 8 or 5, and 1 and 7, 2 and 5. Match these numbers: 29890 and 29390; 72360 and 72860; and 81939 and 87939. Did you see the errors?

In comparing or matching addresses and zip codes in each row of the items, you should always start reading from the left. That is, compare each row of the **Correct List** with each row of the **List to be Checked.** Although the *instruction* for you is to compare the each row of the **List to Be Checked** with the **Correct List** (from right to left), it should be the other way around. **That is, you should compare** each row of the **Correct List** with each row of the **List to Be Checked.** Why? It's because it's not the usual way to look at the addresses and zip codes from the right to the left; it should be from left to right because reading is always done from left to right.

Example:

Postal 473 Battery Test

Part A: Address-Checking Test

| A. No Errors | B. Address Only | C. Zip Code Only | D. Both |

Correct List		*List to Be Checked*	
Address	ZIP Code	Address	ZIP Code
1. 537 Richmond Dr Akron, OH	89965	337 Richmond Dr Akron, OH	89964
2. 1597 Pope Ln Douglas, GA	31535	1897 Pope Ln Douglas, GA	31535
3. 4375 Park Ave Worcester, MA	01610	4375 Park Ave Worcester, MA	01610
4. 4638 College Rd Baltimore, MD	21229-0103	4689 College Rd Baltimore, MD	21229-3019
5. 2069 Pershing Ave Dade City, FL	33525-3012	20668 Pershing Ave Dade City, FL	33526-3012

In a nutshell, you just determine whether the addresses and zip codes in the **Correct List** and **List to Be Checked** are *alike* or *different.* Each row includes the address containing numbers, street names (and abbreviations, Rd for Road, etc.), and city and state names and the ZIP codes consist of five or more numbers. Sometimes the ZIP code contains nine numbers, including the so-called ZIP plus 4 (four numbers).

Actually, it's just wise to remember that there are two columns of addresses and ZIP codes (left column or first column and right column or second column). You should not care whether any of each address or ZIP code belongs to the **Correct List** or to the **List to Be Checked**. If there's any difference in any of the information in each row, there should be an error or errors. Therefore, mark **A** for **No Errors; B** for an error in the **Address Only; C** for an error in the **ZIP Code Only;** and **D** for errors in **both** address and ZIP Code. So it doesn't matter whether you read the information in each row of the addresses and ZIP codes from right to left or from left to right. Just find the error or errors in the address and ZIP code!

12

6 Exam 473 Practice Tests

Part A: Address Checking

Part A: Address-Checking Practice Test 1

This is a practice test containing 60 items or questions. You have to answer these questions in 11 minutes.

What you have to do is to compare each row of the address and zip code in the **Correct List** (left column) to those in the **List to Be Checked** (right column). Determine of they are alike or different. If there are differences, know where the errors are. Mark any of the Delivery Routes **A, B, C,** and **D: A** for **No Errors; B** for an error in the **Address Only; C** for an error in the **Zip Code Only;** and **D,** for errors in **Both** the address and ZIP code.

A. No Errors	B. Address Only	C. ZIP Code Only	D. Both

	Correct List		List to be Checked		
	Address	ZIP Code	Address	ZIP Code	
1.	50378 Bear Dr Park City, UT	84098-3101	50878 Bear Dr Park City, UT	84098-3101	1. ___
2.	89411 Braxton Ct Williamsburg, VA	23185-2183	39411 Braxton Ct Williamsburg, VA	23195-2183	2. ___
3.	2028 Bay Ct Pasadena, TX	77505-0109	2026 Bay Ct Pasadena, TX	77505-0109	3. ___
4.	15982 Townsend Rd Charleston, SC	29406-1102	15982 Townsed Rd Charleston, SC	29406-1102	4. ___
5.	21033 Walnut Dr Hamilton, OH	45011	21933 Walnut Dr Hamilton OH	45011	5. ___
6.	20931 Greenbriar Dr Goldsboro, NC	27534-0102	20931 Greenbriar Dr Goldsboro, NC	27534-0103	6. ___
7.	50921 Coleridge Rd Rochester, NY	14509-2302	50921 Coleridge Dr Rochester, NY	14509-2303	7. ___
8.	29105 Richmond Pl Akron, OH	44303-2109	29105 Richmond Pl Akron, OH	44303-2109	8. ___
9.	3422 Drove Dr Los Angeles, CA	90065	4322 Dove Dr Los Angeles, CA	90065	9. ___
10.	24161 Chapman Orange, CA	92868-4120	24161 Chapman Orange, CA	92868-4120	10. ___

A. No Errors	B. Address Only	C. ZIP Code Only	D. Both

	Correct List		Correct List		
	Address	Zip Code	Address	ZIP Code	Answers
11.	70830 Pepperfield Dr Tampa, FL	33624-2309	70330 Pepperfield Dr Tampa, Fl	33624-2381	11. ____
12	9310 Tuscany Ln Griffin, GA	92868	9310 Tuscany Dr Griffin, GA	92869	12. ____
13.	28014 Madison Ct Champaign, IL	61820-2117	28015 Madison Ct Champaign, IL	61825-2117	13. ____
14.	3815 Shady Grove Rd Rockville, MD	20850-0105	3815 Shady Grove St Rockville, MD	20850-0105	14. ____
15.	3551 Pine View Ct Battle Creek, MI	49017	3551 Pineview Ct Battle Creek, MI	49017	15. ____
16.	31012 Todd St Ypsilanti, MI	48198	31012 Todd St Ypsilanti, MI	48098	16. ____
17.	4109 Mayfair St Waterloo, IA	50701-2131	4109 Mayfair St Waterloo, IA	50701-2131	17. ____
18.	7203 Rock Rd Rockville, MD	20852-4121	7203 Rock Rd Rockville, MD	20852-4122	18. ____
19.	2130 Randall Ln Bloomfield Hills, MI	48304-0120	2130 Randall Ln Bloomfield Hills, MI	48304-0220	19. ____
20	42591 Scott Loop Honolulu, HI	96818	42591 Scott Loop Honolulu, HI	96818	20. ____
21.	2131 Blanchard St Pensacola, F	32505-2109	2131 Blanchard Dr Pensacola, FL	32505-2709	21. ____
22.	7012 Old Ridge Pl Atlanta, GA	30327	7013 Old Ridge Dr Atlanta, GA	30827	22. ____
23.	20831 Princeton Ln Valdosa, GA	30327-2103	20831 Princeton Rd Valdosa, GA	30328-2103	23. ____
24.	7079 Heatherfield Dr Lafayette, IN	47909-1025	7013 Heatherfield Dr Lafayette, IN	47809-1025	24. ____
25.	10254 Thompson Ave Newport, KY	41076	10254 Thompson Rd Newport, KY	41076	25. ____
26.	40120 Bush Ave Chicopee, MA	01013-5121	40120 Bush Ave Chicopee, MA	01013-5121	26. ____
27.	4015 Yonka St Detroit, MI	48234-2120	4016 Yonka St Detroit, MI	48284-2120	27. ____
28.	8530 Thompson Ave Waterbury, CT	06708-2109	8530 Thompson Ave Waterbury, CT	06708-2109	28. ____

A. No Errors		B. Address Only		C. ZIP Code Only		D. Both

	Correct List		List to be Check		

	Address	ZIP Code	Address	ZIP Code	Answers
29.	20512 Pershing Ave Dade City, Fl	33525-3012	20812 Pershing Cir Dade City, FL	33525-3012	29. ___
30.	5021 Jones Wood Rd Monroe, GA	30655-2106	5021 Jones Wood Rd Monroe, GA	30658-2151	30. ___
31.	12698 St James Blvd Rockville, MD	20850	12898 St James Blvd Rockville, MD	20850	31. ___
32.	4345 Park Ave Worcester, MA	01610-4120	4345 Park Ave Worcester, MA	01610-4120	32. ___
33.	5598 Hanna St Fort Wayne, IN	46806-2152	5598 Hanna Rd Fort Wayne, IN	46806-2152	33. ___
34.	17332 US Hwy 60 E Owensboro, KY	42301	17832 US Hwy 60 E Owensboro, KY	42301	34. ___
35.	4638 College Rd Baltimore, MD	21229-0103	4688 College Rd Baltimore, MD	21229-0108	35. ___
36.	4347 Park Ave Worcester, MA	01610-2151	4347 Park Ave Worcester, MA	01610-2151	36. ___
37.	1223 Taylor Ave N Grand Rapids, MI	49505-1256	1223 Taylor Ave N Grand Rapids, MI	49505-1256	37. ___
38.	25980 County Rd 138 Saint Cloud, MN	56301-2051	25980 County St 138 Saint Cloud, MN	56301-2057	38. ___
39.	6298 W 4th St Hattiesburg, MS	39402-1250	6298 W 5th St Hattiesburg, MS	39402-6019	39. ___
40.	1597 Pope Ln Douglas, GA	31535	1897 Pope Ln Douglas, GA	31535	40. ___
41.	14901 Observatory Dr Orlando, FL	32818-2121	14901 Observatory Dr Orlando, FL	32818-2121	41. ___
42.	91431 Baymeadows Rd Jacksonville, FL	32256	91431 Beymeadow Rd Jacksonville, FL	32256	42. ___
43.	17398 Monitor Ave Bakersfield, CA	93307	17898 Monitor Ave Bakersfield, CA	93307	43. ___
44.	13808 Telluride St Brighton, CO	80603-2108	13808 Telluride Rd Brighton, CO	80603-2103	44. ___

A. No Errors	B. Address Only	C. ZIP Code Only	D. Both

	Correct List		List to Be Check	
	Address	ZIP Code	Address	ZIP Code	Answers

	Address	ZIP Code	Address	ZIP Code	Answers
45.	16798 Ponce Leon Blvd Brooksfield, FL	34614	18798 Ponce Leon Blvd Brooksfield, FL	34614	45. ___
46.	1898 7th Ave SE Cedar Rapids, IA	52403	1898 7th Ave SW Cedar Rapids, IA	52408	46. ___
47.	3150 Skylark Ln Newport, KY	41076-0112	2150 Skylark Ln Newport, KY	41076-0115	47. ___
48.	3159 White Oak Ct Denham Springs, LA	70435	3159 White Oak Ct Denham Springs, LA	70435	48. ___
49.	18990 Elmwood Ave Detroit, MI	48207-2108	18990 Elmwood Ave Detroit, MI	48307-2108	49. ___
50.	25778 Timberline Dr Warren, MI	48091	28778 Timberline Dr Warren, MI	48091	50. ___
51.	1109 National Pkwy Fort Lauderdale, FL	33323-3107	1109 National Pkwy Fort Lauderdale, FL	33323-3107	51. ___
52.	5897 "O" St Sacramento, CA	96819-3156	5397 "O" St Sacramento, CA	96819-3156	52. ___
53.	2315 Rockhurst Dr Waterbury, CT	06708-2109	2315 Rockhurst Dr Waterbury, CT	06708-2109	53. ___
54.	8805 Lee Vista Rd Orlando, FL	32829	8805 Lee Vista St Orlando, FL	32929	54. ___
55.	2497 Wallace Rd Griffin, GA	30224-4129	2497 Wallace Ave Griffin, GA	30224-4129	55. ___
56.	1425 111th St Bolingbrook, IL	60440	1625 111th St Bolingbrook, IL	60440	56. ___
57.	8298 Broadacres Rd Shreveport, LA	71119	8298 Broadacres Rd Shreveport, LA	71119	57. ___
58.	12601 Wyoming St Detroit, MI	48238-2106	12801 Wyoming St Detroit, MI	48238-2109	58. ___
59.	12579 Dorchester Ct Saint Paul MN	55124-0110	12579 Dorchester Ct Saint Paul MN	55124-0110	59. ___
60.	2301 15th Ave Longmont, CO	80501	2307 15th Ave Longmont, CO	80501	60. ___

(See the answers to the above questions on page 73.

Postal Test 473

Part A: Address-Checking Practice Test 2

This is a practice test containing 60 items or questions. You have to answer these questions in 11 minutes.

What you have to do is to compare the each row of the address and zip code in the **Correct List** (left column) to those in the **List to Be Checked** (right column). Determine of they are alike or different. If there are differences, know where the errors are. Mark any of the Delivery Routes **A, B, C,** and **D: A** for **No Errors; B** for an error in the **Address Only; C** for an error in the **Zip Code Only;** and **D,** for errors in **Both** the address and ZIP code.

A. No Errors	B. Address Only	C. ZIP Code Only	D. Both

	Correct List		List to Be Checked		Answers
	Address	ZIP Code	Address	ZIP Code	
1.	3145 Sandra Ln Corona, CA	92879-2109	3145 Sandra Ln Corona, CA	93879-2109	1. ___
2.	4402 Asbrook Ln Orlando, FL	32919	4302 Asbrook Ln Orlando, FL	32919	2. ___
3.	91201 Old Ham Dr Indianapolis, IN	46228-0122	91201 Old Ham Dr Indianapolis, IN	46228-0128	3. ___
4.	2108 Vasseur Ave Paduca, KY	42003-2102	2108 Basseur Ave Paduca, KY	42003-2102	4. ___
5.	2345 Church Rd Chesterfield, MO	63005	2435 Church Rd Chesterfield, MO	63003	5. ___
6.	21307 Bluebird Ln Naperville, IL	60565-2801	21307 Bluebird Ln Naperville, IL	60565-2801	6. ___
7.	7821 Compass Ln Tampa, FL	33611-0120	7821 Compass Rd Tampa, FL	33611-0120	7. ___
8.	17854 King St New Iberia, LA	70560	17854 King Ln New Iheria, LA	70568	8. ___
9.	3094 Oakview St Worcester, MA	01605-7021	3194 Oakview St Worcester, MA	01605-7022	9. ___
10	4129 Riverview Ave Saint Paul, MN	55107-1027	4129 Riverview Ave Saint Paul, MN	55107-1037	10. ___
11.	8129 Gladys Ct McDonough, GA	30252-2905	8128 Gladys Ct McDonough, GA	30253-2905	11. ___

A. No Errors	B. Address Only	C. ZIP Code	D. Both

	Correct List		List to Be Checked		
	Address	ZIP Code	Address	ZIP Code	Answers
12.	3451 Belvedere Dr Stratford, CT	06614-2109	3451 Belvedere Dr Stratford, CT	06615-2109	12. ___
13.	76095 Gibson Rd San Francisco, CA	94129-2160	76095 Gibson Rd San Francisco, CA	94129-2160	13. ___
14.	30591 San Juan Dr Anchorage, AK	99504-3106	30691 San Juan Dr Anchorage, AK	99504-3106	14. ___
15.	1678 Brookwood Rd Peoria, IL	61614	1778 Brookwood St Peoria, IL	61615	15. ___
16.	21595 Packard St Rochester, NY	14609-2102	21895 Packard St Rochester, NY	14608-2102	16. ___
17.	28091 Hickory St New Bern, NC	28502	28091 Hickory St New Bern, NC	28502	17. ___
18.	2121 Rolling Hills Dr Kingsport, TN	37660-8126	2121 Rolling Hills Dr Kingsport, TN	37661-8125	18. ___
19.	50605 SW Millen Dr Portland, OR	97224-2101	50605 SW Millen Dr Portland, OR	97224-2101	19. ___
20.	50672 Armstrong Dr Spartanburg, SC	29301-2106	50673 Armstrong Dr Spartanburg, NC	29301-2108	20. ___
21.	50618 Peterson Ct Fort Worth, TX	76177-0102	50618 Peterson Ct Forth Worth, TX	76117-0102	21. ___
22.	87401 Baywood Dr Harrisburgh, PA	17111	87401 Beywood Dr Harrisburgh, PA	17111	22. ___
23.	3194 Beaver Rd Columbus, OH	43213-2104	3195 Beaver Ave Columbus, OH	43213-2104	23. ___
24.	8254 Sandy Creek Raleigh, NC	27615	8254 Sandy Creek Raleigh, NC	27615	24. ___
25.	54902 Bedford Ave Middletown, NY	10940	54902 Bedford Ave Middletown, NY	10940	25. ___
26.	48125 Wisconsin St Middletown, OH	45049-2109	48125 Wisconsin Ln Middletown, OH	45049-2109	26. ___
27.	2586 Sky Park Dr Portland, OR	97504	2586 Sky Park Dr Portland, OR	97504	27. ___

	A. No Errors	B. Address Only	C. ZIP Code Only	D. Both

	Correct List		List to Be Checked	
	Address	ZIP Code	Address	ZIP Code	Answers
28.	9321 Hudson Pl Providence, RI	02905-3102	9321 Hudson Pl Providence, RI	02905-3108	28. ___
29.	17092 Arlington Dr Johnson City, TN	37601-0120	17092 Arlington Dr Johnson City, TN	37601-0120	29. ___
30.	1021 Cypress Brook Cypress, TX 77429	88428	1021 Cypress Brook Cypress, TX	88420	30. ___
31.	10888 Edes Ave Oakland, CA	94603-0530	10888 Edes Ave Oakland, CA	94603-0530	31. ___
32.	5267 Lakesside Dr Lake Wales, FL	33898-2109	5267 Lakeside Dr Lake Wales, FL	33898-2109	32. ___
33.	1100 8th SW Fifton, GA	31794-0581	1100 8th NW Fifton, GA	31894-0581	33. ___
34.	7498 42nd St NE Cedar Rapids, IA	52411	7496 42nd St NE Cedar Rapids, IA	52412	34. ___
35.	4000 N Charles St Baltimore, MD	31535-0210	4000 N Charles St Baltimore, MD	31535-0210	35. ___
36.	4234 Adams Rd Douglas, GA	31535-0320	4238 Adams Rd Douglas, GA	31835-0320	36. ___
37.	3398 E Las Vegas St Colorado Springs, CO	80906	3396 E Las Vegas St Colorado Sprgs, CO	80908	37. ___
38.	25199 Highway 27 Lake Wales, FL	33859	25190 Highway 27 Lake Wales, FL	33859	38. ___
39.	5201 Union Ave Santa Maria, CA	93454-2106	5201 Union Ave Santa Maria, CA	93458-2106	39. ___
40.	2100 Hillside Ave Trenton, IJ	08618	2108 Hillside Rd Trenton, NJ	08614	40. ___
41.	1299 Beverly Rd Asheville, NC	28806-0310	1200 Beverly Rd Asheville, NC	28906-0310	41. ___
42.	6732 Beech St Cincinnati, OH	45217	6832 Beech St Cincinnati, OH	48217	42. ___
43.	6732 E 7th Ct Tulsa, OK	74133	6732 E 7th Ct Tulsa, OK	74133	43. ___

A. No Errors	B. Address Only	C. ZIP Code Only	D. Both

	Correct List		List to Be Checked		Answers
44.	1676 Hagood Ave Columbia, SC	29204	1778 Hagood Ave Columbia, SC	29204	44. ___
45.	899 Cates St Marysville, TN	37803-3192	899 Cates St Marysville, TN	37803-3192	45. ___
46.	31512 N Hwy 303 Grand Prairie, TX	75050	31812 N Hwy 303 Grand Prairie, TX	78050	46. ___
47.	1299 E 1040 N Orem, UT	84097	1299 E 1040 N Orem, UT	84097	47. ___
48.	7300 NE 110th St Vancouver, WA	98662	7800 NE 110th St Vancouver, WA	93662	48. ___
49.	4998 Oakfield Way San Antonio, TX	78250	4998 Oakfield Way San Antonio, TX	78250	49. ___
50.	3741 Woodcrest Ln Virginia Beach, VA	34563-3106	3741 Woodcrest Rd Virginia Beach, VA	38563-3106	50. ___
51.	15882 Paloxy Dr Tyler, TX	75703-0951	15882 Paloxy Dr Tyler, TX	85703-0951	51. ___
52.	13786 83rd Ave E Puyallup, WA	98373 -1220	19897 93rd Ave E Puyallup, WA	98373-1280	52. ___
53.	2007 Tryon St Greer, SC	29651	2008 Tryon Pl Greer, SC	29657	53. ___
54.	3298 Dunaway St Amarillo, TX	79103	3298 Dunaway St Amarillo, TX	98103	54. ___
55.	5297 NW Rogers Ln Lawton, OK	73505	5297 NW Rogers Ln Lawton, OK	73505	55. ___
56.	7398 Overton St Pittsburgh, PA	15218-2109	7399 Overton St Pittsburgh, PA	15218-2106	56. ___
57.	3120 Tudor Pl Chesapeake, VA	23320-4182	3120 Tudor Rd Chesapeake, VA	23320-4102	57. ___
58.	18197 79th Ave E Puyallup, WA	98375-0151	18197 79th Ave E Puyallup, WA	98375-0151	58. ___
59.	5926 Sandy Porks St Raleigh, NC	27615	5926 Sandy Porks St Raleigh, NC	27618	59. ___
60.	7298 E 73rd Pl Tulsa, OK	74133-2691	7299 N 73rd Pl Tulsa, OK	74138-2691	60. ___

(See the answers to the above questions on page 74)

Postal Test 473

Part A: Address-Checking Practice Test 3

This is a practice test containing 60 items or questions. You have to answer these questions in 11 minutes.

What you have to do is to compare the each row of the address and zip code in the **Correct List** (left column) to those in the **List to Be Checked** (right column). Determine of they are alike or different. If there are differences, know where the errors are. Mark any of the Delivery Routes **A, B, C,** and **D: A** for **No Errors; B** for an error in the **Address Only; C** for an error in the **Zip Code Only;** and **D,** for errors in **Both** the address and ZIP code.

A. No Errors	B. Address Only	C. ZIP Code Only	D. Both

	Correct List		List to Be Checked		Answers
	Address	ZIP Code	Address	ZIP Code	
1.	3182 Teakwood Dr Santa Maria, CA	93455-2102	3182 Teakwood Dr Santa Maria, CA	93455-2102	1. ___
2.	25911 Sulivan St Waterbury, CT	06708-0125	25911 Sulvan Rd Waterbury, CT	06708-0125	2. ___
3.	5209 Richmond Wy Commerce, GA	30529	5209 Richmond Rd Commerce, GA	30529	3. ___
4.	30510 Edmonton St Detroit, MI	48204	30510 Edmonton Dr Detroit, MI	48204	4. ___
5.	2812 Roundtree Blvd Ypsilanti, MI	48197-4102	2812 Roundtree Blvd Ypsilanti, MI	48197-4103	5. ___
6.	210 Grand Oak Dr Carbondale, IL	62901-0205	210 Grand Oak Dr Carbondale, IL	62901-0205	6. ___
7.	2014 Sngleton Ave Newport, KY	41076-0326	2014 Singleton Ave New Port, KY	41078-0326	7. ___
8.	38312 Paradise Way Eustis, FL	32736-0106	38312 Paradise Cir Eustia, FL	32730-0106	8. ___
9.	3054 Missouri Ave Los Angeles, CA	90025-1256	3054 Missouri Ave Los Angeles, CA	90025-1256	9. ___
10.	31561 Winnipig St Brighton, CO	80603-0127	31561 Winnipig St Brighton, CO	80803-0127	10. ___
11.	301 Shadowbrook Ct Burlington, NC	27215-0220	307 Shadowcrook Ct Burlington, NC	27215-0220	11. ___

A. No Errors	B. Address Only	C. ZIP Code Only	D. Both

Correct List   *Correct List*

#	Address	ZIP Code	Address	ZIP Code	Answers
12.	3157 Glastonburgh Ln Portland, OR	97224-2146	3157 Glastonburg Dr Portland, OR	97224-2146	12. ___
13.	2725 Manchester Ln Chesapeake, VA	23321	2725 Manchester Rd Chesapeake, VA	23321	13. ___
14.	12254 Parryville Dr Houston, TX	77041-0109	12258 Perryville Dr Houston, TX	77041-0109	14. ___
15.	4254 Westside Dr Olympia, WA	98502-0121	4254 Westside Ln Olympia, WA	98502-0127	15. ___
16.	3152 Stonebrook Rd Charleston, WV	25314-2109	3152 Stonebrook Rd Charleston, WV	25314-2109	16. ___
17.	214 Peacock Dr Fort Worth, TX	76131-0129	214 Peacock Dr Fort Worth, TX	76137-0129	17. ___
18.	30912 Mallard Dr Pittsburg, PA	15238-2012	30912 Malard Dr Pittsburg, PA	15238-2012	18. ___
19.	3152 Bayham Dr Cincinnati, OH	45218	3152 Baham Dr Cincinnati, OH	48218	19. ___
20.	2154 Netherfield Ct Winchester, VA	22602	2154 Netherfield Dr Winchester, VA	22603	20. ___
21.	542 Auburn Dr Madison, WI	53711-0109	542 Auburn Dr Madison, MI	53811-0109	21. ___
22.	50113 NW 32nd Ave Vancouver, WA	98685-2199	50113 NW 33rd Ave Vancouver, WA	98685-2199	22. ___
23.	3452 Castlewood Dr Greenville, SC	29615-2298	3452 Castlewood Dr Greenoak, SC	29615-2298	23. ___
24.	31075 Ottawa St Pittsburg, PA	15211	31075 Ottawa St Pittsburg, PA	15212	24. ___
25.	433 Woodside Dr Oklahoma City, OK	73110-0610	423 Woodside Dr Oklahoma City, OK	73110-0610	25. ___
26.	3154 Kellwood Ct Raleigh, NC	27609-0291	3154 Kellwood Ct Raleigh, SC	27609-0291	26. ___

| A. No Errors | B. Address Only | ZIP Code Only | D. Both |

	Correct List		List to Be Checked		
	Address	ZIP Code	Address	ZIP Code	Answers
27.	12540 Ruthland Ave Buffalo, NY	14212-0029	12540 Ruthlan Ave Buffalo, NY	14212-0028	27. ___
28.	5409 Knoll Crest Ct Boulder, CO	80301-2158	5409 Knoll Crest Ct Boulder, CO	80307-2158	28. ___
29.	6789 S Vassar St Wichita, KS	67218	6788 S Vassar St Wichita, KS	78219	29. ___
30.	9054 Bramble Way Shreveport, LA	71118-0929	9054 Bramble Way Shreveport, LA	71118-0929	30. ___
31.	63990 Lakeside Ln Carbondale, IL	62903-2108	63998 Lakeside St Carbondale, IL	62908-2108	31. ___
32.	1015 US Hwy 319 N Fifton, GA	31794-0129	1015 US Hwy 319 N Fifton, GA	31794-0129	32. ___
33.	150 N Drake Rd Kalamazoo, MI	49009-5201	150 E Drake Rd Kalamazoo, MI	48009-5201	33. ___
34.	3015 Duncan Dr Greenville, MS	38703	3015 Duncan Dr Greenville, MS	38708	34. ___
35.	8531 Fernwood Trl Roswell, GA	30075-2105	8531 Fernwood Trl Roswell, GA	30075-2105	35. ___
36.	1900 Adams Ln Sarasota, FL	34236	1908 Adams Ln Sarasota, FL	34286	36. ___
37.	11990 Drake Rd Kalamazoo, MI	49009-4120	11990 Drake Rd Kalamzoo, MI	49009-4120	37. ___
38.	1343 Colbert Ct Florissant, MO	63031	1348 Colbert Ct Florrisant, MO	63037	38. ___
39.	5011 N Covington Ct Wichita, KS	67212-3012	5011 N Covington Ct Wichita, KS	67212-3012	39. ___
40.	499 Oliver Ct Monroe, LA	71202	499 Oliver Trl Monroe, LA	71203	40. ___
41.	1289 Windsor Rd Wesminster, MD	21158	1288 Windsor St Wesminster, MD	21158	41. ___
42.	1688 S 11th St Greenwood, IN	46526	1689 S 11th St Greenwood, IN	46528	42. ___

A. No Errors	B. Address Only		ZIP Code Only	D. Both

	Correct List		List to Be Checked		
	Address	ZIP Code	Address	ZIP Code	Answers
43.	2911 Cherry Wood Dr Buffalo, NY	142121-0102	2911 Cherry Wood Dr Buffalo, NY	142121-0102	43.___
44.	3569 Apache Dr Johnson City, TN	37604-3107	3560 Apache Dr Johnson City, TN	38604-3107	44.___
45.	29010 Woodside Dr Yorktown, VA	22191-2651	29010 Woodside Dr Yorktown, VA	22191-2651	45.___
46.	2080 Crossbow Ct Fort Worth, TX	76133	2080 Crossbow Ct Fort Worth, TX	76133	46.___
47.	4100 NE 20th St Renton, WA	98059-0621	4108 NE 20th St Renton, WA	98159-0621	47.___
48.	5990 S Rosa Rd Madison, WI	53719	5990 S Rosa Rd Madison, WI	53719	48.___
49.	2290 Crest Dr El Cajon, CA	92021-0934	2290 Crest Dr El Cajon, CA	92022-0934	49.___
50.	3901 McIntosh Plz Newark, DE	19713-0492	3901 McIntosh Pl Newark, DE	19713-0492	50.___
51.	12199 SW 8th Ave Gainsville, FL	32607	12190 SW 8th Ave Gainsville, FL	32807	51.___
52.	7703 Whipple St Chicago, IL	60652-2307	7708 Whippe St Chicago IL	60652-2308	52.___
53.	16199 Old Auburn Rd Fort Wayne, IN	46845	16199 Old Auburn Rd Fort Wayne, IN	46845	53.___
54.	16346 S Butch St Olathe, KS	47892-2109	16346 S Butch St Olathe, KS	47392-2108	54.___
55.	1398 Natchitocks St Monroe, LA	71291	1398 Natchitocks Rd Monroe, LA	71291	55.___
56.	12980 N Windsor Rd Westminster, MD	21158-0721	12980 N Windsor Rd Westminster, MD	21758-0721	56.___
57.	35981 N 32nd St Caldwell, ID	83605	38981 N 32nd St Caldwell, ID	83608	57.___
58.	5199 Sweetser Ave Evansville, IN	47715-2017	5199 Sweetser Ave Evansville, IN	47715-2017	58.___
59.	1489 Walter Jetlon St Paducan, KY	42003	1489 Walter Jetlon St Paducan, KY	42003	59.___
60.	3501 Oliver Ct Shreveport, LA	71202	3501 Oliver Ct Shreveport, LA	71202	60.___

(See the answers to the above questions on page 75.)

Part A: Address-Checking Practice Test 4

This is a practice test containing 60 items or questions. You have to answer these questions in 11 minutes.

What you have to do is to compare the each row of the address and zip code in the **Correct List** (left column) to those in the **List to Be Checked** (right column). Determine of they are alike or different. If there are differences, know where the errors are. Mark any of the Delivery Routes **A, B, C,** and **D: A** for **No Errors; B** for an error in the **Address Only; C** for an error in the **Zip Code Only;** and **D,** for errors in **Both** the address and ZIP code.

A. No Errors	B. Address Only	C. ZIP Code	D. Both

	Correct List		List to Be Checked		
	Address	Zip Code	Address	Zip Code	Answers
1.	26902 Poseidon Dr Havasa City, Al	86406-2102	28902 Poseidon Dr Havassa City, AL	86306-2102	1.____
2.	3201 Duray Pl Los Angeles, CA	90008-0731	3201 Duray Dr Los Angeles, CA	90008-0731	2.____
3.	13700 Livingston Ave Tampa, FL	33613	13700 Livingston Ave Tampa, FL	33613	3.____
4.	1973 N Collington Ave Baltimore, MD	21213-5020	1978 N Collington Ave Baltimore, MD	21218-5020	4.____
5.	1523 Heyward St Columbia, SC	29205	1523 Heyward St Columbia, SC	29208	5.____
6.	1599 S Peach Ave Tyler, TX	75701-2129	1590 S Peach Ave Tyler, TX	75701-2120	6.____
7.	13799 9th Ave W Everett, WA	98204-3109	13899 9th Ave W Everett, WA	98204-3108	7.____
8.	4211 Boxwood Dr Mesquite, TX	75180	4211 Boxwood Dr Mesquite, TX	75180	8.____
9.	5300 Lozzeles Rd Charlotte, NC	28214-5114	5800 Lozzeles Rd Charlotte, NC	28214-5115	9.____
10.	6175 Morroco St Cincinnati, OH	45230	6175 Morroco St Cincinnati, OH	45230	10.____
11.	1199 N 10th St Hagleton, PA	17103-2108	1190 E 10th St Hagleton, PA	17103-2108	11.____
12.	7391 Barnett St Rockhill, SC	29732	7391 Barnett St Rockhill, SC	29732	12.____
13.	1217 River Divide Rd Seviervill, TN	37862-0120	1217 River Divide St Seviervill, TN	37662-0120	13.____

A. No Errors	B. Address Only	C. ZIP Code Only	D. Both

	Corect List		List to Be Checked		
	Address	ZIP Code	Address	ZIP Code	Answers
14.	6408 Boat Club Rd Forth Worth, TX	76179-0197	6408 Boat Club Rd Forth Worth, TX	76179-0198	14.___
15.	7290 Bairbridge St Charlottesville, VA	22902-3023	7290 Bairbridge Rd Charlottesville, VA	22902-3023	15.___
16.	3577 S 93rd St Milwaukee, WI	53228	3577 S 93rd St Milwaukee, WI	53229	16.___
17.	62812 Merchant Way Everett, WA	98208-6109	62812 Merchant Way Everett, WA	98209-6109	17.___
18.	1100 Jeff Davis Ave Selma, AL	36703-2121	1100 Jeff Davis Ave Selma, AL	36703-2127	18.___
19.	2398 Cottonwood St Santa Ana, CA	92705-2109	2398 Cottonwood Pl Santa Ana, CA	92705-2109	19.___
20.	4364 Blackston St S Augusta, GA	30906	4364 Blackston St S Augusta, GA	30906	20.___
21.	3399 S Gayer Rd Kokomo, IN	46902-4201	3398 S Gayer Rd Kokomo, IN	46902-4207	21.___
22.	7306 Hillcrest Dr Lowell, MA	01851	7306 Hillcrest Dr Lowell, MA	01851	22.___
23.	2289 S Drake Rd Kalamazoo, MI	49009-7120	2289 N Drake Rd Kalamazoo, MI	49009-7120	23.___
24.	17990 Marina Dr Slidell, LA	70458-3106	17890 Marina Dr Slidell, LA	70459-3106	24.___
25.	1319 Park Ave Worcester, MA	01610	1319 Park Ave Worcester, MA	01610	25.___
26.	8210 Glenhaven Cir Hattiesburg, MS	39401-5212	8219 Glenhaven Cir Hattiesburg, MS	39401-5212	26.___
27.	7312 Pleasant Knoll Joliet, IL	60435	7312 Pleasant Knoll Joliet, IL	60435	27.___
28.	10597 Blue Hill Rd Baton Raton Rouge, LA	70810	10597 Blue Hill Ln Baton Raton Rouge, LA	90810	28.___
29.	73109 Puckett Pl Covington, GA	30014-7231	73109 Puckett Pl Covington, GA	30014-7237	29.___

	A. No Errors	B. Address Only	C: ZIP Code Only	D. Both

	Correct List		List to Be Checked		Answers
	Address	Zip Code	Address	Zip Code	
30.	699 N Mountan Ave Montclair, NJ	07043-2106	699 S Mountain Ave Montclair, NJ	07043-2106	30.____
31.	6108 S 75th East Ave Tulsa, OK	74133-2109	6108 N 75th East Ave Tulsa, OK	74133-2109	31.____
32.	1299 Valley Rd Montclair, NJ	07043	1299 Valley Rd Montclair, NJ	07043	32.____
33.	15498 Parkview St Houston, TX	77071-2608	15498 Parkview St Houston, TX	78071-2608	33.____
34.	11497 34th St SW Seattle, WA	98146-2109	11497 34th St SW Seattle, WA	09146-2109	34.____
35.	10967 Metcalf St Escondido, CA	92026-0151	10967 Metcalf Rd Escondido, CA	92026-0751	35.____
36.	2199 E Park St Arlington Hts, IL	60004	2199 E Park St Arlington Hts, IL	60004	36.____
37.	3322 Burton St Chicopee, MA	01013	3322 Burton St Chicopee, MA	01013	37.____
38.	2201 Fuller St Hattiesburg, MS	39402-1020	2207 Fuller St Hattiesburg, MS	39408-1020	38.____
39.	69912 Ludwig Ave West Monroe, LA	71292-0129	69912 Ludwig Ave West Monroe, LA	71892-0129	39.____
40.	1700 N School St Honolulu, HI	96819-7130	1700 N School St Honolulu, HI	96819-7130	40.____
41.	10417 Old Decatur Rd Fort Wayne, IN	46806-1028	10417 Old Decator Rd Fort Wayne, IN	46906-1028	41.____
42.	1499 Walter Jetton Rd Paducan, KY	42003-2129	1490 Walter Jetton Paducan, KY	48003-2129	42.____
43.	45598 Murfield Dr Canton, MI	48188-2469	45598 Murfield Dr Canton, MI	48188-2469	43.____
44.	11203 W Florence Ln Boise, ID	48709	11203 W Florence Rd Boise, ID	48709	44.____
45.	2199 SW Filmore St. Topeka, KS	66611	2199 SW Filmore St Topeka, KS	66611	45.____

| A. No Errors | B. Address Only | C: ZIP Code Only | D. Both |

Correct List		List to Be Checked		
Address	ZIP Code	Address	ZIP Code	Answers
46. 1299 New Windsor Rd Westminster, MD	21158-0670	1299 New Windsor Rd Westminster, MD	21158-0670	46.____
47. 289 Stuyvesant Ave Brooklyn, NY	11288	280 Stuyvesant Ave Brooklyn, NY	11288	47.____
48. 1968 Old Mountain Rd Statesville, NC	28677-1020	1968 Old Mountain Ln Statesville, NC	28877-1020	48.____
49. 5797 NE Church St Portland, OR	97224-8010	5797 NE Church St Portland, OR	97224-8010	49.____
50. 1133 Hope St Providence, RI	02906-5021	1138 Hope St Providence, RI	02906-5021	50.____
51. 62980 Davis Ln Austin, TX	78749	62980 Davis Rd Austin, TX	78740	51.____
52. 2299 Wolfsnare Rd Virginia Beach, VA	23454-1030	2290 Wolfsnare Rd Virginia Beach, VA	23454-1030	52.____
53. 7993 Forest Ave Fond Du Lac, WI	54937-0950	7993 Forest Ave Fond Du Lac, WI	54937-0050	53.____
54. 586 Highland Ave Albertville, AL	35950-1020	586 Highland Ave Albertville, AL	35950-1029	54.____
55. 1478 W Emerald Ave Mesa, AZ	85202-7211	1470 W Emerald Ave Mesa, AZ	82202-7211	55.____
56. 3496 Moonbeam Dr Monterey Park, CA	91754-0106	3498 Moonbeam Dr Monterey Park, CA	97754-0106	56.____
57. 13798 Livingstone Ave Tampa, FL	33613-0710	13898 Livingstone Ave Tampa, FL	33618-0710	57.____
58. 8576 Creekview Ct Riverdale, GA	30274-1030	8576 Creekview Ct Riverdale, GA	30274-1030	58.____
59. 3598 Maple Rd Loisville, KY	40299-3341	3598 Maple Rd Loisville, KY	40299-3341	59.____
60. 8699 Military St Detroit, MI	48204	8699 Military St Detroit, MI	48205	60.____

(See the answers to the above questions on page 76.)

Part A: Address-Checking Practice Test 5

This is a practice test containing 60 items or questions. You have to answer these questions in 11 minutes.

What you have to do is to compare the each row of the address and zip code in the **Correct List** (left column) to those in the **List to Be Checked** (right column). Determine of they are alike or different. If there are differences, know where the errors are. Mark any of the Delivery Routes **A, B, C,** and **D: A** for **No Errors; B** for an error in the **Address Only; C** for an error in the **Zip Code Only;** and **D,** for errors in **Both** the address and ZIP code.

A. No Errors	B. Address Only	C. ZIP Code	D. Both

	Correct List		List to Be Checked		
	Address	ZIP Code	Address	ZIP Code	Answers
1.	1598 N Emerson Ave Idaho Falls, ID	83402-0736	1598 N Emerson Ave Idaho Falls, ID	83402-0736	1.___
2.	3659 E County Rd 400 Columbus, OH	47201-2180	3659 E County Rd 400 Columbus, OH	47207-2180	2.___
3.	3099 Belle Chase Hwy Gretna, LA	70053	3090 Belle Chase Hwy Gretna, LA	70953	3.___
4.	73011 Beech St Chicopee, MA	01020-0347	73017 Beech St Chicopee, MA	01020-0347	4.___
5.	30317 Stonetree Cir Rochester, MI	48399	30317 Stonetree Cir Rochester, MI	48399	5.___
6.	12900 Michael Dr Utica, MI	48315-2106	12900 Michael Dr Utica, MI	48315-2106	6.___
7.	1350 Cannon Ave Goldsboro, NC	28143-2189	1350 Cannon Rd Goldsboro, NC	28148-2189	7.___
8.	799 Elm St Salisbury, NC	28144-3107	790 Elm St Salisbury, NC	28144-3107	8.___
9.	12100 Bangor Ave Cleveland, OH	44125	12100 Bangor Ave Cleveland, OH	44725	9.___
10.	1700 W Great Lakes Rd Enid, OK	73703-3091	1700 W Great Lakes Rd Enid, OK	73703-3091	10.___
11.	1100 Fawcett Ave Keesport, PA	15132-1461	1100 Fawcett Rd Keesport, PA	15133-1461	11.___
12.	5208 Bluebird Ln Greer, SC	29650	5208 Bluefird Ln Greer, SC	29650	12.___
13.	2699 Highland Dr Knoxville, TN	37918-0164	2699 Highland Dr Knoxville, TN	38918-0164	13.___

A. No Errors	B. Address Only	C. ZIP Code Only	D. Both

	Correct List		List to Be Checked		
	Address	ZIP Code	Address	ZIP Code	Answers
14.	3109 Winthrop Ave Fort Worth, TX	76116	3109 Winthrop Ave Fort Worth, TX	76116	14.____
15.	8991 E 46th St Ogden, UT	84403-0172	8990 E 4th St Ogden, UT	84403-0173	15.____
16.	2217 S 78th St Yakima, WA	98903-2142	2217 N 78th St Yakima, WA	98903-2143	16.____
17.	1586 S Peach Ave Tyler, TX	75701	1586 S Peach Ave Tyler, TX	75701	17.____
18.	3088 Niagara St Bellingham, WA	98226	3088 Niagara St Bellingham, WA	98226	18.____
19.	5277 Walnut Ave Long Beach, CA	90805-3172	5278 Walnut Ave Long Beach, CA	90805-3172	19.____
20.	15200 Telluride St Brighton, CO	80601-0103	15200 Telluride St Brighton, CO	80601-0103	20.____
21.	6856 N Sterling Ave Tampa, FL	33614-1420	6856 N Sterling Ave Tampa, FL	33614-1428	21.____
22.	2701 Keith Bridge Rd Cumming, GA	30041	2801 Keith Bridge Rd Cumming, GA	30047	22.____
23.	4421 N Broadway St Chicago, IL	60640-7120	4421 N Broadway St Chicago, IL	60640-7120	23.____
24.	2988 Tebbs Ave Indianapolis, IN	46221-2107	2988 Tebbs Ln Indianapolis, IN	46227-2107	24.____
25.	3011 Ford Cir Annapolis, MD	21401	3017 Ford Ctr Annapolis, MD	21409	25.____
26.	2709 Pleasantview Dr Redlands, CA	92374-8120	2709 Pleasantview Dr Redlands, CA	92374-6120	26.____
27.	11788 Eudora Ct Denver, CO	80233-2182	11788 Eudora Ct Denver, CO	80233-2182	27.____
28.	3312 Starfish St Kissimmee, FL	34744-0129	3313 Starfish St Kissimmee, FL	34744-0129	28.____
29.	2799 E Monroe St Springfield, IL	62703-4160	2799 N Monroe St Springfield, IL	62703-4160	29.____

A. No Errors	B. Address Only	C. ZIP Code Only	D. Both

	Correct List		List to Be Checked		
	Address	ZIP Code	Address	ZIP Code	Answers
30.	4731 Rock Creek Dr Jasper, AL	35504-3178	4731 Rock Creek Ln Jasper, AL	35504-3178	30.____
31.	1454 Bryant Ave Bronx, NY	10460-3109	1454 Bryant Ave Bronx, NY	10460-3109	31.____
32.	2432 Sawmill Rd Raleigh, NC	27613	2432 Sawmill Rd Raleigh, NC	27613	32.____
33.	601 E 8th St Portland, OR	97501-3172	601 N 8th St Portland, OR	97801-3172	33.____
34.	2801 Wild Field Dr Warwick, RI	02889-4187	2301 Wild Field Dr Warwick, RI	02889-4181	34.____
35.	7264 Birck Wood Ct Greer, SC	29651-0267	7268 Birch Wood Ct Greer, SC	29651-0267	35.____
36.	2178 Linden Ave Memphis, TN	38104	2178 Linden Ave Memphis, TN	39104	36.____
37.	1374 Creek Stone Ct Park City, UT	84098	1384 Creek Stone Ct Park City, UT	84098	37.____
38.	8401 S 212th St Kent, WA	98031-4122	8401 S 212th St Kent, WA	93031-4122	38.____
39.	6500 James St Mobile, AL	36608-0391	6500 James St Mobile, AL	36608-0391	39.____
40.	1479 W 14th St Wilmington, DE	19806-4121	1479 E 14th St Wilmington, DE	19806-4121	40.____
41.	19500 SW 57th Pl Dunnellon, FL	34431	19500 SW 57th Pl Dunnellon, FL	34431	41.____
42.	1311 Oxford Rd NE Atlanta, GA	30307-7186	1311 Oxford St NE Atlanta, GA	30307-7186	42.____
43.	1227 Spring Rd East Saint Louis, IL	62206-4179	1237 Spring Rd East Saint Louis, IL	62206-4178	43.____
44.	12502 Valley Wood Dr Silver Spring, MD	20906-5108	12502 Valley Wood Dr Silver Spring, MD	20906-5108	44.____
45.	4800 Aleda Ave SE Grand Rapids, MI	49508-2170	4800 Aleda Ave SW Grand Rapids, MI	49508-2170	45.____

A. No Errors	B. Address Only		C. ZIP Code Only	D. Both	
	Correct List			*List to Be Checked*	
	Address	Zip Code		Address	Zip Code	Answers

	Address	Zip Code	Address	Zip Code	
46.	2170 Woodridge Dr Greenwood, SC	29611	2170 Woodridge Dr Greenwood, SC	29611	46.____
47.	1562 Helen Ave North Las Vegas, NV	89032-5108	1563 Helen Ave North Las Vegas, NV	89032-5108	47.____
48.	3189 Birch St Toms River, NJ	08753-2191	3189 Birth St Toms River, NJ	08753-2191	48.____
49.	24401 Grand Central Little Neck, NY	11362-4173	24401 Grand Central Little Neck, NY	11862-4173	49.____
50.	1002 E 11th St Portland, OR	97501-0320	1002 E 11th St Portland, OR	78501-0320	50.____
51.	699 Randolph St Knoxville, TN	39117	690 Randolph St Knoxville, TN	39117	51.____
52.	3059 Wynterset Cir Yorktown, VA	23692-5123	3089 Wynterset Cir Yorktown, VA	28692-5123	52.____
53.	5299 S Birchwood Dr Sioux Falls, SD	57108-0986	5299 S Birthwood Dr Sioux Falls, SD	57108-0986	53.____
54.	5600 Bull Creek Rd Austin, TX	78756-4120	5600 Bull Creek Rd Austin, TX	78756-4220	54.____
55.	4800 Center St Salt Lake City, UT	84107-3760	4300 Center St Salt Lake City, UT	84107-3860	55.____
56.	4999 14th St NW Big Harbor, WA	98329	4999 14th St NE Big Harbor, WA	98329	56.____
57.	1701 Beld St Madison, WI	53713-2170	1701 Beld St Madison, WI	53713-2170	57.____
58.	2702 Poseidon Dr Lake Havasu City, AZ	86404-7180	2702 Poseidon Dr Lake Havasu City, AZ	86404-7180	58.____
59.	2228 Monterey St Bakersfield, CA	93306	2228 Montey St Bakersfield, CA	93806	59.____
60.	2172 N 7th Ave Greeley, CO	80631-6742	2172 N 7th St Greeley, CO	80831-6742	60.____

(See the answers to the above questions on page 77.

Part A: Address-Checking Practice Test 6

This is a practice test containing 60 items or questions. You have to answer these questions in 11 minutes.

What you have to do is to compare the each row of the address and zip code in the **Correct List** (left column) to those in the **List to Be Checked** (right column). Determine of they are alike or different. If there are differences, know where the errors are. Mark any of the Delivery Routes **A, B, C,** and **D: A** for **No Errors; B** for an error in the **Address Only; C** for an error in the **Zip Code Only;** and **D,** for errors in **Both** the address and ZIP code.

A. No Errors	B. Address Only	C. ZIP Code	D. Both

	Correct List		List to be Checked		
	Address	Zip Code	Address	Zip Code	Answers
1.	3149 Robin Hood Dr Modesto, CA	95350-3106	3749 Robinhood Dr Modesto, CA	95350-3106	1. ___
2.	3195 Kellwood Ct Raleigh, NC	27609-0291	3195 Kellwood Ct Raleigh, NC	27809-0291	2. ___
3.	5001 Mount Vernon Pl Rockville, MD	20850	5001 Mount Vernon Pl Rockville, MD	20850	3. ___
4.	1602 Superior Rd Ypsilanti, MI	48198-2105	1602 Superior Rd Ypsilanti, MI	48190-2105	4. ___
5.	2301 Kensington Dr Columbus, OH	43221-0321	2307 Kensington Dr Columbus, OH	43221-0321	5. ___
6.	3346 Thunderbred Ln Plano, TX	75023-0971	3546 Thunderbred Ln Plano, TX	75823-0971	6. ___
7.	3510 Whitestorm Way Virginia Beach, VA	23454-2370	3510 Whitestorm Rd Virginia Beach, WA	23454-2370	7. ___
8.	5209 Harding Pl Nashville, TN	23454	5208 Harding Place Nashville, TN	23484	8. ___
9.	4902 Brentwood Dr Greenwood, SC	29646	4902 Brentwood Dr Greenwood, NC	29846	9. ___
10.	6527 Little League Rd Williamsport, PR	17701-3172	6527 Little League Way Williamsport, PR	17701-3172	10. ___
11.	5021 Grant Ln Sevierville, TN	37876-0429	5021 Grant Ln Sevierville, TN	37876-0429	11. ___
12.	7501 Malood Ct Fontana, CA	92335-7103	7507 Malood Ct Fontana, CA	92335-7103	12. ___
13.	1730 State Ct Bridgeport, CT	06605-3102	1730 State Ct Bridgeport, CT	06605-3102	13. ___

A. No Errors	B. Address Only	C.ZIP Code Only	D. Both

	Correct List		List to Be Checked		
	Address	Zip Code	Address	Zip Code	Answers
14.	7381 Hucklebern Ln Lake Wales, FL	33898-5172	7381 Hucklebern Ln Lake Wales, FL	33898-5172	14. ___
15.	10570 Flat Shoals Rd Covington, GA	30051-2103	10570 Flat Shoals Dr Covington, GA	30081-2103	15. ___
16.	5598 W Jackson St Hayward, CA	94545	5598 W Jackson St Hayward, CA	94546	16. ___
17.	3891 Wall St Waterburg, CT	06704-5109	3897 Wall St Waterburg, CT	06708-5109	17. ___
18.	5721 Woodfield Rd Bloomington, IL	61704-2108	5727 Woodfield Rd Bloomington, IL	61704-2108	18. ___
19.	1900 Greyhound Pass Carmel, IN	61704	1900 Greyhound Pass Carmel, IN	61705	19. ___
20.	4311 W 110th Ter Leanwood, KS	66211-0731	4311 W 110th Ter Leanwood, KS	66211-0731	20. ___
21.	5822 Acorn St Shreveport, LA	71107-0971	5822 Acorn St Shreveport, LA	71107-0971	21. ___
22.	8522 2nd Ave Silver Spring, MD	20910-6206	8522 3rd Ave Silver Spring, MD	20970-6206	22. ___
23.	8501 Elmira St Detroit, MI	48204	8801 Elmira St Detroit, MI	48204	23. ___
24.	6003 Candlewood Dr Minneapolis, MN	55443-8120	6003 Candlewood Ln Minneapolis, MN	55443-8120	24. ___
25.	3439 Greenleaf Ln Columbus, MS	39705	3539 Greenleaf Ln Columbus, MS	39708	25. ___
26.	8402 Chef Menteur St New Orleans, LA	70127-2105	8402 Chef Menteur St New Orleans, LA	70128-2105	26. ___
27.	720 Gannet Ct Bel Air, MD	21015-4129	720 Gannet Dr Bel Air, MD	21015-4129	27. ___
28.	3912 Adams Dr Valdosa, GA	31605	3912 Adams Dr Valdosa, GA	31605	28. ___
29.	8900 220th St Queens Village, NY	11427-5026	8908 220th St Queens Village, NY	11427-5026	29. ___

A. No Errors	B. Address Only	C. ZIP Code Only	D. Both

	Correct List		List to Be Checked		
	Address	Zip Code	Address	Zip Code	Answers
30.	2902 Burchner Blvd Bronx, NY	10465-2103	2902 Burchner Blvd Bronx, NY	10465-2102	30. ___
31.	11702 US Hwy 301 N Lumberton, NC	28358-0529	11703 US Hwy 301 N Lumberton, NC	28359-0529	31. ___
32.	3908 S 74th West Ave Tulsa, OK	74107	3908 N 74th West Ave Tulsa, OK	74108	32. ___
33.	1923 Blackfort St Chattanooga, TN	37404-0371	1928 Blackfort St Chattanooga, TN	37504-0371	33. ___
34.	3909 N Highway 360 Grand Prairie, TX	75052	3909 N Highway 360 Grand Prairie, TX	75052	34. ___
35.	3472 Fawkland Cir Boynton Beach, FL	33426-5102	3472 Fawkland Dr Boynton Beach, FL	33426-5102	35. ___
36.	1429 E Gate Shop Ctr Carbondale, IL	62902	1429 E Gate Shop Ctr Carbondale, IL	62902	36. ___
37.	2684 Armherst Ave Manhattan, KS	66502-8129	2884 Armherst Ave Manhattan, KS	68502-8129	37. ___
38.	11575 Highway Ave Silver Spring, MD	20902-3103	11575 Highway Ave Silver Spring, MD	20902-3103	38. ___
39.	22205 Hall Rd Macomb, MI	48042	22205 Hall Rd Macomb, MI	48043	39. ___
40.	2206 Main St Tupelo, MS	38804-6291	2208 Main St Tupelo, MS	38804-6291	40. ___
41.	1276 S Thomas Ave Yuma, AZ	85364-0681	1276 S Thomas Ave Yuma, CO	85364-0681	41. ___
42.	4647 E Wardlow Rd Long Beach, FL	90808	4647 E Wardlow Rd Long Beach, CA	90308	42. ___
43.	7282 W State Rd 40 Ormond Beach, FL	32174-0617	7282 N State Rd 40 Ormond Beach, FL	32174-0617	43. ___
44.	2872 W 111th Ter Leawood, KS	66211-9320	2872 N 111th Ter Leawood, KS	66211-9320	44. ___
45.	3599 Beverly Pl Shreveport, LA	77105-3177	3599 Beverly Pl Shreveport, LA	77106-3177	45. ___

| A. No Errors | B. Address Only | C. ZIP Code Only | D. Both |

	Correct List		List to Be Checked		D. Both
	Address	Zip Code	Address	Zip Code	Answers
46.	1998 North Ave Columbus, GA	31901-5261	1997 North Ave Columbus, GA	31901-5261	46. ___
47.	1789 W Park Ave Champaign, IL	61821-0031	1789 W Park Ave Champaign, IL	61821-0031	47. ___
48.	2700 Hanna St Fort Wayne, IN	46806-7102	2708 Hanna St Fort Wayne, IN	46806-7102	48. ___
49.	399 Langdon St Somerset, KY	42503	399 Langdon St Somerset, KY	42508	49. ___
50.	3976 Casino Ave Chicopee, MA	01013-2650	3976 Casino Ave Chicopee, MA	01013-2650	50. ___
51.	5823 W Victory Rd Boise, IN	83709-2372	5323 W Victory Rd Boise, IN	88709-2372	51. ___
52.	5001 Maple Ave Newport, KY	41071-0029	5008 Maple Ave New Port, KY	47071-0029	52. ___
53.	2238 Clifton Ave Baltimore, MD	21216	2238 Clifton Ave Baltimore, MD	21216	53. ___
54.	5386 Euclid Ave NE Albuquerque, NM	87110-2181	5886 Euclid Ave NE Albuquerque, NM	87110-2181	54. ___
55.	3029 Bethesda Rd Asheville, NC	28805	3029 Bethesda St Asheville, NC	28805	55. ___
56.	3976 Timberway Sevierville, TN	37876	3976 Timberway Sevierville, TN	37876	56. ___
57.	3741 Rosewood Ln Huntsville, TX	77340-3201	3741 Rosewood Ln Huntsville, TX	77341-3201	57. ___
58.	1827 Court St Richmond, VA	23222-7321	1827 Court Rd Richmond, VA	23322-7321	58. ___
59.	17200 W Capital Dr Brookfield, WI	53045	17200 N Capital Dr Brookfield, WI	53045	59. ___
60.	1775 Ames Ave Cheyeane, WY	82001-3203	1775 Ames Ave Cheyeane, WY	82001-3203	60. ___

(See Answers to the above questions on page 78).

Answers to Questions
Address-Checking Practice Test 1

Answers to Questions
on pages 49 - 52.

1. B		31. B	
2. D		32. A	
3. B		33. B	
4. B		34. B	
5. B		35. D	
6. C		36. A	
7. D		37. A	
8. A		38. D	
9. B		39. D	
10. A		40. B	
11. D		41. A	
12. D		42. B	
13. D		43. B	
14. B		44. D	
15. B		45. B	
16. C		46. D	
17. A		47. D	
18. C		48. A	
19. C		49. C	
20. A		50. B	
21. D		51. A	
22. D		52. B	
23. D		53. A	
24. D		54. D	
25. B		55. B	
26. A		56. B	
27. D		57. A	
28. A		58. D	
29. B		59. A	
30. C		60. B	

Answers to Questions
Address-Checking Practice Test 2

Answers to Questions
on pages 53 - 56

1. C		31. A	
2. B		32. B	
3. C		33. D	
4. B		34. D	
5. D		35. A	
6. A		36. D	
7. B		37. D	
8. D		38. B	
9. D		39. C	
10. C		40. D	
11. D		41. D	
12. C		42. D	
13. A		43. A	
14. B		44. B	
15. D		45. A	
16. D		46. D	
17. A		47. A	
18. C		48. D	
19. A		49. A	
20. D		50. D	
21. D		51. C	
22. B		52. D	
23. B		53. D	
24. A		54. C	
25. A		55. A	
26. B		56. D	
27. A		57. D	
28. C		58. A	
29. A		59. C	
30. D		60. D	

Answers to Questions
Address-Checking Practice Test 3

Answers to Questions
on page 57 - 60

1. A	31. D
2. B	32. A
3. B	33. D
4. B	34. C
5. C	35. A
6. A	36. D
7. D	37. B
8. D	38. D
9. A	39. A
10. C	40. D
11. B	41. B
12. B	42. D
13. B	43. A
14. B	44. D
15. D	45. A
16. A	46. A
17. C	47. D
18. B	48. A
19. D	49. C
20. D	50. B
21. C	51. D
22. B	52. D
23. B	53. A
24. C	54. C
25. B	55. B
26. B	56. C
27. D	57. D
28. C	58. A
29. D	59. A
30. A	60. A

Answers to Questions
Address-Checking Practice Test 4

Answers to Questions
on pages 61 - 64

1. D	31. B
2. B	32. A
3 . A	33. C
4. D	34. C
5. C	35. D
6. D	36. A
7. D	37. A
8. A	38. D
9. D	39. C
10. A	40. A
11. B	41. D
12. A	42. D
13. D	43. A
14. C	44. B
15. B	45. A
16. C	46. A
17. C	47. B
18. C	48. D
19. B	49. A
20. A	50. B
21. D	51. D
22. A	52. B
23. B	53. C
24. D	54. C
25. A	55. D
26. B	56. D
27. A	57. D
28. D	58. A
29. C	59. A
30. B	60. C

Answers to Questions
Address-Checking Practice Test **5**

Answers to Questions
on pages 65 - 68

1. A	31. A
2. C	32. A
3. D	33. D
4. B	34. D
5. A	35. B
6. A	36. C
7. D	37. B
8. B	38. C
9. C	39. A
10. A	40. B
11. D	41. A
12. B	42. B
13. C	43. D
14. A	44. A
15. D	45. B
16. D	46. A
17. A	47. B
18. A	48. B
19. B	49. C
20. A	50. C
21. C	51. B
22. D	52. D
23. A	53. B
24. D	54. C
25. D	55. D
26. C	56. B
27. A	57. A
28. B	58. A
29. B	59. D
30. B	60. D

Answers to Questions
Address-Checking Practice Test 6

Answers to Questions
on pages 69 - 72

1. B	31. D
2. C	32. D
3. A	33. D
4. C	34. A
5. B	35. B
6. D	36. A
7. B	37. D
8. D	38. A
9. D	39. C
10. B	40. B
11. A	41. B
12. B	42. D
13. A	43. B
14. A	44. B
15. D	45. C
16. C	46. B
17. D	47. A
18. B	48. B
19. C	49. C
20. A	50. A
21. A	51. D
22. D	52. D
23. B	53. A
24. B	54. B
25. D	55. B
26. C	56. A
27. B	57. C
28. A	58. D
29. B	59. B
30. C	60. A

13

Part B: Forms Completion

Identification of Information to Complete a Form

Part B: Forms Completion of Test 473 involves the identification of information required to fill out or complete a form. A number of forms with several items or questions, will be shown to you by the US Postal Service so that you can identify the data required to complete the form.

You will be answering 30 items or questions to be finished in 16 minutes. Actually, there are no techniques or strategies needed to complete the form. You just have to understand the questions, and think of the correct information to complete it. Just understand well the questions, and see to it that you give the right information needed to accomplish the form.

A sample of a form used by the US Postal Service is shown below. It's the **Domestic Return Receipt.**

SENDER: *COMPLETE THIS SECTION*	COMPLETE THIS SECTION ON DELIVERY	
■ Complete items 1, 2, and 3. Also complete item 4 if Restricted Delivery is desired.	A. Signature X	☐ Agent ☐ Addressee
■ Print your name and address on the reverse so that we can return the card to you.	B. Received by (*Printed Name*)	C. Date of Delivery
■ Attach this card to the back of the mailpiece, or on the front if space permits.	D. Is delivery address different from item 1? ☐ Yes If YES, enter delivery address below: ☐ No	
1. Article Addressed to:		
	3. Service Type ☐ Certified Mail ☐ Express Mail ☐ Registered ☐ Return Receipt for Merchandise ☐ Insured Mail ☐ C.O.D.	
	4. Restricted Delivery? *(Extra Fee)* ☐ Yes	
2. Article Number *(Transfer from service label)*		

PS Form 3811, February 2004   Domestic Return Receipt   102595-02-M-1540

Application Cards

Tear off this page, fill it out, and turn it in to your Post Office™.

Application for Post Office Box or Caller Service – Part 1

Customer: Complete items 1, 3-6, 14-16, and 18-19.	Post Office: Complete items 2, 7-13, 17 and 20.

1. Name(s) to Which Box Number(s) Is (are) Assigned	2. Box or Caller Numbers
	_____ through _____

3. Name of Person Applying, Title *(if representing an organization)*, and Name of Organization *(if Different From Item 1)*	4a. Will This Box Be Used for: □ Personal Use □ Business Use *(Optional)*
	4b. Email Address *(Optional)*

5. Address *(Number, street, apt. no., city, state, and ZIP Code™)*. When address changes, cross out address here and put new address on back.	6. Telephone Number *(Include area code)*

7. Date Application Received	8. Box Size Needed	9. ID and Physical Address Verified by *(Initials)*	10. Dates of Service
			_____ through _____

11. Two types of identification are required. One must contain a photograph of the adressee(s). Social Security cards, credit cards, and birth certificates are unacceptable as identification. Write in identifiying information. Subject to verification.	12. Check Eligibility for Carrier Delivery □ a. City □ b. Rural □ c. HCR □ d. None	13. Service assigned □ a. Box □ b. Caller □ c. Reserve No.
	14. List name(s) of minors or names of other persons **receiving mail** in individual box. Other persons must present two forms of valid ID. If applicant is a firm, name each member **receiving mail**. Each member must have verifiable ID upon request. *(Continue on reverse side.)*	

WARNING: The furnishing of false or misleading information on this form or omission of information may result in criminal sanctions (including fines and imprisonment) and/or civil sanctions (including multiple damages and civil penalties.) (18 U.S.C. 1001)	15. Signature of Applicant *(Same as Item 3)*. I agree to comply with all Postal Service® rules regarding Post Office box or caller services.

PS Form **1093**, April 2004 *(Page 1 of 2)* (7530-02-000-7165)

Use a separate form for each number or consecutive group of numbers, and type of service. File part 1 alphabetically by customer's name.

1. Which of these should be a correct entry for Box 7?

A. $3.50
B. April 2, 2005
C. Small
D. 3 p.m.

2. Where would you enter the applicant's address?

A. Box 4b
B. Box 5
C. Box 3
D. Box 6

3. Which of these would be a correct entry for Box 8?

A. 12/02/04
B. Medium
C. 2513 Hickory Dr., Farmington Hills, MI 48333
D. $5.00

Application for Post Office™ Box or Caller Service – Part 2

Special Orders

16. Postmaster: The following named persons or representatives of the organization listed below are authorized to **accept** mail addressed to this (these) Post Office box(es) or caller number(s). All names listed must have verifiable ID. *(Continue on reverse side.)*

a. Name of Box Customer *(Same as item 1)*		**Customer Note:**
b. Name(s) of Applicant(s) *(Same as item 3)*		The Postal Service® may consider it valid evidence that a person is authorized to remove mail from the box if that person possesses a key or combination to the box.
c. Other Authorized Representative	d. Other Authorized Representative	20. Post Office Date Stamp
17. Box or Caller Number to Which This Card Applies		
18. Will this box be used for Express Mail® reshipment? *(Check one)* a. Yes ☐ b. No ☐		

WARNING: *The furnishing of false or misleading information on this form or omission of material may result in criminal sanctions (including fines and imprisonment) and/or civil sanctions (including multiple damages and civil penalties.) (18 U.S.C. 1001)*

19. Signature of Applicant *(Same as Item 3)*. I agree to comply with all Postal Service® rules regarding Post Office box or caller services.

Use a separate form for each number or consecutive group of numbers, and type of service. File part 2 by box or caller number.

PS Form **1093,** April 2004 *(Detached from Page 1 of 2)* (7530-02-000-7165)

The above is Part II of an Application for Post Office Box or Caller Service. Here are some questions to be answered.

1. Which of these would require a check mark?

A. Box C

B. Box 20.

C. Box 18

D. Box D

2. Where would you enter the names of persons authorized to remove or get mail from the box?

A. Box 17

B. Box a

C. Box b

D. Boxes c and d

3. Which of these would be a correct entry for Box 18?

A. 2 p.m.

B. 05/29/04

C. 2

D. A check mark

14

Part C: Coding and Memory

The Way to Assign Addresses to Delivery Routes

Postal Test 473 is similar in some ways to the old **470 Battery Test**. The **Memory-for-Address Test** of the old **470 Test** consisted of two Parts: Part A, Practice Test, and Part B: The Actual Test.

Now, **Part C** of the new Test 473 consists of two sections: the **Coding Section** and the **Memory Section**. The Coding Section contains 36 items to be answered or completed in 6 minutes while the Memory Section contains 36 items to be answered in 7 minutes.

During the test, you will be presented with a **Coding Guide**, the first column of which consists of **Address Range** and the second column, **Delivery Route**, represented by letters **A, B, C,** and **D.** You must decide which correct code (or route lettered A, B, C, D, and C), is assigned to each item or address range (containing numbers and names of streets).

You must work on the items as fast and as accurate as you can. But the most important thing to remember is to be able to memorize address ranges containing numbers and names of streets and the delivery routes.

During the first section **(Coding)** of the Part C Test, you will be allowed to look at the coding guide while you are assigning codes, (A, B, C, and D, to each item of the addresses. But you won't be allowed to look at the coding guide while doing the second section **(Memory)** of the Part C Test.

Here's a sample Coding Guide.

Coding Guide	
Address Range	Delivery Route
200 - 4999 Mayfair Rd 61 - 498 Seaweed St 400 - 1399 Oakwood Dr	A
5000 - 6599 Mayfair Rd 500 - 1699 Seaweed St	B
1 - 199 Oven Hill 1400- 7998 Oakwood Dr 200 - 499 Lebanon Blvd	C
All mail matters that don't fall in one of the address ranges listed above.	D

The Coding Guide that the Post Office will give you will be used during the Coding Section test and the Memory Section test of the Part C Test. Create address codes to remember address ranges assigned to routes.

You must memorize the address ranges to be assigned to delivery routes, marked A, B, C, and D. In the above example, all numbers ranging from 200-4999 Mayfair Rd are assigned to Delivery Route "A." All numbers ranging from 500 - 1699 Seaweed St, are assigned to Delivery Route "B."

In memorizing the numbers **14**00 - **79**98 Oakwood Dr and **2**00 - **4**99 Lebanon Blvd, we can shorten them to **14 - 79** Oakwood Dr (remembering that there are two zeroes (00) after 14 and there are a 9 and an 8 (98) after 79 Oakwood Dr. This address range is assigned to Delivery Route C. You may shorten **2**00 - **4**99 Lebanon Blvd to **2 - 4** Lebanon Blvd, remembering that there are two zeroes (00) after 2 and two 9s (99) after 4. Also remember that numbers ranging from 1400 to 7998 Oakwood Dr, are assigned to Delivery route "C" and numbers ranging from 200 to 499 Lebanon are also assigned to Delivery Route "C."

If there's an address range such as 940 Mayfair Rd (between the numbers 200 - 4999 Mayfair Rd, the mail goes to Delivery Route "A." And the list goes on and on.

For strategies for **Coding and Memory Section Tests**, see the next page.

15

Strategies for Coding-Memory Test
Techniques for Memorizing Coding Guides

Part C of the new Test 473 consists of two sections: the **Coding Section** which contains 36 items to be answered or completed in 6 minutes.and the **Memory Section** which contains 36 items to be answered in 7 minutes.

During the test, you will be presented with a **Coding Guide**, the first column of which consists of **Address Range** and the second column, **Delivery Route**, represented by letters **A, B, C,** and **D.** You must decide which correct code (or route lettered A, B, C, or D, is assigned to each item or address range (containing numbers and names of streets).

Actually, techniques for the **Coding-Memory Test** of the Postal 473/473/-C and the **Memory-for-Address Test** of the RCA 460 Exam have similarities and differences.

In the Coding-Memory Test of the 473/473-C Test, you have four choices in answering the questions: Delivery Routes A, B, C, and D. You must determine which route the address range is assigned to. In other words, you will be given numbers of streets that are within certain address ranges. And then identify if the address belongs to Delivery Routes A, B, C, or D. If the address is not within the given address range, then the answer should be D. That is, all mail matters that don't fall in one of the address ranges listed in the Coding Guide, are covered by Route D, which is served by a particular letter carrier.

(Note: In the **Memory-for-Address Test** of the 460 RCA examination, you have to memorize the locations of addresses (numbers and street names) contained in boxes marked A, B, C, D, and E. You will be given an address range such as 4700-5599 Table and you must determine to which box the address range belongs. For instance, the address range 4700-5599 Table may be assigned to Box B. This Memory-for-Address test of the 460 RCA exam is easier than the Coding and Memory Section Test of the Postal 473 Battery Test. Why? Because in the 460 RCA exam, the selection of the answer will be the exact address contained in each box. On the other hand, in the Coding-Memory test of the 473 Battery Test, the numbers given are almost always not the exact numbers mentioned in Coding Guide. The numbers given may just be within the address range. In addition, you must determine if the numbers really fall in any of the address ranges listed.)

Here's a sample Coding Guide:

Coding Guide	
Address Range	Delivery Route
200-4999 Mayfair Rd 61- 498 Seaweed St 400 - 1399 Oakwood Dr	A
5000 - 6599 Mayfair Rd 500 -1699 Seaweed St	B
1 - 199 Oven Hill 1400 - 7998 Oakwood Dr 200 - 499 Lebanon Blvd	C
All mail matters that don't fall in one of the address ranges listed above.	D

The Coding Guide that the Post Office will give you will be used during the **Coding** section and the **Memory** section test. Create address codes to remember address ranges assigned to routes.

You must memorize the address ranges to be assigned to a delivery route to be served by a city or rural carrier letter carrier. In the above example, all numbers ranging from 200- 4999 Mayfair Rd are assigned to Delivery Route "A."

In the same example, all numbers ranging from 500 - 1699 Seaweed St, are assigned to "B" (Delivery Route).

Memorizing the Codes

There are different ways you can do to memorize the codes. Remember, there's a limited time in memorizing the codes and completing the items or questions.

Again, devote most of the 2 minutes and 1 1/2 minutes allowed to the practice test to memorization of the coding guide since this part of the test is not scored. Then you will also be given 3 minutes to memorize the Coding Guide. You will be given 7 minutes to answer the 36 items in the Memory Section part of the Part C test.

Here's a short cut to memorizing the codes.

■ From top to bottom, first memorize the names of the streets (excluding the word "Rd" or "St." or the letter "S" (for South).

Coding Guide	
Address Range	Delivery Route
200 - 4999 Mayfair Rd 61 - 498 Seaweed St 400 - 1399 Oakwood Dr	A
5000 - 6599 Mayfair Rd 500 - 1699 Seaweed St	
1 - 199 Oven Hill 1400 - 7998 Oakwood Dr 200 - 499 Lebanon Blvd	
All mail matters that don't fall in one of the address ranges listed above.	D

■ In remembering the names, associate *Mayfair, Seaweed,* and *Oakwood* to things or objects you know. For instance, imagine some things such as you saw the Broadway show *Mayfair*, then you went to get a string of *seaweeds*, after which you proceeded to the *Oakwood* Hospital. You can do the same with the other names of streets. Things or objects that are imagined are easily remembered or recalled.

■ You may also combine *Mayfair, Seaweed* and *Oakwood* as one word "*Mayseaoak*" combining the three names into one, just using the first syllable of each word. You can do the same thing with the other addresses.

■ In remembering some long numbers, such as **5**00 - **16**99 Seaweed, they may be remembered as **5** and **16** Seaweed, excluding the two 0s (zeroes), but not forgetting that there are two zeroes after the numbers 5 and a 99 after 16 (500 - 1699 Seaweed).

■ In remembering the short numbers, such as the numbers 1 - 199 Oven, memorize 1 - 199 as one string of numbers, 1199. Recall the name Oven by thinking of the oven in your kitchen or wherever.

■ It's common that the last number of the first address range of a street ends with a 9 or 99; for instance 1,299. So the last 2 numbers of the first string of numbers of address range (same street) will naturally end with 2 zeroes (00), for instance 13**99** - 25**00**; if the first strings of numbers end with 2 zeroes, the the next address range will start with an **01** (such as 25**01** and again the next string of numbers will end with 9 or **99**, such as 25**99**.

■ To remember numbers and places, associate them with things or places you know or familiar with you. For instance, you may associate any number or numbers such as street number 1956 as the year you were born or the year you visited your relatives in Haiti or Rome. You may associate the street name Venice being the city where you took a vacation in the year 2000 or whatever date. All depends on events or happenings that took or taking place in your life. Everyone will have his or her own codes to remember or recall things or places. Creating codes to recall things are the instrument to easily recalling numbers, events, things, and places. Things imagined are easily remembered by your own biocomputer.

Address Ranges

In seeing the increasing numbers with regard to address ranges, let's have the following example:

200 - 4999 Mayfair Rd
5000 - 6599 Mayfair Rd

In this case, we should only memorize the numbers **2**00, **49**99, **50**00 and **65**99. Or maybe you can shorten those numbers to **2, 49, 50,** and **65**(99), remembering that there are two zeroes (00) after 2 and 50. Then remember that there are two nines (99) after 49 and 65. Remember that mail from numbers 200 to 4999 will be assigned to Delivery Route "A". That is, numbers below 5000 (200 to 4999) belong to the Delivery Route "A." Then numbers from 5000 to 6599 Mayfair Rd will be served by Delivery Route "B". You may remember 5000 as being the amount you paid for a dress or whatever and you may recall 6599 as 1965 as being the year you were baptized, depending on the event that happened in your life.

When there's an address such as 840 Mayfair Rd, (between the numbers 200 - 4999 Mayfair Rd, (see Coding Guide), all the mail to the address 840 Mayfair Rd) will go to Delivery Route A.

On the other hand, if there's a street such as 6600 Mayfair Rd, you may note that such street address, 6600 Mayfair Rd, does not fall in any of the address ranges served by Delivery Routes A, B, or C. Since such street does not fall in any of the address ranges served by Delivery Route, A, B, or C, the answer is "D."

Summary of Test Strategies and Techniques

■ **Codes:** Use codes for numbers and names of streets to easily remember them.

■ **Shortcut:** Just combine the first syllable of each street name in a box (A, B, C, and D) to remember them.

See the sample Coding Guide on the next page.

Coding Guide	
Address Range	Delivery Route
100 - 2999 Seminol Ln 51 - 298 Ford Pkwy 4001 - 1399 Cambridge Dr	A
3000 - 6599 Seminol Ln 501- 2000 Summerview Dr	B
1 - 199 Hamilton Blvd 300 - 2798 Ford Pkwy 201 - 3000 Jefferson Cir	C
All mail matters that don't fall in one of the address ranges listed above.	D

You can see in the above sample Coding Code the following streets that are covered by different routes (A, B, C, and D): Seminol, Ford, Cambridge, Summerview, Hamilton, and Jefferson. Listed twice are Seminole and Ford.

From top to bottom (Routes A, B, and C), you may combine the first syllables of the streets in the following manner: **SeFordCam, SeSu,** and **HaFordJeff**.

The combined syllables of the above streets are considered as your codes for remembering the streets. In the case of streets such as Seminol Ln, Ford Pkwy, Cambridge Dr., etc., forget about whether the street name is a Ln, Pkwy, Dr or an Ave. Just remember Seminol, Ford, and Cambridge.

In remembering the numbers of Seminol, they may be shortened as follows: **1 - 29** for 100 - **29**99 Seminole (remembering that there are another 0 after 10 and 99 after 29, etc. Remember that almost of the time, address numbers end in **00**, **99**, and **98**. You may note that if the first rows of numbers end in **0** or **00**, the last number of the second pair of numbers of the same route will be **9**, **99** or **98**. If the last number of the first string of numbers ends with a "1" (such as 51 - 298) Ford, the last number of the second string of numbers will end with an even number such as 8 or 0.

■ **Caution:** Once in every five or six numbers, before you mark the *circle* for your answers, be sure that the answer corresponds to the proper *line* of each item. For instance, the marked circle belonging to item number should answer item or question number 9. Sometimes when you're in a hurry, you may mark circles that do not correspond to the questions you're answering. That happened to me once when I took a Postal exam.

■ **Be in a hurry.** Skip the difficult questions you do not know, answer the ones you do know, and time permitting, return to the difficult questions you skipped.

■ **Memorization:** Don't try to write down addresses or notes on the palm of your hand. You'll have no time to do that. You can try to remember only the first or two digits of the address. it's better to remember 1 or 2 digits.

■**Side by side.** Don't place the question sheet and the answer sheet far from each other or far from your body.

16

4 Exam 473 Practice Tests

Part C: Coding-Memory Test

Part C of the new Test 473 consists of two sections: the Coding Section and the Memory Section. The Coding section contains 36 items to be answered or completed in 6 minutes while the Memory Section contains 36 items to be answered in 7 minutes.

It is important to note that you will be presented with a Coding Guide. The first column of the guide consists of Address Range and the second column contains the Delivery Route, represented by letters A, B, C, and D. The procedure is to decide which correct route (marked A, B, C, or D), is assigned to each addresss range (consisting of numbers and names of streets.)

You'll be using the same guide throughout both sections of the Part C Test. Each item or question is an address. You must decide which delivery route serves the address.

Coding Section

The first section of the Part C Test, called Coding Section, actually consists of three segments:

Segment 1: You are given 2 minutes within which to study or memorize the Coding Guide. Also, you have to answer four items as a practice test. Since this is not counted, you may answer only one question and use the time in memorizing the code. You are allowed to look at the Coding Guide as you answer the questions. The same Coding Guide will be used throughout the Coding and Memory tests.

Segment 2: You'll be given 1 1/2 minutes to answer 8 questions on this part of the test. Since this is not scored, you may answer only 2 or 3 questions. You better use the time in memorizing the coding guide.

Segment 3: You have 6 minutes to answer 36 questions. This part of the test is scored or counted. You must mark the circles on the official answer sheet. You'll still be allowed to look at the coding guide as you answer the questions.

When you work on the first section, Coding, of the test, you are allowed to look at the coding guide while you are assigning codes, (A, B, C, and D), to each item of the addresses. However, when you work on the second section (memory), you won't be allowed to look at the coding guide. In other words, memorize the coding guide.

As mentioned, you are given 2 minutes in Segment 1 and another 1 1/2 minutes in Segment 2 (total of 3 1/2 minutes to memorize and answer 4 questions (Segment 1) and 8 questions (Segment 2). After that you are allowed to answer the 36 items in 6 minutes. Since Segment 1 and Segment 2 are not counted or scored, why not use the 3 1/2 minutes to memorize the guiding code? Answers to questions or items (Segment 1 and Segment 2) should be marked on the sample answer sheet at the bottom of the question page. The 36 questions (Segment 3) should, however, be answered on the official answer sheet. After that comes the Memory Test.

Practice Test 1
Part C: Coding and Memory

Segment 1 of Coding Section

Instructions

Segment 1 of the Coding Section test is a 2-minute exercise for memorizing the Coding Guide to be used in answering the questions on this test. Also, you have these 2 minutes to answer 4 questions. Since this part of the test is not scored, you should not work on all of the questions. Just memorize the guide using the techniques mentioned in Chapter 18: **Strategies for the Coding-Memory Test** on pages 85-90. Turn the page to see the Coding Guide.

Part C: Coding & Memory

Segment 1 of Coding Section

Coding Guide	
Address Range	Delivery Route
10 - 299 SW 2nd St **300 - 3**99 Sunset Dr **1 - 24**98 Wetson Rd	A
300 - 899 SW 2nd St 600 - 999 Pine Ridge Dr	B
200 - 1399 Shotgun Rd 400 - 899 Sunset Dr 1 - 1099 S Prospect Ter	C
All mail that doesn't fall in one of the address ranges listed above	D

There are several ways of remembering the above address ranges in different boxes assigned to any of the delivery routes, **A, B, C,** and **D.** We should create so-called extract codes to easily remember the above numbers and streets. You may combine the **first syllables** of the streets.

The codes may be created (from top to bottom) as **2ndSunWet** for SW 2nd Sunset, and Wetson. For the second box, it should be **2ndPine** for SW 2nd, and Pine Ridge. For the third box it should be **ShotSunPros** for Shotgun, Sunset and Prospect.

In remembering the street numbers, you may shorten the numbers in the first box serving as codes, (from top to bottom) as **1 - 2** SW 2nd for 10 - 299 SW 2nd St; **3 - 3** Sunset for 300 - 399 Sunset; and **1 - 24** Wetson for 1 - 2498 Wetson. Then for the second pairs of numbers, you may just remember **99** for **2**99 SW 2nd; **99** for 3**99** Sunset; and **98** for 2498 Wetson..

You may also remember the numbers with this strategy by dividing the group of numbers into three columns. For example, the numbers may be divided as follows:

10	2	99	for 10 - 299 SW SW 2nd St
3(00)	3	99	for 300 - 399 Sunset Dr
1	24	98	for 1 - 2498 Wetson Rd

Part C: Coding and Memory
Practice Test 1

Segment 1 of Coding Section

Questions

Address	Delivery Route			
1. 200 SW 2nd St	A	B	C	D
2. 900 Sunset Dr	A	B	C	D
3. 970 Pine Ridge Dr	A	B	C	D
4. 14000 Shotgun Rd	A	B	C	D

Sample Answer Sheet

1. Ⓐ Ⓑ Ⓒ Ⓓ

2. Ⓐ Ⓑ Ⓒ Ⓓ

3. Ⓐ Ⓑ Ⓒ Ⓓ

4. Ⓐ Ⓑ Ⓒ Ⓓ

The correct answers are 1-A, 2-D, 3-B, and 4-D

Part C: Coding and Memory

Segment 2 of Coding Section

Instructions

Segment 2 of the Coding Section has 8 questions to be answered in 1 1/2 minutes. Of course, you can look at the Coding Guide. Since this part of the test is not scored, you can just answer 2 or 3 questions, then use the time to memorize the guide. You have to mark your answers at the bottom of the sample question page, not on the official answer sheets.

For Segment 2 of the Coding Section, which serves as a practice test, turn the page.

Part C: Coding & Memory

Segment 2 of Coding Section

Coding Guide	
Address Range	Delivery Route
10 - 299 SW 2nd St 300 - 399 Sunset Dr 1 - 2498 Wetson Rd	A
300 - 899 SW 2nd St 600 - 999 Pine Ridge Dr	B
200 - 1399 Shotgun Rd 400 - 899 Sunset Dr 1 - 1099 S Prospect Ter	C
All mail that doesn't fall in one of the address ranges listed above	D

There are addresses that start with number 1; for instance, two of the above address ranges: 1 - 2498 Wetson and 1 - 1099 S Prospect. In the case of these addresses, you may just remember 2498 Wetson and 1099 S Prospect, forgetting about the number 1. In other words, all numbers below 2498 Wetson are assigned to Route A, and all numbers below 1099 S Prospect are covered by Route C. All addresses over the two numbers, 2498 Wetson and 1099 S Prospect, are all assigned to Route D. Why? Because all mail that doesn't fall in one of the address ranges above above are assigned to Route D.

Furthermore, associate the numbers 2498 and 1099 to places or things you are familiar with. For example, you may remember 2498 in this way: you are 24 years old who graduated in college in 1998. You may remember 1099 as the model of your computer's printer or other things you know well. Use your imagination!

Part C: Coding and Memory
Practice Test 1

Segment 2 of Coding Section

Questions

Addresses	Delivery Route				Answers
1. 601 Pine Ridge Dr	A	B	C	D	1. ___
2. 900 Sunset Dr	A	B	C	D	2. ___
3. 350 Wetson Rd	A	B	C	D	3. ___
4. 550 S Prospect Ter	A	B	C	D	4. ___
5. 950 SW 2nd St	A	B	C	D	5. ___
6. 1250 Shotgun Rd	A	B	C	D	6. ___
7. 340 Wetson Rd	A	B	C	D	7. ___
8. 700 Sunset Dr	A	B	C	D	8. ___

Sample Answer Sheet

1. Ⓐ Ⓑ Ⓒ Ⓓ   5. Ⓐ Ⓑ Ⓒ Ⓓ

2. Ⓐ Ⓑ Ⓒ Ⓓ   6. Ⓐ Ⓑ Ⓒ Ⓓ

3. Ⓐ Ⓑ Ⓒ Ⓓ   7. Ⓐ Ⓑ Ⓒ Ⓓ

4. Ⓐ Ⓑ Ⓒ Ⓓ   8. Ⓐ Ⓑ Ⓒ Ⓓ

The correct answers are 1-B, 2-D, 3-A, 4-C, 5-D, 6-C, 7-A, and 8-C

Part C: Coding and Memory

Segment 3 of Coding Section

Instructions

Segment 3 of the Coding Section, Practice Test 1 has 36 questions to be answered in 6 minutes. You can still look at the Coding Guide. It's the real test, therefore, this part of the test is scored. In other words, correct answers are counted. Answer the questions in 6 minutes. You have to mark your answers on the official answer sheets.

For Segment 3 of the Coding Section, go to the next page.

Part C: Coding & Memory

Segment 3 of Coding Section

Coding Guide	
Address Range	Delivery Route
10 - 299 SW 2nd St 300 - 399 Sunset Dr 1 - 2498 Wetson Rd	A
300 - 899 SW 2nd St 600 - 999 Pine Ridge Dr	B
200 - 1399 Shotgun Rd 400 - 899 Sunset Dr 1 - 1099 S Prospect Ter	C
All mail that doesn't fall in one of the address ranges listed above	D

Part C: Coding and Memory
Practice Test 1

Segment 3 of Coding Section

Questions

Address	Delivery Route				Answers
1. 299 SW 2nd St	A	B	C	D	1. ___
2. 870 SW 2nd St	A	B	C	D	2. ___
3. 400 Sunset Dr	A	B	C	D	3. ___
4. 890 Pine Ridge Dr	A	B	C	D	4. ___
5. 1000 S Prospect Ter	A	B	C	D	5. ___
6. 460 Wetson Rd	A	B	C	D	6. ___
7. 1250 Shotgun Rd	A	B	C	D	7. ___
8. 400 Sunset Dr	A	B	C	D	8. ___
9. 2399 Wetson Rd	A	B	C	D	9. ___
10. 780 SW 2nd St	A	B	C	D	10. ___
11. 998 S Prospect Ter	A	B	C	D	11. ___
12. 335 Sunset Dr	A	B	C	D	12. ___
13. 59 S Prospect Ter	A	B	C	D	13. ___
14. 50 SW 2nd St	A	B	C	D	14. ___
15. 800 SW 2nd St	A	B	C	D	15. ___
16. 400 Sunset Dr	A	B	C	D	16. ___
17. 780 Wetson Rd	A	B	C	D	17. ___
18. 959 Shotgun Rd	A	B	C	D	18. ___

Continued on the next page.

Part C: Coding & Memory

Segment 3 of Coding Section

Coding Guide	
Address Range	Delivery Route
10 - 299 SW 2nd St 300 - 399 Sunset Dr 1 - 2498 Wetson Rd	A
300 - 899 SW 2nd St 600 - 999 Pine Ridge Dr	B
200 - 1399 Shotgun Rd 400 - 899 Sunset Dr 1 - 1099 S Prospect Ter	C
All mail that doesn't fall in one of the address ranges listed above	D

Part C: Coding and Memory
Practice Test 1
Continuation

Segment 3 of Coding Section

Questions

Address	Delivery Route				Answers
19. 1299 Shotgun Rd	A'	B	C	D	19. ___
20. 1950 Wetson Rd	A	B	C	D	20. ___
21. 500 SW 2nd St	A	B	C	D	21. ___
22. 1000 Pine Ridge Dr	A	B	C	D	22. ___
23. 275 SW 2nd St	A	B	C	D	23. ___
24. 900 SW 2nd St	A	B	C	D	24. ___
25. 1199 Shotgun Rd	A	B	C	D	25. ___
26. 389 Sunset Dr	A	B	C	D	26. ___
27. 998 S Prospect Ter	A	B	C	D	27. ___
28. 2399 Wetson Rd	A	B	C	D	28. ___
29. 785 Sunset Dr	A	B	C	D	29. ___
30. 400 SW 2nd St	A	B	C	D	30. ___
31. 890 S Prospect Ter	A	B	C	D	31. ___
32. 750 Pine Ridge Dr	A	B	C	D	32. ___
33. 259 SW 2nd St	A	B	C	D	33. ___
34. 55 S Prospect Ter	A	B	C	D	34. ___
35. 95 Wetson Rd	A	B	C	D	35. ___
36. 800 Pine Ridge Dr	A	B	C	D	36. ___

See the answers to the above questions on the next page.

Part C: Coding & Memory

Coding Section

Answers to Questions
Practice Test 1

Segment 3 of Coding Section, 103-105

1. A
2. B
3. C
4. B
5. C
6. A
7. C
8. C
9. A
10. B
11. C
12. A
13. C
14. A
15. B
16. C
17. A
18. C
19. C
20. A
21. B
22. D
23. A
24. D
25. C
26. A
27. C
28. A
29. C
30. B
31. C
32. B
33. A
34. C
35. A
36. B

Part C: Coding and Memory

Memory Section

The second section of Part C, called Memory Section, is composed of four segments, which are as follows:

Segment 1: You'll have 3 minutes to memorize the Coding Guide.

Segment 2: You have 1 1/2 minutes to memorize the Coding Guide and answer the questions. There are 8 questions to be answered. Since this part of the test is not counted or scored, you may just answer 2 or 3   questions. Instead, use the 1 1/2 minutes allowed to this part of the test in memorizing the Coding Guide.

Segment 3: This part of the test gives you 5 minutes to memorize the guide. There are no questions to be answered on this part of the exam.

Segment 4: This is the part that is important. You have 7 minutes to answer 36 questions, without any Coding Guide to look at. You must answer the questions from memory. Also, you must mark the circles for your answers on the official answer sheet, (not on the sample answer sheet on the question page).

As you can see, you have a total of 9 1/2 minutes to memorize the Coding Guide. That's enough time in memorizing the same code. As you may remember, you also have 3 1/2 minutes time to memorize the Coding Guide on the Coding Section of Part C Test.

For **Strategies for Coding-Memory Test,** see page 85-90.

Part C - Coding & Memory
Practice Test #1

Segment 1 of Memory Section

Instructions

Segment 1 of the Memory Section test gives you 3 minutes to memorize the Coding Guide. There will be no questions to be answered. Memorize the guide using the techniques mentioned in Chapter 15: **Strategies for the Coding-Memory Test** on pages 85-90. This same Coding Guide is used throughout this Practice 1 of this Coding and Memory Test. Now, memorize the Coding Code on the next page.

Part C: Coding & Memory
Segment 1 of Memory Section

Coding Guide	
Address Rage	Delivery Route
10 - 299 SW 2nd St 300 - 399 Sunset Dr 1 - 2498 Wetson Rd	A
300 - 899 SW 2nd St 600 - 999 Pine Ridge Dr	B
200 - 1399 Shotgun Rd 400 - 899 Sunset Dr 1 - 1099 S Prospect Ter	C
All mail that doesn't fall in one of the address ranges listed above	D

There are several ways of remembering the above address ranges in different boxes assigned to the delivery routes, **A, B, C,** and **D.** We should create so-called **extract codes** to easily remember the above addresses. You may combine the **first syllables** of the streets.

The codes may be created (from top to bottom) as **2ndSunWet** for SW 2nd, Sunset, and Wetson. For the second box, it should be **2ndPine** for SW 2nd, and Pine Ridge. For the third box it should be **ShoSunPros** for Shotgun, Sunset and Prospect.

In remembering the street numbers, you may shorten the group of numbers in the first box serving as codes, (from top to bottom) as **1 - 2** SW 2nd St for 10 - 299 SW 2nd St; **3 - 3** Sunset for 300 - 399 Sunset; and **1 - 24** Wetson for 1 - 2498 Wetson. Then for the second pairs of numbers, you may just remember **99** for 299 SW 2nd; **99** for 399 Sunset; and **98** for 2498 Wetson Rd.

You may also remember the numbers by dividing the group of numbers into three columns. For example, the numbers may be divided as follows:

10	2	99	for 10 - 299 SW 2nd
3(00)	3	99	for 300 - 399 Sunset
1	24	98	for 1 - 2498 Wetson

Part C: Coding and Memory
Segment 2 of Memory Section

Instructions

Segment 2 of the Memory Section has 8 questions to be answered in 1 1/2 minutes. Of course, you can't look at the Coding Guide. You have to answer the questions from memory. Since this part of the test is not scored, you can just answer 2 or three questions. Instead, use the time to memorize the guide. You have to mark your answers at the bottom of the sample question page, not on the official answer sheets.

For Segment 2 of the Coding Section, which serves as a practice test, turn the next page.

Part C: Coding and Memory
Practice Test 1

Segment 2 of Memory Section

Questions

Address	Delivery Route				Answers
1. 597 S Prospect Ter	A	B	C	D	1. ___
2. 650 Sunset Dr	A	B	C	D	2. ___
3. 2500 Wetson Rd	A	B	C	D	3. ___
4. 900 Sunset Dr	A	B	C	D	4. ___
5. 499 SW 2nd St	A	B	C	D	5. ___
6. 2298 Wetson Rd	A	B	C	D	6. ___
7. 288 SW 2nd St	A	B	C	D	7. ___
8. 870 Pine Ridge Dr	A	B	C	D	8. ___

Sample Answer Sheet

1. (A) (B) (C) (D)
2. (A) (B) (C) (D)
3. (A) (B) (C) (D)
4. (A) (B) (C) (D)
5. (A) (B) (C) (D)
6. (A) (B) (C) (D)
7. (A) (B) (C) (D)
8. (A) (B) (C) (D)

The correct answers are 1-C; 2-C; 3-D; 4-D; 5- B; 6-A; 7-A and 8-B

Part C: Coding and Memory
Segment 3 of Memory Section

Instructions

On Segment 3 of the Memory Section test, you have 5 minutes to memorize the address ranges and routes of the Coding Guide. See it on the next page. There will be no questions to be answered during this memorization period. For the next test, (Segment 4) you don't have to look at the Coding Guide. In other words, you have to answer the questions from memory.

Part C: Coding & Memory
Segment 3 of Memory Section

Coding Guide	
Address Rage	Delivery Route
10 - 299 SW 2nd St 300 - 399 Sunset Dr 1 - 2498 Wetson Rd	A
300 - 899 SW 2nd St 600 - 999 Pine Ridge Dr	B
200 - 1399 Shotgun Rd 400 - 899 Sunset Dr 1 - 1099 S Prospect Ter	C
All mail that doesn't fall in one of the address ranges listed above	D

There are addresses that start with number 1; for instance, two of the above address ranges: 1 - 2498 Wetson and 1 - 1099 S Prospect.   In the case of these addresses, you may just remember 2498 Wetson and 1099 S Prospect, forgetting about the number 1. In other words, all numbers below 2498 Wetson are assigned to Route A, and all numbers below 1099 S Prospect are covered by Route C. All addresses over the two numbers, 2498 Wetson and 1099 S Prospect, are all assigned to Route D. Why? Because all mail that doesn't fall in one of the address ranges above above are assigned to Route D.

Furthermore, associate the numbers 2498 and 1099 to places or things you are familiar with. For example, you may remember 2498 in this w ay: you are 24 years old who graduated in college in 1998. You may remember 1099 as the model of your computer's printer or other things you know well. Use your imagination!

Part C: Coding and Memory

Segment 4 of Memory Section

Instructions

Segment 4 of the Memory Section is the real test. This part is scored and the score adds to your total Test 473 score. You will have 36 questions to be answered in 7 minutes. You should mark the answers on the official answer sheet. Segment 4 of the Memory Section prohibits you from looking at the Coding Guide. You have to answer the questions from memory.

Part C: Coding and Memory
Practice Test 1

Segment 4 of Memory Section

Questions

Address	Delivery Route				Answers
1. 399 Sunset Dr	A	B	C	D	1. ___
2. 1400 Shotgun Rd	A	B	C	D	2. ___
3. 799 Sunset Dr	A	B	C	D	3. ___
4. 690 SW 2nd St	A	B	C	D	4. ___
5. 2000 Wetson Rd	A	B	C	D	5, ___
6. 379 Sunset Dr	A	B	C	D	6. ___
7. 89 S Prospect Ter	A	B	C	D	7. ___
8. 49 Wetson Rd	A	B	C	D	8. ___
9. 1000 Pine Ridge Dr	A	B	C	D	9. ___
10. 170 SW 2nd St	A	B	C	D	10. ___
11. 389 Sunset Dr	A	B	C	D	11. ___
12. 150 SW 2nd St	A	B	C	D	12. ___
13. 1199 Shotgun Rd	A	B	C	D	13. ___
14. 950 Sunset Dr	A	B	C	D	14. ___
15. 198 Wetson Rd	A	B	C	D	15. ___
16. 299 Sunset Dr	A	B	C	D	16. ___
17. 850 Pine Ridge Dr	A	B	C	D	17. ___
18. 89 S Prospect Ter	A	B	C	D	18. ___

Part C: Coding and Memory
Practice Test 1
Continuation

Segment 4 of Memory Section

Questions

Address	Delivery Route				Answers
19. 95 S Prospect Ter	A	B	C	D	19. ___
20. 2398 Wetson Rd	A	B	C	D	20. ___
21. 490 Pine Ridge Dr	A	B	C	D	21. ___
22. 199 SW 2nd St	A	B	C	D	22. ___
23. 1200 S Prospect Ter	A	B	C	D	23. ___
24. 1200 Wetson Rd	A	B	C	D	24. ___
25. 299 Sunset Dr	A	B	C	D	25. ___
26. 799 Sunset Dr	A	B	C	D	26. ___
27. 2199 Wetson Rd	A	B	C	D	27. ___
28. 56 S Prospect Ter	A	B	C	D	28. ___
29. 780 SW 2nd St	A	B	C	D	29. ___
30. 301 Sunset Dr	A	B	C	D	30. ___
31. 450 S Prospect Ter	A	B	C	D	31. ___
32. 899 Pine Ridge Dr	A	B	C	D	32. ___
33. 900 Sunset Dr	A	B	C	D	33. ___
34. 89 Wetson Rd	A	B	C	D	34. ___
35. 699 SW 2nd St	A	B	C	D	35. ___
36. 1000 Pine Ridge Dr	A	B	C	D	36. ___

See the answers to the above questions on the next page

Part C: Coding & Memory

Memory Section

Answers to Questions
Practice Test 1

Segment 4 of Memory Section, p. 116-117

1. A
2. D
3. C
4. B
5. A
6. A
7. C
8. A
9. D
10. A
11. A
12. A
13. C
14. D
15. A
16. D
17. B
18. C
19. C
20. A
21. D
22. A
23. D
24. A
25. D
26. C
27. A
28. C
29. B
30. A
31. C
32. B
33. D
34. A
35. B
36. D

Practice Test 2
Part C - Coding & Memory

Coding Section

The first section of the Part C Test, called Coding Section, actually consists of three segments:

Segment 1: You are given 2 minutes within which to study or memorize the Coding Guide. Also, you have to answer four items as a practice test. Since this is not counted, you may answer only one question and use the time in memorizing the code. You are allowed to look at the Coding Guide as you answer the questions. The same Coding Guide will be used throughout the Coding and Memory tests.

Segment 2: You'll be given 1 1/2 minutes to answer 8 questions on this part of the test. Since this is not scored, you may answer only 2 or 3 questions. You better use the time in memorizing the coding guide.

Segment 3: You have 6 minutes to answer 36 questions. This part of the test is scored or counted. You'll still be allowed to look at the coding guide as you answer the questions. You must mark the circles on the official answer sheet.

When you work on the first section, Coding, of the test, you are allowed to look at the coding guide while you are assigning codes, (A, B, C, and D), to each item of the addresses. However, when you work on the second section (memory), you won't be allowed to look at the coding guide. In other words, memorize the coding guide.

Part C - Coding & Memory

Segment 1 of Coding Section

Instructions

Segment 1 of the Coding Section test is a 2-minute exercise for memorizing the Coding Guide to be used in answering the questions on this test. Also, you have these 2 minutes to answer 4 questions. Since this part of the test is not scored, you should not work on all of the questions. Just memorize the guide using the techniques mentioned in Chapter 18: **Strategies for the Coding-Memory Test** on pages 85-90. Turn the page to see the Coding Guide.

Part C: Coding & Memory

Segment 2 of Coding Section

Coding Guide	
Address Range	Delivery Route
601 - 1299 Chrysler Dr **8**00 - 999 Decator St **8**5 - 2499 Birwood Rd	A
1300 - 1599 Chrysler Dr 12601 - 13599 Blackstone St	B
1 - 1299 Clairmont St 1000 - 2999 Decator St 1 - 1399 Woodward Ave	C
All mail that doesn't fall in one of the address ranges listed above	D

There are several ways of remembering the above address ranges in different boxes assigned to the delivery routes, **A, B, C,** and **D.** We should create so-called **extract codes** to easily remember the above addresses. You may combine the **first syllables** of the streets.

The codes may be created (from time to bottom) as **ChryDeBir** for Chrysler, Decator and Birwood. For the second box, it should be **ChryBlack** for Chrysler and Blackstone. For the third box it should be **ClairDeWood** for Clairmont, Decator and Woodward. Disregard the Dr, St, Ave, etc.

In remembering the street numbers, you may shorten the group of numbers in the first box, serving as codes. You may remember them (from top to bottom) as **6**(01) - **12** Chrysler for 601 - 1299 Chrysler; **8**(00)- **9** Decator for 8(00) - 999 Decator and **8**(5) - 24 Birwood for 85 - 2499 Birwood Rd. Then for the second strings of numbers, you may just remember **99** for 1299 Chrysler; **99** for 99 Decator and 99 for 2499 Birwood. For the second box, you can do the same, such as **13-15** for **13**00 - **15**99 Chrysler Dr, etc.

You may also remember the numbers by dividing the numbers into three columns. For example, the numbers may be divided as follows:

6(01)	12	99	for 601 - 1299 Chrysler Dr
8(00)	9	99	for 800 - 999 Decator St
8(5)	24	99	for 85 - 2499 Birwood Rd

Part C: Coding and Memory
Practice Test 2

Segment 1 of Coding Section

Questions

Address	Delivery Route			
1. 1199 Chrysler Dr	A	B	C	D
2. 1011 Decator St	A	B	C	D
3. 1299 Birwood Rd	A	B	C	D
4. 590 Woodward Ave	A	B	C	D

Sample Answer Sheet

1. Ⓐ Ⓑ Ⓒ Ⓓ

2. Ⓐ Ⓑ Ⓒ Ⓓ

3. Ⓐ Ⓑ Ⓒ Ⓓ

4. Ⓐ Ⓑ Ⓒ Ⓓ

The correct answers are 1-A; 2-C; 3-A; and 4-C.

Part C: Coding and Memory
Segment 2 of Coding Section

Instructions

Segment 2 of the Coding Section has 8 questions to be answered in 1 1/2 minutes. Of course, you can look at the Coding Guide. Since this part of the test is not scored, you can just answer 2 or 3 questions, then use the time to memorize the guide. You have to mark your answers at the bottom of the sample question page, not on the official answer sheets.

For Segment 2 of the Coding Section, which serves as a practice test, turn the page.

Part C: Coding & Memory

Segment 2 of Coding Section

Coding Guide	
Address Range	Delivery Route
601 - 1299 Chrysler Dr 800 - 999 Decator St 85 - 2499 Birwood Rd	A
1300 - 1599 Chrysler Dr 12601 - 13599 Blackstone St	B
1 - 1299 Clairmont St 1000 - 2999 Decator St 1 - 1399 Woodward Ave	C
All mail that doesn't fall in one of the address ranges listed above	D

There are addresses that start with number 1; for instance, two of the above address ranges: 1 - 1299 Clairmont and 1 - 1399 Woodward. In the case of these addresses, you may just remember 1299 Clairmont and 1399 Woodward, **forgetting about the number 1**. In other words, all numbers below 1299 Clairmont are assigned to Route C, and all numbers below 1399 Woodward are also covered by Route C. All addresses over the two numbers, 1299 Clairmont and 1399 Woodward, are all assigned to Route D. Why? Because all mail that doesn't fall in one of the address ranges above are assigned to Route D.

Furthermore, associate the numbers 1299 and 1399 to places or things you are familiar with. For example, you may remember 1299 in this way: you have 12 years of schooling; and you graduated in college in 1999. You may remember 1399 as the model of your HP computer. You may associate the numbers to other significant events in your life. Use your imagination!

Part C: Coding & Memory
Practice Test 2

Segment 2 of Coding Section

Questions

Address	Delivery Route				Answers
1. 3000 Decator St	A	B	C	D	1. ___
2. 1199 Chrysler Dr	A	B	C	D	2. ___
3. 1100 Clairmont St	A	B	C	D	3. ___
4. 96 Woodward Ave	A	B	C	D	4. ___
5. 12900 Blackstone St	A	B	C	D	5. ___
6. 59 Woodward Ave	A	B	C	D	6. ___
7. 3002 Decator St	A	B	C	D	7. ___
8. 1500 Birwood Rd	A	B	C	D	8. ___

Sample Answer Sheet

1. (A)(B)(C)(D)

2. (A)(B)(C)(D)

3. (A)(B)(C)(D)

4. (A)(B)(C)(D)

5. (A)(B)(C)(D)

6. (A)(B)(C)(D)

7. (A)(B)(C)(D)

8. (A)(B)(C)(D)

The correct answers are 1-D; 2-A; 3-C; 4-C; 5-B; 6-C; 7-D; and 8-A.

Part C: Coding and Memory

Segment 3 of Coding Section

Instructions

Segment 3 of the Coding Section, Practice Test 1 has 36 questions to be answered in 6 minutes. You can still look at the Coding Guide. It's the real test, therefore, this part of the test is scored. In other words, correct answers are counted. Answer the questions in 6 minutes. You have to mark your answers on the official answer sheets.

For Segment 3 of the Coding Section, go to the next page.

Part C: Coding and Memory

Segment 3 of Coding Section

Coding Guide	
Address Range	Delivery Route
601 - 1299 Chrysler Dr 800 - 999 Decator St 85 - 2499 Birwood Rd	A
1300 - 1599 Chrysler Dr 12601 - 13599 Blackstone St	B
1 - 1299 Clairmont St 1000 - 2999 Decator St 1 - 1399 Woodward Ave	C
All mail that doesn't fall in one of the address ranges listed above	D

Part C: Coding and Memory
Practice Test 2

Segment 3 of Coding Section

Questions

Address	Delivery Route				Answers
1. 1199 Chrysler Dr	A	B	C	D	1. ___
2. 1400 Woodward Ave	A	B	C	D	2. ___
3. 2299 Birwood Rd	A	B	C	D	3. ___
4. 955 Chrysler Dr	A	B	C	D	4. ___
5. 12900 Blackstone St	A	B	C	D	5. ___
6. 95 Clairmont St	A	B	C	D	6. ___
7. 950 Woodward Ave	A	B	C	D	7. ___
8. 1500 Chrysler Dr	A	B	C	D	8. ___
9. 1298 Woodward Ave	A	B	C	D	9. ___
10. 899 Decator St	A	B	C	D	10. ___
11. 2197 Birwood Rd	A	B	C	D	11. ___
12. 759 Decator St	A	B	C	D	12. ___
13. 1198 Clairmont St	A	B	C	D	13. ___
14. 2398 Birwood Rd	A	B	C	D	14. ___
15. 1159 Decator St	A	B	C	D	15. ___
16. 1300 Chrysler Dr	A	B	C	D	16. ___
17. 12700 Blackstone St	A	B	C	D	17. ___
18. 1500 Birwood Rd	A	B	C	D	18. ___

Practice Test 2
Part C: Coding and Memory
Continuation

Segment 3 of Coding Section

Coding Guide	
Address Range	Delivery Route
601 - 1299 Chrysler Dr 800 - 999 Decator St 85 - 2499 Birwood Rd	A
1300 - 1599 Chrysler Dr 12601 - 13599 Blackstone St	B
1 - 1299 Clairmont St 1000 - 2999 Decator St 1 - 1399 Woodward Ave	C
All mail that doesn't fall in one of the address ranges listed above	D

Part C: Coding and Memory
Practice Test 2
Continuation

Segment 3 of Coding Section

Questions

Address	Delivery Route				Answers
19. 11599 Blackstone St	A	B	C	D	19. ___
20. 1298 Woodward Ave	A	B	C	D	20. ___
21. 95 Birwood Rd	A	B	C	D	21. ___
22. 2897 Decator St	A	B	C	D	22. ___
23. 1499 Chrysler Dr	A	B	C	D	23. ___
24. 12599 Blackstone St	A	B	C	D	24. ___
25. 2798 Decator St	A	B	C	D	25. ___
26. 59 Woodward Ave	A	B	C	D	26. ___
27. 1399 Chrysler Dr	A	B	C	D	27. ___
28. 12798 Blackstone St	A	B	C	D	28. ___
29. 79 Clairmont St	A	B	C	D	29. ___
30. 1199 Chrysler Dr	A	B	C	D	30. ___
31. 900 Decator St	A	B	C	D	31. ___
32. 95 Woodward Ave	A	B	C	D	32. ___
33. 2500 Birwood Rd	A	B	C	D	33. ___
34. 12909 Blackstone St	A	B	C	D	34. ___
35. 89 Clairmont St	A	B	C	D	35. ___
36. 890 Woodward Ave	A	B	C	D	36. ___

See the answers to the above questions on the next page.

Part C: Coding & Memory

Coding Section

Answers to Questions
Practice Test 2

Segment 3 of Coding Section, 131-133

1. A
2. D
3. A
4. A
5. B
6. C
7. C
8. B
9. C
10. A
11. A
12. D
13. C
14. A
15. C
16. B
17. B
18. A
19. D
20. C
21. A
22. C
23. B
24. B
25. C
26. C
27. B
28. B
29. C
30. A
31. A
32. C
33. D
34. B
35. C
36. C

Practice Test 2
Part C: Coding and Memory

Memory Section

The second section of Part C, called Memory Section, is composed of four segments, which are as follows:

Segment 1: You'll have 3 minutes to memorize the Coding Guide.

Segment 2: You have 1 1/2 minutes to memorize the Coding Guide and answer the questions. There are 8 questions to be answered. Since this part of the test is not counted or scored, you may just answer 2 or 3 questions. Instead, use the 1 1/2 minutes allowed to this part of the test in memorizing the Coding Guide.

Segment 3. This part of the test gives you 5 minutes to memorize the guide. There are no questions to be answered on this part of the exam.

Segment 4: This is the segment that is scored or counted. You have 7 minutes to answer 36 questions, without any Coding Guide to look at. You must answer the questions from memory. Also, you must mark the circles for your answers on the official answer sheet, not on the sample answer sheet on the question page.

As you can see, you have a total of 9 1/2 minutes to memorize the Coding Guide. That's enough time in memorizing the code. As you may remember, you also have 3 1/2 minutes time to memorize the Coding Guide on the Coding Section of Part C Test.

For **Strategies for Coding-Memory Test,** see pages 85-90.

Part C: Coding and Memory

Segment 1 of Memory Section

Instructions

Segment 1 of the Memory Section test gives you 3 minutes to memorize the Coding Guide. There will be no questions to be answered. Memorize the guide using the techniques mentioned in Chapter 15: **Strategies for the Coding-Memory Test** on pages 85-90. This same Coding Guide is used throughout this Practice 1 of this Coding and Memory Test. Now, memorize the Coding Code on the next page.

Part C: Coding and Memory

Segment 2 of Memory Section

Coding Guide	
Address Range	Delivery Route
601 - 1299 Chrysler Dr **8**00 - 999 Decator St **8**5 - 2499 Birwood Rd	A
1300 - 1599 Chrysler Dr 12601 - 13599 Blackstone St	B
1 - 1299 Clairmont St 1000 - 2999 Decator St 1 - 1399 Woodward Ave	C
All mail that doesn't fall in one of the address ranges listed above	D

There are several ways of remembering the above address ranges in different boxes assigned to the delivery routes, **A, B, C,** and **D.** We should create so-called **extract codes** to easily remember the above addresses. You may combine the **first syllables** of the streets.

The codes may be created (from time to bottom) as **ChryDeBir** for Chrysler, Decator and Birwood. For the second box, it should be **ChryBlack** for Chrysler and Blackstone. For the third box it should be **ClairDeWood** for Clairmont, Decator and Woodward. Disregard the Dr, St, Ave, etc.

In remembering the street numbers, you may shorten the group of numbers in the first box, serving as codes. You may remember them (from top to bottom) as **6**(01) - **12** Chrysler for 601 - 1299 Chrysler; **8**(00) - **9** Decator for 800 - 999 Decator and **8**(5) - **24** Birwood for 85 - 2499 Birwood. Then for the second pairs of numbers, you may just remember **99** for Chrysler; **99** for 999 Decator and **99** for 2499 Birwood.

You may also remember the numbers by dividing the numbers into three columns. For example, the numbers may be divided as follows:

6(01)	12	99	for 601 - 1299 Chrysler Dr
8(00)	9	99	for 800 - 999 Decator St
8(5)	24	99	for 85 - 2499 Birwood Rd

Part C: Coding and Memory

Segment 2 of Memory Section

Instructions

Segment 2 of the Memory Section has 8 questions to be answered in 1 1/2 minutes. Of course, you can't look at the Coding Guide. You have to answer the questions from memory. Since this part of the test is not scored, you can just answer 2 or 3 questions. Instead, use the time to memorize the guide. You have to mark your answers at the bottom of the sample question page, not on the official answer sheets.

For Segment 2 of the Coding Section, which serves as a practice test, turn the next page.

Part C: Coding and Memory
Practice Test 2

Segment 2 of Memory Section

Questions

Address	Delivery Route				Answers
1. 1200 Woodward Ave	A	B	C	D	1. ___
2. 1399 Chrysler Dr	A	B	C	D	2. ___
3. 2499 Decator St	A	B	C	D	3. ___
4. 99 Clairmont St	A	B	C	D	4. ___
5. 1500 Birwood Rd	A	B	C	D	5. ___
6. 99 Clairmont St	A	B	C	D	6. ___
7. 870 Decator St	A	B	C	D	7. ___
8. 1600 Chrysler Dr	A	B	C	D	8. ___

Sample Answer Sheet

1. (A) (B) (C) (D)

2. (A) (B) (C) (D)

3. (A) (B) (C) (D)

4. (A) (B) (C) (D)

5. (A) (B) (C) (D)

6. (A) (B) (C) (D)

7. (A) (B) (C) (D)

8. (A) (B) (C) (D)

The correct answers are: 1-C; 2-B; 3-C; 4-C; 5-A; 6-C; 7-A; and 8-D.

Part C: Coding and Memory

Segment 3 of Memory Section

Instructions

On Segment 3 of the Memory Section test, you have 5 minutes to memorize the address ranges and routes of the Coding Guide. See it on the next page. There will be no questions to be answered during this memorization period. For the next test, (Segment 4) you don't have to look at the Coding Guide. In other words, you have to answer the questions from memory.

Part C: Coding & Memory

Segment 3 of Memory Section

Coding Guide	
Address Range	Delivery Route
601 - 1299 Chrysler Dr 800 - 999 Decator St 85 - 2499 Birwood Rd	A
1300 - 1599 Chrysler Dr 12601 - 13599 Blackstone St	B
1 - 1299 Clairmont St 1000 - 2999 Decator St 1 - 1399 Woodward Ave	C
All mail that doesn't fall in one of the address ranges listed above	D

There are addresses that start with number 1; for instance, two of the above address ranges: 1 - 1299 Clairmont and 1 - 1399 Woodward. In the case of these addresses, you may just remember 1299 Clairmont and 1399 Woodward, **forgetting about the number 1**. In other words, all numbers below 1299 Clairmont are assigned to Route C, and all numbers below 1399 Woodward are also covered by Route C. All addresses over the two numbers, 1299 Clairmont and 1399 Woodward, are all assigned to Route D. Why? Because all mail that doesn't fall in one of the address ranges above are assigned to Route D.

Furthermore, associate the numbers 1299 and 1399 to places or things you are familiar with. For example, you may remember 1299 in this way: you have 12 years of schooling; and you graduated in college in 1999. You may remember 1399 as the model of your HP computer. You may associate the numbers to other significant events in your life. Use your imagination!

Part C: Coding and Memory

Segment 4 of Memory Section

Instructions

Segment 4 of the Memory Section is the real test. This part is scored and the score adds to your total Test 473 score. You will have 36 questions to be answered in 7 minutes. You should mark the answers on the official answer sheet. Segment 4 of the Memory Section prohibits you from looking at the Coding Guide. You have to answer the questions from memory.

Part C: Coding and Memory
Practice Test 2

Segment 4 of Memory Section

Questions

Address	Delivery Route				Answers
1. 1299 Clairmont St	A	B	C	D	1. ___
2. 14000 Blackstone St	A	B	C	D	2. ___
3. 45 Clairmont St	A	B	C	D	3. ___
4. 1500 Decator St	A	B	C	D	4. ___
5. 1200 Birwood Rd	A	B	C	D	5. ___
6. 14000 Blackstone St	A	B	C	D	6. ___
7. 750 Chrysler Dr	A	B	C	D	7. ___
8. 1400 Birwood Rd	A	B	C	D	8. ___
9. 1100 Clairmont St	A	B	C	D	9. ___
10. 89 Woodward Ave	A	B	C	D	10. ___
11. 1300 Chrysler Dr	A	B	C	D	11. ___
12. 1499 Birwood Rd	A	B	C	D	12. ___
13. 3000 Decator St	A	B	C	D	13. ___
14. 12900 Blackstone St	A	B	C	D	14 ___
15. 2300 Birwood Rd	A	B	C	D	15. ___
16. 1000 Decator St	A	B	C	D	16. ___
17. 70 Woodward Ave	A	B	C	D	17. ___
18. 1350 Chrysler Dr	A	B	C	D	18. ___

Part C: Coding and Memory
Practice Test 2
Continuation

Segment 4 of Memory Section

Questions

Address	Delivery Route				Answers
19. 1199 Chrysler Dr	A	B	C	D	19. ___
20. 14000 Blackstone St	A	B	C	D	20. ___
21. 59 Woodward Ave	A	B	C	D	21. ___
22. 1400 Chrysler Dr	A	B	C	D	22. ___
23. 95 Birwood Rd	A	B	C	D	23. ___
24. 881 Decator St	A	B	C	D	24. ___
25. 85 Clairmont St	A	B	C	D	25. ___
26. 2285 Birwood Rd	A	B	C	D	26. ___
27. 87 Woodward Ave	A	B	C	D	27. ___
28. 2288 Birwood Rd	A	B	C	D	28. ___
29. 1200 Decator St	A	B	C	D	29. ___
30. 99 Clairmont St	A	B	C	D	30. ___
31. 1100 Chrysler Dr	A	B	C	D	31. ___
32. 2398 Birwood Rd	A	B	C	D	32. ___
33. 12700 Blackstone St	A	B	C	D	33. ___
34. 801 Decator St	A	B	C	D	34. ___
35. 1100 Woodward Ave	A	B	C	D	35. ___
36. 95 Birwood Rd	A	B	C	D	36. ___

For answer to the above items, turn the page.

Part C: Coding & Memory
Memory Section

Answers to Questions
Practice Test 2

Segment 4 of Memory Section, 144-145

1. C
2. D
3. C
4. C
5. A
6. D
7. A
8. A
9. C
10. C
11. B
12. A
13. D
14. B
15. A
16. C
17. C
18. B
19. A
20. D
21. C
22. B
23. A
24. A
25. C
26. A
27. C
28. A
29. C
30. C
31. A
32. A
33. B
34. A
35. C
36. A

Practice Test 3
Part C: Coding and Memory

Coding Section

The first section of the Part C Test, called Coding Section, actually consists of three parts:

Segment 1: You are given 2 minutes within which to study or memorize the Coding Guide. Also, you have to answer four items as a practice test. Since this is not counted, you may answer only one question and use the time in memorizing the code. You are allowed to look at the Coding Guide as you answer the questions. The same Coding Guide will be used throughout the Coding and Memory tests.

Segment 2: You'll be given 1 1/2 minutes to answer 8 questions on this part of the test. Since this is not scored, you may answer only 2 or 3 questions. You better use the time in memorizing the coding guide.

Segment 3: You have 6 minutes to answer 36 questions. This part of the test is scored or counted. You must mark the circles on the official answer sheet. You'll still be allowed to look at the coding guide as you answer the items.

When you work on the first section, Coding, of the test, you are allowed to look at the coding guide while you are assigning delivery routes, (A, B, C, and D), to each address range. However, when you work on the second section (memory), you won't be allowed to look at the coding guide. In other words, memorize the coding guide.

Part C: Coding and Memory

Segment 1 of Coding Section

Instructions

Segment 1 of the Coding Section test is a 2-minute exercise for memorizing the Coding Guide to be used in answering the questions on this test. Also, you have these 2 minutes to answer 4 questions. Since this part of the test is not scored, you should not work on all of the questions. Just memorize the guide using the techniques mentioned in Chapter 18: **Strategies for the Coding-Memory Test** on pages 85-90. Turn the page to see the Coding Guide.

Part C: Coding and Memory

Segment 1 of Coding Section

Coding Guide	
Address Range	Delivery Route
50 - 1799 Clark St **100** - 1499 Walter Jetton Blvd **28**00 - 3098 Washington St	A
1800 - 2999 Clark St 300 - 3099 Stafford St	B
1 - 2299 Largo Rd 100 - 4899 Eastlawn St 1500 - 1999 Walter Jetton Blvd	C
All mail that doesn't fall in one of the address ranges listed above	D

There are several ways of remembering the above address ranges in different boxes assigned to the delivery routes, **A, B, C,** and **D.** We should create so-called **extract codes** to easily remember the above addresses. You may combine the **first syllables** of the streets.

The codes may be created (from top to bottom) as **ClarkWalWash** for Clark, Walter Jetton and Washington. For the second box, it should be **ClarkStaf** for Clark and Stafford. For the third box it should be **LarEastWal** for Largo, Eastlawn and Walter Jetton.

In remembering the street numbers, you may shorten the group of numbers in the first box. You may remember them as (from top to bottom) as **5**(0) - **17** Clark for 50 - 1799 Clark; **1**(00) - **14** Walter for 100 - 1499 Walter Jetton; and **28**(00) - **30** Washington for 2800 - 3098 Washington. Then for the second pairs of numbers, you may just remember **99** for 1799 Clark; **99** for 1499 Walter Jetton; and **98** for 3098 Washington. You may also remember the numbers by dividing them into three columns. For example, the numbers may be divided as follows:

5(0)	17	99	for 50 - 1799 Clark St
1(00)	14	99	for 100 - 1499 Walter Jetton Blvd
28(00)	30	98	for 2800 - 3098 Washington

Part C: Coding and Memory
Practice Test 3

Segment 1 of Coding Section

Questions

Address	Delivery Route			
1. 80 Clark St	A	B	C	D
2. 3599 Eastlawn St	A	B	C	D
3. 1500 Stafford St	A	B	C	D
4. 4000 Washington St	A	B	C	D

Sample Answer Sheet

1. Ⓐ Ⓑ Ⓒ Ⓓ

2. Ⓐ Ⓑ Ⓒ Ⓓ

3. Ⓐ Ⓑ Ⓒ Ⓓ

4. Ⓐ Ⓑ Ⓒ Ⓓ

The correct answers are: 1-A; 2-C; 3-B, & 4-D.

Part C: Coding and Memory

Segment 2 of Coding Section

Instructions

Segment 2 of the Coding Section has 8 questions to be answered in 1 1/2 minutes. Of course, you can look at the Coding Guide. Since this part of the test is not scored, you can just answer 2 or 3 questions, then use the time to memorize the guide. You have to mark your answers at the bottom of the sample question page, not on the official answer sheets.

For Segment 2 of the Coding Section, which serves as a practice test, turn the page.

Part C: Coding and Memory

Segment 2 of Coding Section

Coding Guide	
Address Range	Delivery Route
50 - 1799 Clark St 100 - 1499 Walter Jetton Blvd 2800 - 3098 Washington St	A
1800 - 2999 Clark St 300 - 3099 Stafford St	B
1 - 2299 Largo Rd 100 - 4899 Eastlawn St 1500 - 1999 Walter Jetton Blvd	C
All mail that doesn't fall in one of the address ranges listed above	D

There are addresses that start with number 1; for instance, one of the above address ranges: 1 - 2299 Largo. In the case of this address, you may just remember 2299 Largo, forgetting about the number 1. In other words, all numbers below 2299 Largo are assigned to Route C. All numbers over 2299 Largo are all assigned to Route D. Why? Because all mail that doesn't fall in one of the address ranges above are assigned to Route D.

Furthermore, associate the numbers 2299 to places or things you are familiar with. For example, you may remember 2299 in this way: you have lived for 22 years in your current address, and you graduated in college in 1999. Use your imagination!

Part C: Coding and Memory
Practice Test 3

Segment 2 of Coding Section

Questions

	Address	Delivery Route				Answers
1.	2000 Walter Jetton Blvd	A	B	C	D	1. ___
2.	1650 Clark St	A	B	C	D	2. ___
3.	1099 Largo Rd	A	B	C	D	3. ___
4.	1889 Walter Jetton Blvd	A	B	C	D	4. ___
5.	2995 Stafford St	A	B	C	D	5. ___
6.	2889 Washington St	A	B	C	D	6. ___
7.	4809 Eastlawm St	A	B	C	D	7. ___
8.	79 Largo Rd	A	B	C	D	8. ___

Sample Answer Sheet

1. Ⓐ Ⓑ Ⓒ Ⓓ

2. Ⓐ Ⓑ Ⓒ Ⓓ

3. Ⓐ Ⓑ Ⓒ Ⓓ

4. Ⓐ Ⓑ Ⓒ Ⓓ

5. Ⓐ Ⓑ Ⓒ Ⓓ

6. Ⓐ Ⓑ Ⓒ Ⓓ

7. Ⓐ Ⓑ Ⓒ Ⓓ

8. Ⓐ Ⓑ Ⓒ Ⓓ

The correct answers are: 1-D; 2-A; 3-C; 4-C; 5-B; 6-A; 7-C; & 8-C.

Part C: Coding and Memory

Segment 3 of Coding Section

Instructions

Segment 3 of the Coding Section, Practice Test 1 has 36 questions to be answered in 6 minutes. You can still look at the Coding Guide. It's the real test, therefore, this part of the test is scored. In other words, correct answers are counted. Answer the questions in 6 minutes. You have to mark your answers on the official answer sheets.

For Segment 3 of the Coding Section, go to the next page.

Part C: Coding and Memory
Segment 3 of Coding Section

Coding Guide	
Address Range	Delivery Route
50 - 1799 Clark St 100 - 1499 Walter Jetton Blvd 2800 - 3098 Washington St	A
1800 - 2999 Clark St 300 - 3099 Stafford St	B
1 - 2299 Largo Rd 100 - 4899 Eastlawn St 1500 - 1999 Walter Jetton Blvd	C
All mail that doesn't fall in one of the address ranges listed above	D

Part C: Coding and Memory
Practice Test 3

Segment 3 of Coding Section

Questions

Address	Delivery Route				Answers
1. 870 Walter Jetton Blvd	A	B	C	D	1. ___
2. 4999 Eastlawn St	A	B	C	D	2. ___
3. 2000 Largo Rd	A	B	C	D	3. ___
4. 3100 Stafford St	A	B	C	D	4. ___
5. 1550 Largo Rd	A	B	C	D	5. ___
6. 1900 Walter Jetton Blvd	A	B	C	D	6. ___
7. 2098 Washington St	A	B	C	D	7. ___
8. 75 Largo Rd	A	B	C	D	8. ___
9. 2095 Walter Jetton Blvd	A	B	C	D	9. ___
10 1800 Clark St	A	B	C	D	10. ___
11. 500 Eastlawn St	A	B	C	D	11. ___
12. 1759 Clark St	A	B	C	D	12. ___
13. 670 Eastlawn St	A	B	C	D	13. ___
14. 1300 Walter Jetton Blvd	A	B	C	D	14. ___
15. 90 Largo Rd	A	B	C	D	15. ___
16. 4000 Washington St	A	B	C	D	16. ___
17. 900 Stafford St	A	B	C	D	17. ___
18. 799 Eastlawn St	A	B	C	D	18. ___

Part C: Coding and Memory

Segment 3 of Coding Section

Coding Guide	
Address Range	Delivery Route
50 - 1799 Clark St 100 - 1499 Walter Jetton Blvd 2800 - 3098 Washington St	A
1800 - 2999 Clark St 300 - 3099 Stafford St	B
1 - 2299 Largo Rd 100 - 4899 Eastlawn St 1500 - 1999 Walter Jetton Blvd	C
All mail that doesn't fall in one of the address ranges listed above	D

Part C: Coding and Memory
Practice Test 3
Continuation

Segment 3 of Coding Section

Questions

	Address	Delivery Route				Answers
19.	1900 Walter Jetton Blvd	A	B	C	D	19. ___
20.	1699 Clark St	A	B	C	D	20. ___
21.	2189 Largo Rd	A	B	C	D	21. ___
22.	2000 Walter Jetton Blvd	A	B	C	D	22. ___
23.	3100 Washington St	A	B	C	D	23. ___
24.	3789 Eastlawn St	A	B	C	D	24. ___
25.	2299 Stafford St	A	B	C	D	25. ___
26.	3030 Clark St	A	B	C	D	26. ___
27.	1900 Largo Rd	A	B	C	D	27. ___
28.	2998 Washington St	A	B	C	D	28. ___
29.	2050 Walter Jetton Blvd	A	B	C	D	29. ___
30.	4000 Stafford St	A	B	C	D	30. ___
31.	2199 Largo Rd	A	B	C	D	31. ___
32.	4000 Washington St	A	B	C	D	32. ___
33.	5000 Eastlawn St	A	B	C	D	33. ___
34.	2999 Clark St	A	B	C	D	34. ___
35.	1400 Walter Jetton Blvd	A	B	C	D	35. ___
36.	2998 Washington St	A	B	C	D	36. ___

See the answers to the above questions on the next page.

Part C: Coding & Memory

Coding Section

Answers to Questions
Practice Test 3

Segment 3 of Coding Section, p. 159-161

1. A
2. D
3. C
4. D
5. C
6. C
7. D
8. C
9. D
10. B
11. C
12. A
13. C
14. A
15. C
16. D
17. B
18. C
19. C
20. A
21. C
22. D
23. D
24. C
25. B
26. D
27. C
28. A
29. D
30. D
31. C
32. D
33. D
34. B
35. A
36. A

Part C: Coding and Memory
Practice Test 3

Memory Section

The second section of Part C, called Memory Section, is composed of four parts, which are as follows:

Segment 1: You'll have 3 minutes to memorize the Coding Guide.

Segment 2: You have 1 1/2 minutes to memorize the Coding Guide and answer the questions. There are 8 questions to be answered. Since this part of the test is not counted or scored, you may just answer 2 or 3 questions. Instead, use the 1 1/2 minutes allowed to this part of the test in memorizing the Coding Guide.

Segment 3. This part of the test gives you 5 minutes to memorize the guide. There are no questions to be answered on this part of the exam.

Segment 4: This is the part that counts. You have 7 minutes to answer 36 questions, without any Coding Guide to look at. You must answer the questions from memory. Also, you must mark the circles for your answers on the official answer sheet, not on the sample answer sheet on the question page.

As you can see, you have a total of 9 1/2 minutes to memorize the Coding Guide. That's enough time in memorizing the same code. As you may remember, you also have 3 1/2 minutes time to memorize the Coding Guide on the Coding Section of Part C Test.

For **Strategies for Coding-Memory Test,** see pages 85-90.

Part C: Coding and Memory

Segment 1 of Memory Section

Instructions

Segment 1 of the Memory Section test gives you 3 minutes to memorize the Coding Guide. There will be no questions to be answered. Memorize the guide using the techniques mentioned in Chapter 15: **Strategies for the Coding-Memory Test** on pages 85-90. This same Coding Guide is used throughout this Practice 1 of this Coding and Memory Test. Now, memorize the Coding Code on the next page.

Part C: Coding and Memory

Segment 1 of Memory Section

Coding Guide	
Address Range	Delivery Route
50 - 1799 Clark St **100** - 1499 Walter Jetton Blvd **28**00 - 3098 Washington St	A
1800 - 2999 Clark St 300 - 3099 Stafford St	B
1 - 2299 Largo Rd 100 - 4899 Eastlawn St 1500 - 1999 Walter Jetton Blvd	C
All mail that doesn't fall in one of the address ranges listed above	D

There are several ways of remembering the above address ranges in different boxes assigned to the delivery routes, **A, B, C,** and **D.** We should create so-called **extract codes** to easily remember the above addresses. You may combine the **first syllables** of the streets.

The codes may be created (from top to bottom) as **ClarkWalWash** for Clark, Walter Jetton and Washington. For the second box, it should be **ClarkStaf** for Clark and Stafford. For the third box it should be **LarEastWal** for Largo, Eastlawn and Walter Jetton.

In remembering the street numbers, you may shorten the group of numbers in the first box serving as codes. You may remember them as (from top to bottom) as **5**(0) - 17 Clark for 50 - 1799 for Clark; **1**(00) - 14 Walter for 100 - 1499 Walter Jetton; and **28**(00) - 30 Washington for 2800 - 3098 Washington. Then for the second pairs of numbers, you may just remember 99 for 1799 Clark; 99 for 1499 Walter Jetton; and 98 for 3098 Washington. You may also remember the numbers by dividing them into three columns. For example, the numbers may be divided as follows:

5(0)	17	99	for 50 - 1799 Clark St
1(00)	14	99	for 100 - 1499 Walter Jetton Blvd
28(00)	30	98	for 2800 - Washington St

Part C: Coding and Memory

Segment 2 of Memory Section

Instructions

Segment 2 of the Memory Section has 8 questions to be answered in 1 1/2 minutes. Of course, you can't look at the Coding Guide. You have to answer the questions from memory. Since this part of the test is not scored, you can just answer 2 or three questions. Instead, use the time to memorize the guide. You have to mark your answers at the bottom of the sample question page, not on the official answer sheets.

For Segment 2 of the Coding Section, which serves as a practice test, turn the next page.

Part C: Coding and Memory
Practice Test 3

Segment 2 of Memory Section

Questions

Address	Delivery Route				Answers
1. 2290 Walter Jetton Blvd	A	B	C	D	1. ___
2. 1995 Clark St	A	B	C	D	2. ___
3. 1595 Walter Jetton Blvd	A	B	C	D	3. ___
4. 750 Stafford St	A	B	C	D	4. ___
5. 2950 Washington St	A	B	C	D	5. ___
6. 50 Largo Rd	A	B	C	D	6. ___
7. 1699 Clark St	A	B	C	D	7. ___
8. 600 Eastlawn St	A	B	C	D	8. ___

Sample Answer Sheet

1. (A) (B) (C) (D)

2. (A) (B) (C) (D)

3. (A) (B) (C) (D)

4. (A) (B) (C) (D)

5. (A) (B) (C) (D)

6. (A) (B) (C) (D)

7. (A) (B) (C) (D)

8. (A) (B) (C) (D)

The correct answers are: 1-D; 2-B; 3-C; 4-B; 5-A; 6-C; 7-A; & 8-C

Part C: Coding and Memory

Segment 3 of Memory Section

Instructions

On Segment 3 of the Memory Section test, you have 5 minutes to memorize the address ranges and routes of the Coding Guide. See it on the next page. There will be no questions to be answered during this memorization period. For the next test, (Segment 4) you don't have to look at the Coding Guide. In other words, you have to answer the questions from memory.

Part C: Coding and Memory

Segment 3 of Memory Section

Coding Guide	
Address Range	Delivery Route
50 - 1799 Clark St 100 - 1499 Walter Jetton Blvd 2800 - 3098 Washington St	A
1800 - 2999 Clark St 300 - 3099 Stafford St	B
1 - 2299 Largo Rd 100 - 4899 Eastlawn St 1500 - 1999 Walter Jetton Blvd	C
All mail that doesn't fall in one of the address ranges listed above	D

There are addresses that start with number 1; for instance, one of the above address ranges: 1 - 2299 Largo. In the case of this address, you may just remember 2299 Largo, **forgetting about the number 1**. In other words, all numbers below 2299 Largo are assigned to Route C: All numbers over 2299 Largo are all assigned to Route D. Why? Because all mail that doesn't fall in one of the address ranges above are assigned to Route D.

Furthermore, associate the numbers 2299 to places or things you are familiar with. For example, you may remember 2288 in this way: you have lived for 22 years in your current address, and you graduated in college in 1999. Use your imagination!

Part C: Coding and Memory

Segment 4 of Memory Section

Instructions

Segment 4 of the Memory Section is the real test. This part is scored and the score adds to your total Test 473 score. You will have 36 questions to be answered in 7 minutes. You should mark the answers on the official answer sheet. Segment 4 of the Memory Section prohibits you from looking at the Coding Guide. You have to answer the questions from memory.

Part C: Coding and Memory
Practice Test 3

Segment 4 of Memory Section

Questions

Address	Delivery Route				Answers
1. 951 Stafford St	A	B	C	D	1. ___
2. 399 Walter Jetton Blvd	A	B	C	D	2. ___
3. 487 Eastlawn St	A	B	C	D	3. ___
4. 2999 Washington St	A	B	C	D	4. ___
5. 2800 Clark St	A	B	C	D	5. ___
6. 80 Largo Rd	A	B	C	D	6. ___
7. 2000 Walter Jetton Blvd	A	B	C	D	7. ___
8. 2997 Stafford St	A	B	C	D	8. ___
9. 289 Stafford St	A	B	C	D	9. ___
10. 4890 Eastlawn St	A	B	C	D	10. ___
11. 1700 Walter Jetton Blvd	A	B	C	D	11. ___
12. 4799 Eastlawn St	A	B	C	D	12. ___
13. 49 Clark St	A	B	C	D	13. ___
14 400 Stafford St	A	B	C	D	14. ___
15. 2900 Washington St	A	B	C	D	15. ___
16. 2300 Eastlawn St	A	B	C	D	16. ___
17 1398 Walter Jetton Blvd	A	B	C	D	17. ___
18. 95 Clark St	A	B	C	D	18. ___

Part C: Coding and Memory
Practice Test 3
Continuation

Segment 4 of Memory Section

Questions

Address	Delivery Route				Answers
19. 3500 Washington St	A	B	C	D	19. ___
20. 395 Stafford St	A	B	C	D	20. ___
21. 89 Largo Rd	A	B	C	D	21. ___
22. 129 Walter Jetton Blvd	A	B	C	D	22. ___
23. 47 Clark St	A	B	C	D	23. ___
24. 2000 Walter Jetton Blvd	A	B	C	D	24. ___
25. 19 Largo Rd	A	B	C	D	25. ___
26. 50 Clark St	A	B	C	D	26. ___
27. 3198 Eastlawn St	A	B	C	D	27. ___
28. 500 Stafford St	A	B	C	D	28. ___
29. 3199 Clark St	A	B	C	D	29. ___
30. 2905 Washington St	A	B	C	D	30. ___
31. 180 Clark St	A	B	C	D	31. ___
32. 3000 Walter Jetton Blvd	A	B	C	D	32. ___
33. 1500 Clark St	A	B	C	D	33. ___
34 300 Eastlawn St	A	B	C	D	34. ___
35. 2596 Stafford St	A	B	C	D	35. ___
36. 85 Largo Rd	A	B	C	D	36. ___

See the answers to the above questions on the next page.

Part C: Coding & Memory

Memory Section

Answers to Questions
Practice Test 3

Segment 4 of Memory Section, p. 172-173

1. B
2. A
3. C
4. A
5. B
6. C
7. D
8. B
9. D
10. C
11. C
12. C
13. D
14. B
15. A
16. C
17. A
18. A
19. D
20. B
21. C
22. A
23. D
24. D
25. C
26. A
27. C
28. B
29. D
30. A
31. A
32. D
33. A
34. C
35. B
36. C

Practice Test 4
Part C: Coding and Memory

Coding Section

The first section of the Part C Test, called Coding Section, actually consists of three segments:

Segment 1: You are given 2 minutes within which to study or memorize the Coding Guide. Also, you have to answer four items as a practice test. Since this is not counted, you may answer only one question and use the time in memorizing the code. You are allowed to look at the Coding Guide as you answer the questions. The same Coding Guide will be used throughout the Coding and Memory tests.

Segment 2: You'll be given 1 1/2 minutes to answer 8 questions on this part of the test. Since this is not scored, you may answer only 2 or 3 questions. You better use the time in memorizing the coding guide.

Segment 3: You have 6 minutes to answer 36 questions. This part of the test is scored or counted. You must mark the circles on the official answer sheet.

When you work on the first section, Coding, of the test, you are allowed to look at the Coding Guide while you are assigning address ranges to delivery routes, (A, B, C, and D). However, when you work on the second section (memory), you won't be allowed to look at the Coding Guide. In other words, memorize the coding guide.

Part C: Coding and Memory

Segment 1 of Coding Section

Instructions

Segment 1 of the Coding Section test is a 2-minute exercise for memorizing the Coding Guide to be used in answering the questions on this test. Also, you have these 2 minutes to answer 4 questions. Since this part of the test is not scored, you should not work on all of the questions. Just memorize the guide using the techniques mentioned in Chapter 18: **Strategies for the Coding-Memory Test** on pages 85-90. Turn the page to see the Coding Guide.

Part C: Coding and Memory

Segment 1 of Coding Section

Coding Guide	
Address Range	Delivery Route
20 - **8**99 Hasting St 1- 799 Farwell Dr **60**00 - 10099 High St	A
900 - 1899 Hasting St 201 - 900 Lumber St	B
1- 500 Laurel St 800 - 999 Farwell Dr 81 - 2000 Highway 41 N	C
All mail that doesn't fall in one of the address ranges listed above	D

There are several ways of remembering the above address ranges in different boxes assigned to the delivery routes, **A, B, C,** and **D.** We should create so-called **extract codes** to easily remember the above addresses. You may combine the **first syllables** of the streets.

The codes may be created (from top to bottom) as **HasFarHigh** for Hasting St, Farwell Dr and High St. For the second box, it should be **HasLum** for Hasting St and Lumber St. For the third box it should be **LauFarHigh** for Laurel St, Farwell Dr and Highway 41 N.

In remembering the street numbers, you may shorten the group of numbers in the first box. You may remember them (from top to bottom) as **2**(0) - **8** Hasting for 20 - 899 for Hasting; **1 - 7** Farwell for 1 - 799 Farwell; and **60**(00) - **100** High for 6000 - 10099 High. Then for the second pairs of numbers, you may just remember **99** for Hasting; **99** for Farwell; and **99** for High. You may also remember the numbers by dividing them into three columns. For example, the numbers may be divided as follows:

2(0)	8	99	for 20 - 899 Hasting St
1	7	99	for 1 - 799 Farwell Dr
60(00)	100	99	for 6000 - 10099 High St

Part C: Coding and Memory
Practice Test 4

Segment 1 of Coding Section

Questions

Address	Delivery Route			
1. 37 Hasting St	A	B	C	D
2. 22 Laurel St	A	B	C	D
3. 300 Farwell Dr	A	B	C	D
4. 1997 Highway 41 N	A	B	C	D

Sample Answer Sheet

1. Ⓐ Ⓑ Ⓒ Ⓓ

2. Ⓐ Ⓑ Ⓒ Ⓓ

3. Ⓐ Ⓑ Ⓒ Ⓓ

4. Ⓐ Ⓑ Ⓒ Ⓓ

The correct answers are: 1-A; 2-C; 3-A; & 4-C.

Part C: Coding and Memory

Segment 2 of Coding Section

Instructions

Segment 2 of the Coding Section has 8 questions to be answered in 1 1/2 minutes. Of course, you can look at the Coding Guide. Since this part of the test is not scored, you can just answer 2 or 3 questions, then use the time to memorize the guide. You have to mark your answers at the bottom of the sample question page, not on the official answer sheets.

For Segment 2 of the Coding Section, which serves as a practice test, turn the page.

Part C: Coding and Memory

Segment 2 of Coding Section

Coding Guide	
Address Range	Delivery Route
20 - 899 Hasting St 1 - 799 Farwell Dr 6000 - 10099 High St	A
900 - 1899 Hasting St 201 - 900 Lumber St	B
1 - 500 Laurel St 800 - 999 Farwell Dr 81 - 2000 Highway 41 N	C
All mail that doesn't fall in one of the address ranges listed above	D

There are addresses that start with number 1; for instance, two of the above address ranges: 1 - 799 Farwell and 1 - 500 Laurel. In the case of these addresses you may just remember 1 - 799 Farwell and 1 - 500 Laurel, **forgetting about the number 1.** In other words, all numbers below 799 Farwell are assigned to Route A, and all numbers below 500 Laurel are assigned to Route C. All numbers above 799 Farwell 500 Laurel are all covered by Route D. Why? Because all mail that doesn't fall in one of the address ranges above are assigned to Route D.

Furthermore, associate the numbers 799 to places or things you are familiar with. For example, you may remember 799 in this way: you have 7 brothers and sisters and the youngest finished her elementary school years in 1999. You may remember 500 by associating it with Fortune 500 or what. Think about it.

Part C: Coding and Memory
Practice Test 4

Segment 2 of Coding Section

Questions

Address	Delivery Route				Answers
1. 90 Farwell Dr	A	B	C	D	1. ___
2. 278 Hasting St	A	B	C	D	2. ___
3. 395 Laurel St	A	B	C	D	3. ___
4. 295 Highway 41 N	A	B	C	D	4. ___
5. 38 Farwell Dr	A	B	C	D	5. ___
6. 231 Laurel St	A	B	C	D	6. ___
7. 2001 Highway 41 N	A	B	C	D	7. ___
8. 899 Lumber St	A	B	C	D	8. ___

Sample Answer Sheet

1. Ⓐ Ⓑ Ⓒ Ⓓ

2. Ⓐ Ⓑ Ⓒ Ⓓ

3. Ⓐ Ⓑ Ⓒ Ⓓ

4. Ⓐ Ⓑ Ⓒ Ⓓ

5. Ⓐ Ⓑ Ⓒ Ⓓ

6. Ⓐ Ⓑ Ⓒ Ⓓ

7. Ⓐ Ⓑ Ⓒ Ⓓ

8. Ⓐ Ⓑ Ⓒ Ⓓ

The correct answers are: 1-A; 2-A; 3-C; 4-C; 5-A; 6-C; 7-D; and 8-B

Part C: Coding and Memory

Segment 3 of Coding Section

Instructions

Segment 3 of the Coding Section, Practice Test 1 has 36 questions to be answered in 6 minutes. You can still look at the Coding Guide. It's the real test, therefore, this part of the test is scored. In other words, correct answers are counted. Answer the questions in 6 minutes. You have to mark your answers on the official answer sheets.

For Segment 3 of the Coding Section, go to the next page.

Part C: Coding and Memory

Segment 3 of Coding Section

Coding Guide	
Address Range	Delivery Route
20 - 899 Hasting St 1 - 799 Farwell Dr 6000 - 10099 High St	A
900 - 1899 Hasting St 201 - 900 Lumber St	B
1 - 500 Laurel St 800 - 999 Farwell Dr 81 - 2000 Highway 41 N	C
All mail that doesn't fall in one of the address ranges listed above	D

Part C: Coding and Memory
Practice Test 4

Segment 3 of Coding Section

Questions

Address	Delivery Route				Answers
1. 801 Farwell Dr	A	B	C	D	1. ___
2. 6700 High St	A	B	C	D	2. ___
3. 299 Lumber St	A	B	C	D	3. ___
4. 800 Laurel St	A	B	C	D	4. ___
5. 1998 Hasting St	A	B	C	D	5. ___
6. 899 Farwell Dr	A	B	C	D	6. ___
7. 701 Lumber St	A	B	C	D	7. ___
8. 1788 Hasting St	A	B	C	D	8. ___
9. 1800 Highway 41 N	A	B	C	D	9. ___
10. 750 Farwell Dr	A	B	C	D	10. ___
11. 1501 Highway 41 N	A	B	C	D	11. ___
12. 1999 Hasting St	A	B	C	D	12. ___
13. 801 Farwell Dr	A	B	C	D	13. ___
14. 786 Lumber St	A	B	C	D	14. ___
15. 901 Farwell Dr	A	B	C	D	15. ___
16. 10100 High St	A	B	C	D	16. ___
17. 899 Lumber St	A	B	C	D	17. ___
18. 2001 Highway 41 N	A	B	C	D	18. ___

Part C: Coding and Memory

Segment 3 of Coding Section

Coding Guide	
Address Range	Delivery Route
20 - 899 Hasting St 1 - 799 Farwell Dr 6000 - 10099 High St	A
900 - 1899 Hasting St 201 - 900 Lumber St	B
1 - 500 Laurel St 800 - 999 Farwell Dr 81 - 2000 Highway 41 N	C
All mail that doesn't fall in one of the address ranges listed above	D

Part C: Coding and Memory
Practice Test 4
Continuation

Segment 3 of Coding Section

Questions

Address	Delivery Route				Answers
19. 223 Hasting St	A	B	C	D	19. ___
20. 9000 High St	A	B	C	D	20. ___
21. 2002 Highway 41 N	A	B	C	D	21. ___
22. 801 Lumber St	A	B	C	D	22. ___
23. 699 Farwell Dr	A	B	C	D	23. ___
24. 2010 Highway 41 N	A	B	C	D	24. ___
25. 778 Lumber St	A	B	C	D	25. ___
26. 800 Hasting St	A	B	C	D	26. ___
27. 400 Laurel St	A	B	C	D	27. ___
28. 476 Farwell Dr	A	B	C	D	28. ___
29. 1799 Hasting St	A	B	C	D	29. ___
30. 21 Laurel St	A	B	C	D	30. ___
31. 11500 High St	A	B	C	D	31. ___
32. 94 Highway 41 N	A	B	C	D	32. ___
33. 1999 Hasting St	A	B	C	D	33. ___
34. 300 Lumber St	A	B	C	D	34. ___
35. 27 Hasting St	A	B	C	D	35. ___
36. 1500 Highway 41 N	A	B	C	D	36. ___

See the answers to the above questions on the next page.

Part C: Coding & Memory

Coding Section

Answers to Questions
Practice Test 4

Segment 3 of Coding Section, p. 187-189

1. C
2. A
3. B
4. D
5. D
6. C
7. B
8. B
9. C
10. A
11. C
12. D
13. C
14. B
15. C
16. D
17. B
18. D
19. A
20. A
21. D
22. B
23. A
24. D
25. B
26. A
27. C
28. A
29. B
30. C
31. D
32. C
33. D
34. B
35. A
36. C

Practice Test 4
Part C: Coding and Memory

Memory Section

The second section of Part C, called Memory Section, is composed of four parts or segments, which are as follows:

Segment 1: You'll have 3 minutes to memorize the Coding Guide.

Segment 2: You have 1 1/2 minutes to memorize the Coding Guide and answer the questions. There are 8 questions to be answered. Since this part of the test is not counted or scored, you may just answer 2 or 3 questions. Instead, use the 1 1/2 minutes allowed to this part of the test in memorizing the Coding Guide.

Segment 3. This segment is a 5-minute study time to memorize the guide. There are no questions to be answered on this part of the exam.

Segment 4: This is the part that counts. You have 7 minutes to answer 36 questions, without any Coding Guide to look at. You must answer the questions from memory. Also, you must mark the circles for your answers on the official answer sheet.

As you can see, you have a total of 9 1/2 minutes to memorize the Coding Guide. That's enough time in memorizing the same code. As you may remember, you also have 3 1/2 minutes time to memorize the Coding Guide on the Coding Section of Part C Test.

For **Strategies for Memory Section Test,** see pages 85-90.

Part C: Coding and Memory

Segment 1 of Memory Section

Instructions

Segment 1 of the Memory Section test gives you 3 minutes to memorize the Coding Guide. There will be no questions to be answered. Memorize the guide using the techniques mentioned in Chapter 15: **Strategies for the Coding-Memory Test** on pages 85-90. This same Coding Guide is used throughout this Practice 1 of this Coding and Memory Test. Now, memorize the Coding Code on the next page.

Part C: Coding and Memory

Segment 1 of Memory Section

Coding Guide	
Address Range	Delivery Route
20 - 899 Hasting St 1 - 799 Farwell Dr **60**00 - 10099 High St	A
900 - 1899 Hasting St 201 - 900 Lumber St	B
1 - 500 Laurel St 800 - 999 Farwell Dr 81 - 2000 Highway 41 N	C
All mail that doesn't fall in one of the address ranges listed above	D

There are several ways of remembering the above address ranges in different boxes assigned to the delivery routes, **A, B, C,** and **D.** We should create so-called **extract codes** to easily remember the above addresses. You may combine the **first syllables** of the streets..

The codes may be created (from top to bottom) as **HasFarHigh** for Hasting St, Farwell Dr and High St. For the second box, it should be **HasLum** for Hasting St and Lumber St. For the third box it should be **LauFarHigh** for Laurel St, Farwell Dr and Highway 41 N.

In remembering the street numbers, you may shorten the group of numbers in the first box serving as codes. You may remember them (from top to bottom) as **2**(0) - **8** Hasting for 20 - 899 Hasting; **1 - 7** Farwell for 1 - 799 Farwell; and **60**(00) - **100** High for 6000 - 10099 High. Then for the second pairs of numbers, you may just remember **99** for Hasting; **99** for Farwell and **99** for High. You may also remember the numbers by dividing them into three columns. For example, the numbers may be divided as follows:

2(0)	8	99	for 20 - 899 Hasting St
1	7	99	for 1 - 799 Farwell Dr
60(00)	100	99	for 6000 - 10099 High St

Part C: Coding and Memory

Segment 2 of Memory Section

Instructions

Segment 2 of the Memory Section has 8 questions to be answered in 1 1/2 minutes. Of course, you can't look at the Coding Guide. You have to answer the questions from memory. Since this part of the test is not scored, you can just answer 2 or three questions. Instead, use the time to memorize the guide. You have to mark your answers at the bottom of the sample question page, not on the official answer sheets.

For Segment 2 of the Coding Section, which serves as a practice test, turn the next page.

Part C: Coding and Memory
Practice Test 4

Segment 2 of Memory Section

Questions

Address	Delivery Route				Answers
1. 36 Hasting St	A	B	C	D	1. ___
2. 600 Laurel St	A	B	C	D	2. ___
3. 1599 Highway 41 N	A	B	C	D	3. ___
4. 351 Lumber St	A	B	C	D	4. ___
5. 81 Farwell Dr	A	B	C	D	5. ___
6. 6100 High St	A	B	C	D	6. ___
7. 1900 Hasting St	A	B	C	D	7. ___
8. 59 Laurel St	A	B	C	D	8. ___

Sample Answer Sheet

1. (A) (B) (C) (D)

2. (A) (B) (C) (D)

3. (A) (B) (C) (D)

4. (A) (B) (C) (D)

5. (A) (B) (C) (D)

6. (A) (B) (C) (D)

7. (A) (B) (C) (D)

8. (A) (B) (C) (D)

The correct answers are: 1-A; 2-D; 3-C; 4-B; 5-A; 6-A; 7-D; and 8-C.

Part C: Coding and Memory

Segment 3 of Memory Section

Instructions

On Segment 3 of the Memory Section test, you have 5 minutes to memorize the address ranges and routes of the Coding Guide. See it on the next page. There will be no questions to be answered during this memorization period. For the next test, (Segment 4) you don't have to look at the Coding Guide. In other words, you have to answer the questions from memory.

Part C: Coding and Memory

Segment 3 of Memory Section

Coding Guide	
Address Range	Delivery Route
20 - 899 Hasting St 1 - 799 Farwell Dr 6000 - 10099 High St	A
900 - 1899 Hasting St 201 - 900 Lumber St	B
1 - 500 Laurel St 800 - 999 Farwell Dr 81 - 2000 Highway 41 N	C
All mail that doesn't fall in one of the address ranges listed above	D

There are addresses that start with number 1; for instance, the above address ranges: 1 - 799 Farwell and 1 - 500 Laurel. In the case of these addresses you may just remember 1 - 799 Farwell and 1 - 500 Laurel, forgetting about the number 1. In other words, all numbers below 799 Farwell are assigned to Route A, and all numbers below 500 Laurel are assigned to Route C. All numbers above 799 Farwell and 500 Laurel are all assigned to Route D. Why? Because all mail that doesn't fall in one of the address ranges above are assigned to Route D.

Furthermore, associate the numbers 799 to places or things you are familiar with. For example, you may remember 799 in this way: you have 7 brothers and sisters and the youngest finished her elementary school years in 1999. You may remember 500 by associating it with Fortune 500 or what. Associate the numbers with things or places you remember well.

Part C: Coding and Memory

Segment 4 of Memory Section

Instructions

Segment 4 of the Memory Section is the real test. This part is scored and the score adds to your total Test 473 score. You will have 36 questions to be answered in 7 minutes. You should mark the answers on the official answer sheet. Segment 4 of the Memory Section prohibits you from looking at the Coding Guide. You have to answer the questions from memory.

Part C: Coding and Memory
Practice Test 4

Segment 4 of Memory Section

Questions

Address	Delivery Route				Answers
1. 801 Lumber St	A	B	C	D	1. ___
2. 899 Farwell Dr	A	B	C	D	2. ___
3. 7000 High St	A	B	C	D	3. ___
4. 1000 Highway 41 N	A	B	C	D	4. ___
5. 11099 High St	A	B	C	D	5. ___
6. 87 Highway 41 N	A	B	C	D	6. ___
7. 1599 Hasting St	A	B	C	D	7. ___
8. 650 Farwell Dr	A	B	C	D	8. ___
9. 401 Laurel St	A	B	C	D	9. ___
10. 1000 Farwell Dr	A	B	C	D	10. ___
11. 395 Lumber St	A	B	C	D	11. ___
12. 798 Hasting St	A	B	C	D	12. ___
13. 491 Laurel St	A	B	C	D	13. ___
14. 1050 Lumber St	A	B	C	D	14. ___
15. 50 Laurel St	A	B	C	D	15. ___
16. 1777 Hasting St	A	B	C	D	16. ___
17. 1700 Highway 41 N	A	B	C	D	17. ___
18. 1070 Farwell Dr	A	B	C	D	18. ___

Part C: Coding and Memory
Practice Test 4
Continuation

Segment 4 of Memory Section
Continuation

Questions

Address	Delivery Route				Answers
19. 800 Farwell Dr	A	B	C	D	19 ___
20. 2001 Highway 41 N	A	B	C	D	20. ___
21. 900 Lumber St	A	B	C	D	21. ___
22. 590 Laurel St	A	B	C	D	22. ___
23. 651 Farwell Dr	A	B	C	D	23. ___
24. 1999 Hasting St	A	B	C	D	24. ___
25. 600 Laurel St	A	B	C	D	25. ___
26. 95 Highway 41 N	A	B	C	D	26. ___
27. 10100 High St	A	B	C	D	27. ___
28. 401 Lumber St	A	B	C	D	28. ___
29. 1001 Farwell Dr	A	B	C	D	29. ___
30. 1700 Hasting St	A	B	C	D	30. ___
31. 50 Laurel St	A	B	C	D	31. ___
32. 801 Farwell Dr	A	B	C	D	32. ___
33. 899 Hasting St	A	B	C	D	33. ___
34. 901 Lumber St	A	B	C	D	34. ___
35. 995 Farwell Dr	A	B	C	D	35. ___
36. 7000 High St	A	B	C	D	36. ___

See the answers to the above questions on the next page.

Part C: Coding & Memory

Memory Section

Answers to Questions
Practice Test 4

Segment 4 of Memory Section, p. 200-201

1. B
2. C
3. A
4. C
5. D
6. C
7. B
8. A
9. C
10. D
11. B
12. A
13. C
14. D
15. C
16. B
17. C
18. D
19. C
20. D
21. B
22. D
23. A
24. D
25. D
26. C
27. D
28. B
29. D
30. B
31. C
32. C
33. A
34. D
35. C
36. A

17

D. Inventory of Personal Experiences

And Characteristics

Part B that involves **inventory of personal experiences and characteristics** contains 236 test items to be finished in 90 minutes. That's one and a half hours of evaluating personal characteristics, experiences, tendencies or feelings as related to doing work as an employee of the United States Postal Service.

This portion of the test is divided into three sections. Each section contains several items with response choices. For instance, the **first section** may contain items with response choices, such as "Strongly Agree" to "Strongly Disagree". The **second section** may have items with four response choices, from "Very" Often" to "Rarely or Never". And the **third section** may consist of items with four to nine response choices.

Actually, it's hard to prepare for the Part D of Postal 473 Test. It's because there are no correct or wrong answers. You simply may select the best answer that may reflect your feelings on how you assess your own personal characteristics and experiences that may relate to what's happening in a Postal work setting or how you may react with Postal co-workers.

However, I would like to familiarize you with the types of questions you may encounter on this part of the test. Of course, you will be given different questions during the test.

Here are some sample questions:

I. Agree/Disagree Section

1. You do not like other workers to intervene in your work.
A. Strongly Agree
B. Agree
C. Disagree
D. Strongly Disagree

2. Family problems should not be discussed in work place.

A. Strongly Agree
B. Agree
C. Disagree
D. Strongly Disagree

II. Frequency Section

1. You schedule your work ahead of time.
A. Very Often
B. Often
C. Sometimes
D. Rarely

2. There should be a division of labor in the work place, doing your own things.

A. Very often
B. Often
C. Sometimes
D. Rarely

III. Experience Section

1. What type of work do you like best?

A. Work that requires physical efforts.
B. Work that needs stretching of hands and feet.
C. Work that requires you doing your own while sitting or standing.
D. Doing the same work every day.
E. Would not mind doing any of these.
F. Not sure

2. What type of work do you like the least?

A. Work that requires a lot of time standing.
B. Work that requires a lot of time sitting down.
C. Work that needs too much concentration
D. Doing the same tasks every day.
E. Doesn't care doing any of these.
F. Not sure

18 18

460 RCA Examination

A Test for Rural Carrier Associate Applicants

The 460 Examination is a test for Rural Carrier Associate applicants. The rural carrier associates are substitutes of regular rural carriers serving the remote areas of the United States.

Regular rural carriers mostly come from the ranks of rural carrier associates who take Exam 460. That is, rural carrier associates, who substitute during vacations or absences of regular or permanent rural carriers, are promoted to the positions of regular carriers when positions become available due to retirement, death, or transfer of regular rural carriers.

Exam 460 covers the following parts:

Part A: Address Checking
Part B: Memory for Address
Part C: Number Series
Part D: Following Oral Instructions

Part A: Address-Checking Test

In this part of the test, you will have to determine whether two addresses are alike (Letter "A" for Alike) or different (Letter "D" for Different) You have to select one answer from two choices. On the other hand, in the Address-Checking Test of Exam 473/473-C Battery Test, you have to select one answer from a selection of four choices, answering the questions with "A" for "No Errors"; "B" for "Address Only Errors"; "C" for "Zip Code Only" and "D" for Both (Address and ZIP Code errors). Thus, the two address-checking tests have similarities and differences. It is interesting to note that the address-checking test for RCA 460 Test is easier than the 473/473-C Battery Test because in the 460 Test, you have to answer the question with only two choices, "A" or "D".

Part B: Memory-for-Address Test

In this part of the test, you will have to memorize the locations of names of streets and numbers (A, B, C, D, or E) of 25 addresses shown in five boxes. You will be given a list of street names and numbers with address ranges, and you have to determine in which box the street name or address is contained.

Part C: Number Series Test

For each series of question, there is at the left a series of numbers which follow some definite order and at the right five sets of two numbers. You are to see the numbers in the series at the left and find out what order they follow. You then may decide what the two numbers in that series would be if the same order were continued.

Part D: Following Oral Instructions

In this part of the test, you will be instructed to follow some directions by writing in a test booklet and then on an actual answer sheet.

Sample Questions
460 Rural Carrier Associate Exam
U.S. Postal Service

TEST INSTRUCTIONS

During the test session, it will be your responsibility to pay close attention to what the examiner has to say and to follow all instructions. One of the purposes of the test is to see how quickly and accurately you can work. Therefore, each part of the test will be carefully timed. You will not **START** until being told to do so. Also, when you are told to **STOP**, you must immediately **STOP** answering the questions. When you are told to work on a particular part of the examination, regardless of which part, you are to work on that part **ONLY**. **If you finish a part before time is called, you may review your answers for that part, but you will not go on or back to any other part.** **Failure to follow ANY** directions given to you by the examiner may be grounds for disqualification. Instructions read by the examiner are intended to ensure that each applicant has the same fair and objective opportunity to compete in the examination.

SAMPLE QUESTIONS

Study carefully before the examination.

The following questions are like the ones that will be on the test. Study these carefully. This will give you practice with the different kinds of questions and show you how to mark your answers.

Part A: Address Checking

In this part of the test, you will have to decide whether two addresses are alike or different. If the two addresses are exactly *Alike* in every way, darken circle A for the question. If the two addresses are *Different* in any way, darken circle D for the question.

Mark your answers to these sample questions on the Sample Answer Grid at the right.

1...2134 S 20th St   2134 S 20th St

Since the two addresses are exactly alike, mark A for
question 1 on the Sample Answer Grid.

Sample Answer Grid		
1	Ⓐ	Ⓓ
2	Ⓐ	Ⓓ
3	Ⓐ	Ⓓ
4	Ⓐ	Ⓓ
5	Ⓐ	Ⓓ

2...4608 N Warnock St   4806 N Warnock St

3...1202 W Girard Dr   1202 W Girard Rd

4...Chappaqua NY 10514   Chappaqua NY 10514

5...2207 Markland Ave   2207 Markham Ave

The correct answers to questions 2 to 5 are: 2D, 3D, 4A, and 5D.

Your score on Part A of the actual test will be based on the number of wrong answers as well as on the number of right answers. Part A is scored right answers minus wrong answers. Random guessing should not help your score. For the Part A test, you will have six minutes to answer as many of the 95 questions as you can. It will be to your advantage to work as quickly and as accurately as possible. You will not be expected to be able to answer all the questions in the time allowed.

Part B: Memory for Addresses

In this part of the test, you will have to memorize the locations (A, B, C, D, or E) of 25 addresses shown in five boxes, like those below. For example, "Sardis" is in Box C, "6800–6999 Table" is in Box B, etc. (The addresses in the actual test will be different.)

A	B	C	D	E
4700–5599 Table	6800–6999 Table	5600–6499 Table	6500–6799 Table	4400–4699 Table
Lismore	Kelford	Joel	Tatum	Ruskin
5600–6499 West	6500–6799 West	6800–6999 West	4400–4699 West	4700–5599 West
Hesper	Musella	Sardis	Porter	Nathan
4400–4699 Blake	5600–6499 Blake	6500–6799 Blake	4700–5599 Blake	6800–6999 Blake

Study the locations of the addresses for five minutes. As you study, silently repeat these to yourself. Then cover the boxes and try to answer the questions below. Mark your answers for each question by darkening the circle as was done for questions 1 and 2.

1. Musella
2. 4700–5599 Blake
3. 4700–5599 Table
4. Tatum
5. 4400–4699 Blake
6. Hesper
7. Kelford
8. Nathan
9. 6500–6799 Blake
10. Joel
11. 4400–4699 Blake
12. 6500–6799 West
13. Porter
14. 6800–6999 Blake

Sample Answer Grid			
1 (A) ● (C) (D) (E)	5 (A) (B) (C) (D) (E)	9 (A) (B) (C) (D) (E)	13 (A) (B) (C) (D) (E)
2 (A) (B) (C) ● (E)	6 (A) (B) (C) (D) (E)	10 (A) (B) (C) (D) (E)	14 (A) (B) (C) (D) (E)
3 (A) (B) (C) (D) (E)	7 (A) (B) (C) (D) (E)	11 (A) (B) (C) (D) (E)	
4 (A) (B) (C) (D) (E)	8 (A) (B) (C) (D) (E)	12 (A) (B) (C) (D) (E)	

The correct answers for questions 3 to 14 are: 3A, 4D, 5A, 6A, 7B, 8E, 9C, 10C, 11A, 12B, 13D, and 14E.

During the examination, you will have three practice exercises to help you memorize the location of addresses shown in five boxes. After the practice exercises, the actual test will be given. Part B is scored right answers minus one-fourth of the wrong answers. Random guessing should not help your score. But, if you can eliminate one or more alternatives, it is to your advantage to guess. For the Part B test, you will have five minutes to answer as many of the 88 questions as you can. It will be to your advantage to work as quickly and as accurately as you can. You will not be expected to be able to answer all the questions in the time allowed.

Part C: Number Series

For each *Number Series* question there is at the left a series of numbers which follow some definite order and at the right five sets of two numbers each. You are to look at the numbers in the series at the left and find out what order they follow. Then decide what the next two numbers in that series would be if the same order were continued. Mark your answers on the Sample Answer Grid.

1. 1 2 3 4 5 6 7 .... A) 1 2   B) 5 6   C) 8 9   D) 4 5   E) 7 8

The numbers in this series are increasing by 1. If the series were continued for two more numbers, it would read: 1 2 3 4 5 6 7 8 9. Therefore the correct answer is 8 and 9 and you should have darkened C for question 1.

2. 15 14 13 12 11 10 9 .... A) 2 1   B) 17 16   C) 8 9   D) 8 7   E) 9 8

The numbers in this series are decreasing by 1. If the series were continued for two more numbers, it would read: 15 14 13 12 11 10 9 8 7. Therefore the correct answer is 8 and 7 and you should have darkened D for question 2.

3. 20 20 21 21 22 22 23 .... A) 23 23   B) 23 24   C) 19 19   D) 22 23   E) 21 22

Each number in this series is repeated and then increased by 1. If the series were continued for two more numbers, it would read: 20 20 21 21 22 22 23 23 24. Therefore the correct answer is 23 and 24 and you should have darkened B for question 3.

4. 17 3 17 4 17 5 17 .... A) 6 17   B) 6 7   C) 17 6   D) 5 6   E) 17 7

This series is the number 17 separated by numbers increasing by 1, beginning with the number 3. If the series were continued for two more numbers, it would read: 17 3 17 4 17 5 17 6 17. Therefore the correct answer is 6 and 17 and you should have darkened A for question 4.

5. 1 2 4 5 7 8 10 .... A) 11 12   B) 12 14   C) 10 13   D) 12 13   E) 11 13

The numbers in this series are increasing first by 1 (plus 1) and then by 2 (plus 2). If the series were continued for two more numbers, it would read: 1 2 4 5 7 8 10 (plus 1) *11* and (plus 2) *13*. Therefore the correct answer is 11 and 13 and you should have darkened E for question 5.

Now read and work sample questions 6 through 10 and mark your answers on the Sample Answer Grid.

6. 21 21 20 20 19 19 18 .... A) 18 18   B) 18 17   C) 17 18   D) 17 17   E) 18 19

7. 1 22 1 23 1 24 1 .... A) 26 1   B) 25 26   C) 25 1   D) 1 26   E) 1 25

8. 1 20 3 19 5 18 7 .... A) 8 9   B) 8 17   C) 17 10   D) 17 9   E) 9 18

9. 4 7 10 13 16 19 22 .... A) 23 26   B) 25 27   C) 25 26   D) 25 28   E) 24 27

10. 30 2 28 4 26 6 24 .... A) 23 9   B) 26 8   C) 8 9   D) 26 22   E) 8 22

Sample Answer Grid
6 (A)(B)(C)(D)(E)   8 (A)(B)(C)(D)(E)   9 (A)(B)(C)(D)(E)   10 (A)(B)(C)(D)(E)
7 (A)(B)(C)(D)(E)

The correct answers to sample questions 6 to 10 are: 6B, 7C, 8D, 9D and 10E. Explanations follow.

6. Each number in the series repeats itself and then decreases by 1 or minus 1; *21* (repeat) *21* (minus 1) *20* (repeat) *20* (minus 1) *19* (repeat) *19* (minus 1) *18* (repeat) *?* (minus 1) *?*

7. The number 1 is separated by numbers which begin with 22 and increased by 1; *1 22 1* (increase 22 by 1) *23 1* (increase 23 by 1) *24 1* (increase 24 by 1) *?*

8. This is best explained by two alternating series — one series starts with 1 and increases by 2 or plus 2; the other series starts with 20 and decreases by 1 or minus 1.

$$1 \quad \wedge \quad 3 \quad \wedge \quad 5 \quad \wedge \quad 7 \quad \wedge \quad ?$$
$$20 \qquad 19 \qquad 18 \qquad ?$$

9. This series of numbers increases by 3 (plus 3) beginning with the first number — *4 7 10 13 16 19 22 ? ?*

10. Look for two alternating series — one series starts with 30 and decreases by 2 (minus 2); the other series starts with 2 and increases by 2 (plus 2).

Now try questions 11 to 15.

11. 5 6 20 7 8 19 9 . . . . A) 10 18   B) 18 17   C) 10 17   D) 18 19   E) 10 11

12. 4 6 9 11 14 16 19 . . . . A) 21 24   B) 22 25   C) 20 22   D) 21 23   E) 22 24

13. 8 8 1 10 10 3 12 . . . . A) 13 13   B) 12 5   C) 12 4   D) 13 5   E) 4 12

14. 10 12 50 15 17 50 20 . . . . A) 50 21   B) 21 50   C) 50 22   D) 22 50   E) 22 24

15. 20 21 23 24 27 28 32 33 38 39 .   A) 45 46   B) 45 52   C) 44 45   D) 44 49   E) 40 46

Sample Answer Grid
11 (A)(B)(C)(D)(E)   13 (A)(B)(C)(D)(E)   14 (A)(B)(C)(D)(E)   15 (A)(B)(C)(D)(E)
12 (A)(B)(C)(D)(E)

The correct answers to the sample questions above are: 11A, 12A, 13B, 14D and 15A.

It will be to your advantage to answer every question in Part C that you can, since your score on this part of the test will be based on the number of questions that you answer correctly. Answer first those questions which are easiest for you. For the Part C test, you will have 20 minutes to answer as many of the 24 questions as you can.

Part D: Following Oral Instructions

In this part of the test, you will be told to follow directions by writing in a test booklet and then on an answer sheet. The test booklet will have lines of material like the following five samples:

SAMPLE 1.   5__

SAMPLE 2.   1   6   4   3   7

SAMPLE 3.   D   B   A   E   C

SAMPLE 4.   (8__) (5__) (2__) (9__) (10__)

SAMPLE 5.   (7__) [6__] (1__) [12__]

To practice this part of the test, tear off page 11. Then have somebody read the instructions to you and you follow the instructions. When he or she tells you to darken the space on the Sample Answer Grid, use the one on this page.

Sample Answer Grid			
1 (A)(B)(C)(D)(E)	4 (A)(B)(C)(D)(E)	7 (A)(B)(C)(D)(E)	10 (A)(B)(C)(D)(E)
2 (A)(B)(C)(D)(E)	5 (A)(B)(C)(D)(E)	8 (A)(B)(C)(D)(E)	11 (A)(B)(C)(D)(E)
3 (A)(B)(C)(D)(E)	6 (A)(B)(C)(D)(E)	9 (A)(B)(C)(D)(E)	12 (A)(B)(C)(D)(E)

Your score for part D will be based on the number of questions that you answer correctly. Therefore, if you are not sure of an answer, it will be to your advantage to guess. Part D will take about 25 minutes.

KEEP THESE INSTRUCTIONS FOR FUTURE REFERENCE. YOUR PARTICIPATION AND COOPERATION IN THIS POSTAL EXAM IS APPRECIATED.

Instructions to be read **(the words in parentheses should NOT be read aloud)**

You are to follow the instructions that I shall read to you. I cannot repeat them.

Look at the samples. Sample 1 has a number and a line beside it. On the line write A as in ace. **(Pause 2 seconds.)** Now on the Sample Answer Grid, find the number 5 **(pause 2 seconds)** and darken the letter you just wrote on the line. **(Pause 2 seconds.)**

Look at Sample 2. **(Pause slightly.)** Draw a line under the third number. **(Pause 2 seconds.)** Now look on the Sample Answer Grid, find the number under which you just drew a line and darken B as in boy. **(Pause 5 seconds.)**

Look at the letters in Sample 3. **(Pause slightly.)** Draw a line under the third letter in the line. **(Pause 2 seconds.)** Now on your Sample Answer Grid, find number 9 **(pause 2 seconds)** and darken the letter under which you drew a line. **(Pause 5 seconds.)**

Look at the five circles in Sample 4. **(Pause slightly.)** Each circle has a number and a line in it. Write D as in dog on the line in the last circle. **(Pause 2 seconds.)** Now on the Sample Answer Grid, darken the number-letter combination that is in the circle you just wrote in. **(Pause 5 seconds.)**

Look at Sample 5. **(Pause slightly.)** There are two circles and two boxes of different sizes with numbers in them. **(Pause slightly.)** If 4 is more than 2 and if 5 is less than 3, write A as in ace in the smaller circle. **(Pause slightly.)** Otherwise write C as in car in the larger box. **(Pause 2 seconds.)** Now on the Sample Grid, darken the number-letter combination in the box or circle in which you just wrote. **(Pause 5 seconds.)**

Now look at the Sample Answer Grid. **(Pause slightly.)** You should have darkened 4B, 5A, 9A, 10D, and 12C on the Sample Answer Grid. **(If the person preparing to take the examination made any mistakes, try to help him or her see why he or she made the wrong marks.)**

460 RCA Examination

Techniques for Address-Checking

And Practice Tests

The *Address-Checking Test* forms Part A of the 460 examination. This test is given to applicants for rural carriere associates. On this test, you must determine whether two addresses are *alike* or *different.* It's like comparing sexy Sharon Stone with sassy Drew Barrymore, the size of their bodies, the shape of their legs or noses, and so on. In comparing addresses, too, you are to see how they are alike or different. If they are alike in numbers, roads, streets, or spelling, you answer **A** (for alike); if they are different in numbers, roads, streets, or spelling, you answer **D** (for different).

You're Not a Walkathon Participant

If you had plenty of time to take this test, as if participating in a walkhathon, you might score 100%. But you are racing against time; there is a time limit to answer the items or questions. You must compare 95 sets of addresses in only 6 minutes. In other words, you are like in a participant in a Grand Prix race. Your eyes must zoom from left to right in seconds! To finish comparing the 95 sets of addresses, you must take less than 4 seconds to answer each question, including the marking of circles on the answer sheet. (See **How to Mark Circles on the Answer Sheet**, page 35.) The examiner may tell you, however, that you don't have to answer all the questions (few do) to make a high score.

Let Your Fingers Do the Walking

In comparing addresses (in two columns), you can point at the streets and the numbers with your fingers. Place the little finger of your nonwriting hand on one column of addresses and your index finger of the same hand on the other column. Move your hand downward as you make comparisons, while your right hand marks the answer sheets.

Widen the Focus of Your Eyes!

Pretend that you're driving a car. Your sight is focused to the front as far as you can see, but you can still see to your left and to your right. You don't need the eyes of an E.T. to do this, but do remember that comparing addresses is faster than the so-called speed reading. If possible, just make one or two "eye sweeps" of the addresses.

Things to Do, In a Nutshell

■ Compare the two addresses (left and right) by one or two eye sweeps of the line. It's also a good idea to fold the paper so that the number, for instance, "2134" of the second address will be near the "St." or "Rd." of the first address (on the same line, of course). It's like taking a photo of an excited Bill Clinton and Hillary Rodman at their anniversary ball—you want them to be close together so that you can get a good close-up shot. The question sheet and the answer sheet should be lying side by side; the question sheet on your non-writing side, the answer sheet on your writing side. In this way, your sight doesn't travel too far. Don't jerk your neck from left to right as you read; just let your eyes do the sweeping. While you do this, hold your pencil in your writing hand and don't move your nonwriting hand from the answer sheet. Then move it downward as you mark a circle with two or three strikes by your writing hand. Be sure that the line you are marking corresponds to the question you are answering.

■ **Spellings:** Note the spellings of street, city, state, and numbers in the ZIP code. Sometimes the first address has a ZIP code of 48012 and the second address has a ZIP code of 48021.

■ **Differences:** Most of the time there are differences in abbreviations, such as St., Rd., or Ave. Sometimes the first address (left) is abbreviated as St. and the second address (right) is abbreviated as Rd., or vice versa.

■ **Guide:** It's best to use a bookmark or some other kind of guide with your nonwriting hand: place it just below the line you are comparing and slide it straight down to the next line as you continue with the test. This prevents you from comparing the first address or number with an address or number in the wrong line. You can also place the little finger of your nonwriting hand on the left column and the index finger of the same hand on the right column of addresses. Move your nonwriting hand downward as you make the comparisons, while you mark the answers with your writing hand.

How to Compare the Addresses

There are four ways to compare the addresses. Use whichever is most comfortable for you:

First Way: Compare the two addresses by moving your eyes from left to right; that is, compare the address on the left to the one on the right. Make *one* or *two* "eye sweeps" of the addresses. It's like sweeping snow from your car, but you do it in a snap. If possible, the "eye sweep" should be faster than the speed of sound.

Example:

2134 S 20th St   2134 S 20th St

Since the addresses are alike, the answer is *A*.

Second Way: Focus your sight on the space between the two addresses. You can look at the addresses simultaneously from the center. With this method you can get a complete view of both addresses, like looking at Bo Derek and Raquel Welch at the same time while they are smiling at you.

Example:

7507 Wyngate Dr ● 7505 Wyngate Dr

Since the street numbers are different, the answer is *D*.

Third Way: First, compare only the street name and the abbreviations: *St, Rd,* or *Ave.* If they are alike, then compare the street numbers on the left to the numbers on the right. If they are alike, answer *A*.

Example:
2207 Markland Ave   2207 Markham

When you use the third way in this example, first compare the street name and the abbreviation *Rd* or *Ave*. Since there's a difference in street names (one is Mark*land* and the other is Mark*ham)*, you immediately mark circle *D*, meaning that they are different. Do not continue comparing anymore, but proceed at once to the next line or number. If the street names are alike, then compare the left-hand numbers to the numbers on the right. If they are still alike, answer *A;* if the figures are different, answer *D*.

Fourth Way: This can be discussed by analyzing the example below.

Example:

5428 N Shelbourne Rd   5482   N   Shelbourne   Rd

You compare the numbers at the left to the numbers at right, ignoring the initial, street name, and abbreviation (Rd. etc.). Once you see a difference *(28* and *82)* darken circle *D* right away. Do not go on to compare the street names because you've already found a difference between the *two* addresses. In a nutshell, differences may occur in numbers, abbreviations, or names.

Address-Checking Practice Test

Work—6 Minutes

These addresses are like the ones in the address-checking test.

Decide whether the two addresses are *Alike* or *Different*. If they are *Alike,* darken or mark space A; if they are *Different,* darken space D. Mark the answers on the answer sheet to the right. Work as fast as you can without making too any errors. Work exactly 6 minutes.

ANSWER SHEET

#	Address 1	Address 2	Test A	Test B
1.	1405 Hickory Rd NW	1504 Hickory Rd NW	Ⓐ Ⓓ	Ⓐ Ⓓ
2.	1354 Central Park W	1354 Central Park W	Ⓐ Ⓓ	Ⓐ Ⓓ
3.	500 Court Rd NE	500 Court RD NW	Ⓐ Ⓓ	Ⓐ Ⓓ
4.	East Point, MI 48021	East Pointe, MI 48031	Ⓐ Ⓓ	Ⓐ Ⓓ
5.	35016 S Main St	35015 S Main St	Ⓐ Ⓓ	Ⓐ Ⓓ
6.	Bay Pines, FL 33503	Bay Pines, FL 33503	Ⓐ Ⓓ	Ⓐ Ⓓ
7.	3653 Peasant Run Ave	3653 Pleasant Run Ave	Ⓐ Ⓓ	Ⓐ Ⓓ
8.	154 S Washington Sq	154 N Washington Sq	Ⓐ Ⓓ	Ⓐ Ⓓ
9.	3531 McWeeney Rd	3531 McWeeney Rd	Ⓐ Ⓓ	Ⓐ Ⓓ
10.	7535 Cedar Ln	7535 Cedar St	Ⓐ Ⓓ	Ⓐ Ⓓ
11.	Meridian, Idaho 83645	Meridian, Idaho 83345	Ⓐ Ⓓ	Ⓐ Ⓓ
12.	Manson, NC 27553	Manson, NC 27553	Ⓐ Ⓓ	Ⓐ Ⓓ
13.	2105 W 18th Ave	2103 W 18th Ave	Ⓐ Ⓓ	Ⓐ Ⓓ
14.	3153 Carter Dr	3157 Carter Dr	Ⓐ Ⓓ	Ⓐ Ⓓ
15.	98354 Hopeville Ln	98354 Hopeville Ln	Ⓐ Ⓓ	Ⓐ Ⓓ
16.	15315 N Audrey Rd	15815 N Audrey Rd	Ⓐ Ⓓ	Ⓐ Ⓓ
17.	31543 Stony Brook	31543 Stony Brook	Ⓐ Ⓓ	Ⓐ Ⓓ
18.	Southfield, MI 48075	Southfield, MI 48073	Ⓐ Ⓓ	Ⓐ Ⓓ
19.	11359 N Tulipe St	11359 S Tulipe St	Ⓐ Ⓓ	Ⓐ Ⓓ
20.	31547 Country Club Rd	31547 Country Club Rd	Ⓐ Ⓓ	Ⓐ Ⓓ
21.	80329 Guillian Rdg	80329 Guillian Rdg	Ⓐ Ⓓ	Ⓐ Ⓓ
22.	93178 Herschel Plaza	98178 Hershel Plaza	Ⓐ Ⓓ	Ⓐ Ⓓ
23.	5462 Audobon Ct	5462 Audobon Ct	Ⓐ Ⓓ	Ⓐ Ⓓ
24.	89354 Ocean Blvd	19354 Ocean Blvd	Ⓐ Ⓓ	Ⓐ Ⓓ
25.	77331 SW Teppert St	77381 SW Teppert St	Ⓐ Ⓓ	Ⓐ Ⓓ
26.	315 Bensen Pky	315 Bensen Pky	Ⓐ Ⓓ	Ⓐ Ⓓ
27.	20361 Alexander St	20361 Alexander Ave	Ⓐ Ⓓ	Ⓐ Ⓓ
28.	3154 S Colorado Rd	3154 N Colorado Rd	Ⓐ Ⓓ	Ⓐ Ⓓ
29.	9156 N Placid Ln	9156 S Placid Ln	Ⓐ Ⓓ	Ⓐ Ⓓ
30.	1120 Kenilworth Ct	1120 Kenilworth Ct	Ⓐ Ⓓ	Ⓐ Ⓓ
31.	87104 Tulip Pky	87104 Tulip Rd	Ⓐ Ⓓ	Ⓐ Ⓓ
32.	2465 Cornplakes Sq	2465 Cornplakes Sq	Ⓐ Ⓓ	Ⓐ Ⓓ
33.	9037 Delaware Ave	9038 Delaware Ave	Ⓐ Ⓓ	Ⓐ Ⓓ
34.	3154 N Lancaster	3154 N Lancaster	Ⓐ Ⓓ	Ⓐ Ⓓ
35.	3698 Stonybrook Sq	3698 Stonybrook Sq	Ⓐ Ⓓ	Ⓐ Ⓓ
36.	3154 E Jefferson St	3154 E Jefferson St	Ⓐ Ⓓ	Ⓐ Ⓓ
37.	8634 19th Ave SW	8634 19th Ave SE	Ⓐ Ⓓ	Ⓐ Ⓓ
38.	2654 Avenue NW	3645 Avenue NW	Ⓐ Ⓓ	Ⓐ Ⓓ
39.	3545 Monticello Ct	3545 Montecello Ct	Ⓐ Ⓓ	Ⓐ Ⓓ
40.	46017 Thunder Hill	46017 Thunder Hill	Ⓐ Ⓓ	Ⓐ Ⓓ

Go on to the next number on the next page.

41. 8761 Woodridge Ave	8761 Woodrige Rd	41 Ⓐ Ⓓ	41 Ⓐ Ⓓ
42, 11253 Lovers Ln	11253 Lovers Ln	42 Ⓐ Ⓓ	42 Ⓐ Ⓓ
43. 7718 Rolling Hills NW	7718 Rolling Hills SE	43 Ⓐ Ⓓ	43 Ⓐ Ⓓ
44. 3838 Edgecom View	3383 Edgecom View	44 Ⓐ Ⓓ	44 Ⓐ Ⓓ
45. 7634 5th Ave S	7634 5th Ave S	45 Ⓐ Ⓓ	45 Ⓐ Ⓓ
46. 1873 7th St SW	1878 7th St SW	46 Ⓐ Ⓓ	46 Ⓐ Ⓓ
47. 3838 Oceanside Blvd	3838 Oceanside Blvd	47 Ⓐ Ⓓ	47 Ⓐ Ⓓ
48. 9835 Frescot Ct E	9835 Frescot CT W	48 Ⓐ Ⓓ	48 Ⓐ Ⓓ
49. 43735 Belleview N	43735 Belleview N	49 Ⓐ Ⓓ	49 Ⓐ Ⓓ
50. 3549 Eastland Dr E	3549 Eastland Dr W	50 Ⓐ Ⓓ	50 Ⓐ Ⓓ
51. 860 Rolling Acres W	860 Rolling Acres W	51 Ⓐ Ⓓ	51 Ⓐ Ⓓ
52. 9117 Surf St	9117 Surf St	52 Ⓐ Ⓓ	52 Ⓐ Ⓓ
53. 3938 Woodridge Ct	3938 Woodridge Ct	53 Ⓐ Ⓓ	53 Ⓐ Ⓓ
54. 9304 Yarbu St	9304 Yarbugh St	54 Ⓐ Ⓓ	54 Ⓐ Ⓓ
55. 11397 Edgeman Blvd S	11395 Edgeman Blvd S	55 Ⓐ Ⓓ	55 Ⓐ Ⓓ
56. 62660 High Noon Rd	62669 High Noon Rd	56 Ⓐ Ⓓ	56 Ⓐ Ⓓ
57. 2951 Lamaro Cove	2551 Lamaro Cove	57 Ⓐ Ⓓ	57 Ⓐ Ⓓ
58. 5066 Laurel Cir	5066 Laurel Cir	58 Ⓐ Ⓓ	58 Ⓐ Ⓓ
59. Ashburn, Virginia 22111	Ashburne, Virginia 22111	59 Ⓐ Ⓓ	59 Ⓐ Ⓓ
60. 1703 Allensville St	1708 Allensville St	60 Ⓐ Ⓓ	60 Ⓐ Ⓓ
61. 58356 Deerfield Cir	58356 Deerfield Cir	61 Ⓐ Ⓓ	61 Ⓐ Ⓓ
62. 3259 Rolling Stone Ct	3259 Rolling Stone Ct	62 Ⓐ Ⓓ	62 Ⓐ Ⓓ
63. 9306 High St SW	9307 High St SW	63 Ⓐ Ⓓ	63 Ⓐ Ⓓ
64. 305 Kentucky Ave	305 Kentucky Ave	64 Ⓐ Ⓓ	64 Ⓐ Ⓓ
65. 2548 Redesco Rd	2548 Redesco Sq	65 Ⓐ Ⓓ	65 Ⓐ Ⓓ
66. 2088 N Melendreso St	2089 N Melendreso St	66 Ⓐ Ⓓ	66 Ⓐ Ⓓ
67. 5983 Aroma Blvd	5983 Aroma Blvd	67 Ⓐ Ⓓ	67 Ⓐ Ⓓ
68. 3784 Lincoln Ave	3785 Lincoln Ave	68 Ⓐ Ⓓ	68 Ⓐ Ⓓ
69. 7835 Malcom Rd	7838 Malcom Rd	69 Ⓐ Ⓓ	69 Ⓐ Ⓓ
70. 2549 Montgomery Ave	2549 Montgomery Cir	70 Ⓐ Ⓓ	70 Ⓐ Ⓓ
71. 250 Virginia St W	250 Virginia St W	71 Ⓐ Ⓓ	71 Ⓐ Ⓓ
72. 13286 E Ausburn St	13286 W Ausburne St	72 Ⓐ Ⓓ	72 Ⓐ Ⓓ
73. 934 Lenoxin Cir SW	934 Lenoxin Cir SW	73 Ⓐ Ⓓ	73 Ⓐ Ⓓ
74. 1035 Lovers Ln W	1085 Lovers Ln W	74 Ⓐ Ⓓ	74 Ⓐ Ⓓ
75. 937 W Waterford Rd	937 W Waterford Rd	75 Ⓐ Ⓓ	75 Ⓐ Ⓓ
76. 3087 E Bellevue Hill	3087 W Bellevue Hill	76 Ⓐ Ⓓ	76 Ⓐ Ⓓ
77. 6943 6th Ave N	6948 6th Ave N	77 Ⓐ Ⓓ	77 Ⓐ Ⓓ
78 . 2052 Hubert Ave	2052 Hubert Ave	78 Ⓐ Ⓓ	78 Ⓐ Ⓓ
79. 983 SW Campbell Rd	983 SW Campbell Rd	79 Ⓐ Ⓓ	79 Ⓐ Ⓓ
80. 4088 4th Ave W	4088 4th Ave SE	80 Ⓐ Ⓓ	80 Ⓐ Ⓓ
81. 22011 Crossroad Ave	22011 Crossroad Ave	81 Ⓐ Ⓓ	81 Ⓐ Ⓓ
82. 1342 Northwest St	1342 Northeast St	82 Ⓐ Ⓓ	82 Ⓐ Ⓓ
83. 2057 Tender Rd	2057 Tender Rd	83 Ⓐ Ⓓ	83 Ⓐ Ⓓ
84. 3522 Bleeker Cove	3522 Bleeker Cove	84 Ⓐ Ⓓ	84 Ⓐ Ⓓ
85. 3154 Pittsburg Ct	3134 Pitsburg Ct	85 Ⓐ Ⓓ	85 Ⓐ Ⓓ
86. 5497 Gilmore Sq	5495 Gilmore Sq	86 Ⓐ Ⓓ	86 Ⓐ Ⓓ
87. 3921 Melendres Ave	3921 Melendres Ave	87 Ⓐ Ⓓ	87 Ⓐ Ⓓ
88. 5834 SW 7th Ave	5835 SW 7th Ave	88 Ⓐ Ⓓ	88 Ⓐ Ⓓ
89. 8640 Cherry Hill	8640 Cherry Hill	89 Ⓐ Ⓓ	89 Ⓐ Ⓓ

Go on to the next number on the next page.

90. 306 Calihan Ave E	306 Calihan Ave W	90	Ⓐ Ⓓ	90	Ⓐ Ⓓ
91. 3040 Makiling Ct	3040 Makiling Sq	91	Ⓐ Ⓓ	91	Ⓐ Ⓓ
92. 1555 Rectory Pl	1555 Rectory Pl	92	Ⓐ Ⓓ	92	Ⓐ Ⓓ
93. 3056 Bradley Ave	3056 Bradley Ave	93	Ⓐ Ⓓ	93	Ⓐ Ⓓ
94. 3054 Gangho Cir W	3054 Gangho Cir E	94	Ⓐ Ⓓ	94	Ⓐ Ⓓ
95. 97711 Acres Rd	97711 Acres Rd	95	Ⓐ Ⓓ	95	Ⓐ Ⓓ

STOP

If you finish before the time is up, check your answers for Part A.

Do not go to any other part.

(See the correct answers on the next page.

Correct Answers

Address-Checking Test

1. D	25. D	49. A	73. A
2. A	26. A	50. D	74. D
3. D	27. D	51. A	75. A
4. D	28. D	52. A	76. D
5. D	29. D	53. A	77. D
6. A	30. A	54. D	78. A
7. D	31. D	55. D	79. A
8. D	32. A	56. D	80. D
9. A	33. D	57. D	81. A
10. D	34. A	58. A	82. D
11. D	35. A	59. D	83. A
12. A	36. A	60. D	84. A
13. D	37. D	61. A	85. D
14. D	38. D	62. A	86. D
15. A	39. D	63. D	87. A
16. D	40. A	64. A	88. D
17. A	41. D	65. D	89. A
18. D	42. A	66. D	90. D
19. D	43. D	67. A	91. D
20. A	44. D	68. D	92. A
21. A	45. A	69. D	93. A
22. D	46. D	70. D	94. D
23. A	47. A	71. A	95. A
24. D	48. D	72. D	

Address-Checking Practice Test

Work—6 Minutes

These addresses are like the ones in the adress-checking test.

Decide whether the two addresses are *Alike* or *Different*. If they are Alike, darken or mark space A; if they are *Different,* darken space D. Mark the answers on the answer sheet to the right. Work as fast as you can without making too many errors. Work exactly 6 minutes.

ANSWER SHEET

#	Address 1	Address 2	Test A	Test B
1.	1545 Harrison Ave	1543 Harrison Ave	1 Ⓐ Ⓓ	1 ⒶⒹ
2.	94375 Forrest Pl SW	94375 Forrest Pl SW	2 ⒶⒹ	2 ⒶⒹ
3.	3598 Lassie Rd W	3598 Lassie Rd W	3 ⒶⒹ	3 ⒶⒹ
4.	5071 Nesika Bay Sq	5077 Nesika Bay SQ	4 ⒶⒹ	4 ⒶⒹ
5.	3857 Blackberry Ln E	5857 Blackberry Ln W	5 ⒶⒹ	5 ⒶⒹ
6.	3547 Sherman Oaks St	3547 Sherman Oaks St	6 ⒶⒹ	6 ⒶⒹ
7.	9763 Clay Pky W	8653 Ckay Pkwy W	7 ⒶⒹ	7 ⒶⒹ
8.	308 S Lincolnside Dr	308 S Lincolnside Dr	8 ⒶⒹ	8 ⒶⒹ
9.	836 Sundae Sq N	836 Sundae Sq S	9 ⒶⒹ	9 ⒶⒹ
10.	3547 E Brighton Rd	3547 E Brighton Rd	10 ⒶⒹ	10 ⒶⒹ
11.	9836 W Falkner St	9836 E Falkner St	11 ⒶⒹ	11 ⒶⒹ
12.	5945 Stevens Rd	4945 Stevens Rd	12 ⒶⒹ	12 ⒶⒹ
13.	9003 Underwood St	9003 Underwood St	13 ⒶⒹ	13 ⒶⒹ
14.	4846 Blanchard Ave	4846 Glanchard Ave	14 ⒶⒹ	14 ⒶⒹ
15.	93658 Mt. Elena Sq	93658 Mt. Elena Dr	15 ⒶⒹ	15 ⒶⒹ
16.	354 W Boston Way	354 E Boston Way	16 ⒶⒹ	16 ⒶⒹ
17.	1919 Sievers Pky	1919 Stevers Pkwy	17 ⒶⒹ	17 ⒶⒹ
18.	3785 Apache Drum Rd	3785 Apache Dr Rd	18 ⒶⒹ	18 ⒶⒹ
19.	301 Bryan Ct	301 Bryan Ct	19 ⒶⒹ	19 ⒶⒹ
20.	9381 Agatha Pass Way	9331 Agatha Pass Way	20 ⒶⒹ	20 ⒶⒹ
21.	3547 Brownsville St	3547 Bronsville St	21 ⒶⒹ	21 ⒶⒹ
22.	3078 13th Ave SW	3073 13th Ave SW	22 ⒶⒹ	22 ⒶⒹ
23.	234 Creol Pass	234 Creole Pass	23 ⒶⒹ	23 ⒶⒹ
24.	7878 Burnett Dr	7878 Burnett Dr	24 ⒶⒹ	24 ⒶⒹ
25.	235 Dixon	235 Dixon	25 ⒶⒹ	25 ⒶⒹ
26.	9478 Wicker Way	9478 Wicker Way	26 ⒶⒹ	26 ⒶⒹ
27.	3054 17th St	3054 17th St	27 ⒶⒹ	27 ⒶⒹ
28.	37854 Bonn Ave	37854 Bonn Ave	28 ⒶⒹ	28 ⒶⒹ
29.	9076 Bingham Dr	9076 Bighan Dr	29 ⒶⒹ	29 ⒶⒹ
30.	3175 Walnut	3175 Walnut	30 ⒶⒹ	30 ⒶⒹ
31.	347 Bridgeview Ave	347 Bridgeview Rd	31 ⒶⒹ	31 ⒶⒹ
32.	9048 3rd Avenue SE	9048 3rd Avenue SE	32 ⒶⒹ	32 ⒶⒹ
33.	3250 Grant S	3250 Grant W	33 ⒶⒹ	33 ⒶⒹ
34.	1867 Pinecone Creek	1867 Pinecone Creek	34 ⒶⒹ	34 ⒶⒹ
35.	3065 Simon Blvd	3065 Simon Blvd	35 ⒶⒹ	35 ⒶⒹ
36.	3545 Armstrong Rd	3545 Armstrong Rdg	36 ⒶⒹ	36 ⒶⒹ
37.	16459 Rudolf Rdg	16459 Rudolf Rdg	37 ⒶⒹ	37 ⒶⒹ
38.	3649 Campbell Way	3669 Campbell Way	38 ⒶⒹ	38 ⒶⒹ
39.	3965 Simon Ave	9363 Simon Ave	39 ⒶⒹ	39 ⒶⒹ
40.	3548 Walnut Rd	3548 Walnut Rd	40 ⒶⒹ	40 ⒶⒹ

Go on to the next nmber on the next page.

41. 35646 W Armstrong St	35648 W Armstrong Sq	41 Ⓐⓓ	41 Ⓐⓓ
42. 3759 N Ford	3759 N Ford	42 Ⓐⓓ	42 Ⓐⓓ
43. 3584 Rose S	3584 Rose N	43 Ⓐⓓ	43 Ⓐⓓ
44. 40647 S Philips	40647 S Philips	44 Ⓐⓓ	44 Ⓐⓓ
45. 4657 Scotts Bluff	4657 Scotts Bluff	45 Ⓐⓓ	45 Ⓐⓓ
46. 9486 Beechnut St	9486 Beechnut Ct	46 Ⓐⓓ	46 Ⓐⓓ
47. 7786 Maleroy Ct	7788 Maleroy Ct	47 Ⓐⓓ	47 Ⓐⓓ
48. 36547 Keyport Rd	36547 Keyport Rd	48 Ⓐⓓ	48 Ⓐⓓ
49. 6458 47th Ave W	6458 47th Ave W	49 Ⓐⓓ	49 Ⓐⓓ
50. 308 King Dr	308 King Dr	50 Ⓐⓓ	50 Ⓐⓓ
51. 5496 Franklin Cove	5496 Franklin Cove	51 Ⓐⓓ	51 Ⓐⓓ
52. 8745 Cactus Ave	8745 Cactus Ave S	52 Ⓐⓓ	52 Ⓐⓓ
53. 35648 W Glenn	35648 S. Glenn	53 Ⓐⓓ	53 Ⓐⓓ
54. 8475 E Cherokee	8475 E Cherokee	54 Ⓐⓓ	54 Ⓐⓓ
55. 48757 Roxbury Sq	48757 Roxbury Sq	55 Ⓐⓓ	55 Ⓐⓓ
56. 9475 Lawrence Ct	9473 Lawrence Ct	56 Ⓐⓓ	56 Ⓐⓓ
57. 35548 Bauxite Sq	35548 Bauxite Sq	57 Ⓐⓓ	57 Ⓐⓓ
58. 3756 Pearl Bay	3756 Pearl Bay	58 Ⓐⓓ	58 Ⓐⓓ
59. 30657 Plymouth Rock	30655 Plymouth Rock	59 Ⓐⓓ	59 Ⓐⓓ
60. 9486 Pleasant Rdg	9486 Pleasant Rd	60 Ⓐⓓ	60 Ⓐⓓ
61. 32875 Clifton Blvd	32875 Clifton Blvd	61 Ⓐⓓ	61 Ⓐⓓ
62. 307 Paramount W	307 Paramount W	62 Ⓐⓓ	62 Ⓐⓓ
63. 9468 Cottonwood Cove	9463 Cottonwood Sq	63 Ⓐⓓ	63 Ⓐⓓ
64. 3757 E Atchinson	3757 E Atchinson	64 Ⓐⓓ	64 Ⓐⓓ
65. 3756 Sheridan St	3758 Sheridan St	65 Ⓐⓓ	65 Ⓐⓓ
66. 5476 Bloomfield Rd	5476 Bloomfield Rd	66 Ⓐⓓ	66 Ⓐⓓ
67. 396547 Highland	396547 Highland	67 Ⓐⓓ	67 Ⓐⓓ
68. 5430 Shellfield SW	5430 Shellfield SW	68 Ⓐⓓ	68 Ⓐⓓ
69. 37546 Taft Ave E	37546 Taft Ave W	69 Ⓐⓓ	69 Ⓐⓓ
70. 307 Panama Park	307 Panama Park	70 Ⓐⓓ	70 Ⓐⓓ
71. 68456 Bayview St.	68456 Bayview St	71 Ⓐⓓ	71 Ⓐⓓ
72. 305 Ballard Sq E	305 Ballard Sq E	72 Ⓐⓓ	72 Ⓐⓓ
73. 38656 Rose Rd	38656 Rose Rd	73 Ⓐⓓ	73 Ⓐⓓ
74. 9357 Armstrong Ave	9357 Armstrong Ave	74 Ⓐⓓ	74 Ⓐⓓ
75. 3547 Madonna Way	3547 Madonna Way	75 Ⓐⓓ	75 Ⓐⓓ
76. 39658 Victor Sq	39658 Victor Sq	76 Ⓐⓓ	76 Ⓐⓓ
77. 458 N Hermosillo Ct	458 N Hemosillo Ct	77 Ⓐⓓ	77 Ⓐⓓ
78. 3233 Teppert	3233 Teppert	78 Ⓐⓓ	78 Ⓐⓓ
79. 3065 Salty Bay Sq	3063 Salty Bay Sq	79 Ⓐⓓ	79 Ⓐⓓ
80. 9654 Audubon Blvd	9654 Audubon Blvd	80 Ⓐⓓ	80 Ⓐⓓ
81. 3054 Sleepy Hollow	3054 Sleep Holly	81 Ⓐⓓ	81 Ⓐⓓ
82. 3258 Pine Way St	3253 Pine Way St	82 Ⓐⓓ	82 Ⓐⓓ
83. 3547 Bums Ct W	3547 Bums Ct W	83 Ⓐⓓ	83 Ⓐⓓ
84. 30645 Mountainside View	30643 Mountainside View	84 Ⓐⓓ	84 Ⓐⓓ
85. 354 Carlson St W	354 Carlson St W	85 Ⓐⓓ	85 Ⓐⓓ
86. 659 Brooks Shield N	659 Brooks Shield N	86 Ⓐⓓ	86 Ⓐⓓ
87. 3645 Stevens Rd	3647 Stevesn Rd W	87 Ⓐⓓ	87 Ⓐⓓ
88. 3547 Alderwood W	3547 Alderwood W	88 Ⓐⓓ	88 Ⓐⓓ
89. 3543 Pineapple Cove	3543 Pineapple Cove	89 Ⓐⓓ	89 Ⓐⓓ

Go on the next number on the next page.

90. 3540 Francisco Sq	3540 Francisco Sq	90 Ⓐ Ⓓ	90 Ⓐ Ⓓ
91. 6486 Pleasan Rd	8486 Pleasant Sq	91 Ⓐ Ⓓ	91 Ⓐ Ⓓ
92. 3547 Sutter Ave	3547 Sutter Ave	92 Ⓐ Ⓓ	92 Ⓐ Ⓓ
93. 3547 Mango Sq	3547 Mango Sq	93 Ⓐ Ⓓ	93 Ⓐ Ⓓ
94. 54 5 Marina Dr	545 Marina St	94 Ⓐ Ⓓ	94 Ⓐ Ⓓ
95. 65406 Marine Way	65406 Marine Way	95 Ⓐ Ⓓ	95 Ⓐ Ⓓ

STOP

If you finish before the time is up, check your answers for Part A

Do not go to any other part.

(See the correct answers on the next page.)

Correct Answers

Address-Checking Test

1. D	25. A	49. A	73. A
2. A	26. A	50. A	74. A
3. A	27. A	51. A	75. A
4. D	28. A	52. D	76. A
5. D	29. D	53. D	77. D
6. A	30. A	54. A	78. A
7. D	31. D	55. A	79. D
8. A	32. A	56. D	80. A
9. D	33. D	57. A	81. D
10. A	34. A	58. A	82. D
11. D	35. A	59. D	83. A
12. D	36. D	60. D	84. D
13. A	37. A	61. A	85. A
14. D	38. D	62. A	86. A
15. D	39. D	63. D	87. D
16. D	40. A	64. A	88. A
17. D	41. D	65. D	89. A
18. D	42. A	66. A	90. A
19. A	43. D	67. A	91. D
20. D	44. A	68. A	92. A
21. D	45. A	69. D	93. A
22. D	46. D	70. A	94. D
23. D	47. D	71. A	95. A
24. A	48. A	72. A	

Address-Checking Practice Test

Work—6 Minutes

These addresses are like the ones in the address-checking test.

Decide whether the two addresses are *Alike* or *Different*. If they are *Alike*, darken or mark space A; if they are *Different*, darken space D. Mark the answers on the answer sheet to the right. Work as fast as you can without making too many errors. Work Exactly 6 minutes.

			Test A	Test B
1.	3854 Carson S	3854 Carson S	1 Ⓐ Ⓓ	1 Ⓐ Ⓓ
2.	9046 Los Padres Cir	9048 Los Padres Cir	2 Ⓐ Ⓓ	2 Ⓐ Ⓓ
3.	354 S Luverne Rd	354 S Luverne Rd	3 Ⓐ Ⓓ	3 Ⓐ Ⓓ
4.	3548 Kimberly Sq	3548 Kimberly Sq	4 Ⓐ Ⓓ	4 Ⓐ Ⓓ
5.	253 Larami Rd N	258 Larami Rd N	5 Ⓐ Ⓓ	5 Ⓐ Ⓓ
6.	9461 S Audubon	9461 S Audubon	6 Ⓐ Ⓓ	6 Ⓐ Ⓓ
7.	3547 La Cross Dr	3547 La Cross Dr	7 Ⓐ Ⓓ	7 Ⓐ Ⓓ
8.	547 Salty Bay Rd	547 Salty Bay Rd	8 Ⓐ Ⓓ	8 Ⓐ Ⓓ
9.	36548 Harrison Cir	36543 Harrison Cir	9 Ⓐ Ⓓ	9 Ⓐ Ⓓ
10.	547 S Gregory Park	547 S Gregory Park	10 Ⓐ Ⓓ	10 Ⓐ Ⓓ
11.	658 S Salem Ln	658 S Salem Ln	11 Ⓐ Ⓓ	11 Ⓐ Ⓓ
12.	7845 S Liberty Pl	7845 N Liberty Pl	12 Ⓐ Ⓓ	12 Ⓐ Ⓓ
13.	745 Olympic Way	745 Olympic Way	13 Ⓐ Ⓓ	13 Ⓐ Ⓓ
14.	5478 Monterrey Rd	5478 Monterrey Rd	14 Ⓐ Ⓓ	14 Ⓐ Ⓓ
15	986 S Ocean Blvd	986 N Ocean Blvd	15 Ⓐ Ⓓ	15 Ⓐ Ⓓ
16.	389 S Placid Plaza	389 N Placid Plaza	16 Ⓐ Ⓓ	16 Ⓐ Ⓓ
17.	9475 Olympic Cove	7475 Olympic Cove	17 Ⓐ Ⓓ	17 Ⓐ Ⓓ
18.	346 S Blanchard Ct	346 S Blanchard Ct	18 Ⓐ Ⓓ	18 Ⓐ Ⓓ
19.	8764 Jensen Way	3764 Jensen Way	19 Ⓐ Ⓓ	19 Ⓐ Ⓓ
20.	3754 Hayes Point	8754 Hayes Point	20 Ⓐ Ⓓ	20 Ⓐ Ⓓ
21.	8457 Galveston Blvd	8457 Galveston Hwy	21 Ⓐ Ⓓ	21 Ⓐ Ⓓ
22.	8475 NE Wilmoth	8475 NE Wilmont	22 Ⓐ Ⓓ	22 Ⓐ Ⓓ
23.	3503 O'Neal Rd	3503 O'Neal Rd	23 Ⓐ Ⓓ	23 Ⓐ Ⓓ
24.	1057 S Pierce Ct	1057 N Pierce Ct	24 Ⓐ Ⓓ	24 Ⓐ Ⓓ
25 .	3854 Monroe NW	3854 Monroe NW	25 Ⓐ Ⓓ	25 Ⓐ Ⓓ
26.	79845 Bonn Blvd	79845 Bonn Blvd	26 Ⓐ Ⓓ	26 Ⓐ Ⓓ
27.	3015 Holiday Inn Dr	3015 Holiday Inn Dr	27 Ⓐ Ⓓ	27 Ⓐ Ⓓ
28.	4961 Warner St	8961 Warner St	28 Ⓐ Ⓓ	28 Ⓐ Ⓓ
29.	5488 Wellington Way	5488 Wellington Way	29 Ⓐ Ⓓ	29 Ⓐ Ⓓ
30.	466 S Terrace	466 S Terrace	30 Ⓐ Ⓓ	30 Ⓐ Ⓓ
31.	4466 Jackson Rd W	4466 Jackson Rd E	31 Ⓐ Ⓓ	31 Ⓐ Ⓓ
32.	4455 Concord Blvd	4455 Concord Pky	32 Ⓐ Ⓓ	32 Ⓐ Ⓓ
33.	776 Symington St	767 Symington St	33 Ⓐ Ⓓ	33 Ⓐ Ⓓ
34.	8811 Carver Cove	8811 Carver Cove	34 Ⓐ Ⓓ	34 Ⓐ Ⓓ
35.	8835 Joplin Ct	8885 Joplin Ct	35 Ⓐ Ⓓ	35 Ⓐ Ⓓ
36.	9947 S Lighthouse Ln	9947 S Lighthouse Ln	36 Ⓐ Ⓓ	36 Ⓐ Ⓓ
37.	6649 Main St	6649 Main St	37 Ⓐ Ⓓ	37 Ⓐ Ⓓ
38.	9488 32nd Ave S	9483 32nd Ave S	38 Ⓐ Ⓓ	38 Ⓐ Ⓓ
39.	1143 S Greenbriar Ct	1149 S Greenbriar Ct	39 Ⓐ Ⓓ	39 Ⓐ Ⓓ
40.	766 Hazel Park	766 Hazel Park	40 Ⓐ Ⓓ	40 Ⓐ Ⓓ

Go on to the next number on the next page.

#	Address 1	Address 2			
41.	8976 S Lester	8976 S Lester	41 Ⓐ Ⓓ	41 Ⓐ Ⓓ
42.	389 Hubert Rd	389 Hubert Rd	42 Ⓐ Ⓓ	42 Ⓐ Ⓓ
43.	8881 Melvin Way	8881 Melvin Way	43 Ⓐ Ⓒ	43 Ⓐ Ⓓ
44.	76459 Ronald St	76459 Ronald Dr	44 Ⓐ Ⓓ	44 Ⓐ Ⓓ
45.	3887 Saint Peter Dr	3887 Saint Peter Dr	45 Ⓐ Ⓓ	45 Ⓐ Ⓓ
46.	4152 Melrose Park	4152 Melrose Park	46 Ⓐ Ⓓ	46 Ⓐ Ⓓ
47.	4648 Crestwood N	4643 Crestwood N	47 Ⓐ Ⓓ	47 Ⓐ Ⓓ
48.	37647 Stables St	37647 Stables Rd	48 Ⓐ Ⓓ	48 Ⓐ Ⓓ
49.	3754 S Belair Blvd	3754 S Belaire Blvd	49 Ⓐ Ⓓ	49 Ⓐ Ⓓ
50.	370 E Essex St	370 W Essex St	50 Ⓐ Ⓓ	50 Ⓐ Ⓓ
51.	3654 S Mathews	3654 S Mathew	51 Ⓐ Ⓓ	51 Ⓐ Ⓓ
52.	94745 Severance Ct	94745 Severance Ct	52 Ⓐ Ⓓ	52 Ⓐ Ⓓ
53.	4538 Wheeler Way	4538 Wheeler Way	53 Ⓐ Ⓓ	53 Ⓐ Ⓓ
54.	794 Norfolk Ave	794 Norfolk Ave	54 Ⓐ Ⓓ	54 Ⓐ Ⓓ
55.	578 7th Ave NW	578 7th Ave SW	55 Ⓐ Ⓓ	55 Ⓐ Ⓓ
56.	3904 12th St. SW	3904 12th St SE	56 Ⓐ Ⓓ	56 Ⓐ Ⓓ
57.	3547 S Wendover	3547 S Wendover	57 Ⓐ Ⓓ	57 Ⓐ Ⓓ
58.	448 E Lincoln Sq	448 E Lincoln Sq	58 Ⓐ Ⓓ	58 Ⓐ Ⓓ
59.	354 St. Peter St E	354 St Peter St E	59 Ⓐ Ⓓ	59 Ⓐ Ⓓ
60.	3308 Essex Ct	3308 Essex Ct	60 Ⓐ Ⓓ	60 Ⓐ Ⓓ
61.	947 E Amherst	947 W Amherst	61 Ⓐ Ⓓ	61 Ⓐ Ⓓ
62.	7987 Elizabeth Ln	7987 Elizabeth Ln	62 Ⓐ Ⓓ	62 Ⓐ Ⓓ
63.	3649 Montrose Rd	3649 Montrose Rd	63 Ⓐ Ⓓ	63 Ⓐ Ⓓ
64.	396 Montreal Pl	3946 Montreal Pl	64 Ⓐ Ⓓ	64 Ⓐ Ⓓ
65.	4497 Clayton Ct	4497 Clayton St	65 Ⓐ Ⓓ	65 Ⓐ Ⓓ
66.	436 Ontario Way	486 Ontario Way	66 Ⓐ Ⓓ	66 Ⓐ Ⓓ
67.	94876 S Olmstead	94876 N Olmstead	67 Ⓐ Ⓓ	67 Ⓐ Ⓓ
68.	3540 Brooks Shield	3540 Brooks Shield	68 Ⓐ Ⓓ	68 Ⓐ Ⓓ
69.	9887 Cortland Dr	9837 Cortland Dr	69 Ⓐ Ⓓ	69 Ⓐ Ⓓ
70.	397 S Hamilton Ln	397 S Hamilton Ln	70 Ⓐ Ⓓ	70 Ⓐ Ⓓ
71.	547 E Vernon	547 S Vernon	71 Ⓐ Ⓓ	71 Ⓐ Ⓓ
72.	7845 S Perry Dr	7845 N Perry Dr	72 Ⓐ Ⓓ	72 Ⓐ Ⓓ
73.	4457 Old Hickory	4487 Old Hickory	73 Ⓐ Ⓓ	73 Ⓐ Ⓓ
74.	5645 N Dolomite Dr	5645 S Dolomite Dr	74 Ⓐ Ⓓ	74 Ⓐ Ⓓ
75.	3540 S Hampstead Pl	3540 S Hampstead Pl	75 Ⓐ Ⓓ	75 Ⓐ Ⓓ
76.	35489 E Clinton Sq	85489 E Clinton Sq	76 Ⓐ Ⓓ	76 Ⓐ Ⓓ
77.	3548 Bush Hwy	3548 Bush Hwy	77 Ⓐ Ⓓ	77 Ⓐ Ⓓ
78.	3540 S Kendall	3540 S Kendall	78 Ⓐ Ⓓ	78 Ⓐ Ⓓ
79.	3540 Battlecreek Rd	354 Battlecreeek Rd	79 Ⓐ Ⓓ	79 Ⓐ Ⓓ
80.	5469 Bismark Park	5489 Bismark Park	80 Ⓐ Ⓓ	80 Ⓐ Ⓓ
81.	84645 Pocahontas Hwy	84645 Pocahontas Hwy	81 Ⓐ Ⓓ	81 Ⓐ Ⓓ
82.	3954 Wasbash Rd	3854 Wasbash Rd	82 Ⓐ Ⓓ	82 Ⓐ Ⓓ
83.	4965 Bancroft Pky	4965 Gancroft Pky	83 Ⓐ Ⓓ	83 Ⓐ Ⓓ
84.	3547 S Windsor Ave	3547 S Windsor Ave	84 Ⓐ Ⓓ	84 Ⓐ Ⓓ
85.	6947 Hiawatha Way	6947 Hiawatha Way	85 Ⓐ Ⓓ	85 Ⓐ Ⓓ
86.	3540 E Lucerne Dr	3540 E Lucerne Dr	86 Ⓐ Ⓓ	86 Ⓐ Ⓓ
87.	4645 Marshall Park	4645 Marshal Park	87 Ⓐ Ⓓ	87 Ⓐ Ⓓ
88.	3545 Janet Pl	3548 Janet Pl	88 Ⓐ Ⓓ	88 Ⓐ Ⓓ
89.	9943 Lucern Way	9943 Lucern Way	89 Ⓐ Ⓓ	89 Ⓐ Ⓓ

Go on to the next number on the next page.

90. 3369 S Laverne Rd	3369 S Laverne St	90 Ⓐ Ⓓ	90 Ⓐ Ⓓ
91. 6536 Sta. Ana Rd	6536 Sta. Ana St	91 Ⓐ Ⓓ	91 Ⓐ Ⓓ
92. 7659 5th Ave SW	7659 5th Ave SE	92 Ⓐ Ⓓ	92 Ⓐ Ⓓ
93. 36450 S Marshall	36450 S Marshall	93 Ⓐ Ⓓ	93 Ⓐ Ⓓ
94. 4783 Randolph Hwy	4783 Randolf Hwy	94 Ⓐ Ⓓ	94 Ⓐ Ⓓ
95. 6459 Bismark Cove	6459 Bismark Cove	95 Ⓐ Ⓓ	95 Ⓐ Ⓓ

STOP

If you finish before the time is up, check your answers for Part A.

Do not go to any other part.

(See the correct answers on the next page.)

Correct Answers

Address-Checking Test

1. A	25. A	49. D	73. D
2. D	26. A	50. D	74. D
3. A	27. A	51. D	75. A
4. A	28. D	52. A	76. D
5. D	29. A	53. A	77. A
6. A	30. A	54. A	78. A
7. A	31. D	55. D	79. D
8. A	32. D	56. D	80. D
9. D	33. D	57. A	81. A
10. A	34. A	58. A	82. D
11. A	35. D	59. A	83. D
12. D	36. A	60. A	84. A
13. A	37. A	61. D	85. A
14. A	38. D	62. A	86. A
15. D	39. D	63. A	87. D
16. D	40. A	64. D	88. D
17. D	41. A	65. D	89. A
18. A	42. A	66. D	90. D
19. D	43. A	67. D	91. D
20. D	44. D	68. A	92. D
21. D	45. A	69. D	93. A
22. D	46. A	70. A	94. D
23. A	47. D	71. D	95. A
24. D	48. D	72. D	

Address-Checking Practice Test

Work—6 Minutes

These addresses are like the ones in the address-checking test.

Decide whether the two addresses are *Alike* or *Different*. if they are *Alike,* darken or mark space A; if they are *Different* darken Space D. Mark the answers on the answer sheet to the right. Work as fast as you can without making too many errors. Work exactly 6 minutes.

			Test A		Test B
1.	3540 Willow SW	3540 Willo SE	1 Ⓐ Ⓓ	1	Ⓐ Ⓓ
2.	3548 Santa Cruz Bay	3548 Santa Cruz Bay	2 Ⓐ Ⓓ	2	Ⓐ Ⓓ
3.	9375 Hollister Rd	9375 Hollister St	3 Ⓐ Ⓓ	3	Ⓐ Ⓓ
4.	65499 Grandview Dr	65499 Grandview Dr	4 Ⓐ Ⓓ	4	Ⓐ Ⓓ
5.	385 Evangeline St	385 Evangeline St	5 Ⓐ Ⓓ	5	Ⓐ Ⓓ
6.	9354 Briarcliff View	9354 Briarcliff View	6 Ⓐ Ⓓ	6	Ⓐ Ⓓ
7.	39547 Memphis Rd	39547 Memphis St	7 Ⓐ Ⓓ	7	Ⓐ Ⓓ
8.	1978 Briarwood Cir	1978 Briarwood Cir	8 Ⓐ Ⓓ	8	Ⓐ Ⓓ
9.	3954 Peppermint	3954 Peppermint	9 Ⓐ Ⓓ	9	Ⓐ Ⓓ
10.	3549 Woodward Ave	3549 Woodward Ave	10 Ⓐ Ⓓ	10	Ⓐ Ⓓ
11.	23323 Teppert St	23328 Teppert St	11 Ⓐ Ⓓ	11	Ⓐ Ⓓ
12.	4488 Campbell	4488 Campbell	12 Ⓐ Ⓓ	12	Ⓐ Ⓓ
13.	8745 S Copper Creek	8745 N Copper Creek	13 Ⓐ Ⓓ	13	Ⓐ Ⓓ
14.	865 12th Mile S	865 12th Mile S	14 Ⓐ Ⓓ	14	Ⓐ Ⓓ
15.	647 Morning Breeze	647 Morning Breese	15 Ⓐ Ⓓ	15	Ⓐ Ⓓ
16.	9481 Bownsville Cove	9481 Brownsville Cove	16 Ⓐ Ⓓ	16	Ⓐ Ⓓ
17.	1054 Gainsville Rd	1054 Gainsville Rd	17 Ⓐ Ⓓ	17	Ⓐ Ⓓ
18.	6493 Parker Cir	6493 Parker Cir	18 Ⓐ Ⓓ	18	Ⓐ Ⓓ
19.	9454 Alexandria St	9454 Alexandra Dr	19 Ⓐ Ⓓ	19	Ⓐ Ⓓ
20.	7845 Crescent View	7845 Crescent View	20 Ⓐ Ⓓ	20	Ⓐ Ⓓ
21.	9450 Darwin St	9450 Darwin Sq	21 Ⓐ Ⓓ	21	Ⓐ Ⓓ
22.	390 Pandora Rd	390 Pandora Rd	22 Ⓐ Ⓓ	22	Ⓐ Ⓓ
23.	5403 Gilbert St	5408 Gilbert St	23 Ⓐ Ⓓ	23	Ⓐ Ⓓ
24.	38545 Santa Fe Cir	33545 Santa Fe Cir	24 Ⓐ Ⓓ	24	Ⓐ Ⓓ
25.	3054 S Daytona St	3054 S Daytona St	25 Ⓐ Ⓓ	25	Ⓐ Ⓓ
26.	9467 Guadalupe Loop	9467 Guadalupe Loop	26 Ⓐ Ⓓ	26	Ⓐ Ⓓ
27.	10545 Tallahasse Ln	10548 Tallsahasse Ln	27 Ⓐ Ⓓ	27	Ⓐ Ⓓ
28.	54065 Redfield SW	54065 Redfield SW	28 Ⓐ Ⓓ	28	Ⓐ Ⓓ
29.	8351 Greenfield Sq	3351 Greenfield Sq	29 Ⓐ Ⓓ	29	Ⓐ Ⓓ
30.	8354 52nd Ave S	8354 52nd Ave S	30 Ⓐ Ⓓ	30	Ⓐ Ⓓ
31.	8540 Sleepy Hollow	8540 Sleepy Hollow	31 Ⓐ Ⓓ	31	Ⓐ Ⓓ
32.	3954 Hubert Dr	3954 Hubert Dr	32 Ⓐ Ⓓ	32	Ⓐ Ⓓ
33.	5482 Durhamn Rd	5482 Durham Rd	33 Ⓐ Ⓓ	33	Ⓐ Ⓓ
34.	9354 Maleroy	9354 Maleroy	34 Ⓐ Ⓓ	34	Ⓐ Ⓓ
35.	3367 Franklin S	3367 Franklin N	35 Ⓐ Ⓓ	35	Ⓐ Ⓓ
36.	3954 E Beechnut	3954 E Beechnut	36 Ⓐ Ⓓ	36	Ⓐ Ⓓ
37.	9461 Falcon Crest	9461 Falcon Crest	37 Ⓐ Ⓓ	37	Ⓐ Ⓓ
38.	94564 Carver Pl	94564 Carver Pl	38 Ⓐ Ⓓ	38	Ⓐ Ⓓ
39.	7735 Keyport Point	7733 Keyport Point	39 Ⓐ Ⓓ	39	Ⓐ Ⓓ
40.	9454 Scotts Bluff N	9454 Scotts Bluff S	40 Ⓐ Ⓓ	40	Ⓐ Ⓓ

Go on to the next number on the next page.

41.	3300 Boston Harbor	3300 Boston Harbor	41	Ⓐ Ⓓ	41	Ⓐ Ⓓ
42.	93547 St John	93547 St John	42	Ⓐ Ⓓ	42	Ⓐ Ⓓ
43.	9476 Eagle View	9476 Eagle View	43	Ⓐ Ⓓ	43	Ⓐ Ⓓ
44.	3054 Blanchard Dr	3054 Blanchard Cir	44	Ⓐ Ⓓ	44	Ⓐ Ⓓ
45.	3377 Alderwood Ln	3377 Alderwood Ln	45	Ⓐ Ⓓ	45	Ⓐ Ⓓ
46.	5667 Sievers Rd	5661 Sievers Rd	46	Ⓐ Ⓓ	46	Ⓐ Ⓓ
47.	9457 S Burnett	9457 N Burnett	47	Ⓐ Ⓓ	47	Ⓐ Ⓓ
48.	6573 Dixon Rd	6573 Dixon Rd	48	Ⓐ Ⓓ	48	Ⓐ Ⓓ
49.	8477 Covington Ln	8477 Covington Ln	49	Ⓐ Ⓓ	49	Ⓐ Ⓓ
50.	3549 E Amhurst Creek	3549 W Amherst Creek	50	Ⓐ Ⓓ	50	Ⓐ Ⓓ
51.	9474 Melbourne Ave	9474 Melborne Ave	51	Ⓐ Ⓓ	51	Ⓐ Ⓓ
52.	3549 Granite View	3549 Gratite View	52	Ⓐ Ⓓ	52	Ⓐ Ⓓ
53.	3047 Diamond Crest	3047 Diamond Crest	53	Ⓐ Ⓓ	53	Ⓐ Ⓓ
54.	39540 Central Plaza	30540 Central Plaza	54	Ⓐ Ⓓ	54	Ⓐ Ⓓ
55.	3540 Blake Rd	3540 Blake Rd	55	Ⓐ Ⓓ	55	Ⓐ Ⓓ
56.	3054 Cooper SW	3054 Cooper SE	56	Ⓐ Ⓓ	56	Ⓐ Ⓓ
57.	745 Knoll Hwy	745 Knoll Hwy	57	Ⓐ Ⓓ	57	Ⓐ Ⓓ
58.	5400 Birmingham Park	5400 Biningham Park	58	Ⓐ Ⓓ	58	Ⓐ Ⓓ
59.	3954 Grant Pl	3954 Grant Pl	59	Ⓐ Ⓓ	59	Ⓐ Ⓓ
60.	45451 7th Ave SW	45451 7th Ave SE	60	Ⓐ Ⓓ	60	Ⓐ Ⓓ
61.	3054 Bridgeview St	3054 Bridgeview St	61	Ⓐ Ⓓ	61	Ⓐ Ⓓ
62.	3954 Armistice	3954 Armistice	62	Ⓐ Ⓓ	62	Ⓐ Ⓓ
63.	541 S Averley	541 N Averley	63	Ⓐ Ⓓ	63	Ⓐ Ⓓ
64.	3005 Flint SW	8005 Flint SW	64	Ⓐ Ⓓ	64	Ⓐ Ⓓ
65.	39651 Chrysler Rd	39651 Chrysler Rd	65	Ⓐ Ⓓ	65	Ⓐ Ⓓ
66.	3301 Ford Pky	3301 Ford Pky	66	Ⓐ Ⓓ	66	Ⓐ Ⓓ
67.	7731 Armstrong Dr	7731 Armstrong Dr	67	Ⓐ Ⓓ	67	Ⓐ Ⓓ
68.	33901 King St	33907 King Sq	68	Ⓐ Ⓓ	68	Ⓐ Ⓓ
69.	310 Amapola Rd	310 Anapola Rd	69	Ⓐ Ⓓ	69	Ⓐ Ⓓ
70.	3016 Straton Lake	3016 Straton Lake	70	Ⓐ Ⓓ	70	Ⓐ Ⓓ
71.	3011 Belmont Way	3011 Belmont Way	71	Ⓐ Ⓓ	71	Ⓐ Ⓓ
72.	318 S Marine	318 N Marine	72	Ⓐ Ⓓ	72	Ⓐ Ⓓ
73.	3105 N Foster Ave	3105 N Foster Ave	73	Ⓐ Ⓓ	73	Ⓐ Ⓓ
74.	3016 Knottingham	3016 Knottingham	74	Ⓐ Ⓓ	74	Ⓐ Ⓓ
75.	7861 Bell St	7861 Bell St	75	Ⓐ Ⓓ	75	Ⓐ Ⓓ
76.	3810 Jerriman S	3810 Jerriman N	76	Ⓐ Ⓓ	76	Ⓐ Ⓓ
77.	3106 Knickerbocker	3106 Knickerbocker	77	Ⓐ Ⓓ	77	Ⓐ Ⓓ
78.	1154 R Johnston	1154 R Johnston	78	Ⓐ Ⓓ	78	Ⓐ Ⓓ
79.	31545 Dorchester	31545 Darchester	79	Ⓐ Ⓓ	79	Ⓐ Ⓓ
80.	3154 Ft. Hamilton	3154 Ft Hamilton	80	Ⓐ Ⓓ	80	Ⓐ Ⓓ
81.	3190 S Boulder	3190 S Boulder	81	Ⓐ Ⓓ	81	Ⓐ Ⓓ
82.	3106 NW 157th St	8315 SW 157th St	82	Ⓐ Ⓓ	82	Ⓐ Ⓓ
83.	3154 Evergreen	3154 Evergreen	83	Ⓐ Ⓓ	83	Ⓐ Ⓓ
84.	3154 Rosengarden	3154 Rosengarden	84	Ⓐ Ⓓ	84	Ⓐ Ⓓ
85.	3965 Lumberville N	3965 Lumberville S	85	Ⓐ Ⓓ	85	Ⓐ Ⓓ
86.	316 Markham S	316 Markam S	86	Ⓐ Ⓓ	86	Ⓐ Ⓓ
87.	3188 Warnock Creek	3188 Warnock Creek	87	Ⓐ Ⓓ	87	Ⓐ Ⓓ
88.	3110 Kessler Nook	3110 Kessler Nook	88	Ⓐ Ⓓ	88	Ⓐ Ⓓ
89.	3388 Ovington Park	3388 Ovington Park	89	Ⓐ Ⓓ	89	Ⓐ Ⓓ

Go on to the next number on the next page.

90. 3100 Catalina Cir	3100 Catalina Cir	90 Ⓐ Ⓓ	90 Ⓐ Ⓓ
91. 9615 Dorchester	9615 Darchester	91 Ⓐ Ⓓ	91 Ⓐ Ⓓ
92. 3110 Blake E	3110 Blake S	92 Ⓐ Ⓓ	92 Ⓐ Ⓓ
93. 3174 Empire St	8174 Empire St	93 Ⓐ Ⓓ	93 Ⓐ Ⓓ
94. 1947 Hampton Ave	1847 Hampton Ave	94 Ⓐ Ⓓ	94 Ⓐ Ⓓ
95. 31054 Hancock	31054 Hamcock	95 Ⓐ Ⓓ	95 Ⓐ Ⓓ

STOP

If you finish before the time is up, check your answers for Part A.

Do not go to any other part.

(See the correct answers on the next page.)

Correct Answers

Address-Checking Test

1. D		49. A	73. A
2. A	25. A	50. D	74. A
3. D	26. A	51. D	75. A
4. A	27. D	52. D	76. D
5. A	28. A	53. A	77. A
6. A	29. D	54. D	78. A
7. D	30. A	55. A	79. D
8. A	31. A	56. D	80. A
9. A	32. A	57. A	81. A
10. A	33. D	58. D	82. D
11. D	34. A	59. A	83. A
12. A	35. D	60. D	84. A
13. D	36. A	61. A	85. D
14. A	37. A	62. A	86. D
15. D	38. A	63. D	87. A
16. D	39. D	64. D	88. A
17. A	40. D	65. A	89. A
18. A	41. A	66. A	90. A
19. D	42. A	67. A	91. D
20. A	43. A	68. D	92. D
21. D	44. D	69. D	93. D
22. A	45. A	70. A	94. D
23. D	46. D	71. A	95. D
24. D	47. D	72. D	
	48. A		

Address-Checking Practice Test

Work—6 Minutes

These addresses are like the ones in the address-checking test.

Decide whether the two addresses are *Alike* or *Different.* If they are *Alike,* darken or mark space A; if they are *Different,* darken space D. Mark the answers on the answer sheet to the right. Work as fast as you can without making too many errors. Work exactly 6 minutes.

			Test A	Test B
1.	76386 Island Park	76386 Island Park	1 Ⓐ Ⓓ	1 Ⓐ Ⓓ
2.	3540 S Hotel Rd	9540 S Hotel Rd	2 Ⓐ Ⓓ	2 Ⓐ Ⓓ
3.	3964 Missouri Ct	3964 Misouri Ct	3 Ⓐ Ⓓ	3 Ⓐ Ⓓ
4.	93645 Harness St	93647 Harness St	4 Ⓐ Ⓓ	4 Ⓐ Ⓓ
5.	3540 Raffles Blvd	3540 Raffles Blvd	5 Ⓐ Ⓓ	5 Ⓐ Ⓓ
6.	350 N Westminster	350 N Westminster	6 Ⓐ Ⓓ	6 Ⓐ Ⓓ
7.	3064 Columbia Dr	3064 Columbia Dr	7 Ⓐ Ⓓ	7 Ⓐ Ⓓ
8.	5400 Cordelia NW	5400 Cordelia NE	8 Ⓐ Ⓓ	8 Ⓐ Ⓓ
9.	1649 Kauai Rd	1649 Kauai Rd	9 Ⓐ Ⓓ	9 Ⓐ Ⓓ
10.	3540 Cadiz Way	3540 Cadiz Way	10 Ⓐ Ⓓ	10 Ⓐ Ⓓ
11.	3889 Stockbridge S	3839 Stockbridge S	11 Ⓐ Ⓓ	11 Ⓐ Ⓓ
12.	4401 E Cadiz Ln	4401 S Cadiz Ln	12 Ⓐ Ⓓ	12 Ⓐ Ⓓ
13.	35400 Morris Ave	35400 Morris Ave	13 Ⓐ Ⓓ	13 Ⓐ Ⓓ
14.	3054 Hampton Rd	3054 Hanpton Rd	14 Ⓐ Ⓓ	14 Ⓐ Ⓓ
15.	3358 Marina Rd	3353 Marina Rd	15 Ⓐ Ⓓ	15 Ⓐ Ⓓ
16.	30658 Windmill Ave	30658 Windmill Ave	16 Ⓐ Ⓓ	16 Ⓐ Ⓓ
17.	7883 Markham Way	7883 Markhan Way	17 Ⓐ Ⓓ	17 Ⓐ Ⓓ
18.	30654 Warnock St	30654 Warnock St	18 Ⓐ Ⓓ	18 Ⓐ Ⓓ
19.	5400 Berkshire Sq	5400 Berkshire Sq	19 Ⓐ Ⓓ	19 Ⓐ Ⓓ
20.	9365 Columbia Dr	9365 Columbia Ave	20 Ⓐ Ⓓ	20 Ⓐ Ⓓ
21.	8835 Doughty Hwy	8835 Doughty Hwy	21 Ⓐ Ⓓ	21 Ⓐ Ⓓ
22.	3047 Jerriman Pky	3047 Jerriman Pky	22 Ⓐ Ⓓ	22 Ⓐ Ⓓ
23.	6589 Nautilus Castle	6539 Nautilus Castle	23 Ⓐ Ⓓ	23 Ⓐ Ⓓ
24.	4054 Red Light	4058 Red Light	24 Ⓐ Ⓓ	24 Ⓐ Ⓓ
25.	385 S Blue Moon	385 S Blue Moon	25 Ⓐ Ⓓ	25 Ⓐ Ⓓ
26.	3054 Green Lagoon	3058 Green Lagoon	26 Ⓐ Ⓓ	26 Ⓐ Ⓓ
27.	3064 Kalamazoo Rd	3064 Kalamazoo St	27 Ⓐ Ⓓ	27 Ⓐ Ⓓ
28.	6540 Catalunia Dr	6540 Catalunia Dr	28 Ⓐ Ⓓ	28 Ⓐ Ⓓ
29.	9463 Delaware Creek	9469 Delaware Creek	29 Ⓐ Ⓓ	29 Ⓐ Ⓓ
30.	3054 LaSalle Village	3054 LaSale Village	30 Ⓐ Ⓓ	30 Ⓐ Ⓓ
31.	5405 Hamilton Way	5405 Hamilton Way	31 Ⓐ Ⓓ	31 Ⓐ Ⓓ
32.	5481 Montana Dr	5481 Montana Dr	32 Ⓐ Ⓓ	32 Ⓐ Ⓓ
33.	8954 Doughty Way	8957 Doughty Hwy	33 Ⓐ Ⓓ	33 Ⓐ Ⓓ
34.	3054 Christy St	3054 Christy St	34 Ⓐ Ⓓ	34 Ⓐ Ⓓ
35.	3437 Glendale Rd	5437 Glendale St	35 Ⓐ Ⓓ	35 Ⓐ Ⓓ
36.	43065 7th Ave W	40368 7th Ave W	36 Ⓐ Ⓓ	36 Ⓐ Ⓓ
37.	3054 MacDonald Vlg	3054 MacDonald Vlg	37 Ⓐ Ⓓ	37 Ⓐ Ⓓ
38.	30547 Keating E	30547 Keating W	38 Ⓐ Ⓓ	38 Ⓐ Ⓓ
39.	3054 Carter Dr	3057 Carter Dr	39 Ⓐ Ⓓ	39 Ⓐ Ⓓ
40.	3068 E Evanston	3063 Evanston	40 Ⓐ Ⓓ	40 Ⓐ Ⓓ

Go on to the next number on the next page.

41.	64506 Pittmar Dr	64506 Pittmar Dr	41	Ⓐ Ⓓ	41	Ⓐ Ⓓ
42.	3540 Chamber Ln	3540 Chamber Ln	42	Ⓐ Ⓓ	42	Ⓐ Ⓓ
43.	3954 Central Sq	3954 Central Sq	43	Ⓐ Ⓓ	43	Ⓐ Ⓓ
44.	944 S Apple Rdge	944 S Apple Rdg	44	Ⓐ Ⓓ	44	Ⓐ Ⓓ
45.	4867 Tripp Rd	4887 Tripp Rd	45	Ⓐ Ⓓ	45	Ⓐ Ⓓ
46.	1469 Brayton Cir	1469 Brytom Cir	46	Ⓐ Ⓓ	46	Ⓐ Ⓓ
47.	4954 Crestlane Rd	4954 Crestlane Rd	47	Ⓐ Ⓓ	47	Ⓐ Ⓓ
48.	3054 Wilmington Pl	3054 Wilmington Pl	48	Ⓐ Ⓓ	48	Ⓐ Ⓓ
49.	7697 Brooklyn Bridge	7697 Brooklyn Bridge	49	Ⓐ Ⓓ	49	Ⓐ Ⓓ
50.	85349 Williston St	85349 Williston St	50	Ⓐ Ⓓ	50	Ⓐ Ⓓ
51.	5831 Medford Dr	5831 Melford Dr	51	Ⓐ Ⓓ	51	Ⓐ Ⓓ
52.	9485 Tuyvesant Way	9485 Tuysevent Way	52	Ⓐ Ⓓ	52	Ⓐ Ⓓ
53.	5948 Briarcliff St	5948 Briarcliff St	53	Ⓐ Ⓓ	53	Ⓐ Ⓓ
54.	4057 59th St W	4057 59th St E	54	Ⓐ Ⓓ	54	Ⓐ Ⓓ
55.	57849 Prince Rd	57849 Prince Rd	55	Ⓐ Ⓓ	55	Ⓐ Ⓓ
56.	4857 Welch Sq	4857 Welch Sq	56	Ⓐ Ⓓ	56	Ⓐ Ⓓ
57.	59846 Interlaken	53846 Interlaken	57	Ⓐ Ⓓ	57	Ⓐ Ⓓ
58.	3857 Rugby St	3857 Rugby St	58	Ⓐ Ⓓ	58	Ⓐ Ⓓ
59.	4395 Boutinville	4395 Boutinville	59	Ⓐ Ⓓ	59	Ⓐ Ⓓ
60.	294 76th Ave SW	294 76th Ave SW	60	Ⓐ Ⓓ	60	Ⓐ Ⓓ
61.	8823 Pleasant Run	8828 Pleasant Run	61	Ⓐ Ⓓ	61	Ⓐ Ⓓ
62.	4867 Old Coral Rd	4867 Old Coral Rd	62	Ⓐ Ⓓ	62	Ⓐ Ⓓ
63.	4856 Chessnut Way	4356 Chessnut Way	63	Ⓐ Ⓓ	63	Ⓐ Ⓓ
64.	475 Penn Sq	475 Penn Sq	64	Ⓐ Ⓓ	64	Ⓐ Ⓓ
65.	4057 Mountainville	4057 Mountainville	65	Ⓐ Ⓓ	65	Ⓐ Ⓓ
66.	4005 Bryant Rd	4008 Bryant Rd	66	Ⓐ Ⓓ	66	Ⓐ Ⓓ
67.	4481 Carmen Cove	4482 Carmen Cove	67	Ⓐ Ⓓ	67	Ⓐ Ⓓ
68.	497 S Elmhurst	497 S Elmhurst	68	Ⓐ Ⓓ	68	Ⓐ Ⓓ
69.	3751 Spring Valley	3751 Spring Valley	69	Ⓐ Ⓓ	69	Ⓐ Ⓓ
70.	4477 Sycamore Rd	4477 Sycamore St	70	Ⓐ Ⓓ	70	Ⓐ Ⓓ
71.	8845 Massachusettes	8848 Massachusettes	71	Ⓐ Ⓓ	71	Ⓐ Ⓓ
72.	405 SE Griffin Way	405 SW Griffin Way	72	Ⓐ Ⓓ	72	Ⓐ Ⓓ
73.	4054 Crossroad Pky	4054 Crossroad Pky	73	Ⓐ Ⓓ	73	Ⓐ Ⓓ
74.	4976 Kempner Dr	4976 Kempner Sq	74	Ⓐ Ⓓ	74	Ⓐ Ⓓ
75.	9451 Stephenway Hwy	9451 Stephenway Pky	75	Ⓐ Ⓓ	75	Ⓐ Ⓓ
76.	8830 Runyon Way	8830 Runyon Way	76	Ⓐ Ⓓ	76	Ⓐ Ⓓ
77.	7740 Sedgewick St	7740 Sedgewick St	77	Ⓐ Ⓓ	77	Ⓐ Ⓓ
78.	8847 Upper Loop Dr	8347 Upper Loop Dr	78	Ⓐ Ⓓ	78	Ⓐ Ⓓ
79.	3754 Westchester Rd	3754 Westchester Rd	79	Ⓐ Ⓓ	79	Ⓐ Ⓓ
80.	9973 Bisbee Creek	9973 Bisbeek Creek	80	Ⓐ Ⓓ	80	Ⓐ Ⓓ
81.	4956 Kneeland Way S	4956 Kneeland Way S	81	Ⓐ Ⓓ	81	Ⓐ Ⓓ
82.	6947 LeRoy Rdg	6947 LeRoy Brdg	82	Ⓐ Ⓓ	82	Ⓐ Ⓓ
83.	4954 Honeybee Cir	4954 Honebee Cir	83	Ⓐ Ⓓ	83	Ⓐ Ⓓ
84.	7745 Kneeland Ct	7745 Kneeland Ct	84	Ⓐ Ⓓ	84	Ⓐ Ⓓ
85.	3354 Upperhill Way	3354 Uppperhill Hwy	85	Ⓐ Ⓓ	85	Ⓐ Ⓓ
86.	46549 Moseman Rd	46549 Moseman Rd	86	Ⓐ Ⓓ	86	Ⓐ Ⓓ
87.	449 17th Ave SW	449 17th Ave SE	87	Ⓐ Ⓓ	87	Ⓐ Ⓓ
88.	5478 Curtis Way	5478 Curtis Way	88	Ⓐ Ⓓ	88	Ⓐ Ⓓ
89.	54854 Gedney Rd	54854 Gedney Rd	89	Ⓐ Ⓓ	89	Ⓐ Ⓓ

Go on to the next number on the next page.

90. 68893 Hudson Bay	68893 Hudson Bay	90 Ⓐ Ⓓ	90 Ⓐ Ⓓ
91. 44054 Palmer Rd	44054 Palmer Rd	91 Ⓐ Ⓓ	91 Ⓐ Ⓓ
92. 9943 Evangeline Sq	9943 Evangeline Sq	92 Ⓐ Ⓓ	92 Ⓐ Ⓓ
93. 4467 Lorezo Rd	4467 Lorenzo Rd	93 Ⓐ Ⓓ	93 Ⓐ Ⓓ
94. 9947 Robbin W	9847 Robbin W	94 Ⓐ Ⓓ	94 Ⓐ Ⓓ
95. 4471 S Lawton Sq	4471 N Lawton Sq	95 Ⓐ Ⓓ	95 Ⓐ Ⓓ

If you finish before the time is up, check your answers for Part A.

STOP

If you finish before the time is up, check your answers for Part A.

Do not go to any other part.

(See the correct answers on the next page.)

Correct Answers

Address-Checking Test

1. A	25. A	49. A	73. A
2. D	26. D	50. A	74. D
3. D	27. D	51. D	75. D
4. D	28. A	52. D	76. A
5. A	29. D	53. A	77. A
6. A	30. D	54. D	78. D
7. A	31. A	55. A	79. A
8. D	32. A	56. A	80. D
9. A	33. D	57. D	81. A
10. A	34. A	58. A	82. D
11. D	35. D	59. A	83. D
12. D	36. D	60. A	84. A
13. A	37. A	61. D	85. D
14. D	38. D	62. A	86. A
15. D	39. D	63. D	87. D
16. A	40. D	64. A	88. A
17. D	41. A	65. A	89. A
18. A	42. A	66. D	90. A
19. A	43. A	67. D	91. A
20. D	44. A	68. A	92. A
21. A	45. D	69. A	93. D
22. A	46. D	70. D	94. D
23. D	47. A	71. D	95. D
24. D	48. A	72. D	

Address-Checking Practice Test
Work—6 Minutes

These addresses are like the ones in the address-checking test.

Decide whether the two addresses are *Alike* or *Different.* If they are *Alike,* darken or mark space A; if they are *Different,* darken space D. Mark the answers on the answer sheet to the right. Work as fast as you can without making too many errors. Work exactly 6 minutes.

ANSWER SHEET

			Test A	Test B
1.	405 Winter Rd NW	405 Winter Rd NW	1 Ⓐ Ⓓ	1 Ⓐ Ⓓ
2.	607 S Calaveras Rd	607 S Calaveras Rd	2 Ⓐ Ⓓ	2 Ⓐ Ⓓ
3.	8406 La Casa St	8406 La Cosa St	3 Ⓐ Ⓓ	3 Ⓐ Ⓓ
4.	121 N Rippon St	121 N Rippon St	4 Ⓐ Ⓓ	4 Ⓐ Ⓓ
5.	Wideman Ark	Wiseman Ark	5 Ⓐ Ⓓ	5 Ⓐ Ⓓ
6.	Sodus NY 14551	Sodus NY 14551	6 Ⓐ Ⓓ	6 Ⓐ Ⓓ
7.	3429 Hermosa Dr	3429 Hermoso Dr	7 Ⓐ Ⓓ	7 Ⓐ Ⓓ
8.	3628 S Zeeland St	3268 S Zealand St	8 Ⓐ Ⓓ	8 Ⓐ Ⓓ
9.	1330 Cheverly Ave NE	1330 Cheverly Ave NE	9 Ⓐ Ⓓ	9 Ⓐ Ⓓ
10.	1689 N Derwood Dr	1689 N Derwood Dr	10 Ⓐ Ⓓ	10 Ⓐ Ⓓ
11.	3886 Sunrise Ct	3886 Sunrise Ct	11 Ⓐ Ⓓ	11 Ⓐ Ⓓ
12.	635 La Calle Mayor	653 La Calle Mayor	12 Ⓐ Ⓓ	12 Ⓐ Ⓓ
13.	2560 Lansford Pl	2560 Lansford St	13 Ⓐ Ⓓ	13 Ⓐ Ⓓ
14.	4631 Central Ave	4631 Central Ave	14 Ⓐ Ⓓ	14 Ⓐ Ⓓ
15.	Mason City Iowa 50401	Mason City Iowa 50401	15 Ⓐ Ⓓ	15 Ⓐ Ⓓ
16.	758 Los Arboles Ave SE	758 Los Arboles Ave SW	16 Ⓐ Ⓓ	16 Ⓐ Ⓓ
17.	3282 E Downington St	3282 E Dunnington St	17 Ⓐ Ⓓ	17 Ⓐ Ⓓ
18.	7117 N Burlingham Ave	7117 N Burlingham Ave	18 Ⓐ Ⓓ	18 Ⓐ Ⓓ
19.	32 Oaklawn Blvd	32 Oakland Blvd	19 Ⓐ Ⓓ	19 Ⓐ Ⓓ
20.	1274 Manzana Rd	1274 Manzana Rd	20 Ⓐ Ⓓ	20 Ⓐ Ⓓ
21.	4598 E Kenilworth Dr	4598 E Kenilworth Dr	21 Ⓐ Ⓓ	21 Ⓐ Ⓓ
22.	Dayton Okla 73449	Dagton Okla 73449	22 Ⓐ Ⓓ	22 Ⓐ Ⓓ
23.	1172 W 83rd Ave	1127 W 83rd Ave	23 Ⓐ Ⓓ	23 Ⓐ Ⓓ
24.	6434 E Pulaski St	6434 E Pulaski Ct	24 Ⓐ Ⓓ	24 Ⓐ Ⓓ
25.	2764 N Rutherford Pl	2764 N Rutherford Pl	25 Ⓐ Ⓓ	25 Ⓐ Ⓓ
26.	565 Greenville Blvd SE	565 Greenview Blvd SE	26 Ⓐ Ⓓ	26 Ⓐ Ⓓ
27.	Washington DC 20013	Washington DC 20018	27 Ⓐ Ⓓ	27 Ⓐ Ⓓ
28.	3824 Massasoit St	3824 Massasoit St	28 Ⓐ Ⓓ	28 Ⓐ Ⓓ
29.	22 Sagnaw Pkwy	22 Saganaw Pkwy	29 Ⓐ Ⓓ	29 Ⓐ Ⓓ
30.	Byram Conn 10573	Byram Conn 10573	30 Ⓐ Ⓓ	30 Ⓐ Ⓓ
31.	1928 S Fairfield Ave	1928 S Fairfield St	31 Ⓐ Ⓓ	31 Ⓐ Ⓓ
32.	36218 Overhills Dr	36218 Overhills Dr	32 Ⓐ Ⓓ	32 Ⓐ Ⓓ
33.	516 Avenida de Las Am	516 Avenida de Las Am	33 Ⓐ Ⓓ	33 Ⓐ Ⓓ
34.	7526 Naraganset Pl SW	7526 Naraganset Pl SW	34 Ⓐ Ⓓ	34 Ⓐ Ⓓ
35.	52626 W Ogelsby Dr	52626 W Ogelsby Dr	35 Ⓐ Ⓓ	35 Ⓐ Ⓓ
36.	1003 Winchester Rd	1003 Westchester RD	36 Ⓐ Ⓓ	36 Ⓐ Ⓓ
37.	3478 W Cavanaugh Ct	3478 W Cavenaugh Ct	37 Ⓐ Ⓓ	37 Ⓐ Ⓓ
38.	Kendall Calif 90551	Kendell Calif 90551	38 Ⓐ Ⓓ	38 Ⓐ Ⓓ
39.	225 El Camino Blvd	225 El Camino Ave	39 Ⓐ Ⓓ	39 Ⓐ Ⓓ
40.	7310 Via delos Pisos	7310 Via de los Pinos	40 Ⓐ Ⓓ	40 Ⓐ Ⓓ

Go on to the next number on the next page.

41.	1987 Wellington Ave SW	1987 Wellington Ave SW	41 Ⓐ Ⓓ	41 Ⓐ Ⓓ
42.	3124 S 71st St	3142 S 71st St	42 Ⓐ Ⓓ	42 Ⓐ Ⓓ
43.	729 Lincolnwood Blvd	729 Lincolnwood Blvd	43 Ⓐ Ⓓ	43 Ⓐ Ⓓ
44.	1166 N Beaumont Dr	1166 S Beaumont Dr	44 Ⓐ Ⓓ	44 Ⓐ Ⓓ
45.	3224 W Winecona Pl	3224 W Winecona Pl	45 Ⓐ Ⓓ	45 Ⓐ Ⓓ
46.	608 Calle Bienvenida	607 Calle Bienvenida	46 Ⓐ Ⓓ	46 Ⓐ Ⓓ
47.	La Molte Iowa 52045	La Molte Iowa 52045	47 Ⓐ Ⓓ	47 Ⓐ Ⓓ
48.	8625 Armitage Ave NW	8625 Armitage Ave NW	48 Ⓐ Ⓓ	48 Ⓐ Ⓓ
49.	2343 Broadview Ave	2334 Broadview Ave	49 Ⓐ Ⓓ	49 Ⓐ Ⓓ
50.	4279 Sierra Grande Ave	4279 Sierra Grande Dr	50 Ⓐ Ⓓ	50 Ⓐ Ⓓ
51.	165 32nd Ave	165 32nd Ave	51 Ⓐ Ⓓ	51 Ⓐ Ⓓ
52.	12742 N Deerborn St	12724 N Deerborn St	52 Ⓐ Ⓓ	52 Ⓐ Ⓓ
53.	114 Estancia Ave	141 Estancia Ave	53 Ⓐ Ⓓ	53 Ⓐ Ⓓ
54.	351 S Berwyn Rd	351 S Berwyn Pl	54 Ⓐ Ⓓ	54 Ⓐ Ⓓ
55.	7732 Avenida Manana SW	7732 Avenida Manana SW	55 Ⓐ Ⓓ	55 Ⓐ Ⓓ
56.	6337 C St SW	6337 G St SW	56 Ⓐ Ⓓ	56 Ⓐ Ⓓ
57.	57895 E Drexyl Ave	58795 E Drexyl Ave	57 Ⓐ Ⓓ	57 Ⓐ Ⓓ
58.	Altro Tex 75923	Altra Tex 75923	58 Ⓐ Ⓓ	58 Ⓐ Ⓓ
59.	3465 S Nashville St	3465 N Nashville St	59 Ⓐ Ⓓ	59 Ⓐ Ⓓ
60.	1226 Odell Blvd NW	1226 Oddell Blvd NW	60 Ⓐ Ⓓ	60 Ⓐ Ⓓ
61.	94002 Chappel Ct	94002 Chappel Ct	61 Ⓐ Ⓓ	61 Ⓐ Ⓓ
62.	512 La Vega Dr	512 La Veta Dr	62 Ⓐ Ⓓ	62 Ⓐ Ⓓ
63.	8774 W Winona Pl	8774 R Winona	63 Ⓐ Ⓓ	63 Ⓐ Ⓓ
64.	6431 Ingleside St SE	6431 Ingleside St SE	64 Ⓐ Ⓓ	64 Ⓐ Ⓓ
65.	2270 N Leanington St	2270 N Leanington St	65 Ⓐ Ⓓ	65 Ⓐ Ⓓ
66.	235 Calle de Vecinos	235 Calle de Vecinos	66 Ⓐ Ⓓ	66 Ⓐ Ⓓ
67.	3987 E Westwood Ave	3987 W Westwood Ave	67 Ⓐ Ⓓ	67 Ⓐ Ⓓ
68.	Skamokawa Wash	Skamohawa Wash	68 Ⓐ Ⓓ	68 Ⓐ Ⓓ
69.	2674 E Champlain Cir	2764 E Champlain Cir	69 Ⓐ Ⓓ	69 Ⓐ Ⓓ
70.	8751 Elmhurst Blvd	8751 Elmwood Blvd	70 Ⓐ Ⓓ	70 Ⓐ Ⓓ
71.	6649 Solano Dr	6649 Solana Dr	71 Ⓐ Ⓓ	71 Ⓐ Ⓓ
72.	4423 S Escenaba St	4423 S Escenaba St	72 Ⓐ Ⓓ	72 Ⓐ Ⓓ
73.	1198 N St NW	1198 M St NW	73 Ⓐ Ⓓ	73 Ⓐ Ⓓ
74.	Sparta GA	Sparta Va	74 Ⓐ Ⓓ	74 Ⓐ Ⓓ
75.	96753 Wrightwood Ave	96753 Wrightwood Ave	75 Ⓐ Ⓓ	75 Ⓐ Ⓓ
76.	2445 Sangamow Ave SE	2445 Sangamow Ave SE	76 Ⓐ Ⓓ	76 Ⓐ Ⓓ
77.	5117 E 67 Pl	5171 E 67 Pl	77 Ⓐ Ⓓ	77 Ⓐ Ⓓ
78.	847 Mesa Grande Pl	847 Mesa Grande Ct	78 Ⓐ Ⓓ	78 Ⓐ Ⓓ
79.	1100 Cermaken St	1100 Cermaker St	79 Ⓐ Ⓓ	79 Ⓐ Ⓓ
80.	321 Tijeras Ave NW	321 Tijeras Ave NW	80 Ⓐ Ⓓ	80 Ⓐ Ⓓ
81.	3405 Prospect St	3405 Prospect St	81 Ⓐ Ⓓ	81 Ⓐ Ⓓ
82.	6643 Burlington Pl	6643 Burlingtown Pl	82 Ⓐ Ⓓ	82 Ⓐ Ⓓ
83.	851 Esperanza Blvd	851 Esperanza Blvd	83 Ⓐ Ⓓ	83 Ⓐ Ⓓ
84.	Jenkinjones W Va	Jenkinjones W Va	84 Ⓐ Ⓓ	84 Ⓐ Ⓓ
85.	1006 Pennsylvania Ave	1008 Pennsylvania Ave	85 Ⓐ Ⓓ	85 Ⓐ Ⓓ
86.	2924 26th St N	2929 26th St N	86 Ⓐ Ⓓ	86 Ⓐ Ⓓ
87.	7115 Highland Dr	7115 Highland Dr	87 Ⓐ Ⓓ	87 Ⓐ Ⓓ
88.	Chaptico MD	Chaptica MD	88 Ⓐ Ⓓ	88 Ⓐ Ⓓ
89.	3508 Camron Mills Rd	3508 Camron Mills Rd	89 Ⓐ Ⓓ	89 Ⓐ Ⓓ

Go on to the next number on the next page.

90.	67158 Capston Dr	67158 Capston Dr	90 Ⓐ Ⓓ	90 Ⓐ Ⓓ
91.	3613 S Taylor Ave	3631 S Taylor Ave	91 Ⓐ Ⓓ	91 Ⓐ Ⓓ
92.	2421 Menokin Dr	2421 Menokin Dr	92 Ⓐ Ⓓ	92 Ⓐ Ⓓ
93.	3226 M St NW	3226 N St NW	93 Ⓐ Ⓓ	93 Ⓐ Ⓓ
94.	1201 S Court House Rd	1201 S Court House Rd	94 Ⓐ Ⓓ	94 Ⓐ Ⓓ
95.	Findlay Ohio 45840	Findley Ohio 45840	95 Ⓐ Ⓓ	95 Ⓐ Ⓓ

STOP
If you finish before the time is up, check your answers for Part A.
Do not go to any other part.

(See the correct answers on the next page.)

Correct Answers

Address-Checking Test

1. A	25. A	49. D	73. D
2. A	26. D	50. D	74. D
3. D	27. D	51. A	75. A
4. A	28. A	52. D	76. A
5. D	29. D	53. D	77. D
6. A	30. A	54. D	78. D
7. D	31. D	55. A	79. D
8. D	32. A	56. D	80. A
9. A	33. A	57. D	81. A
10. A	34. A	58. D	82. D
11. A	35. A	59. D	83. A
12. D	36. D	60. D	84. A
13. D	37. D	61. A	85. D
14. A	38. D	62. D	86. D
15. A	39. D	63. D	87. A
16. D	40. D	64. A	88. D
17. D	41. A	65. A	89. A
18. A	42. D	66. A	90. A
19. D	43. A	67. D	91. D
20. A	44. D	68. D	92. A
21. A	45. A	69. D	93. D
22. D	46. D	70. D	94. A
23. D	47. A	71. D	95. D
24. D	48. A	72. A	

Memory-for-Address Test

Tips, Strategies & Practice Tests

The *Memory-for-Address Test* forms Part B of the **460 Battery Test.** In this part of the test, you must memorize the locations (A, B, C, D, or E) of 25 addresses shown in 5 boxes. You'll be sent a sample test when you file an application for examinations. But the addresses in the actual test will be different from your sample test.

In determining in which box each address is located, you must memorize every address in the 5 boxes. The location of the addresses is easy to memorize if you use some strategies. Based on my experience in postal test taking, I have developed the following strategies for memory-for-address test:

■ **Shortcut:** Just remember the *first two numbers* in each address in a box and the *first syllable* of each name in the same box. For examples, Hubert and Lester are *Hu-Les* when combined. In answering, read only the first two numbers of each address and the first syllable of the name of street, and answer the question by marking the correct circle. Proceed immediately to the next number: You don't have to use a bookmark or any guide in your nonwriting hand. Just point the index finger of that hand to the name or address you are working on. Immediately place the tip of your pencil in your writing hand on the next line on the answer sheet, as you move your nonwriting hand's index finger downward.

■ **Caution:** Once in every five or six numbers, before you mark the circle, be sure that the *circle* corresponds to the proper *line*. That is, the circle belonging to item number 9, for instance, should answer question number 9. Sometimes when you're in a hurry, you may mark circles that do not correspond to the questions you're answering. That happened to me once.

■ **Be in a hurry:** Skip the questions you don't know. Go back to them, however, if you finish working on the test early.

■ **Memorization:** Don't try to write down addresses or notes on your palm. You'll have no time to do that. You can try to remember only the *first digit* of each address, but the trouble is that sometimes the first digits are the same. It's better to remember *two* numbers.

■ **Side by side:** Don't place the question sheet and the answer sheet far from each other or far from your body. Your eyes must not travel long distances. If you don't follow this advice, it's like traveling to Africa instead of to California!

Memory-for-Address Test

In the example below, there are various techniques for memorizing the names and addresses in five minutes.

A	B	C	D	E
1700-2599 Wood Dushore 8500-8699 Lang Lott 6200-6399 James	2700-3299 Wood Jeriel 8700-9399 Lang Vanna 5700-6199 James	1300-1699 Wood Levering 9400-9499 Lang Ekron 6400-6499 James	3300-3599 Wood Bair 8000-8499 Lang Viborg 5000-5699 James	2600-2699 Wood Danby 9500-9999 Lang Lycan 4700-4999 James

The best thing to do is to remember only *two* numbers, the *first two* digits of the addresses. Combine the *first* syllables of the two names in each box, to make it only one name; example, *DusLot (Dus*hore and *Lott.)*

For Box A	Box B	Box C	Box D	Box E
17	27	13	33	26
85	87	94	80	95
62	57	64	50	47

To remember the names:

Box A	Box B	Box C	Box D	Box E
Dus Lot	Je Va	LeEk	BaVi	DanLy

Decide which is the best way for you to memorize the numbers above: from **top** to **bottom** or from **left to right.**

One way is from **top** to **botttom,** by boxes.

A	B	C	D	E
17 ⬇	27 ⬇	13 ⬇	33 ⬇	26 ⬇
85 ⬇	87 ⬇	94 ⬇	80 ⬇	95 ⬇
62 ⬇	57 ⬇	64 ⬇	50 ⬇	47 ⬇
DusLot ▸	JeVa ▸	LeEk ▸	BaVi ▸	DanLy ▸

Memorize the combined names from **left to right.**

Another way is to memorize *A* and *B* **vertically** and *C, D,* and *E* **horizontally.**

A	B	C	D	E
17 ⬇	27 ⬇	13 ▸	33 ▸	26
85 ⬇	87 ⬇	94 ▸	80 ▸	95
62 ⬇	57 ⬇	64 ▸	50 ▸	47
DusLot ▸	JeVa ▸	LeEk ▸	BaVi ▸	DanLy

Important! Important! Important!

Lately, the U.S. Postal Service has been including two or three "same numbers" in the addresses in the five boxes (Memory-for-Address test).

This creates confusion. (You cannot just remember the *first two numbers*. You must remember the *first two numbers*, along with the name of the *street*.

Part B: Memory for Addresses

In this part of the test, you will have to memorize the locations (A, B, C, D, or E) of 25 addresses shown in five boxes, like those below. For example, "Sardis" is in Box C, "6800-6999 Table" is in Box B, etc. (The addresses in the actual test will be different.)

A	B	C	D	E
4700-5599 Table	6800-6999 Table	5600-6499 Table	6500-6799 Table	4400-4699 Table
Lismore	Kelford	Joel	Tatum	Ruskin
5600-6499 West	6500-6799 West	6800-6999 West	4400-4699 West	4700-5599 West
Hesper	Musella	Sardis	Porter	Nathan
4400-4699 Blake	5600-6499 Blake	6500-6799 Blake	4700-5599 Blake	6800-6999 Blake

If you examine the boxes above, you'll see the identical numbers:

1. Three 4700-5599s:
4700-5599 Table (Box A), 4700-5599 Blake (Box D), and 4700-5599 Table (Box E);

2. Three 5600-6499s:
5600-6499 West (A), 5600-6499 Blake (B), and 5600-6499 Table (C);

3. Three 4400-4699s:
4400-4699 Blake (A), 4400-4699 West (D), 4400-4699 Table (E);

4. Three 6800-6999s:
6800-6999 Table (B), 6800-6999 West (C), and 6800-6999 Blake (E).

5. And *three* 6500-6799s:
6500-6799 West (B), 6500-6799 Blake (C) and 6500-6799 Table (D).

Instruction: To avoid confusion and to remember to which box the numbers belong, remember the *first two numbers* along with the name of the *streets*:

Example: 47 Table (Box A); 47 Blake (Box D) and 47 West (Box E).

For Box A, for instance, you may remember the numbers and names of streets as follows (Box A):

A	B	C	D	E
47 Table	68 Table	56 Table	65 Table	44 Table
56 West	65 West	68 West	44 West	47 West
44 Blake	56 Blake	65 Blake	47 Blake	68 Blake
LisHe	KelMu	JoSar	TaPor	RusNa

LisHe (Combination of the first syllables of Lismore and Hesper.)
You may memorize the *first two numbers* vertically; for example, 47, 56, 44. Then remember that in every box the *first street* is **Table**; the *second*, **West**, and the *third*, **Blake.** Or you may find your own way of memorizing them.

How to Remember
Names and Numbers

In memorizing numbers or names, associate them with numbers or names familiar to you, so that you can retrieve them instantly from your mind. Visualize! A thing visualized is not usually forgotten. That is, create key words or extraction codes. In entering information into a computer, you need to have a *code* so that you can retrieve the information. Without it, you cannot retrieve the facts and figures you stored on the disk. Your brain, which is your own computer, operates in the same way.

Use Your Imagination

To memorize Box A, for example, I'll remember *17* as the age of a beautiful teenaged girl living in the neighborhood; I'll remember *85* (1985) as the year I invaded Grenada; and *62* (1962) as the year my wife and I promised to each other *"to love and cherish, for better or worse, till death do us part."* I'll remember *Dus-Lot* by visualizing that I'll go to the *lot* which is full of *dust* to play games.

Since you have to memorize the names and addresses in five boxes in five minutes, you'll have to memorize each box in sixty seconds. Actually, you'll do the memorization in eight minutes, including the three minutes for the practice test. But don't rely on that. Count on only five minutes. I have done it and many of my students have done it. If the computer can do it, your brain can do it, too!

In your case, think of years or numbers that you can associate with the numbers in Box A. For example, your youngest brother or sister may be *17* years old (or make him or her 17), you visited Beirut in year *85 (1985),* and for *62,* you may remember that the Texas Rangers won the World Series in 1962. You may remember *Dus-Lot* by recalling the name *Dusty* Baker, who has a *lot* of chewing gum in his mouth. Or you may recall names of your friends which sound like *Dus* or *Lot.*

Associate Numbers
with Things or Events

You can think of many things. Associate numbers with age, weight, height, numbers of floors in buildings, dates, or events. Associate names with well-known personalities: actors, actresses, politicians, athletes, and others.

When you see the number, you can associate it easily with things familiar to you. Associate it with the first thing that comes into your mind. Different people will usually have different key numbers or key words.

In a nutshell, you'll have to remember only the first two numbers of addresses and the first syllables of two names. Forget about the street names, such as Wood or Lang. *Combine two names* into *one* and kill two birds with one stone. Imagine too that you're writing numbers and names on an invisible computer screen!

Combine Two Names Into One.

Memory-for-Address Test

Work—3 Minutes

Answer each question on a piece of paper to show the letter of the box in which the address belongs.
Try to remember the location of as many addresses as you can. If you are not sure of an address, guess.
Work only three minutes.

A	B	C	D	E
1800-2499 Wood Lott 7500-8799 Lang Dushore 6400-6599 James	2200-3199 Wood Vanna 8600-9299 Lang Jeriel 5400-6299 James	1200-1599 Wood Ekron 7400-9399 Lang Levering 6100-6499 James	3100-3699 Wood Viborg 8000-8299 Lang Valley 5500-5899 James	2700-2799 Wood Lycan 5600-9999 Lang Danby 4500-4699 James

1. 1800-2499 Wood
2. 2700-2799 Wood
3. Danby
4. 8600-9299 Lang
5. Lott
6. 6400-6599 James
7. Vanna
8. 6100-6499James
9. 8000-8299 Lang
10. Levering
11. 5600-9999 Lang
12. 8600-9299 Lang
13. Lott
14. 4500-4699 James
15. Ekron
16. 5500-5899 James
17. Jeriel
18. Dushore
19. 6400-6599 James
20. Viborg
21. 7500-8799 Lang
22. Danby
23. 4500-4699 James
24. 5500-5899 James

25. 2200-3199 Wood
26. Viborg
27. 7500-8799 Lang
28. Lycan
29. 5600-9999 Lang
30. 2200-3199 Wood
31. Levering
32. 2700-2799 Wood
33. 5500-5899 James
34. Vanna
35. 4500-4699 James
36. Dushore
37. 7500-8799 Lang
38. 6400-6599 James
39. 2700-2799 Wood
40. Valley
41. 8600-9299 Lang
42. Lycan
43. Vanna
44. 8000-8299 Lang
45. 2700-2799 Wood
46. Valley
47. Dushore
48. 7500-8799 Lang

49. Levering
50. 6400-6599 James
51. 5600-9999 Lang
52. 4500-4699 James
53. Jeriel
54. 7400-9399 Lang
55. Dushore
56. 3100-3699 Wood
57. 2200-3199 Wood
58. Valley
59. 6400-6599 James
60. Danby
61. 7400-9399 Lang
62. 5500-5899 James
63. Jeriel
64. 2200-3199 Wood
65. Viborg
66. 8000-8299 Lang
67. Ekron
68. 5400-6299 James
69. 5600-9999 Lang
70. 6400-6599 James
71. 2700-2799 Wood
72. Valley

73. Lott
74. Danby
75. 1800-2499 Wood
76. 8600-9299 Lang
77. 6100-6499 James
78. Lycan
79. 5400-6299 James
80. 6100-6499 James
81. Vanna
82. 7400-9399 Lang
83. 3100-3699 Wood
84. 4500-4699 James
85. 2200-3199 Wood
86. 6400-6599 james
87. Ekron
88. 8600-9299 Lang

STOP

When the time is up, go on to the next page for the correct answers.

(**Author's Note:** The sample test above is known as the memory-for-address test in the 470 Battery Test and the 460 Rural Carrier Associate Exam. This Part B is considered as a practice test. You'll be allowed to look at the names and addresses in the boxes, as you are instructed to answer as many questions as possible in three minutes. In the next part, however, you will be asked to answer all the 88 questions in five minutes and you won't be allowed to look at the names and addresses. During the three-minute practice test, answer only a few questions. Spend most of the three minutes in memorizing the placement of numbers and names (just the first two numbers of each address and the first syllables of names, combining two syllables into one. Now, answer a few questions and memorize the names and addresses in preparation for the next part. (**See Memory-for-Address Test: Tips & Strategies, page 243.**)

Correct Answers

Memory-for-Address Test

1. A	31. C	61. C
2. E	32. E	62. D
3. E	33. D	63. B
4. B	34. B	64. B
5. A	35. E	65. D
6. A	36. A	66. D
7. B	37. A	67. C
8. C	38. A	68. B
9. D	39. E	69. E
10. C	40. D	70. A
11. E	41. B	71. E
12. B	42. E	72. D
13. A	43. B	73. A
14. E	44. D	74. E
15. C	45. E	75. A
16. D	46. D	76. B
17. B	47. A	77. C
18. A	48. A	78. E
19. A	49. C	79. B
20. D	50. A	80. C
21. A	51. E	81. B
22. E	52. E	82. C
23. E	53. B	83. D
24. D	54. C	84. E
25. B	55. A	85. B
26. D	56. D	86. A
27. A	57. B	87. C
28. E	58. D	88. B
29. E	59. A	
30. B	60. E	

Memory-for-Address Test

Work—5 Minutes

This is the section that counts.

Decide in which box each name or address belongs. Don't look back at the boxes with the addresses in them. Work 5 minutes. For each question, mark the answers on the answer sheet to the right.

ANSWER SHEET

	Test A	Test B
1. Ekron	1 Ⓐ Ⓑ Ⓒ Ⓓ Ⓔ	1 Ⓐ Ⓑ Ⓒ Ⓓ Ⓔ
2. 4500-4699 James	2 Ⓐ Ⓑ Ⓒ Ⓓ Ⓔ	2 Ⓐ Ⓑ Ⓒ Ⓓ Ⓔ
3. 1800-2499 Wood	3 Ⓐ Ⓑ Ⓒ Ⓓ Ⓔ	3 Ⓐ Ⓑ Ⓒ Ⓓ Ⓔ
4. Dushore	4 Ⓐ Ⓑ Ⓒ Ⓓ Ⓔ	4 Ⓐ Ⓑ Ⓒ Ⓓ Ⓔ
5. 8600-9299 Lang	5 Ⓐ Ⓑ Ⓒ Ⓓ Ⓔ	5 Ⓐ Ⓑ Ⓒ Ⓓ Ⓔ
6. 5400-5899 James	6 Ⓐ Ⓑ Ⓒ Ⓓ Ⓔ	6 Ⓐ Ⓑ Ⓒ Ⓓ Ⓔ
7. Levering	7 Ⓐ Ⓑ Ⓒ Ⓓ Ⓔ	7 Ⓐ Ⓑ Ⓒ Ⓓ Ⓔ
8. 6400-6599 James	8 Ⓐ Ⓑ Ⓒ Ⓓ Ⓔ	8 Ⓐ Ⓑ Ⓒ Ⓓ Ⓔ
9. Viborg	9 Ⓐ Ⓑ Ⓒ Ⓓ Ⓔ	9 Ⓐ Ⓑ Ⓒ Ⓓ Ⓔ
10. 2200-3199 Wood	10 Ⓐ Ⓑ Ⓒ Ⓓ Ⓔ	10 Ⓐ Ⓑ Ⓒ Ⓓ Ⓔ
11. 5400-6299 James	11 Ⓐ Ⓑ Ⓒ Ⓓ Ⓔ	11 Ⓐ Ⓑ Ⓒ Ⓓ Ⓔ
12. Lycan	12 Ⓐ Ⓑ Ⓒ Ⓓ Ⓔ	12 Ⓐ Ⓑ Ⓒ Ⓓ Ⓔ
13. 6400-6599 James	13 Ⓐ Ⓑ Ⓒ Ⓓ Ⓔ	13 Ⓐ Ⓑ Ⓒ Ⓓ Ⓔ
14. 8000-8299 Lang	14 Ⓐ Ⓑ Ⓒ Ⓓ Ⓔ	14 Ⓐ Ⓑ Ⓒ Ⓓ Ⓔ
15. 8600-9299 Lang	15 Ⓐ Ⓑ Ⓒ Ⓓ Ⓔ	15 Ⓐ Ⓑ Ⓒ Ⓓ Ⓔ
16. Dushore	16 Ⓐ Ⓑ Ⓒ Ⓓ Ⓔ	16 Ⓐ Ⓑ Ⓒ Ⓓ Ⓔ
17. 1200-1599 Wood	17 Ⓐ Ⓑ Ⓒ Ⓓ Ⓔ	17 Ⓐ Ⓑ Ⓒ Ⓓ Ⓔ
18. Levering	18 Ⓐ Ⓑ Ⓒ Ⓓ Ⓔ	18 Ⓐ Ⓑ Ⓒ Ⓓ Ⓔ
19. 8600-9299 Lang	19 Ⓐ Ⓑ Ⓒ Ⓓ Ⓔ	19 Ⓐ Ⓑ Ⓒ Ⓓ Ⓔ
20. 1200-1599 Wood	20 Ⓐ Ⓑ Ⓒ Ⓓ Ⓔ	20 Ⓐ Ⓑ Ⓒ Ⓓ Ⓔ
21. Danby	21 Ⓐ Ⓑ Ⓒ Ⓓ Ⓔ	21 Ⓐ Ⓑ Ⓒ Ⓓ Ⓔ
22. 2700-2799 Wood	22 Ⓐ Ⓑ Ⓒ Ⓓ Ⓔ	22 Ⓐ Ⓑ Ⓒ Ⓓ Ⓔ
23. Vanna	23 Ⓐ Ⓑ Ⓒ Ⓓ Ⓔ	23 Ⓐ Ⓑ Ⓒ Ⓓ Ⓔ
24. 6400-6599 James	24 Ⓐ Ⓑ Ⓒ Ⓓ Ⓔ	24 Ⓐ Ⓑ Ⓒ Ⓓ Ⓔ
25. Levering	25 Ⓐ Ⓑ Ⓒ Ⓓ Ⓔ	25 Ⓐ Ⓑ Ⓒ Ⓓ Ⓔ
26. 3100-3699 Wood	26 Ⓐ Ⓑ Ⓒ Ⓓ Ⓔ	26 Ⓐ Ⓑ Ⓒ Ⓓ Ⓔ
27. Lott	27 Ⓐ Ⓑ Ⓒ Ⓓ Ⓔ	27 Ⓐ Ⓑ Ⓒ Ⓓ Ⓔ
28. 1800-2499 Wood	28 Ⓐ Ⓑ Ⓒ Ⓓ Ⓔ	28 Ⓐ Ⓑ Ⓒ Ⓓ Ⓔ
29. 7400-9399 Lang	29 Ⓐ Ⓑ Ⓒ Ⓓ Ⓔ	29 Ⓐ Ⓑ Ⓒ Ⓓ Ⓔ
30. Jeriel	30 Ⓐ Ⓑ Ⓒ Ⓓ Ⓔ	30 Ⓐ Ⓑ Ⓒ Ⓓ Ⓔ
31. 5400-6299 James	31 Ⓐ Ⓑ Ⓒ Ⓓ Ⓔ	31 Ⓐ Ⓑ Ⓒ Ⓓ Ⓔ
32. 4500-4699 James	32 Ⓐ Ⓑ Ⓒ Ⓓ Ⓔ	32 Ⓐ Ⓑ Ⓒ Ⓓ Ⓔ
33. 5600-9999 Lang	33 Ⓐ Ⓑ Ⓒ Ⓓ Ⓔ	33 Ⓐ Ⓑ Ⓒ Ⓓ Ⓔ
34. 7400-9399 Lang	34 Ⓐ Ⓑ Ⓒ Ⓓ Ⓔ	34 Ⓐ Ⓑ Ⓒ Ⓓ Ⓔ
35. 8600-9299 Lang	35 Ⓐ Ⓑ Ⓒ Ⓓ Ⓔ	35 Ⓐ Ⓑ Ⓒ Ⓓ Ⓔ
36. Viborg	36 Ⓐ Ⓑ Ⓒ Ⓓ Ⓔ	36 Ⓐ Ⓑ Ⓒ Ⓓ Ⓔ
37. 5600-9999 Lang	37 Ⓐ Ⓑ Ⓒ Ⓓ Ⓔ	37 Ⓐ Ⓑ Ⓒ Ⓓ Ⓔ
38. Jeriel	38 Ⓐ Ⓑ Ⓒ Ⓓ Ⓔ	38 Ⓐ Ⓑ Ⓒ Ⓓ Ⓔ
39. 1800-2499 Wood	39 Ⓐ Ⓑ Ⓒ Ⓓ Ⓔ	39 Ⓐ Ⓑ Ⓒ Ⓓ Ⓔ
40. 8000-8299 Lang	40 Ⓐ Ⓑ Ⓒ Ⓓ Ⓔ	40 Ⓐ Ⓑ Ⓒ Ⓓ Ⓔ

Go on to the next number on the next page.

41. Danby	41 Ⓐ Ⓑ Ⓒ Ⓓ Ⓔ	41 Ⓐ Ⓑ Ⓒ Ⓓ Ⓔ
42. 5400-6299 James	42 Ⓐ Ⓑ Ⓒ Ⓓ Ⓔ	42 Ⓐ Ⓑ Ⓒ Ⓓ Ⓔ
43. Ekron	43 Ⓐ Ⓑ Ⓒ Ⓓ Ⓔ	43 Ⓐ Ⓑ Ⓒ Ⓓ Ⓔ
44. 8000-8299 Lang	44 Ⓐ Ⓑ Ⓒ Ⓓ Ⓔ	44 Ⓐ Ⓑ Ⓒ Ⓓ Ⓔ
45. Lott	45 Ⓐ Ⓑ Ⓒ Ⓓ Ⓔ	45 Ⓐ Ⓑ Ⓒ Ⓓ Ⓔ
46. 5500-9999 Lang	46 Ⓐ Ⓑ Ⓒ Ⓓ Ⓔ	46 Ⓐ Ⓑ Ⓒ Ⓓ Ⓔ
47. Ekron	47 Ⓐ Ⓑ Ⓒ Ⓓ Ⓔ	47 Ⓐ Ⓑ Ⓒ Ⓓ Ⓔ
48. 8000-8299 Lang	48 Ⓐ Ⓑ Ⓒ Ⓓ Ⓔ	48 Ⓐ Ⓑ Ⓒ Ⓓ Ⓔ
49. 5400-6299 James	49 Ⓐ Ⓑ Ⓒ Ⓓ Ⓔ	49 Ⓐ Ⓑ Ⓒ Ⓓ Ⓔ
50. 2200-3199 Wood	50 Ⓐ Ⓑ Ⓒ Ⓓ Ⓔ	50 Ⓐ Ⓑ Ⓒ Ⓓ Ⓔ
51. Valley	51 Ⓐ Ⓑ Ⓒ Ⓓ Ⓔ	51 Ⓐ Ⓑ Ⓒ Ⓓ Ⓔ
52. 1800-2499 Wood	52 Ⓐ Ⓑ Ⓒ Ⓓ Ⓔ	52 Ⓐ Ⓑ Ⓒ Ⓓ Ⓔ
53. 7500-8799 Lang	53 Ⓐ Ⓑ Ⓒ Ⓓ Ⓔ	53 Ⓐ Ⓑ Ⓒ Ⓓ Ⓔ
54. 8000-8299 Lang	54 Ⓐ Ⓑ Ⓒ Ⓓ Ⓔ	54 Ⓐ Ⓑ Ⓒ Ⓓ Ⓔ
55. Levering	55 Ⓐ Ⓑ Ⓒ Ⓓ Ⓔ	55 Ⓐ Ⓑ Ⓒ Ⓓ Ⓔ
56. 8000-8299 Lang	56 Ⓐ Ⓑ Ⓒ Ⓓ Ⓔ	56 Ⓐ Ⓑ Ⓒ Ⓓ Ⓔ
57. 5500-5899 James	57 Ⓐ Ⓑ Ⓒ Ⓓ Ⓔ	57 Ⓐ Ⓑ Ⓒ Ⓓ Ⓔ
58. 3100-3699 Wood	58 Ⓐ Ⓑ Ⓒ Ⓓ Ⓔ	58 Ⓐ Ⓑ Ⓒ Ⓓ Ⓔ
59. 5400-6299 James	59 Ⓐ Ⓑ Ⓒ Ⓓ Ⓔ	59 Ⓐ Ⓑ Ⓒ Ⓓ Ⓔ
60. 3100-3699 Wood	60 Ⓐ Ⓑ Ⓒ Ⓓ Ⓔ	60 Ⓐ Ⓑ Ⓒ Ⓓ Ⓔ
61. 4500-4699 James	61 Ⓐ Ⓑ Ⓒ Ⓓ Ⓔ	61 Ⓐ Ⓑ Ⓒ Ⓓ Ⓔ
62. 2700-2799 Wood	62 Ⓐ Ⓑ Ⓒ Ⓓ Ⓔ	62 Ⓐ Ⓑ Ⓒ Ⓓ Ⓔ
63. 1200-1599 Wood	63 Ⓐ Ⓑ Ⓒ Ⓓ Ⓔ	63 Ⓐ Ⓑ Ⓒ Ⓓ Ⓔ
64. Valley	64 Ⓐ Ⓑ Ⓒ Ⓓ Ⓔ	64 Ⓐ Ⓑ Ⓒ Ⓓ Ⓔ
65. 7500-8799 Lang	65 Ⓐ Ⓑ Ⓒ Ⓓ Ⓔ	65 Ⓐ Ⓑ Ⓒ Ⓓ Ⓔ
66. 6100-6499 James	66 Ⓐ Ⓑ Ⓒ Ⓓ Ⓔ	66 Ⓐ Ⓑ Ⓒ Ⓓ Ⓔ
67. 8000-8299 Lang	67 Ⓐ Ⓑ Ⓒ Ⓓ Ⓔ	67 Ⓐ Ⓑ Ⓒ Ⓓ Ⓔ
68. 5600-9999 Lang	68 Ⓐ Ⓑ Ⓒ Ⓓ Ⓔ	68 Ⓐ Ⓑ Ⓒ Ⓓ Ⓔ
69. Levering	69 Ⓐ Ⓑ Ⓒ Ⓓ Ⓔ	69 Ⓐ Ⓑ Ⓒ Ⓓ Ⓔ
70. 7400-9399 Lang	70 Ⓐ Ⓑ Ⓒ Ⓓ Ⓔ	70 Ⓐ Ⓑ Ⓒ Ⓓ Ⓔ
71. Valley	71 Ⓐ Ⓑ Ⓒ Ⓓ Ⓔ	71 Ⓐ Ⓑ Ⓒ Ⓓ Ⓔ
72. 5400-6299 James	72 Ⓐ Ⓑ Ⓒ Ⓓ Ⓔ	72 Ⓐ Ⓑ Ⓒ Ⓓ Ⓔ
73. 3100-3699 Wood	73 Ⓐ Ⓑ Ⓒ Ⓓ Ⓔ	73 Ⓐ Ⓑ Ⓒ Ⓓ Ⓔ
74. 6400-6599 James	74 Ⓐ Ⓑ Ⓒ Ⓓ Ⓔ	74 Ⓐ Ⓑ Ⓒ Ⓓ Ⓔ
75. 5400-6299 James	75 Ⓐ Ⓑ Ⓒ Ⓓ Ⓔ	75 Ⓐ Ⓑ Ⓒ Ⓓ Ⓔ
76. 2200-3199 Wood	76 Ⓐ Ⓑ Ⓒ Ⓓ Ⓔ	76 Ⓐ Ⓑ Ⓒ Ⓓ Ⓔ
77. 5600-9999 Lang	77 Ⓐ Ⓑ Ⓒ Ⓓ Ⓔ	77 Ⓐ Ⓑ Ⓒ Ⓓ Ⓔ
78. Dushore	78 Ⓐ Ⓑ Ⓒ Ⓓ Ⓔ	78 Ⓐ Ⓑ Ⓒ Ⓓ Ⓔ
79. 3100-3699 Wood	79 Ⓐ Ⓑ Ⓒ Ⓓ Ⓔ	79 Ⓐ Ⓑ Ⓒ Ⓓ Ⓔ
80. 2200-3199 Wood	80 Ⓐ Ⓑ Ⓒ Ⓓ Ⓔ	80 Ⓐ Ⓑ Ⓒ Ⓓ Ⓔ
81. 8600-9299 Lang	81 Ⓐ Ⓑ Ⓒ Ⓓ Ⓔ	81 Ⓐ Ⓑ Ⓒ Ⓓ Ⓔ
82. Lycan	82 Ⓐ Ⓑ Ⓒ Ⓓ Ⓔ	82 Ⓐ Ⓑ Ⓒ Ⓓ Ⓔ
83. 7400-9399 Lang	83 Ⓐ Ⓑ Ⓒ Ⓓ Ⓔ	83 Ⓐ Ⓑ Ⓒ Ⓓ Ⓔ
84. 5600-9999 Lang	84 Ⓐ Ⓑ Ⓒ Ⓓ Ⓔ	84 Ⓐ Ⓑ Ⓒ Ⓓ Ⓔ
85. 7400-9399 Lang	85 Ⓐ Ⓑ Ⓒ Ⓓ Ⓔ	85 Ⓐ Ⓑ Ⓒ Ⓓ Ⓔ
86. 4500-4699 James	86 Ⓐ Ⓑ Ⓒ Ⓓ Ⓔ	86 Ⓐ Ⓑ Ⓒ Ⓓ Ⓔ
87. 8600-9299 Lang	87 Ⓐ Ⓑ Ⓒ Ⓓ Ⓔ	87 Ⓐ Ⓑ Ⓒ Ⓓ Ⓔ
88. Viborg	88 Ⓐ Ⓑ Ⓒ Ⓓ Ⓔ	88 Ⓐ Ⓑ Ⓒ Ⓓ Ⓔ

Correct Answers

Memory-for-Address Test

1. C		31. B		61. E	
2. E		32. E		62. E	
3. A		33. E		63. C	
4. A		34. C		64. D	
5. B		35. B		65. A	
6. B		36. D		66. C	
7. C		37. E		67. D	
8. A		38. B		68. E	
9. D		39. A		69. C	
10. B		40. D		70. C	
11. B		41. E		71. D	
12. E		42. B		72. B	
13. A		43. C		73. D	
14. D		44. D		74. A	
15. B		45. A		75. B	
16. A		46. E		76. B	
17. C		47. C		77. E	
18. C		48. D		78. A	
19. B		49. B		79. D	
20. C		50. B		80. B	
21. E		51. D		81. B	
22. E		52. A		82. E	
23. B		53. A		83. C	
24. A		54. D		84. E	
25. C		55. C		85. C	
26. D		56. D		86. E	
27. A		57. D		87. B	
28. A		58. D		88. D	
29. C		59. B			
30. B		60. D			

Memory-for-Address Test
Work—3 Minutes

Answer each question on a piece of paper to show the letter of the box in which the address belongs.
Try to remember the location of as many addresses as you can. If you are not sure of an address, guess.
Work only three minutes.

A	B	C	D	E
1500-2599 Blake Cathy 5500-8799 Beach Baker 3400-6599 Walker	1200-3599 Blake Cedar 4600-9599 Beach Forter 1400-2299 Walker	3200-1899 Blake Halstead 6400-9599 Beach Winter 5500-6499 Walker	2100-3599 Blake Hotel 7000-8599 Beach Central 1500-1899 Walker	3500-2999 Blake Tatum 7500-9999 Beach River 2500-4999 Walker

1. 5500-8799 Beach
2. Winter
3. 3200-1899 Blake
4. River
5. 3500-2999 Blake
6. 1400-2299 Walker
7. Baker
8. 3200-1899 Blake
9. 2500-4999 Walker
10. Halsted
11. 700-8599 Beach
12. 5500-4999 Walker
13. Cedar
14. 4600-9599 Beach
15. Cathy
16. 2100-3599 Blake
17. 7500-9999 Beach
18. 4600-9599 Beach
19. 7000-8599 Beach
20. 3400-6599 Walker
21. 3200-1899 Blake
22. Halsted
23. 3500-2999 Blake
24. 1400-2299 Walker

25. 6400-9599 Beach
26. 5500-6499 Walker
27. 3500-2999 Blake
28. Halsted
29. 1400-2299 Walker
30. 1500-2599 Blake
31. Forter
32. 7000-8599 Beach
33. Tatum
34. 3200-1899 Blake
35. Cedar
36. 7000-8599 Beach
37. Winter
38. 1200-3599 Blake
39. Central
40. 4600-9599 Beach
41. Hotel
42. 7500-9999 Beach
43. 1400-2299 Walker
44. 1500-2599 Blake
45. 2100-3599 Blake
46. 7500-9999 Beach
47. 6400-9599 Beach
48. River

49. 7500-9999 Beach
50. 1500-2599 Blake
51. 1200-3599 Blake
52. 1500-1899 Walker
53. 3500-299 Blakel
54. Baker
55. Cedar
56. 1400-2299 Walker
57. 2100-3599 Blake
58. 4600-9599 Beach
59. Cathy
60. 2500-4999 Walker
61. 1200-3599 Blake
62. Forter
63. 3400-6599 Walker
64. 7000-8599 Beach
65. 1400-2299 Walker
66. 3500-2999 Blake
67. Baker
68. 1500-2599 Blake
69. Halsted
70. 5500-6499 Walker
71. 7500-9999 Beach
72. 1200-3599 Blake

73. River
74. 7000-8599 Beach
75. 1400-2299 Walker
76. 3400-6599 Walker
77. Cedar
78. Hotel
79. 3400-6599 Walker
80. Halsted
81. 1200-3599 Blake
82. 5500-6499 Walker
83. 7500-9999 Beach
84. Forter
85. Winter
86. 1500-2599 Blake
87. 3400-6599 Walker
88. 7000-8599 Beach

STOP

When the time is up, go on to the next page for the correct answers.

(**Author's Note:** The sample test above is known as the memory-for-address test in the 470 Battery Test and the 460 Rural Carrier Associate Exam. This Part B is considered as a practice test. You'll be allowed to look at the names and addresses in the boxes, as you are instructed to answer as many questions as possible in three minutes. In the next part, however, you will be asked to answer all the 88 questions in five minutes and you won't be allowed to look at the names and addresses. During the three-minute practice test, answer only a few questions. Spend most of the three minutes in memorizing the placement of numbers and names (just the first two numbers of each address and the first syllables of names, combining two syllables into one. Now, answer a few questions and memorize the names and addresses in preparation for the next part. (**See Memory-for-Address Test: Tips & Strategies, page 243.**)

Correct Answers

Memory-for-Address Test

1. A	31. B	61. B
2. C	32. D	62. B
3. C	33. E	63. A
4. E	34. C	64. D
5. E	35. B	65. B
6. B	36. D	66. E
7. A	37. C	67. A
8. C	38. B	68. A
9. E	39. D	69. C
10. C	40. B	70. C
11. D	41. D	71. E
12. E	42. E	72. B
13. B	43. B	73. E
14. B	44. A	74. E
15. A	45. D	75. B
16. D	46. E	76. A
17. E	47. C	77. B
18. B	48. E	78. D
19. D	49. E	79. A
20. A	50. A	80. C
21. C	51. B	81. B
22. C	52. D	82. C
23. E	53. E	83. E
24. B	54. A	84. B
25. C	55. B	85. C
26. C	56. B	86. A
27. E	57. D	87. A
28. C	58. B	88. D
29. B	59. A	
30. A	60. E	

Memory-for-Address Test

Work—5 Minutes

This is the section that counts.

Decide in which box each name or address belongs. Don't look back at the boxes with the addresses in them. Work 5 minutes. For each question, mark the answers on the answer sheet to the right.

ANSWER SHEET

		Test A		Test B
1.	7500-9999 Beach	1 Ⓐ Ⓑ Ⓒ Ⓓ Ⓔ	1 Ⓐ Ⓑ Ⓒ Ⓓ Ⓔ
2.	Cathy	2 Ⓐ Ⓑ Ⓒ Ⓓ Ⓔ	2 Ⓐ Ⓑ Ⓒ Ⓓ Ⓔ
3.	2100-3599 Blake	3 Ⓐ Ⓑ Ⓒ Ⓓ Ⓔ	3 Ⓐ Ⓑ Ⓒ Ⓓ Ⓔ
4.	7500-9999 Beach	4 Ⓐ Ⓑ Ⓒ Ⓓ Ⓔ	4 Ⓐ Ⓑ Ⓒ Ⓓ Ⓔ
5.	3400-6599 Walker	5 Ⓐ Ⓑ Ⓒ Ⓓ Ⓔ	5 Ⓐ Ⓑ Ⓒ Ⓓ Ⓔ
6.	Halsted	6 Ⓐ Ⓑ Ⓒ Ⓓ Ⓔ	6 Ⓐ Ⓑ Ⓒ Ⓓ Ⓔ
7.	1400-2299 Walker	7 Ⓐ Ⓑ Ⓒ Ⓓ Ⓔ	7 Ⓐ Ⓑ Ⓒ Ⓓ Ⓔ
8.	Tatum	8 Ⓐ Ⓑ Ⓒ Ⓓ Ⓔ	8 Ⓐ Ⓑ Ⓒ Ⓓ Ⓔ
9.	3200-1899 Blake	9 Ⓐ Ⓑ Ⓒ Ⓓ Ⓔ	9 Ⓐ Ⓑ Ⓒ Ⓓ Ⓔ
10.	River	10 Ⓐ Ⓑ Ⓒ Ⓓ Ⓔ	10 Ⓐ Ⓑ Ⓒ Ⓓ Ⓔ
11.	3400-6599 Walker	11 Ⓐ Ⓑ Ⓒ Ⓓ Ⓔ	11 Ⓐ Ⓑ Ⓒ Ⓓ Ⓔ
12.	7000-8599 Beach	12 Ⓐ Ⓑ Ⓒ Ⓓ Ⓔ	12 Ⓐ Ⓑ Ⓒ Ⓓ Ⓔ
13.	Winter	13 Ⓐ Ⓑ Ⓒ Ⓓ Ⓔ	13 Ⓐ Ⓑ Ⓒ Ⓓ Ⓔ
14.	4600-9599 Beach	14 Ⓐ Ⓑ Ⓒ Ⓓ Ⓔ	14 Ⓐ Ⓑ Ⓒ Ⓓ Ⓔ
15.	6400-9599 Beach	15 Ⓐ Ⓑ Ⓒ Ⓓ Ⓔ	15 Ⓐ Ⓑ Ⓒ Ⓓ Ⓔ
16.	Cathy	16 Ⓐ Ⓑ Ⓒ Ⓓ Ⓔ	16 Ⓐ Ⓑ Ⓒ Ⓓ Ⓔ
17.	2100-3599 Blake	17 Ⓐ Ⓑ Ⓒ Ⓓ Ⓔ	17 Ⓐ Ⓑ Ⓒ Ⓓ Ⓔ
18.	7000-8599 Beach	18 Ⓐ Ⓑ Ⓒ Ⓓ Ⓔ	18 Ⓐ Ⓑ Ⓒ Ⓓ Ⓔ
19.	Cedar	19 Ⓐ Ⓑ Ⓒ Ⓓ Ⓔ	19 Ⓐ Ⓑ Ⓒ Ⓓ Ⓔ
20.	1400-2299 Walker	20 Ⓐ Ⓑ Ⓒ Ⓓ Ⓔ	20 Ⓐ Ⓑ Ⓒ Ⓓ Ⓔ
21.	River	21 Ⓐ Ⓑ Ⓒ Ⓓ Ⓔ	21 Ⓐ Ⓑ Ⓒ Ⓓ Ⓔ
22.	2100-3599 Blake	22 Ⓐ Ⓑ Ⓒ Ⓓ Ⓔ	22 Ⓐ Ⓑ Ⓒ Ⓓ Ⓔ
23.	5500-6499 Walker	23 Ⓐ Ⓑ Ⓒ Ⓓ Ⓔ	23 Ⓐ Ⓑ Ⓒ Ⓓ Ⓔ
24.	2100-3599 Blake	24 Ⓐ Ⓑ Ⓒ Ⓓ Ⓔ	24 Ⓐ Ⓑ Ⓒ Ⓓ Ⓔ
25.	7500-9999 Beach	25 Ⓐ Ⓑ Ⓒ Ⓓ Ⓔ	25 Ⓐ Ⓑ Ⓒ Ⓓ Ⓔ
26.	Winter	26 Ⓐ Ⓑ Ⓒ Ⓓ Ⓔ	26 Ⓐ Ⓑ Ⓒ Ⓓ Ⓔ
27.	4600-9599 Beach	27 Ⓐ Ⓑ Ⓒ Ⓓ Ⓔ	27 Ⓐ Ⓑ Ⓒ Ⓓ Ⓔ
28.	3200-1899 Blake	28 Ⓐ Ⓑ Ⓒ Ⓓ Ⓔ	28 Ⓐ Ⓑ Ⓒ Ⓓ Ⓔ
29.	Central	29 Ⓐ Ⓑ Ⓒ Ⓓ Ⓔ	29 Ⓐ Ⓑ Ⓒ Ⓓ Ⓔ
30.	Forter	30 Ⓐ Ⓑ Ⓒ Ⓓ Ⓔ	30 Ⓐ Ⓑ Ⓒ Ⓓ Ⓔ
31.	7500-9999 Beach	31 Ⓐ Ⓑ Ⓒ Ⓓ Ⓔ	31 Ⓐ Ⓑ Ⓒ Ⓓ Ⓔ
32.	2100-3599 Blake	32 Ⓐ Ⓑ Ⓒ Ⓓ Ⓔ	32 Ⓐ Ⓑ Ⓒ Ⓓ Ⓔ
33.	1500-2599 Blake	33 Ⓐ Ⓑ Ⓒ Ⓓ Ⓔ	33 Ⓐ Ⓑ Ⓒ Ⓓ Ⓔ
34.	7000-8599 Beach	34 Ⓐ Ⓑ Ⓒ Ⓓ Ⓔ	34 Ⓐ Ⓑ Ⓒ Ⓓ Ⓔ
35.	7500-9999 Beach	35 Ⓐ Ⓑ Ⓒ Ⓓ Ⓔ	35 Ⓐ Ⓑ Ⓒ Ⓓ Ⓔ
36.	1500-1899 Walker	36 Ⓐ Ⓑ Ⓒ Ⓓ Ⓔ	36 Ⓐ Ⓑ Ⓒ Ⓓ Ⓔ
37.	5500-8799 Beach	37 Ⓐ Ⓑ Ⓒ Ⓓ Ⓔ	37 Ⓐ Ⓑ Ⓒ Ⓓ Ⓔ
38.	Hotel	38 Ⓐ Ⓑ Ⓒ Ⓓ Ⓔ	38 Ⓐ Ⓑ Ⓒ Ⓓ Ⓔ
39.	1200-3599 Blake	39 Ⓐ Ⓑ Ⓒ Ⓓ Ⓔ	39 Ⓐ Ⓑ Ⓒ Ⓓ Ⓔ
40.	River	40 Ⓐ Ⓑ Ⓒ Ⓓ Ⓔ	40 Ⓐ Ⓑ Ⓒ Ⓓ Ⓔ

Go on to the next number on the next page.

#	Address	Answer 1	Answer 2
41.	2500-4999 Walker	41 Ⓐ Ⓑ Ⓒ Ⓓ Ⓔ	41 Ⓐ Ⓑ Ⓒ Ⓓ Ⓔ
42.	Forter	42 Ⓐ Ⓑ Ⓒ Ⓓ Ⓔ	42 Ⓐ Ⓑ Ⓒ Ⓓ Ⓔ
43.	Central	43 Ⓐ Ⓑ Ⓒ Ⓓ Ⓔ	43 Ⓐ Ⓑ Ⓒ Ⓓ Ⓔ
44.	1400-2299 Walker	44 Ⓐ Ⓑ Ⓒ Ⓓ Ⓔ	44 Ⓐ Ⓑ Ⓒ Ⓓ Ⓔ
45.	7500-9999 Beach	45 Ⓐ Ⓑ Ⓒ Ⓓ Ⓔ	45 Ⓐ Ⓑ Ⓒ Ⓓ Ⓔ
46.	2100-3599 Blake	46 Ⓐ Ⓑ Ⓒ Ⓓ Ⓔ	46 Ⓐ Ⓑ Ⓒ Ⓓ Ⓔ
47.	6400-9599 Beach	47 Ⓐ Ⓑ Ⓒ Ⓓ Ⓔ	47 Ⓐ Ⓑ Ⓒ Ⓓ Ⓔ
48.	Halsted	48 Ⓐ Ⓑ Ⓒ Ⓓ Ⓔ	48 Ⓐ Ⓑ Ⓒ Ⓓ Ⓔ
49.	Baker	49 Ⓐ Ⓑ Ⓒ Ⓓ Ⓔ	49 Ⓐ Ⓑ Ⓒ Ⓓ Ⓔ
50.	1200-3599 Blake	50 Ⓐ Ⓑ Ⓒ Ⓓ Ⓔ	50 Ⓐ Ⓑ Ⓒ Ⓓ Ⓔ
51.	1500-1899 Walker	51 Ⓐ Ⓑ Ⓒ Ⓓ Ⓔ	51 Ⓐ Ⓑ Ⓒ Ⓓ Ⓔ
52.	1400-2299 Walker	52 Ⓐ Ⓑ Ⓒ Ⓓ Ⓔ	52 Ⓐ Ⓑ Ⓒ Ⓓ Ⓔ
53.	3200-1899 Blake	53 Ⓐ Ⓑ Ⓒ Ⓓ Ⓔ	53 Ⓐ Ⓑ Ⓒ Ⓓ Ⓔ
54.	Central	54 Ⓐ Ⓑ Ⓒ Ⓓ Ⓔ	54 Ⓐ Ⓑ Ⓒ Ⓓ Ⓔ
55.	4600-9599 Beach	55 Ⓐ Ⓑ Ⓒ Ⓓ Ⓔ	55 Ⓐ Ⓑ Ⓒ Ⓓ Ⓔ
56.	Tatum	56 Ⓐ Ⓑ Ⓒ Ⓓ Ⓔ	56 Ⓐ Ⓑ Ⓒ Ⓓ Ⓔ
57.	Baker	57 Ⓐ Ⓑ Ⓒ Ⓓ Ⓔ	57 Ⓐ Ⓑ Ⓒ Ⓓ Ⓔ
58.	5500-6499 Walker	58 Ⓐ Ⓑ Ⓒ Ⓓ Ⓔ	58 Ⓐ Ⓑ Ⓒ Ⓓ Ⓔ
59.	3400-6599 Walker	59 Ⓐ Ⓑ Ⓒ Ⓓ Ⓔ	59 Ⓐ Ⓑ Ⓒ Ⓓ Ⓔ
60.	6400-9599 Beach	60 Ⓐ Ⓑ Ⓒ Ⓓ Ⓔ	60 Ⓐ Ⓑ Ⓒ Ⓓ Ⓔ
61.	Halsted	61 Ⓐ Ⓑ Ⓒ Ⓓ Ⓔ	61 Ⓐ Ⓑ Ⓒ Ⓓ Ⓔ
62.	5500-6499 Walker	62 Ⓐ Ⓑ Ⓒ Ⓓ Ⓔ	62 Ⓐ Ⓑ Ⓒ Ⓓ Ⓔ
63.	7500-9999 Beach	63 Ⓐ Ⓑ Ⓒ Ⓓ Ⓔ	63 Ⓐ Ⓑ Ⓒ Ⓓ Ⓔ
64.	Forter	64 Ⓐ Ⓑ Ⓒ Ⓓ Ⓔ	64 Ⓐ Ⓑ Ⓒ Ⓓ Ⓔ
65.	3500-2999 Blake	65 Ⓐ Ⓑ Ⓒ Ⓓ Ⓔ	65 Ⓐ Ⓑ Ⓒ Ⓓ Ⓔ
66.	3400-6599 Walker	66 Ⓐ Ⓑ Ⓒ Ⓓ Ⓔ	66 Ⓐ Ⓑ Ⓒ Ⓓ Ⓔ
67.	Cedar	67 Ⓐ Ⓑ Ⓒ Ⓓ Ⓔ	67 Ⓐ Ⓑ Ⓒ Ⓓ Ⓔ
68.	7500-9999 Beach	68 Ⓐ Ⓑ Ⓒ Ⓓ Ⓔ	68 Ⓐ Ⓑ Ⓒ Ⓓ Ⓔ
69.	River	69 Ⓐ Ⓑ Ⓒ Ⓓ Ⓔ	69 Ⓐ Ⓑ Ⓒ Ⓓ Ⓔ
70.	6400-9599 Beach	70 Ⓐ Ⓑ Ⓒ Ⓓ Ⓔ	70 Ⓐ Ⓑ Ⓒ Ⓓ Ⓔ
71.	3500-2999 Blake	71 Ⓐ Ⓑ Ⓒ Ⓓ Ⓔ	71 Ⓐ Ⓑ Ⓒ Ⓓ Ⓔ
72.	1400-2299 Walker	72 Ⓐ Ⓑ Ⓒ Ⓓ Ⓔ	72 Ⓐ Ⓑ Ⓒ Ⓓ Ⓔ
73.	Winter	73 Ⓐ Ⓑ Ⓒ Ⓓ Ⓔ	73 Ⓐ Ⓑ Ⓒ Ⓓ Ⓔ
74.	1400-2299 Walker	74 Ⓐ Ⓑ Ⓒ Ⓓ Ⓔ	74 Ⓐ Ⓑ Ⓒ Ⓓ Ⓔ
75.	3400-6599 Walker	75 Ⓐ Ⓑ Ⓒ Ⓓ Ⓔ	75 Ⓐ Ⓑ Ⓒ Ⓓ Ⓔ
76.	6400-9599 Beach	76 Ⓐ Ⓑ Ⓒ Ⓓ Ⓔ	76 Ⓐ Ⓑ Ⓒ Ⓓ Ⓔ
77.	Tatum	77 Ⓐ Ⓑ Ⓒ Ⓓ Ⓔ	77 Ⓐ Ⓑ Ⓒ Ⓓ Ⓔ
78.	1200-3599 Blake	78 Ⓐ Ⓑ Ⓒ Ⓓ Ⓔ	78 Ⓐ Ⓑ Ⓒ Ⓓ Ⓔ
79.	7500-9999 Beach	79 Ⓐ Ⓑ Ⓒ Ⓓ Ⓔ	79 Ⓐ Ⓑ Ⓒ Ⓓ Ⓔ
80.	Forter	80 Ⓐ Ⓑ Ⓒ Ⓓ Ⓔ	80 Ⓐ Ⓑ Ⓒ Ⓓ Ⓔ
81.	River	81 Ⓐ Ⓑ Ⓒ Ⓓ Ⓔ	81 Ⓐ Ⓑ Ⓒ Ⓓ Ⓔ
82.	5500-8799 Beach	82 Ⓐ Ⓑ Ⓒ Ⓓ Ⓔ	82 Ⓐ Ⓑ Ⓒ Ⓓ Ⓔ
83.	2100-3599 Blake	83 Ⓐ Ⓑ Ⓒ Ⓓ Ⓔ	83 Ⓐ Ⓑ Ⓒ Ⓓ Ⓔ
84.	1400-2299 Walker	84 Ⓐ Ⓑ Ⓒ Ⓓ Ⓔ	84 Ⓐ Ⓑ Ⓒ Ⓓ Ⓔ
85.	7500-9999 Beach	85 Ⓐ Ⓑ Ⓒ Ⓓ Ⓔ	85 Ⓐ Ⓑ Ⓒ Ⓓ Ⓔ
86.	Baker	86 Ⓐ Ⓑ Ⓒ Ⓓ Ⓔ	86 Ⓐ Ⓑ Ⓒ Ⓓ Ⓔ
87.	1200-3599 Blake	87 Ⓐ Ⓑ Ⓒ Ⓓ Ⓔ	87 Ⓐ Ⓑ Ⓒ Ⓓ Ⓔ
88.	2500-49999 Walker	88 Ⓐ Ⓑ Ⓒ Ⓓ Ⓔ	88 Ⓐ Ⓑ Ⓒ Ⓓ Ⓔ

Go on to the next number on the next page.

STOP

If you finish before the time is up,

go back and check your answers.

(See the correct answers on the next page.)

Correct Answers

Memory-for-Address Test

1. E	31. E	61. C
2. A	32. D	62. C
3. D	33. A	63. E
4. E	34. D	64. B
5. A	35. E	65. E
6. C	36. D	66. A
7. B	37. A	67. B
8. E	38. D	68. E
9. C	39. B	69. E
10. E	40. E	70. C
11. A	41. E	71. E
12. D	42. B	72. B
13. C	43. D	73. C
14. B	44. B	74. B
15. C	45. E	75. A
16. A	46. D	76. C
17. D	47. C	77. E
18. D	48. C	78. B
19. B	49. A	79. E
20. B	50. B	80. B
21. E	51. D	81. E
22. D	52. B	82. A
23. C	53. C	83. D
24. D	54. D	84. B
25. E	55. B	85. E
26. C	56. E	86. A
27. B	57. A	87. B
28. C	58. C	88. E
29. D	59. A	
30. B	60. C	

Memory-for-Address Test
Work—3 Minutes

Answer each question on a piece of paper to show the letter of the box in which the address belongs.
Try to remember the location of as many addresses as you can. If you are not sure of an address, guess.
Work only three minutes.

A	B	C	D	E
1200-2599 Drake Weber 1500-1799 Palmer Dewey 4400-6599 Pine	2400-3599 Drake Baker 3600-4599 Palmer Madison 1400-2599 Pine	3200-5599 Drake Hillside 1640-2599 Palmer Dexter 4500-6599 Pine	2100-3599 Drake Ceres 6000-7599 Palmer Bayview 4200-5999 Pine	1700-2599 Drake Girard 3500-9999 Palmer Herald 3400-4599 Pine

1. Hillside
2. 2100-3599 Drake
3. 3500-9999 Palmer
4. 3600-4599 Palmer
5. 4500-6599 Pine
6. 1500-1799 Palmer
7. 3200-5599 Drake
8. Madison
9. 6000-7599 Palmer
10. 1400-2599 Pine
11. 3400-4599 Pine
12. 2400-3599 Drake
13. Dewey
14. Baker
15. 1700-2599 Drake
16. 1400-2599 Pine
17. 4400-6599 Pines
18. 3200-5599 Drake
19. 1500-1799 Palmer
20. Hillside
21. Ceres
22. 2400-3599 Drake
23. 4400-6599 Pine
24. Girard

25. 1640-2599 Palmer
26. 3200-5599 Drake
27. Baker
28. 3500-9999 Palmer
29. 4400-6599 Pine
30. Weber
31. 1400-2599 Pine
32. 2400-3599 Drake
33. 3400-4599 Pine
34. Dewey
35. 3600-4599 Palmer
36. 4400-6599 Pine
37. 2100-3599 Drake
38. 3400-4599 Pine
39. Baker
40. 1200-2599 Drake
41. 2400-3599 Drake
42. Madison
43. 6000-7599 Palmer
44. 2400-3599 Drake
45. Dexter
46. 1700-2599 Drake
47. Madison
48. Bayview

49. 3500-9999 Palmer
50. 4400-6599 Pine
51. 1640-2599 Palmer
52. 3600-4599 Palmer
53. 1700-2599 Drake
54. 2400-3599 Drake
55. 1400-2599 Pine
56. 4400-6599 Pine
57. Baker
58. 3600-4599 Palmer
59. 4400-6599 Pine
60. 3600-4599 Palmer
61. 3500-9999 Palmer
62. Dewey
63. 4200-5999 Pine
64. Hillside
65. 3200-5599 Drake
66. Dewey
67. 4400-6599 Pine
68. 1200-2599 Drake
69. Herald
70. Dexter
71. 2100-3599 Drake
72. 1700-2599 Drake

73. Bayview
74. 2400-3599 Drake
75. 1400-2599 Pine
76. Weber
77. Hillside
78. 4500-6599 Pine
79. 3500-9999 Palmer
80. 1400-2599 Pine
81. 3200-5599 Drake
82. 1500-1799 Palmer
83. 2100-3599 Drake
84. 1640-2599 Palmer
85. Ceres
86. 3600-4599 Palmer
87. Girard
88. 3200-5599 Drake

STOP

When the time is up, go on to the next page for the correct answers.

(**Author's Note:** The sample test above is known as the memory-for-address test in the 470 Battery Test and the 460 Rural Carrier Associate Exam. This Part B is considered as a practice test. You'll be allowed to look at the names and addresses in the boxes, as you are instructed to answer as many questions as possible in three minutes. In the next part, however, you will be asked to answer all the 88 questions in five minutes and you won't be allowed to look at the names and addresses. During the three-minute practice test, answer only a few questions. Spend most of the three minutes in memorizing the placement of numbers and names (just the first two numbers of each address and the first syllables of names, combining two syllables into one. Now, answer a few questions and memorize the names and addresses in preparation for the next part. (**See Memory-for-Address Test: Tips & Strategies, page 243.**)

Correct Answers

Memory-for-Address Test

1. C	31. B	61. E
2. D	32. B	62. A
3. E	33. E	63. D
4. B	34. A	64. C
5. C	35. B	65. C
6. A	36. A	66. A
7. C	37. D	67. A
8. B	38. E	68. A
9. D	39. B	69. E
10. B	40. A	70. C
11. E	41. B	71. D
12. B	42. B	72. E
13. A	43. D	73. D
14. B	44. B	74. B
15. E	45. C	75. B
16. B	46. E	76. A
17. A	47. B	77. C
18. C	48. D	78. C
19. A	49. E	79. E
20. C	50. A	80. B
21. D	51. C	81. C
22. B	52. B	82. A
23. A	53. E	83. D
24. E	54. B	84. C
25. C	55. B	85. D
26. C	56. A	86. B
27. B	57. B	87. E
28. E	58. B	88. C
29. A	59. A	
30. A	60. B	

Memory-for-Address Test

Work—5 Minutes

This is the section that counts.

Decide in which box each name or address belongs. Don't look back at the boxes with the addresses in them. Work 5 minutes. For each question, mark the answers on the answer sheet to the right.

ANSWER SHEET

	Test A	Test B
1. 1700-2599 Drake	1 Ⓐ Ⓑ Ⓒ Ⓓ Ⓔ	1 Ⓐ Ⓑ Ⓒ Ⓓ Ⓔ
2. Bayview	2 Ⓐ Ⓑ Ⓒ Ⓓ Ⓔ	2 Ⓐ Ⓑ Ⓒ Ⓓ Ⓔ
3. 1500-1799 Palmer	3 Ⓐ Ⓑ Ⓒ Ⓓ Ⓔ	3 Ⓐ Ⓑ Ⓒ Ⓓ Ⓔ
4. 4200-4599 Pine	4 Ⓐ Ⓑ Ⓒ Ⓓ Ⓔ	4 Ⓐ Ⓑ Ⓒ Ⓓ Ⓔ
5. Baker	5 Ⓐ Ⓑ Ⓒ Ⓓ Ⓔ	5 Ⓐ Ⓑ Ⓒ Ⓓ Ⓔ
6. 1640-2599 Palmer	6 Ⓐ Ⓑ Ⓒ Ⓓ Ⓔ	6 Ⓐ Ⓑ Ⓒ Ⓓ Ⓔ
7. Girard	7 Ⓐ Ⓑ Ⓒ Ⓓ Ⓔ	7 Ⓐ Ⓑ Ⓒ Ⓓ Ⓔ
8. 4400-6599 Pine	8 Ⓐ Ⓑ Ⓒ Ⓓ Ⓔ	8 Ⓐ Ⓑ Ⓒ Ⓓ Ⓔ
9. 2100-3599 Drake	9 Ⓐ Ⓑ Ⓒ Ⓓ Ⓔ	9 Ⓐ Ⓑ Ⓒ Ⓓ Ⓔ
10. 2400-3599 Drake	10 Ⓐ Ⓑ Ⓒ Ⓓ Ⓔ	10 Ⓐ Ⓑ Ⓒ Ⓓ Ⓔ
11. Herald	11 Ⓐ Ⓑ Ⓒ Ⓓ Ⓔ	11 Ⓐ Ⓑ Ⓒ Ⓓ Ⓔ
12. 4200-5999 Pine	12 Ⓐ Ⓑ Ⓒ Ⓓ Ⓔ	12 Ⓐ Ⓑ Ⓒ Ⓓ Ⓔ
13. 3600-4599 Palmer	13 Ⓐ Ⓑ Ⓒ Ⓓ Ⓔ	13 Ⓐ Ⓑ Ⓒ Ⓓ Ⓔ
14. Hillside	14 Ⓐ Ⓑ Ⓒ Ⓓ Ⓔ	14 Ⓐ Ⓑ Ⓒ Ⓓ Ⓔ
15. 2400-3599 Drake	15 Ⓐ Ⓑ Ⓒ Ⓓ Ⓔ	15 Ⓐ Ⓑ Ⓒ Ⓓ Ⓔ
16. 4400-6599 Pine	16 Ⓐ Ⓑ Ⓒ Ⓓ Ⓔ	16 Ⓐ Ⓑ Ⓒ Ⓓ Ⓔ
17. Ceres	17 Ⓐ Ⓑ Ⓒ Ⓓ Ⓔ	17 Ⓐ Ⓑ Ⓒ Ⓓ Ⓔ
18. 3500-9999 Palmer	18 Ⓐ Ⓑ Ⓒ Ⓓ Ⓔ	18 Ⓐ Ⓑ Ⓒ Ⓓ Ⓔ
19. 4400-6599 Pine	19 Ⓐ Ⓑ Ⓒ Ⓓ Ⓔ	19 Ⓐ Ⓑ Ⓒ Ⓓ Ⓔ
20. 3600-4599 Palmer	20 Ⓐ Ⓑ Ⓒ Ⓓ Ⓔ	20 Ⓐ Ⓑ Ⓒ Ⓓ Ⓔ
21. 6000-7599 Palmer	21 Ⓐ Ⓑ Ⓒ Ⓓ Ⓔ	21 Ⓐ Ⓑ Ⓒ Ⓓ Ⓔ
22. 1700-2599 Drake	22 Ⓐ Ⓑ Ⓒ Ⓓ Ⓔ	22 Ⓐ Ⓑ Ⓒ Ⓓ Ⓔ
23. 1400-2599 Pine	23 Ⓐ Ⓑ Ⓒ Ⓓ Ⓔ	23 Ⓐ Ⓑ Ⓒ Ⓓ Ⓔ
24. Dexter	24 Ⓐ Ⓑ Ⓒ Ⓓ Ⓔ	24 Ⓐ Ⓑ Ⓒ Ⓓ Ⓔ
25. 4200-5999 Pine	25 Ⓐ Ⓑ Ⓒ Ⓓ Ⓔ	25 Ⓐ Ⓑ Ⓒ Ⓓ Ⓔ
26. Baker	26 Ⓐ Ⓑ Ⓒ Ⓓ Ⓔ	26 Ⓐ Ⓑ Ⓒ Ⓓ Ⓔ
27. 1400-2599 Pine	27 Ⓐ Ⓑ Ⓒ Ⓓ Ⓔ	27 Ⓐ Ⓑ Ⓒ Ⓓ Ⓔ
28. 1640-2599 Palmer	28 Ⓐ Ⓑ Ⓒ Ⓓ Ⓔ	28 Ⓐ Ⓑ Ⓒ Ⓓ Ⓔ
29. Herald	29 Ⓐ Ⓑ Ⓒ Ⓓ Ⓔ	29 Ⓐ Ⓑ Ⓒ Ⓓ Ⓔ
30. 4500-6599 Pine	30 Ⓐ Ⓑ Ⓒ Ⓓ Ⓔ	30 Ⓐ Ⓑ Ⓒ Ⓓ Ⓔ
31. 3200-5599 Drake	31 Ⓐ Ⓑ Ⓒ Ⓓ Ⓔ	31 Ⓐ Ⓑ Ⓒ Ⓓ Ⓔ
32. 4200-5999 Pine	32 Ⓐ Ⓑ Ⓒ Ⓓ Ⓔ	32 Ⓐ Ⓑ Ⓒ Ⓓ Ⓔ
33. 2400-3599 Drake	33 Ⓐ Ⓑ Ⓒ Ⓓ Ⓔ	33 Ⓐ Ⓑ Ⓒ Ⓓ Ⓔ
34. 1640-2599 Palmer	34 Ⓐ Ⓑ Ⓒ Ⓓ Ⓔ	34 Ⓐ Ⓑ Ⓒ Ⓓ Ⓔ
35. Dexter	35 Ⓐ Ⓑ Ⓒ Ⓓ Ⓔ	35 Ⓐ Ⓑ Ⓒ Ⓓ Ⓔ
36. 1400-2599 Pine	36 Ⓐ Ⓑ Ⓒ Ⓓ Ⓔ	36 Ⓐ Ⓑ Ⓒ Ⓓ Ⓔ
37. 3400-4599 Pine	37 Ⓐ Ⓑ Ⓒ Ⓓ Ⓔ	37 Ⓐ Ⓑ Ⓒ Ⓓ Ⓔ
38. 1500-1799 Palmer	38 Ⓐ Ⓑ Ⓒ Ⓓ Ⓔ	38 Ⓐ Ⓑ Ⓒ Ⓓ Ⓔ
39. 3600-4599 Palmer	39 Ⓐ Ⓑ Ⓒ Ⓓ Ⓔ	30 Ⓐ Ⓑ Ⓒ Ⓓ Ⓔ
40. 1500-1799 Palmer	40 Ⓐ Ⓑ Ⓒ Ⓓ Ⓔ	40 Ⓐ Ⓑ Ⓒ Ⓓ Ⓔ

Go on to the next number on the next page.

41. Ceres	41 Ⓐ Ⓑ Ⓒ Ⓓ Ⓔ	41 Ⓐ Ⓑ Ⓒ Ⓓ Ⓔ
42. Madison	42 Ⓐ Ⓑ Ⓒ Ⓓ Ⓔ	42 Ⓐ Ⓑ Ⓒ Ⓓ Ⓔ
43. Girard	43 Ⓐ Ⓑ Ⓒ Ⓓ Ⓔ	43 Ⓐ Ⓑ Ⓒ Ⓓ Ⓔ
44. 3600-4599 Palmer	44 Ⓐ Ⓑ Ⓒ Ⓓ Ⓔ	44 Ⓐ Ⓑ Ⓒ Ⓓ Ⓔ
45. 4400-6599 Pine	45 Ⓐ Ⓑ Ⓒ Ⓓ Ⓔ	45 Ⓐ Ⓑ Ⓒ Ⓓ Ⓔ
46. 3200-5599 Drake	46 Ⓐ Ⓑ Ⓒ Ⓓ Ⓔ	46 Ⓐ Ⓑ Ⓒ Ⓓ Ⓔ
47. 1700-2599 Drake	47 Ⓐ Ⓑ Ⓒ Ⓓ Ⓔ	47 Ⓐ Ⓑ Ⓒ Ⓓ Ⓔ
48. 3400-4599 Pine	48 Ⓐ Ⓑ Ⓒ Ⓓ Ⓔ	48 Ⓐ Ⓑ Ⓒ Ⓓ Ⓔ
49. 4500-6599 Pine	49 Ⓐ Ⓑ Ⓒ Ⓓ Ⓔ	49 Ⓐ Ⓑ Ⓒ Ⓓ Ⓔ
50. 3600-4599 Palmer	50 Ⓐ Ⓑ Ⓒ Ⓓ Ⓔ	50 Ⓐ Ⓑ Ⓒ Ⓓ Ⓔ
51. 4400-6599 Pine	51 Ⓐ Ⓑ Ⓒ Ⓓ Ⓔ	51 Ⓐ Ⓑ Ⓒ Ⓓ Ⓔ
52. 2100-3599 Drake	52 Ⓐ Ⓑ Ⓒ Ⓓ Ⓔ	52 Ⓐ Ⓑ Ⓒ Ⓓ Ⓔ
53. 1640-2599 Palmer	53 Ⓐ Ⓑ Ⓒ Ⓓ Ⓔ	53 Ⓐ Ⓑ Ⓒ Ⓓ Ⓔ
54. Dewey	54 Ⓐ Ⓑ Ⓒ Ⓓ Ⓔ	54 Ⓐ Ⓑ Ⓒ Ⓓ Ⓔ
55. Madison	55 Ⓐ Ⓑ Ⓒ Ⓓ Ⓔ	55 Ⓐ Ⓑ Ⓒ Ⓓ Ⓔ
56. 1500-1799 Palmer	56 Ⓐ Ⓑ Ⓒ Ⓓ Ⓔ	56 Ⓐ Ⓑ Ⓒ Ⓓ Ⓔ
57. 2100-3599 Drake	57 Ⓐ Ⓑ Ⓒ Ⓓ Ⓔ	57 Ⓐ Ⓑ Ⓒ Ⓓ Ⓔ
58. Herald	58 Ⓐ Ⓑ Ⓒ Ⓓ Ⓔ	58 Ⓐ Ⓑ Ⓒ Ⓓ Ⓔ
59. 1640-2599 Palmer	59 Ⓐ Ⓑ Ⓒ Ⓓ Ⓔ	59 Ⓐ Ⓑ Ⓒ Ⓓ Ⓔ
60. Dexter	60 Ⓐ Ⓑ Ⓒ Ⓓ Ⓔ	60 Ⓐ Ⓑ Ⓒ Ⓓ Ⓔ
61. 1400-2599 Pine	61 Ⓐ Ⓑ Ⓒ Ⓓ Ⓔ	61 Ⓐ Ⓑ Ⓒ Ⓓ Ⓔ
62. 2100-3599 Drake	62 Ⓐ Ⓑ Ⓒ Ⓓ Ⓔ	62 Ⓐ Ⓑ Ⓒ Ⓓ Ⓔ
63. Herald	63 Ⓐ Ⓑ Ⓒ Ⓓ Ⓔ	63 Ⓐ Ⓑ Ⓒ Ⓓ Ⓔ
64. 3200-5599 Drake	64 Ⓐ Ⓑ Ⓒ Ⓓ Ⓔ	64 Ⓐ Ⓑ Ⓒ Ⓓ Ⓔ
65. 4500-6599 Pine	65 Ⓐ Ⓑ Ⓒ Ⓓ Ⓔ	65 Ⓐ Ⓑ Ⓒ Ⓓ Ⓔ
66. 6000-7599 Palmer	66 Ⓐ Ⓑ Ⓒ Ⓓ Ⓔ	66 Ⓐ Ⓑ Ⓒ Ⓓ Ⓔ
67. 1640-2599 Palmer	67 Ⓐ Ⓑ Ⓒ Ⓓ Ⓔ	67 Ⓐ Ⓑ Ⓒ Ⓓ Ⓔ
68. 4500-6599 Pine	68 Ⓐ Ⓑ Ⓒ Ⓓ Ⓔ	68 Ⓐ Ⓑ Ⓒ Ⓓ Ⓔ
69. Dewey	69 Ⓐ Ⓑ Ⓒ Ⓓ Ⓔ	69 Ⓐ Ⓑ Ⓒ Ⓓ Ⓔ
70. 1200-2599 Drake	70 Ⓐ Ⓑ Ⓒ Ⓓ Ⓔ	70 Ⓐ Ⓑ Ⓒ Ⓓ Ⓔ
71. 3500-9999 Palmer	71 Ⓐ Ⓑ Ⓒ Ⓓ Ⓔ	71 Ⓐ Ⓑ Ⓒ Ⓓ Ⓔ
72. 1700-2599 Drake	72 Ⓐ Ⓑ Ⓒ Ⓓ Ⓔ	72 Ⓐ Ⓑ Ⓒ Ⓓ Ⓔ
73. 4200-5999 Pine	73 Ⓐ Ⓑ Ⓒ Ⓓ Ⓔ	73 Ⓐ Ⓑ Ⓒ Ⓓ Ⓔ
74. Madison	74 Ⓐ Ⓑ Ⓒ Ⓓ Ⓔ	74 Ⓐ Ⓑ Ⓒ Ⓓ Ⓔ
75. 1200-2599 Drake	75 Ⓐ Ⓑ Ⓒ Ⓓ Ⓔ	75 Ⓐ Ⓑ Ⓒ Ⓓ Ⓔ
76. Hillside	76 Ⓐ Ⓑ Ⓒ Ⓓ Ⓔ	76 Ⓐ Ⓑ Ⓒ Ⓓ Ⓔ
77. 3600-4599 Palmer	77 Ⓐ Ⓑ Ⓒ Ⓓ Ⓔ	77 Ⓐ Ⓑ Ⓒ Ⓓ Ⓔ
78. Bayview	78 Ⓐ Ⓑ Ⓒ Ⓓ Ⓔ	78 Ⓐ Ⓑ Ⓒ Ⓓ Ⓔ
79. 3600-4599 Palmer	79 Ⓐ Ⓑ Ⓒ Ⓓ Ⓔ	79 Ⓐ Ⓑ Ⓒ Ⓓ Ⓔ
80. 2100-3599 Drake	80 Ⓐ Ⓑ Ⓒ Ⓓ Ⓔ	80 Ⓐ Ⓑ Ⓒ Ⓓ Ⓔ
81. 4400-6599 Pine	81 Ⓐ Ⓑ Ⓒ Ⓓ Ⓔ	81 Ⓐ Ⓑ Ⓒ Ⓓ Ⓔ
82. 1640-2599 Palmer	82 Ⓐ Ⓑ Ⓒ Ⓓ Ⓔ	82 Ⓐ Ⓑ Ⓒ Ⓓ Ⓔ
83. 1700-2599 Drake	83 Ⓐ Ⓑ Ⓒ Ⓓ Ⓔ	83 Ⓐ Ⓑ Ⓒ Ⓓ Ⓔ
84. Madison	84 Ⓐ Ⓑ Ⓒ Ⓓ Ⓔ	84 Ⓐ Ⓑ Ⓒ Ⓓ Ⓔ
85. 4500-6599 Pine	85 Ⓐ Ⓑ Ⓒ Ⓓ Ⓔ	85 Ⓐ Ⓑ Ⓒ Ⓓ Ⓔ
86. Girard	86 Ⓐ Ⓑ Ⓒ Ⓓ Ⓔ	86 Ⓐ Ⓑ Ⓒ Ⓓ Ⓔ
87. 2400-3599 Drake	87 Ⓐ Ⓑ Ⓒ Ⓓ Ⓔ	87 Ⓐ Ⓑ Ⓒ Ⓓ Ⓔ
88. Dewey	88 Ⓐ Ⓑ Ⓒ Ⓓ Ⓔ	88 Ⓐ Ⓑ Ⓒ Ⓓ Ⓔ

Go on to the next number on the next page.

STOP

If you finish before the time is up,

go back and check your answers.

(See the correct answers on the next page.)

Correct Answers

Memory-for-Address Test

1. E	31. C	61. B
2. D	32. D	62. D
3. A	33. B	63. E
4. D	34. C	64. C
5. B	35. C	65. C
6. C	36. B	66. D
7. E	37. E	67. C
8. A	38. A	68. C
9. D	39. B	69. A
10. B	40. A	70. A
11. E	41. D	71. E
12. D	42. B	72. E
13. B	43. E	73. D
14. C	44. B	74. B
15. B	45. A	75. A
16. A	46. C	76. C
17. D	47. E	77. B
18. E	48. E	78. D
19. A	49. C	79. B
20. B	50. B	80. D
21. D	51. A	81. A
22. E	52. D	82. C
23. B	53. C	83. E
24. C	54. A	84. B
25. D	55. B	85. C
26. B	56. A	86. E
27. B	57. D	87. B
28. C	58. E	88. A
29. E	59. C	
30. C	60. C	

Memory-for-Address Test

Work—3 Minutes

Answer each question on a piece of paper to show the letter of the box in which the address belongs. Try to remember the location of as many addresses as you can. If you are not sure of an address, guess. Work only three minutes.

A	B	C	D	E
1500-2399 Bell Cadiz 5500-8599 Carter Wilton 3300-3589 Huber	2500-3599 Bell Windell 1600-2499 Carter Vernon 8100-8499 Huber	2200-2699 Bell Madison 3700-9899 Carter Atlantic 6500-6499 Huber	3400-3699 Bell Alden 7099-8999 Carter Lucy 4400-5399 Huber	7200-8799 Bell Livonia 4500-9999 Carter Perry 3500-4699 Huber

1. 2500-3599 Bell
2. 7099-8999 Carter
3. Lucy
4. Wilton
5. 3500-4699 Huber
6. 1600-2499 Carter
7. Lucy
8. 3500-4699 Huber
9. 2500-3599 Bell
10. 1600-2499 Carter
11. Alden
12. 3400-3699 Bell
13. 1600-2499 Carter
14. 3700-9899 Carter
15. 8100-8499 Huber
16 Perry
17. Madison
18. 2500-3599 Bell
19. 3300-3589 Huber
20. 3700-9899 Carter
21. 2500-3599 Bell
22. 1600-2499 Carter
23. 7200-8799 Bell
24. 7099-8999 Carter

25. Livonia
26. 4400-5399 Hubert
27. Windell
28. 1500-2399 Bell
29. 2200-2699 Bell
30. 5500-8599 Carter
31. 4500-9999 Carter
32. 8100-8499 Huber
33. 7099-9899 Carter
34. 7200-8799 Bell
35. Madison
36. Vernon
37. 3400-3699 Bell
38. Windell
39. 3300-3589 Huber
40. 5500-8599 Carter
41. 2500-3599 Bell
42. 3400-3699 Bell
43. Lucy
44. 7200-8799 Bell
45. 3500-6499 Huber
46. 8100-8499 Huber
47. Windell
48. 2200-2699 Bell

49. Cadiz
50. Vernon
51. 3700-9899 Carter
52. Lucy
53. 3500-4699 Huber
54. 6500-6499 Huber
55. 3400-3699 Bell
56. 3300-3589 Huber
57. 7099-8999 Carter
58. 4500-9999 Carter
59. Vernon
60. 2200-2699 Bell
61. 7099-8999 Carter
62. 4500-9999 Carter
63. 2200-2699 Bell
64. 3700-9899 Carter
65. 4400-5399 Huber
66. 5500-8599 Carter
67. 3400-3699 Bell
68 . 4500-9999 Carter
69. 2500-3599 Bell
70. Atlantic
71. 3300-3589 Huber
72. Alden

73. 7200-8799 Bell
74. Lucy
75. 2200-2699 Bell
76. Vernon
77. 7099-8999 Carter
78. 6500-6499 Huber
79. 4400-5399 Huber
80. 7200-8799 Bell
81. 2500-3599 Bell
82. 8100-8499 Huber
83. Alden
84. 3400-3699 Bell
85. 3500-4699 Huber
86. 1500-2399 Bell
87. Atlantic
88. 1600-2499 Carter

STOP

When the time is up, go on to the next page for the correct answers.

(**Author's Note:** The sample test above is known as the memory-for-address test in the 470 Battery Test and the 460 Rural Carrier Associate Exam. This Part B is considered as a practice test. You'll be allowed to look at the names and addresses in the boxes, as you are instructed to answer as many questions as possible in three minutes. In the next part, however, you will be asked to answer all the 88 questions in five minutes and you won't be allowed to look at the names and addresses. During the three-minute practice test, answer only a few questions. Spend most of the three minutes in memorizing the placement of numbers and names (just the first two numbers of each address and the first syllables of names, combining two syllables into one. Now, answer a few questions and memorize the names and addresses in preparation for the next part. (**See Memory-for-Address Test: Tips & Strategies,** page 243.)

Correct Answers

Memory-for-Address Test

1. B	31. E	61. D
2. D	32. B	62. E
3. D	33. D	63. C
4. A	34. E	64. C
5. E	35. C	65. D
6. B	36. B	66. A
7. D	37. D	67. D
8. E	38. B	68. E
9. B	39. A	69. B
10. B	40. A	70. C
11. D	41. B	71. A
12. D	42. D	72. D
13. B	43. D	73. E
14. C	44. E	74. D
15. B	45. E	75. C
16. E	46. B	76. B
17. C	47. B	77. D
18. B	48. C	78. C
19. A	49. A	79. D
20. C	50. B	80. E
21. B	51. C	81. B
22. B	52. D	82. B
23. E	53. E	83. D
24. D	54. C	84. D
25. E	55. D	85. E
26. D	56. A	86. A
27. B	57. D	87. C
28. A	58. E	88. B
29. C	59. B	
30. A	60. C	

Memory-for-Address Test

Work—5 Minutes

This is the section that counts.

Decide in which box each name or address belongs. Don't look back at the boxes with the addresses in them. Work 5 minutes. For each question, mark the answers on the answer sheet to the right.

ANSWER SHEET

	Test A	Test B
1. 7200-8799 Bell	1 Ⓐ Ⓑ Ⓒ Ⓓ Ⓔ	1 Ⓐ Ⓑ Ⓒ Ⓓ Ⓔ
2. Atlantic	2 Ⓐ Ⓑ Ⓒ Ⓓ Ⓔ	2 Ⓐ Ⓑ Ⓒ Ⓓ Ⓔ
3. 1500-2399 Bell	3 Ⓐ Ⓑ Ⓒ Ⓓ Ⓔ	3 Ⓐ Ⓑ Ⓒ Ⓓ Ⓔ
4. 4400-5399 Huber	4 Ⓐ Ⓑ Ⓒ Ⓓ Ⓔ	4 Ⓐ Ⓑ Ⓒ Ⓓ Ⓔ
5. Livonia	5 Ⓐ Ⓑ Ⓒ Ⓓ Ⓔ	5 Ⓐ Ⓑ Ⓒ Ⓓ Ⓔ
6. 1600-2499 Carter	6 Ⓐ Ⓑ Ⓒ Ⓓ Ⓔ	6 Ⓐ Ⓑ Ⓒ Ⓓ Ⓔ
7. Madison	7 Ⓐ Ⓑ Ⓒ Ⓓ Ⓔ	7 Ⓐ Ⓑ Ⓒ Ⓓ Ⓔ
8. 3300-3589 Huber	8 Ⓐ Ⓑ Ⓒ Ⓓ Ⓔ	8 Ⓐ Ⓑ Ⓒ Ⓓ Ⓔ
9. 1600-2499 Carter	9 Ⓐ Ⓑ Ⓒ Ⓓ Ⓔ	9 Ⓐ Ⓑ Ⓒ Ⓓ Ⓔ
10. Perry	10 Ⓐ Ⓑ Ⓒ Ⓓ Ⓔ	10 Ⓐ Ⓑ Ⓒ Ⓓ Ⓔ
11. 4400-5399 Huber	11 Ⓐ Ⓑ Ⓒ Ⓓ Ⓔ	11 Ⓐ Ⓑ Ⓒ Ⓓ Ⓔ
12. 4500-9999 Carter	12 Ⓐ Ⓑ Ⓒ Ⓓ Ⓔ	12 Ⓐ Ⓑ Ⓒ Ⓓ Ⓔ
13. 2500-3599 Bell	13 Ⓐ Ⓑ Ⓒ Ⓓ Ⓔ	13 Ⓐ Ⓑ Ⓒ Ⓓ Ⓔ
14. Vernon	14 Ⓐ Ⓑ Ⓒ Ⓓ Ⓔ	14 Ⓐ Ⓑ Ⓒ Ⓓ Ⓔ
15. 3300-3589 Huber	15 Ⓐ Ⓑ Ⓒ Ⓓ Ⓔ	15 Ⓐ Ⓑ Ⓒ Ⓓ Ⓔ
16. 3400-3699 Bell	16 Ⓐ Ⓑ Ⓒ Ⓓ Ⓔ	16 Ⓐ Ⓑ Ⓒ Ⓓ Ⓔ
17. 4500-9999 Carter	17 Ⓐ Ⓑ Ⓒ Ⓓ Ⓔ	17 Ⓐ Ⓑ Ⓒ Ⓓ Ⓔ
18. 4400-5399 Huber	18 Ⓐ Ⓑ Ⓒ Ⓓ Ⓔ	18 Ⓐ Ⓑ Ⓒ Ⓓ Ⓔ
19. Madison	19 Ⓐ Ⓑ Ⓒ Ⓓ Ⓔ	19 Ⓐ Ⓑ Ⓒ Ⓓ Ⓔ
20. Wilton	20 Ⓐ Ⓑ Ⓒ Ⓓ Ⓔ	20 Ⓐ Ⓑ Ⓒ Ⓓ Ⓔ
21. 5500-8599 Carter	21 Ⓐ Ⓑ Ⓒ Ⓓ Ⓔ	21 Ⓐ Ⓑ Ⓒ Ⓓ Ⓔ
22. 3700-9899 Carter	22 Ⓐ Ⓑ Ⓒ Ⓓ Ⓔ	22 Ⓐ Ⓑ Ⓒ Ⓓ Ⓔ
23. 7200-8799 Bell	23 Ⓐ Ⓑ Ⓒ Ⓓ Ⓔ	23 Ⓐ Ⓑ Ⓒ Ⓓ Ⓔ
24. Atlantic	24 Ⓐ Ⓑ Ⓒ Ⓓ Ⓔ	24 Ⓐ Ⓑ Ⓒ Ⓓ Ⓔ
25. 3300-3589 Huber	25 Ⓐ Ⓑ Ⓒ Ⓓ Ⓔ	25 Ⓐ Ⓑ Ⓒ Ⓓ Ⓔ
26. 3500-4699 Huber	26 Ⓐ Ⓑ Ⓒ Ⓓ Ⓔ	26 Ⓐ Ⓑ Ⓒ Ⓓ Ⓔ
27. 1500-2399 Bell	27 Ⓐ Ⓑ Ⓒ Ⓓ Ⓔ	27 Ⓐ Ⓑ Ⓒ Ⓓ Ⓔ
28. 7099-8999 Carter	28 Ⓐ Ⓑ Ⓒ Ⓓ Ⓔ	28 Ⓐ Ⓑ Ⓒ Ⓓ Ⓔ
29. 3500-4699 Huber	29 Ⓐ Ⓑ Ⓒ Ⓓ Ⓔ	29 Ⓐ Ⓑ Ⓒ Ⓓ Ⓔ
30. 3700-9899 Carter	30 Ⓐ Ⓑ Ⓒ Ⓓ Ⓔ	30 Ⓐ Ⓑ Ⓒ Ⓓ Ⓔ
31. Vernon	31 Ⓐ Ⓑ Ⓒ Ⓓ Ⓔ	31 Ⓐ Ⓑ Ⓒ Ⓓ Ⓔ
32. 3300-3589 Huber	32 Ⓐ Ⓑ Ⓒ Ⓓ Ⓔ	32 Ⓐ Ⓑ Ⓒ Ⓓ Ⓔ
33. Alden	33 Ⓐ Ⓑ Ⓒ Ⓓ Ⓔ	33 Ⓐ Ⓑ Ⓒ Ⓓ Ⓔ
34. 3500-4699 Huber	34 Ⓐ Ⓑ Ⓒ Ⓓ Ⓔ	34 Ⓐ Ⓑ Ⓒ Ⓓ Ⓔ
35. Windell	35 Ⓐ Ⓑ Ⓒ Ⓓ Ⓔ	35 Ⓐ Ⓑ Ⓒ Ⓓ Ⓔ
36. 6500-6499 Huber	36 Ⓐ Ⓑ Ⓒ Ⓓ Ⓔ	36 Ⓐ Ⓑ Ⓒ Ⓓ Ⓔ
37. 3400-3699 Bell	37 Ⓐ Ⓑ Ⓒ Ⓓ Ⓔ	37 Ⓐ Ⓑ Ⓒ Ⓓ Ⓔ
38. 1600-2499 Carter	38 Ⓐ Ⓑ Ⓒ Ⓓ Ⓔ	38 Ⓐ Ⓑ Ⓒ Ⓓ Ⓔ
39. Atlantic	39 Ⓐ Ⓑ Ⓒ Ⓓ Ⓔ	39 Ⓐ Ⓑ Ⓒ Ⓓ Ⓔ
40. 8100-8499 Huber	40 Ⓐ Ⓑ Ⓒ Ⓓ Ⓔ	40 Ⓐ Ⓑ Ⓒ Ⓓ Ⓔ

Go on to the next number on the next page.

41. 3400-3699 Bell	41 Ⓐ Ⓑ Ⓒ Ⓓ Ⓔ	41 Ⓐ Ⓑ Ⓒ Ⓓ Ⓔ
42. 3700-9899 Carter	42 Ⓐ Ⓑ Ⓒ Ⓓ Ⓔ	42 Ⓐ Ⓑ Ⓒ Ⓓ Ⓔ
43. Alden	43 Ⓐ Ⓑ Ⓒ Ⓓ Ⓔ	43 Ⓐ Ⓑ Ⓒ Ⓓ Ⓔ
44. Wilton	44 Ⓐ Ⓑ Ⓒ Ⓓ Ⓔ	44 Ⓐ Ⓑ Ⓒ Ⓓ Ⓔ
45. 7099-8999 Carter	45 Ⓐ Ⓑ Ⓒ Ⓓ Ⓔ	45 Ⓐ Ⓑ Ⓒ Ⓓ Ⓔ
46. 8100-8499 Huber	46 Ⓐ Ⓑ Ⓒ Ⓓ Ⓔ	46 Ⓐ Ⓑ Ⓒ Ⓓ Ⓔ
47. 4500-9999 Carter	47 Ⓐ Ⓑ Ⓒ Ⓓ Ⓔ	47 Ⓐ Ⓑ Ⓒ Ⓓ Ⓔ
48. 7200-8799 Bell	48 Ⓐ Ⓑ Ⓒ Ⓓ Ⓔ	48 Ⓐ Ⓑ Ⓒ Ⓓ Ⓔ
49. Atlantic	49 Ⓐ Ⓑ Ⓒ Ⓓ Ⓔ	49 Ⓐ Ⓑ Ⓒ Ⓓ Ⓔ
50. Windell	50 Ⓐ Ⓑ Ⓒ Ⓓ Ⓔ	50 Ⓐ Ⓑ Ⓒ Ⓓ Ⓔ
51. 3300-3589 Huber	51 Ⓐ Ⓑ Ⓒ Ⓓ Ⓔ	51 Ⓐ Ⓑ Ⓒ Ⓓ Ⓔ
52. 3400-3699 Bell	52 Ⓐ Ⓑ Ⓒ Ⓓ Ⓔ	52 Ⓐ Ⓑ Ⓒ Ⓓ Ⓔ
53. 6500-6499 Huber	53 Ⓐ Ⓑ Ⓒ Ⓓ Ⓔ	53 Ⓐ Ⓑ Ⓒ Ⓓ Ⓔ
54. Lucy	54 Ⓐ Ⓑ Ⓒ Ⓓ Ⓔ	54 Ⓐ Ⓑ Ⓒ Ⓓ Ⓔ
55. 4400-5399 Huber	55 Ⓐ Ⓑ Ⓒ Ⓓ Ⓔ	55 Ⓐ Ⓑ Ⓒ Ⓓ Ⓔ
56. 2200-2699 Bell	56 Ⓐ Ⓑ Ⓒ Ⓓ Ⓔ	56 Ⓐ Ⓑ Ⓒ Ⓓ Ⓔ
57. Perry	57 Ⓐ Ⓑ Ⓒ Ⓓ Ⓔ	57 Ⓐ Ⓑ Ⓒ Ⓓ Ⓔ
58. 4400-5399 Huber	58 Ⓐ Ⓑ Ⓒ Ⓓ Ⓔ	58 Ⓐ Ⓑ Ⓒ Ⓓ Ⓔ
59. 6500-6499 Huber	59 Ⓐ Ⓑ Ⓒ Ⓓ Ⓔ	59 Ⓐ Ⓑ Ⓒ Ⓓ Ⓔ
60. 7200-8799 Bell	60 Ⓐ Ⓑ Ⓒ Ⓓ Ⓔ	60 Ⓐ Ⓑ Ⓒ Ⓓ Ⓔ
61. 4400-5399 Huber	61 Ⓐ Ⓑ Ⓒ Ⓓ Ⓔ	61 Ⓐ Ⓑ Ⓒ Ⓓ Ⓔ
62. 6500-6499 Huber	62 Ⓐ Ⓑ Ⓒ Ⓓ Ⓔ	62 Ⓐ Ⓑ Ⓒ Ⓓ Ⓔ
63. 3400-3699 Bell	63 Ⓐ Ⓑ Ⓒ Ⓓ Ⓔ	63 Ⓐ Ⓑ Ⓒ Ⓓ Ⓔ
64. Livonia	64 Ⓐ Ⓑ Ⓒ Ⓓ Ⓔ	64 Ⓐ Ⓑ Ⓒ Ⓓ Ⓔ
65. 3700-9899 Carter	65 Ⓐ Ⓑ Ⓒ Ⓓ Ⓔ	65 Ⓐ Ⓑ Ⓒ Ⓓ Ⓔ
66. Vernon	66 Ⓐ Ⓑ Ⓒ Ⓓ Ⓔ	66 Ⓐ Ⓑ Ⓒ Ⓓ Ⓔ
67. 3700-9899 Carter	67 Ⓐ Ⓑ Ⓒ Ⓓ Ⓔ	67 Ⓐ Ⓑ Ⓒ Ⓓ Ⓔ
68. 2500-3599 Bell	68 Ⓐ Ⓑ Ⓒ Ⓓ Ⓔ	68 Ⓐ Ⓑ Ⓒ Ⓓ Ⓔ
69. 3400-3699 Bell	69 Ⓐ Ⓑ Ⓒ Ⓓ Ⓔ	69 Ⓐ Ⓑ Ⓒ Ⓓ Ⓔ
70. 5500-8599 Carter	70 Ⓐ Ⓑ Ⓒ Ⓓ Ⓔ	70 Ⓐ Ⓑ Ⓒ Ⓓ Ⓔ
71. 1600-2499 Carter	71 Ⓐ Ⓑ Ⓒ Ⓓ Ⓔ	71 Ⓐ Ⓑ Ⓒ Ⓓ Ⓔ
72. Atlantic	72 Ⓐ Ⓑ Ⓒ Ⓓ Ⓔ	72 Ⓐ Ⓑ Ⓒ Ⓓ Ⓔ
73. 3300-3589 Huber	73 Ⓐ Ⓑ Ⓒ Ⓓ Ⓔ	73 Ⓐ Ⓑ Ⓒ Ⓓ Ⓔ
74. 7099-8999 Carter	74 Ⓐ Ⓑ Ⓒ Ⓓ Ⓔ	74 Ⓐ Ⓑ Ⓒ Ⓓ Ⓔ
75. 4500-9999 Carter	75 Ⓐ Ⓑ Ⓒ Ⓓ Ⓔ	75 Ⓐ Ⓑ Ⓒ Ⓓ Ⓔ
76. 2500-3599 Bell	76 Ⓐ Ⓑ Ⓒ Ⓓ Ⓔ	76 Ⓐ Ⓑ Ⓒ Ⓓ Ⓔ
77. 8100-8499 Huber	77 Ⓐ Ⓑ Ⓒ Ⓓ Ⓔ	77 Ⓐ Ⓑ Ⓒ Ⓓ Ⓔ
78. Alden	78 Ⓐ Ⓑ Ⓒ Ⓓ Ⓔ	78 Ⓐ Ⓑ Ⓒ Ⓓ Ⓔ
79. 3300-3589 Huber	79 Ⓐ Ⓑ Ⓒ Ⓓ Ⓔ	79 Ⓐ Ⓑ Ⓒ Ⓓ Ⓔ
80. Lucy	80 Ⓐ Ⓑ Ⓒ Ⓓ Ⓔ	80 Ⓐ Ⓑ Ⓒ Ⓓ Ⓔ
81. 4500-9999 Carter	81 Ⓐ Ⓑ Ⓒ Ⓓ Ⓔ	81 Ⓐ Ⓑ Ⓒ Ⓓ Ⓔ
82. 4400-5399 Huber	82 Ⓐ Ⓑ Ⓒ Ⓓ Ⓔ	82 Ⓐ Ⓑ Ⓒ Ⓓ Ⓔ
83. 6500-6499 Huber	83 Ⓐ Ⓑ Ⓒ Ⓓ Ⓔ	83 Ⓐ Ⓑ Ⓒ Ⓓ Ⓔ
84. 5500-8599 Carter	84 Ⓐ Ⓑ Ⓒ Ⓓ Ⓔ	84 Ⓐ Ⓑ Ⓒ Ⓓ Ⓔ
85. 7099-8999 Carter	85 Ⓐ Ⓑ Ⓒ Ⓓ Ⓔ	85 Ⓐ Ⓑ Ⓒ Ⓓ Ⓔ
86. 4500-9999 Carter	86 Ⓐ Ⓑ Ⓒ Ⓓ Ⓔ	86 Ⓐ Ⓑ Ⓒ Ⓓ Ⓔ
87. 3500-4699 Huber	87 Ⓐ Ⓑ Ⓒ Ⓓ Ⓔ	87 Ⓐ Ⓑ Ⓒ Ⓓ Ⓔ
88. 2500-3599 Bell	88 Ⓐ Ⓑ Ⓒ Ⓓ Ⓔ	88 Ⓐ Ⓑ Ⓒ Ⓓ Ⓔ

Go on to the next number on the next page.

STOP

If you finish before the time is up,

go back and check your answers.

(See the correct answers on the next page.)

Correct Answers

Memory-for-Address Test

1. E	31. B	61. D
2. C	32. A	62. C
3. A	33. D	63. D
4. D	34. E	64. E
5. E	35. B	65. C
6. B	36. C	66. B
7. C	37. D	67. C
8. A	38. B	68. B
9. B	39. C	69. D
10. E	40. B	70. A
11. D	41. D	71. B
12. E	42. C	72. C
13. B	43. D	73. A
14. B	44. A	74. D
15. A	45. D	75. E
16. D	46. B	76. B
17. E	47. E	77. B
18. D	48. E	78. D
19. C	49. C	79. A
20. A	50. B	80. D
21. A	51. A	81. E
22. C	52. D	82. D
23. E	53. C	83. C
24. C	54. D	84. A
25. A	55. D	85. D
26. E	56. C	86. E
27. A	57. E	87. E
28. D	58. D	88. B
29. E	59. C	
30. C	60. E	

460 RCA Examination

Number Series Test 21

Series of Numbers That Progresses and Follows Definite Order

The *Number Series Test* involves a series of numbers that follows some definite pattern. For each number series question, there is a series of numbers that progresses from left to right and follows some definite order. All you must do is to determine what the next two last numbers or the last two pairs of numbers will be if the same order is continued. The test, which is considered nonverbal, measures your ability to find the "missing link."

Here are some strategies:

Strategy 1: Find the rule that creates the series of numbers.

Strategy 2: Found out which number comes next or is missing.

Strategy 3: Find the patterns used.

In this test, you'll discover that the pattern or the relationship may involve the use of the following:

- addition
- subtraction
- multiplication
- division
- squaring
- cubing
- square root
- cube root

At first, the sequence of numbers is easier to determine. For instance, the number may increase by 2, 4, 5, etc.; sometimes, the number may decrease by 1, 3, 5, etc. But sometimes, the series involves the alternating uses of addition and subtraction, which may appear a little more complex.

Simple Number Series. Each of the three sample questions below gives a series of seven numbers. Each number follows a certain pattern or order. Choose what will be the next one or two numbers in that series if the pattern is continued.

1.   6   8   10   12   14   16   18   ....

273

A) 22
B) 20
C) 24
D) 21
E) 23

In this question, the pattern is to add 2 to each number: 6 + 2 = 8; 8 + 2 = 10; 10 + 2 = 12; 12 + 2 14; 14 + 2 = 16; 16 + 2 = 18. The next number in the series is 18 + 2 which equals 20. B is the correct answer. Here's how it's done:

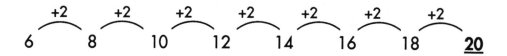

2.   7   9   12   15   17   20   23   ...

A) 29
B) 27
C) 26
D) 25
E) 39

In this question, the pattern is to add 2 to the first number (7 + 2 = 9); add 3 to the second number (9 + 3 = 12; add 3 to the third number (12 + 3 = 15); add 2 to the fourth number (15 + 2 = 17); add 3 to the fifth number (17 + 3 = 20); add 3 to the sixth number (20 + 3) = 23). To continue the series, add 2 to the next number (23 + 2) = 25). D is the correct answer. Here's how it's done:

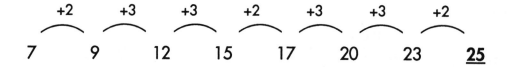

As you can see, the order or pattern is to add 2 once, then add 3 twice. Get it?

3.   9   10   8   9   7   8   6   ...   ...

A) 7
B) 5
C) 9

D) 8
E) 6

In this question, the pattern is to add 1 to the first number, subtract 2 from the next, add 1, subtract 2, and so on. (9 + 1 = 10; 10 - 2 = 8; 8 + 1 = 9; 9 - 2 = 7; 7 + 1 = 8; 8 - 2 = 6; 6 + 1 = 7). Thus A is the correct answer. Here's how it's done:

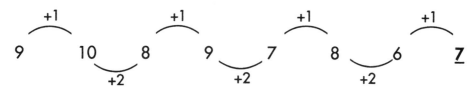

Complex Number Series. These questions are more difficult and the correct answer must be chosen from sets of two numbers. Your job is to select the correct set of two numbers.

The technique used in this type of question is to compare the first number to the third number, the second to the fourth, the third to the fifth, and so on. To make it easier, draw lines to join the numbers as you analyze the pattern. So that you won't be confused, draw the lines both above and below the numbers. (When you finish answering the questions, you may erase these lines on the question or answer sheet. It's as simple as connecting Monday to Wednesday, Wednesday to Friday, Tuesday to Thursday, and Thursday to Saturday. Then all you have to do is find the pattern within each group of numbers.

1. 7   13   8   15   10   17   13   19   17   ...   ...

A) 23   24
B) 21   22
C) 25   26
D) 27   28
E) 28   30

There two patterns in this series. Add 2 to the second, fourth, sixth, and the eight numbers and add to the first, third, fifth, seventh, and ninth numbers as follows: + 1, + 2, +3, +4, +5. B is the correct answer. Here's how it's done:

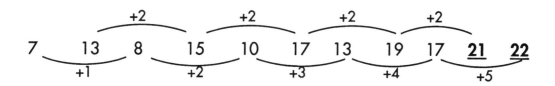

2.   1   7   2   6   4   5   7   4   ...   ...

A) 13 3
B) 15 2
C) 11 3
D) 17 2
E) 12 2

For the first, third, fifth, and seventh numbers, you must to add 1, add 2, add 3, and add 4. For the second, fourth, sixth, and eight numbers, subtract 1 each time. C is the correct answer. Here's how it's done:

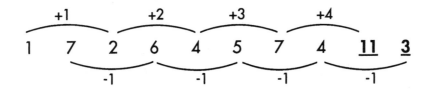

In this test, you are allotted 20 minutes to complete 24 number series questions. In other words, if you have a hard time on a particular question, skip it and go to the next number, etc. Then if you have enough time left, go back to any of the unanswered questions.

Number Series
Practice Test

1. 8 14 9 16 11 18 14 20 18 ... ... 1. .... A) 24 22   C) 22 30   E) 20 23
   B) 22 23   D) 16 22

2. 12 17 12 16 12 15 12   ... ... 2. .... A) 12 13   C) 14 12   E) 14 13
   B) 12 14   D) 13 14

3. 12 3 4 12 5 6 12 ... ... 3. .... A) 6 7   C) 7 8   E) 7 12
   B) 7 7   D) 12 7

4. 1 5 3 7 5 9 7 ... ... 4. .... A) 5 3   C) 11 15   E) 5 9
   B) 11 9   D) 9 11

5. 5 8 10 13 15 18 ... ... 5. .... A) 21 24   C) 20 22   E) 19 21
   B) 20 23   D) 21 23

6. 20 7 17 19 6 16 18 ... ... 6. .... A) 5 17   C) 17 5   E) 5 15
   B) 4 14   D) 15 17

7. 8 9 10 6 7 8 4 ... ... 7. .... A) 5 6   C) 6 7   E) 5 3
   B) 6 4   D) 4 5

8. 17 4 5 17 6 7 17 ... ... 8. .... A) 8 9   C) 17 6   E) 17 8
   B) 8 8   D) 7 8

9. 19 8 7 18 9 8 17 10 9 ... ... 9. .... A) 16 9   C) 18 11   E) 16 11
   B) 18 10   D) 18 9

10. 11 18 12 19 13 20 14 ... ... 10. .... A) 21 15   C) 14 21   E) 15 16
    B) 14 15   D) 15 21

11. 18 17 11 16 15 12 14 ... ... 11. .... A) 11 13   C) 13 13   E) 13 11
    B) 15 11   D) 11 15

12. 15 7 14 8 13 9 12 ... ... 12. .... A) 10 13   C) 12 11   E) 11 10
    B) 10 12   D) 10 11

13. 15 26 24 23 21 20 18 ... ... 13. .... A) 17 15   C) 16 15   E) 13 14
    B) 16 14   D) 19 17

14. 23 29 28 21 27 26 18 25 24 14 23 ... ... 14. .... A) 18 17   C) 13 12   E) 22 9
    B) 24 10   D) 23 21

15. 10 8 13 11 16 14 19 17 22 ... ... 15. .... A) 25 20   C) 20 25   E) 23 26
    B) 20 23   D) 25 28

(See the correct answers on page 142.)

Number Series Practice Test

Here's how it's done.

1. 8   14   9   16   11   18   14   20   18   **22**   **23**

2. 12   17   12   16   12   15   12   **14**   **12**

3. 12   3   4   12   5   6   12   **7**   **8**

4. 1   5   3   7   5   9   7   **11**   **9**

5. 5   8   10   13   15   18   **20**   **23**

6. 20   7   17   19   6   16   18   **5**   **15**

7. 8   9   10   6   7   8   4   **5**   **6**

8. 17   4   5   17   6   7   17   **8**   **9**

+1 +1 +1

9. 19 8 7 18 9 8 17 10 9 **16** **11**

-1 -1 -1

+1 +1 +1 +1

10. 11 18 12 19 13 20 14 **21** **15**

+1 +1 +1

+1 +1

11. 18 17 11 16 15 12 14 **13** **13**

-1 -1 -1

+1 +1 +1

12. 15 7 14 8 13 9 12 **10** **11**

-1 -1 -1 -1

-3 -3 -3

13. 15 26 24 23 21 20 18 **17** **15**

-3 -3 -3

-2 -3 -4 -5

14. 23 29 28 21 27 26 18 25 24 14 23 **22** **9**

-1 -1 -1 -1

+3 +3 +3 +3

15. 10 8 13 11 16 14 19 17 22 **20** **25**

+3 +3 +3 +3 +3

Correct Answers

Number Series Test

1. 22 23	8. 8 9
2. 14 12	9. 16 11
3. 7 8	10. 21 15
4. 11 9	11. 13 13
5. 20 23	12. 10 11
6. 5 15	13. 17 15
7. 5 6	14. 22 9
	15. 20 25

Following Oral Instructions Test

Instructions to Be Followed by Job Applicants

Part D of the 460 RCA Exam consists of the *Following Oral Instructions Test* that involves directions to be given by the examiner to job applicants. When the examiner talks, you listen. If you don't, that's the end of the story; you will fail on this exam. It's because during the test, direction for answering questions will be given orally, and if you miss those questions, the examiner will not repeat them. You better listen carefully to the instructions, and follow them.

The suggested answers to each questions are lettered. You choose the *best* answer, whichever it is.

To practice for the test, you might have a friend read the directions to you, while you mark your answers on the sample answer sheet on page 2.

You will be told to follow directions by writing in a test booklet and then on an answer sheet. The test booklet will have lines of material like the following four samples:

SAMPLE 8. 5 _____

SAMPLE 9. 1 6 4 3 7

SAMPLE 10. D B A E C

SAMPLE 11. (8__) (5__) (2__) (9__) (10__)

SAMPLE 12. (7__) [6__] (1__) [12__]

To practice this test, tear off page 3. Then have somebody read the instructions to you. When you are told to darken a space on the sample answer sheet, use the one on this page.

```
┌─────────────────────────────────────────┐
│          Sample Answer Sheet             │
│                                          │
│  1 Ⓐ Ⓑ Ⓒ Ⓓ Ⓔ      7 Ⓐ Ⓑ Ⓒ Ⓓ Ⓔ      │
│                                          │
│  2 Ⓐ Ⓑ Ⓒ Ⓓ Ⓔ      8 Ⓐ Ⓑ Ⓒ Ⓓ Ⓔ      │
│                                          │
│  3 Ⓐ Ⓑ Ⓒ Ⓓ Ⓔ      9 Ⓐ Ⓑ Ⓒ Ⓓ Ⓔ      │
│                                          │
│  4 Ⓐ Ⓑ Ⓒ Ⓓ Ⓔ     10 Ⓐ Ⓑ Ⓒ Ⓓ Ⓔ      │
│                                          │
│  5 Ⓐ Ⓑ Ⓒ Ⓓ Ⓔ     11 Ⓐ Ⓑ Ⓒ Ⓓ Ⓔ      │
│                                          │
│  6 Ⓐ Ⓑ Ⓒ Ⓓ Ⓔ     12 Ⓐ Ⓑ Ⓒ Ⓓ Ⓔ      │
└─────────────────────────────────────────┘
```

Instructions to be read (the words in parentheses should not be read aloud):

You are to follow the instructions that I shall read to you. I cannot repeat them.

Look at the samples. Sample 1 has a number and a line beside it. On the line write an A. (Pause 2 seconds.) Now on the sample answer sheet, find number 5 (pause 2 seconds) and darken the space for the letter you just wrote on the line. (Pause 2 seconds.)

Look at Sample 2. (Pause slightly.) Draw a line under the third number. (Pause 2 seconds.) Now look on the sample answer sheet, find the number under which you just drew a line, and darken space B as in "baker" for that number. (Pause 5 seconds.)

Look at Sample 3. (Pause slightly.) Draw a line under the third letter in the line. (Pause 2 seconds.) Now on your answer sheet, find number 9 (pause 2 seconds) and darken the space for the letter under which you drew a line. (Pause 5 seconds.)

Look at the five circles in Sample 4. (Pause slightly.) Each circle has a number and a line in it. Write D as in "dog" on the blank in the last circle. (Pause 2 seconds.) Now on the sample answer sheet, darken the space for the number-letter combination that is in the circle you just wrote in (pause 5 seconds.)

Now look at the sample answer sheet. (Pause slightly.) You should have darkened spaces 4B, 5A, 9A, and 10D on the sample answer sheet. (If the person preparing to take the examination made any mistakes, try to help him see why he made wrong marks.)

Examination 710 23

Data Conversion Operator, Clerk-Typist & Clerk Stenographer

(Data Conversion Operator, Clerk-Typist, Clerk Stenographer)

The following questions are samples of the types of questions that will be used on Examination 710. Study these questions carefully. Each question has several suggested answers. You are to decide which one is the **best answer**. Next, on the Sample Answer Sheet below, find the answer space that is numbered the same number as the question, then darken the space that is lettered the same as the answer you have selected. After you have answered all the questions, compare your answers with the ones given in the Correct Answers to Sample Questions below the Sample Answer Sheets.

Sample Questions 1 through 14 - **Clerical Aptitude**

In Sample Questions 1 through 3 below, there is a name or code in a box at the left, and four other names or codes in alphabetical or numerical order at the right. Find the correct space for the boxed name or number so that it will be in alphabetical and/or numerical order with the others and mark the letter of that space as your answer on your Sample Answer Sheet below.

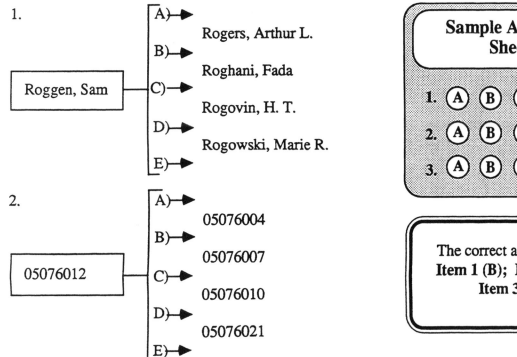

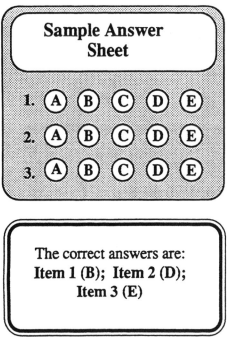

Sample Answer Sheet

1. (A) (B) (C) (D) (E)
2. (A) (B) (C) (D) (E)
3. (A) (B) (C) (D) (E)

The correct answers are:
Item 1 (B); Item 2 (D);
Item 3 (E)

3.

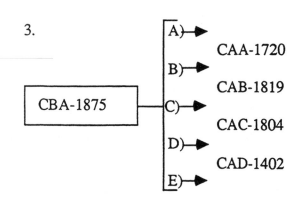

CAA-1720

CAB-1819

CBA-1875

CAC-1804

CAD-1402

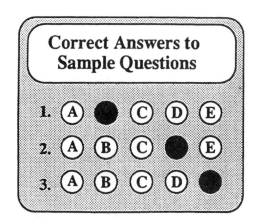

Sample Questions 4 through 8 require you to compare names, addresses, or codes. In each line across the page, there are three names, addresses or codes that are much alike. Compare the three and decide which ones are exactly alike. On the Sample Answer Sheet at the bottom, mark the answers:

A   if **ALL THREE** names, addresses, or codes are exactly **ALIKE**
B   if only the **FIRST** and **SECOND** names, addresses, or codes are exactly **ALIKE**
C   if only the **FIRST** and **THIRD** names, addresses, or codes are exactly **ALIKE**
D   if only the **SECOND** and **THIRD** names, addresses, or codes are exactly **ALIKE**
E   if **ALL THREE** names, addresses, or codes are **DIFFERENT**

4.	Helene Bedell	Helene Beddell	Helene Beddell
5.	F. T. Wedemeyer	F. T. Wedemeyer	F. T. Wedmeyer
6.	3214 W. Beaumont St.	3214 Beaumount St.	3214 Beaumont St.
7.	BC 3105T-5	BC 3015T-5	BC 3105T-5
8.	4460327	4460327	4460327

For the next two questions, find the correct spelling of the word and darken the appropriate answer space on your Sample Answer Sheet. If none of the alternatives are correct, darken Space D.

9.   A) accomodate
     B) acommodate
     C) accommadate
     D) none of the above

10. A) manageble
     B) manageable
     C) manegeable
     D) none of the above

Sample Answer Sheet

4. (A) (B) (C) (D) (E)
5. (A) (B) (C) (D) (E)
6. (A) (B) (C) (D) (E)
7. (A) (B) (C) (D) (E)
8. (A) (B) (C) (D) (E)
9. (A) (B) (C) (D)
10. (A) (B) (C) (D)

The correct answers are:
Item 4 (D);
Item 5 (B);
Item 6 (E);
Item 7 (C);
Item 8 (A);
Item 9 (D);
Item 10 (B)

Correct Answers to Sample Questions

4. (A) (B) (C) ● (E)
5. (A) ● (C) (D) (E)
6. (A) (B) (C) (D) ●
7. (A) (B) ● (D) (E)
8. ● (B) (C) (D) (E)
9. (A) (B) (C) ●
10. (A) ● (C) (D)

For Questions 11 through 14, perform the computation as indicated in the question and find the answer among the list of alternative responses. Mark your Sample Answer Sheet A, B, C, or D for the correct answer; or, if your answer is not among these, mark E for that question.

11.   32 + 26 =

    A)   69
    B)   59
    C)   58
    D)   54
    E)   none of the above

12.   57 - 15 =

    A)   72
    B)   62
    C)   54
    D)   44
    E)   none of the above

13.   23 x 7 =

    A)   164
    B)   161
    C)   154
    D)   141
    E)   none of the above

14.   160 / 5 =

    A)   32
    B)   30
    C)   25
    D)   21
    E)   none of the above

Sample Answer Sheet

11. (A) (B) (C) (D) (E)
12. (A) (B) (C) (D) (E)
13. (A) (B) (C) (D) (E)
14. (A) (B) (C) (D) (E)

The correct answers are:
**Item 11 (C); Item 12 (E);
Item 13 (B); Item 14 (A)**

Correct Answers to Sample Questions

11. (A) (B) ● (D) (E)
12. (A) (B) (C) (D) ●
13. (A) ● (C) (D) (E)
14. ● (B) (C) (D) (E)

Sample Questions 15 through 22 - **Verbal Abilities**

Sample items 15 through 17 below test the ability to follow instructions. They direct you to mark a specific number and letter combination on your Sample Answer Sheet. The answers that you are instructed to mark are, for the most part, NOT in numerical sequence (·i.e., you would not use Number 1 on your answer sheet to answer Question 1; Number 2 for Question 2, etc.). Instead, you must mark the number and space specifically designated in each test question.

Sample Answer Sheet

15. (A) (B) (C) (D) (E)
16. (A) (B) (C) (D) (E)
17. (A) (B) (C) (D) (E)

15. Look at the letters below. Draw a circle around the middle letter. Now, on your Sample Answer Sheet, find Number 16 and darken the space for the letter you just circled.

    R   C   H

The correct answers are:
**Item 15 (B); Item 16 (C);
Item 17 (A)**

16. Draw a line under the number shown below that is more than 10 but less than 20. Find that number on your Sample Answer Sheet, and darken Space A.

    5   9   17   22

17. Add the numbers 11 and 4 and write your answer on the blank line below. Now find this number on your Sample Answer Sheet and darken the space for the second letter in the alphabet.

    _____

Correct Answers to Sample Questions

15. (A) ● (C) (D) (E)
16. (A) (B) ● (D) (E)
17. ● (B) (C) (D) (E)

Answer the remaining Sample Test Questions on the Sample Answer Sheet in numerical sequence (i.e., Number 18 on the Sample Answer Sheet for Question 18; Number 19 for Question 19, etc.).

Select the sentence below which is most appropriate with respect to grammar, usage, and punctuation suitable for a formal letter or report.

18.   A) He should of responded to the letter by now.
      B) A response to the letter by the end of the week.
      C) The letter required his immediate response.
      D) A response by him to the letter is necessary.

In questions 19 and 20 below, you will be asked to decide what the highlighted word means.

19.   The payment was **authorized** yesterday. **Authorized** most nearly means

      A) expected
      B) approved
      C) refunded
      D) received

20.   Please **delete** the second paragraph. **Delete** most nearly means

      A) type
      B) read
      C) edit
      D) omit

In questions 21 and 22 below, you are asked to read a paragraph, then answer the question that follows it.

Sample Answer Sheet

18. (A) (B) (C) (D)
19. (A) (B) (C) (D)
20. (A) (B) (C) (D)

The correct answers are:
**Item 18 (C);   Item 19 (B);
Item 20 (D)**

Corrected Answers to Sample Questions

18. (A) (B) ● (D)
19. (A) ● (C) (D)
20. (A) (B) (C) ●

21. "Window Clerks working for the Postal Service have direct financial responsibility for the selling of postage. In addition, they are expected to have a thorough knowledge concerning the acceptability of all material offered by customers for mailing. Any information provided to the public by these employees must be completely accurate."

The paragraph best supports the statement that Window Clerks

A) must account for the stamps issued to them for sale
B) have had long training in other Postal Service jobs
C) must help sort mail to be delivered by carriers
D) inspect the contents of all packages offered for mailing

22. "The most efficient method for performing a task is not always easily determined. That which is economical in terms of time must be carefully distinguished from that which is economical in terms of expended energy. In short, the quickest method may require a degree of physical effort that may be neither essential nor desirable."

The paragraph best supports the statement that

A) it is more efficient to perform a task slowly than rapidly
B) skill in performing a task should not be acquired at the expense of time
C) the most efficient execution of a task is not always the one done in the shortest time
D) energy and time cannot both be considered in the performance of a single task

Sample Answer Sheet

21. Ⓐ Ⓑ Ⓒ Ⓓ
22. Ⓐ Ⓑ Ⓒ Ⓓ

The correct answers are:
Item 21 (A); Item 22 (C)

Corrected Answers to Sample Questions

21. ● Ⓑ Ⓒ Ⓓ
22. Ⓐ Ⓑ ● Ⓓ

UNITED STATES
POSTAL SERVICE

Sample Questions for Stenography
Examination 711

The sample below shows the length of material dictated. Have someone dictate the passage to you so that you can see how well prepared you are to take dictation at 80 words a minute. Each pair of lines is dictated in 10 seconds. Dictate periods, but not commas. Read the exercise with the expression the punctuation indicates.

I realize that this practice dictation is not a part of the examination	10 sec.
proper and is not to be scored.(Period) When making a study of the private	20 sec.
pension structure and its influence on turnover. the most striking feature is its	30 sec.
youth.(Period) As has been shown, the time of greatest growth began just a few years	40 sec.
ago.(Period) The influence that this growth has had on the labor market and	50 sec.
worker attitudes is hard to assess, partly because the effects have not yet fully	1 min.
evolved and many are still in the growing stage.(Period) Even so, most pension	10 sec.
plans began with much more limited gains than they give now.(Period) For example,	20 sec.
as private plans mature they grant a larger profit and a greater range of gains to	30 sec.
more workers and thereby become more important.(Period) Plans which protect accrued pension	40 sec.
credits are rather new and are being revised in the light of past trends.(Period)	50 sec.
As informal and formal information on pension plans spreads, the workers become more	2 min.
aware of the plans and their provisions increase, their impact on employee attitudes	10 sec.
and decisions will no doubt become stronger.(Period) Each year, more and more workers	20 sec.
will be retiring with a private pension, their firsthand knowledge of the benefits to	30 sec.
be gained from private pensions will spread to still active workers.(Period) Thus, workers	40 sec.
may less often view pensions as just another part of the security package	50 sec.
based on service and more often see them as unique benefits.(Period)	3 min.

On the back page, the TRANSCRIPT and WORD LIST for part of the above dictation are similar to those each competitor will receive for the dictation test. Many words have been omitted from the TRANSCRIPT. Compare your notes with it. When you come to a blank space in the TRANSCRIPT, decide which word (or words) belongs in the space. Look for the missing word in the WORD LIST. Notice what letter is printed beside the word. Write that letter in the blank. B is written in blank 1 to show how you are to record your choice. Write E if the exact answer is NOT in the WORD LIST. You may also write the word (or words) or the shorthand for it, if you wish. The same choice may belong in more than one blank.

EFFECTIVE APRIL 1993

ALPHABETIC WORD LIST

Write E if the answer is NOT listed.

at - D	make - A
attitudes - C	making - B
be - B	market - B
been - C	markets - D
began - D	marking - D
being - A	never - B
completely - A	not - D
examination - A	over - C
examine - B	part - C
examining - D	partly - D
feat - A	pension - C
feature - C	practical - C
full - B	practice - B
fully - D	private - D
greater - D	proper - C
grow - B	section - D
growing - C	so - B
had - D	still - A
has - C	structure - D
has been - B	structured - B
has had - A	to - D
has made - A	to be - C
in - C	trial - A
in part - B	turn - D
influence - A	turnover - B
labor - C	values - A
main - B	yet - C

TRANSCRIPT

B
I realize that this ----- dictation is ----- a ----- of the
                 1   2   3

----- ----- and is ----- ----- scored.
  4   5   6   7

When ----- a ----- of the ----- ----- ----- and its
      8   9   10 11 12

----- on -----, the most striking ----- is its youth. As
13   14   15

----- shown, the time of ----- growth began just a few
16   17

years ago. The ----- that this growth ----- on the labor
            18   19

----- and worker ----- is hard to assess, ----- because
20   21   22

the effects have not yet ----- evolved and many are ----
                   23   24

in the ----- stage....
      25

(For the next sentences there would be another WORD LIST, if the entire sample dictation were transcribed.)

You will be given an answer sheet like the sample at the left, below, on which your answers can be scored by machine. Each number on the answer sheet stands for the blank with the same number in the transcript. Darken the space below the letter that is the same as the letter you wrote in the transcript. If you have not finished writing letters in the blanks in the transcript, or if you wish to make sure that you have lettered them correctly, you may continue to use your notes after you begin marking the answer sheet.

Answer Sheet for Sample Transcript

#		#	
1	A B C D E	14	A B C D E
2	A B C D E	15	A B C D E
3	A B C D E	16	A B C D E
4	A B C D E	17	A B C D E
5	A B C D E	18	A B C D E
6	A B C D E	19	A B C D E
7	A B C D E	20	A B C D E
8	A B C D E	21	A B C D E
9	A B C D E	22	A B C D E
10	A B C D E	23	A B C D E
11	A B C D E	24	A B C D E
12	A B C D E	25	A B C D E
13	A B C D E		

Correct Answers for Sample Transcript

#		#	
1	A **B** C D E	14	A **B** C D E
2	A B C **D** E	15	A B **C** D E
3	A B **C** D E	16	A **B** C D E
4	**A** B C D E	17	A B C D **E**
5	A B **C** D E	18	**A** B C D E
6	A B C **D** E	19	**A** B C D E
7	A B **C** D E	20	A **B** C D E
8	A **B** C D E	21	A B **C** D E
9	A B C D **E**	22	A B C **D** E
10	A B C **D** E	23	A B C **D** E
11	A B **C** D E	24	**A** B C D E
12	A B C **D** E	25	A B **C** D E
13	**A** B C D E		

Analyzing Examination 710

Clerical Aptitude, Verbal Abilities & Typing Test

I. Clerical Aptitude

Sample Questions 1 through 14

In sample questions 1 through 3, there is a name or a code in a box at the left. There are also four other names or codes in alphabetical or numeral order at the right. All you have to do is find out the appropriate place (A to D) at right, so that it will be in alphabetical and/or numerical order with the others. Mark the letter of that space as your answer on the sample answer sheet. In other words, know how to alphabetize or do numerical arrangement.

You are required by sample questions 4 through 8 to compare names, addresses, and codes. In each line across the page, there are three names, addresses, or codes that are much alike. You must compare the three and decide which ones are exactly alike or the same. You must answer A, B, C, D, or E.

On the same sample answer sheet at the right, mark the answer as follows:

A   If **ALL THREE** names, addresses, or codes are exactly **ALIKE**
B   If only the **FIRST** and **SECOND** names, addresses, or codes are exactly **ALIKE**
C   If only the **FIRST** and **THIRD** names, addresses, or codes are exactly **ALIKE**
D   If only the **SECOND** and **THIRD** names, addresses, or codes are exactly **ALIKE**
E   If **ALL THREE** names, addresses, or codes are **DIFERENT**

To make it easier for me to answer the questions, I developed my own system of memorization and comparison. Here is my code, which is easy to remember.

A = 123 (first, second, and third alike)
B = 12 (first and second alike)
C = 13 (first and third alike)
D = 23 (second and third alike)
E =   0 (all different)

(Note: This examination is for Data Conversion Operator, Clerk-Typist, and Clerk-Stenographer)

It is to be emphasized that you'll look for names, addresses, and codes that are ALIKE, except answer E. In other words, in answering E, you look for those names, and addresses, and codes that are all different. Memorize and use my code for this kind of test.

Examples:

4. Helene Bedell	Helene Beddell	Helene Beddell
5. F. T. Wedemeyer	F. T. Wedemeyer	F. T. Wedmeyer
6. 3214 W. Beaumont St.	3214 Beaumount St.	3214 Beaumont St.
7. BC 3105T-5	BC 3015T-5	BC 3105T-5
8. 4460327	4460327	4460327

General Rule: In comparing names or numbers, compare the first column with the second column, then the second with the third. So that you won't get confused, place a minus sign (- for different) or a plus sign (+ for alike) between the first column and the second column and between the second column and the third column. These plus and minus signs are my own codes, not the Postal Service's.

Example 1: (No. 4)

Helen Bedell   -   Helene Beddell   +   Helene Beddell

The code is 23 (second and third alike), so the answer is D.

In the above example, the first and second columns are different (the first column has one *d*, while the second column has a double *d*) and the second and third columns are alike (both have a double *d*). You must not compare the third and first columns to see whether they are different or alike. In short, the third and first columns are different. Hence, the answer is D (code 23).

Example 2: (No. 5)

F. T. Wedemeyer   +   F. T. Wedemeyer   -   F. T. Wedmeyer

In the above example, the first and second columns are alike (with a plus sign) and the second and third columns are different, the third column having only three *e*'s (with a minus sign). You don't need to compare the third column with the first. It is understood that they are different.

The code is 12 (first and second columns are alike). The correct answer is B.

Example 3: (No.6)

3214 W. Beaumont St.   -   3214 Beaumount St.   -   3214 Beaumont St.

If the first and the second columns are different (with a minus sign), and the third and second columns, are different, the code is 0 (all are different). As you can see, the first column has a direction, which is W (West), while the second and third columns have different spellings of streets. The second street is spelled "Beau*mount*) while the third is spelled "Beau*mont*." The correct answer is E, the code being 0.

Example 4: (No. 7)

BC 3105T-5   -   BC 3015T-5   -   BC 3105T-5

In the above example, the first and second columns are different (with a minus sign) and the second and third are different (with a minus sign). You still need to compare the third column with the first, to see if there is any similarity or difference. The first and third columns have the same letters and figures. So the code is 13 (first and third are alike). Therefore, the correct answer is C.

Example 5: (No.) 8

4460327   +   4460327   +   4460327

As you can see, the first and second columns (with a plus sign) are alike and the second and third columns are alike (with a plus sign). Since they are alike, the code is 123 (first, second, and third columns are alike). So the correct answer is A.

As explained in the above examples, you have to know which columns are alike.

After writing the answers, you should erase the plus and minus signs you made on the question sheet. However, if you have no more time to do it, then leave them alone.

Spelling

(See **Spelling Techniques**.)

For the next two questions, find the correct spelling of the word and darken the appropriate answer space on your sample answer sheet. If none of the alternatives are correct, darken Space D.

9.
A) accomodate
B) acommodate
C) accommadate
D) none of the above

10.
A) manageble
B) manageable
C) manegeable
D) none of the above

If you are practicing speed reading, you can glance at the words from A to D in a snap in the above example (question 9). You can immediately disregard A, B, and C because merely by looking at them you'll know they are awkwardly spelled. Pronounce the words to yourself and you'll know what I mean. D is the correct answer. As to question 10, B is the correct answer. The words *manage* and *able* are combined.

Arithmetic

For questions 11 through 14, perform the computation as indicated in the question and find the answer among the list of alternative responses. Mark your sample answer sheet A, B, C, or D for the correct answer; or if your answer is not among these, mark E for that question.

11.

$32 + 26 =$

A) 69
B) 59
C) 58
D) 54
E) none of the above

12.

$57 - 15 =$

A) 72
B) 62
C) 54
D) 44
E) none of the above

13.

23 x 7 =

A) 164
B) 161
C) 154
D) 141
E) none of the above

14.

160/5 =

A) 32
B) 30
C) 25
D) 21
E) none of the above

Now, for the analyses of questions 11 to 14.

You don't need to be an Einstein to score high on arithmetic tests. What you need to do is use some techniques and try them out with your own biocomputer. The Postal Service gives only simple mathematical problems, and you can surely make a perfect score if you have enough time to answer the questions. The problem is that time is limited, so you have to use some techniques to beat the system.

11. Addition problem (32 + 26):

```
  32
+ 26
  58
```

The numbers 32 and 26 are to be added together. The solution to the addition, 58 in this case, is called the "sum."

If the problem is as simple as this, without any carrying, you can simply add the numbers mentally from left to right—not

Sample Answer Sheet

11. Ⓐ Ⓑ Ⓒ Ⓓ Ⓔ
12. Ⓐ Ⓑ Ⓒ Ⓓ Ⓔ
13. Ⓐ Ⓑ Ⓒ Ⓓ Ⓔ
14. Ⓐ Ⓑ Ⓒ Ⓓ Ⓔ

The correct answers are:
**Item 11 (C); Item 12 (E);
Item 13 (B); Item 14 (A)**

Correct Answers to Sample Questions

11. Ⓐ Ⓑ ● Ⓓ Ⓔ
12. Ⓐ Ⓑ Ⓒ Ⓓ ●
13. Ⓐ ● Ⓒ Ⓓ Ⓔ
14. ● Ⓑ Ⓒ Ⓓ Ⓔ

from right to left, which is taught in school. It's much simpler and faster from left to right.

12. Subtraction problem (57 - 15):

```
 57
-15
 42
```

The number 15 is to be subtracted from 57. Simply deduct 1 from 5 and 5 from 7 (starting from the left, because you don't need borrowing. If you need to borrow, then start from right to left).

13. In the multiplication problem (23 x 7):

```
 23
 x7
161
```

In a simple multiplication problem like this, try to work mentally to save time. (When you write it down, you spend several seconds. Think to yourself, 7 x 3 = 21 (just remember 1 and carry 2): 7 x 2 = 14 + 2 = 16. Put the 1 after 16 and the answer is 161 or B.

14. Division problem (160/5):

5/160 = 32

The division given in the sample test is as simple as this, but remember, there's a time limit. You can do the division mentally, too by dividing 16 by 5 = 3 (with the extra 1). Place the extra 1 before 0 and the answer is 10. Dividing 10 by 5 = 2. Put 2 after 3 and the answer is 32 or A.

*(Also see **Numbers and Mathematics,** and **Strategies for Standardized Tests,** Solving Mathematics Problems.)*

II. Verbal Abilities

Sample questions 15 through 22

Sample questions 15 through 17 below tests the ability to follow instructions. They direct you to mark a specific number and letter combination on your sample answer sheet. The answers that you are instructed to mark are, for the most part, NOT in numerical sequence (i.e., you would not use number 1 on your answer sheet to answer question 1; number 2 for question 2, etc.). Instead, you must mark the number and space specifically designated in each test question, as specified in the following sample questions:

15. Look at the letters below. Draw a circle around the middle letter. Now, on your sample answer sheet, find Number 16 and darken the space for the letter you just circled.

R   C   H

So you darken the circle with letter C on number 16. In other words, you are not told to darken the letter C on number 15. The answer to question 15 is to be marked on number 16. So number 16 has C as the answer. How about the answer to number 15? Just continue.

16. Draw a line under the number shown below that is more than 10 but less than 20. Find that number on your sample sheet, and darken space A.

5   9   17   22

So the answer to question number 16 is to be marked on question number 17, which is A. So darken space A on Number 17. In other words, the answer to question number 16 is A, which happened to be on number 17.

17. Add the numbers 11 and 4 and write your answer on the blank line below. Now find this number on your sample answer sheet and darken the space for the second letter in the alphabet.

_____

Add 11 and 4 and the answer is 15. So find number 15 on the sample answer sheet. Darken the second letter in the alphabet, which happens to be B. So darken space B on number 15.

Sample Answer Sheet

15. (A) (B) (C) (D) (E)
16. (A) (B) (C) (D) (E)
17. (A) (B) (C) (D) (E)

The correct answers are:
**Item 15 (B);   Item 16 (C);
Item 17 (A)**

Correct Answers to Sample Questions

15. (A) ● (C) (D) (E)
16. (A) (B) ● (D) (E)
17. ● (B) (C) (D) (E)

In other words, the darkening of spaces started from number 16, then to number 17 and back to number 15. As you can see, the questions are easy to answer but the Postal Service is trying to confuse you and me!

Answer the remaining sample test questions on the sample answer sheet in numerical sequence (i.e., number 18 on the sample answer sheet for question 18; number 19 for question 19, etc.).

Select the sentence below that is the most appropriate with respect to grammar, usage, and punctuation for a formal letter or report.

18.

A) He should be of responded to the letter by now.
B) A response to the letter by the end of the week.
C) The letter required his immediate response.
D) A response by him to the letter is necessary.

If you analyze the sentences, you'll see the question A is awkward and question B is incomplete. So neither of them is the answer. C is grammatically correct. D, although a complete sentence, seems to be awkward, too. So C is the answer. Darken space C.

In questions 19 and 20 below, you'll be asked to decide what the highlighted word means:

19. The payment was **authorized** yesterday. **Authorized** means

---

Sample Answer Sheet

18. Ⓐ Ⓑ Ⓒ Ⓓ
19. Ⓐ Ⓑ Ⓒ Ⓓ
20. Ⓐ Ⓑ Ⓒ Ⓓ

The correct answers are:
Item 18 (C); Item 19 (B);
Item 20 (D)

Corrected Answers to Sample Questions

18. Ⓐ Ⓑ ⬤ Ⓓ
19. Ⓐ ⬤ Ⓒ Ⓓ
20. Ⓐ Ⓑ Ⓒ ⬤

A) expected
B) approved
C) refunded
D) received

In an instance, you'll know that *approved* (B) is the answer. Why? Because *expected, refunded,* and *received,* mean something else.

20. Please *delete* the second paragraph. *Delete* most nearly means

A) type
B) read
C) edit
D) omit

The letters *de* before *lete* indicate a negative action. That is, *de* means *from* which may mean take it out or away from something. So naturally, omit or D is the correct answer.

In questions 21 and 22 below, you are asked to read a paragraph, then answer the question that follows it:

21. "Window clerks working for the Postal Service have direct financial responsibility for the selling of postage. In addition, they are expected to have a thorough knowledge concerning the acceptability of all material offered by customers for mailing. Any information provided to the public by these employees must be completely accurate."

The paragraph best supports the statement that window clerks

A) must account for stamps issued to them for sale
B) have had long training in other Postal Service jobs
C) must help sort mail to be delivered by carriers
D) inspect the contents of all packages offered for mailing

(Reading Comprehension)

In choosing answers to reading comprehension questions, look for the main idea in the statement. In question 20, look for the main idea in the statement "Window clerks...." If you read it carefully, you'll see that the main point in the paragraph is the financial responsibility for the selling of postage. Hence, "A) must account for the stamps issued to them for sale" best supports the statement about Window Clerks.

22. "The most efficient method for performing a task is not always easily determined. That which is economical in terms of time must be carefully distinguished from that which is economical in terms of expended energy. In short, the quickest method may require a degree of physical effort that may be neither essential nor desirable."

The paragraph best supports the statement that

A) it is more efficient to perform a task slowly than rapidly

B) skill in performing a task should not be acquired at the expense of time

C) the most efficient execution of a task is not always the one done in the shortest time

D) energy and time cannot both be considered in the performance of a single task

If you analyze the statement in question 22, the sentence "the most efficient method for performing a task is not always easily determined" clearly indicates that it is the main idea in the statement. As you'll note, there's the word *efficient* in the first sentence of the statement and there's also the word *efficient* in two answer choices: "A) it is more efficient to perform a task slowly than rapidly" and "C) the most efficient execution of a task is not always the one done in the shortest time." So the correct answer is from either these two choices. And it is. C is the correct answer.

Sample Answer Sheet

21. Ⓐ Ⓑ Ⓒ Ⓓ
22. Ⓐ Ⓑ Ⓒ Ⓓ

The correct answers are:
Item 21 (A); Item 22 (C)

Corrected Answers to Sample Questions

21. ● Ⓑ Ⓒ Ⓓ
22. Ⓐ Ⓑ ● Ⓓ

Typing Test

As an applicant, you must show that you can type forty words per minute for five minutes with no more than two errors. Space, paragraph, spell, punctuate, capitalize, and begin and end each line precisely as shown in the exercise.

In the examination, you will have five minutes in which to copy the test exercise. When you complete the exercise, simply double space and begin again. In the test you must type at least sixteen lines to be eligible in speed. At that minimum speed, your paper should not have more than two errors. The number of errors permitted increases with the number of words typed.

Below is an example of the type of material that appears on the typing test:

> This is an example of the type of material which will be presented to you as the actual typewriting examination. Each competitor will be required to typewrite the practice material exactly as it appears on the copy. You are to space, capitalize, punctuate, spell, and begin and end each line exactly as it is presented in the copy. Each time you reach the end of the paragraph you should begin again and continue to practice typing the practice paragraph on scratch paper until the examiner tells you to stop. You are advised that it is more important to type accurately than to type rapidly.

I must repeat that to be a clerk-typist or mark-up clerk, automated, you should type at least forty words per minute and pass the last part of the exam: the typing test. I usually type fifty to sixty words per minute accurately, so whenever I take this typing test, and I have already made one mistake, I try to increase my speed to type more words. For example, when I took an automated mark-up clerk exam in Michigan (including the typing test), I increased my speed as soon as I knew I had made one error. I typed about sixty words per minute with only two errors. You are allowed more errors if you type more than forty words per minute.

Techniques

Try to be at the examination room at least thirty minutes before the test time. Select a typewriter that you like; remember, it will be your word processor, which will produce at least forty words per minute.

From the looks of the machine, you'll know whether you like it and it likes you. Check out the size and shape. Place your fingers in the proper places; see if they fit the keys. See if all the parts work: release the margins and make new ones, especially for the paragraph. How about the spaces? Is the typewriter set for the single space? How about the ribbon? Is it new? If the typewriter is an electric one, it might have a film ribbon, which is no problem.

Gentle Touch

Now feel the keys; be gentle with them. Feel how they react to your touch; touch every part, including the carriage return. Do you like the way it responds to your touch?

Probably, you are now breathing fast. Try typing some words, slowly. Then make a few strong strokes; see if the keys respond quickly to your strokes, or if they like your touch. Now you know your partner; you know which parts are sensitive and which aren't. You know where to touch it and when to touch it.

Now you are ready for your test. Concentrate hard and don't look at any other typewriter. Stare at your typewriter as if it's staring at you too. Say to your partner, "We'll make it."

Take Your Time

When the examiner says "Start!" don't rush and type at full speed. Although your fingers may be trembling and you may be breathing fast, make your every move correct and don't let your fingers slip from the keys. Be gentle with them, and as you become familiar with your typewriter's sensitiveness, you'll know when and how fast to make your move. Little by little, as you make your strokes, you'll notice that you are moving *with* your typewriter.

Little by little, you can increase your speed, but try to be accurate. You have now regained your composure and confidence.

Type in small groups of letters: example: ma-te-ri-al, ex-am-in-a-tion, par-a-graph, im-por-tune. (Forget the hyphen; it's invisible.) Now you are on the way to your destiny!

Answer Want Ads

To become an expert in taking typing tests, answer want ads for typists in the newspapers and tell the advertiser you want to take a typing test. Take the tests for practice only. Make it a routine until you don't get nervous anymore.

When the time comes for your postal typing test, tell yourself, "This is *not* a test. This is the real thing. This is it!"

(Data Conversion Operator)

SAMPLE ITEMS FOR COMPUTER BASED TEST 714

The CB 714 is a computer administered and scored exam. Applicants are assisted with the start-up of the exam and with the exam instructions. **You do not need prior experience on a computer terminal to take this test.**

The exam contains a list of alphanumeric postal data entry items just as you see in the sample items below. Applicants must demonstrate that they can type these items on the computer terminal at the following rate(s) based on the requirements of the position. The lower level passing rate is 5 correct lines per minute. The higher level passing rate is 7 correct lines per minute. Credit is given only for correctly typed lines. Practice for the exam by typing the sample provided below.

Type each line as shown in the exercise, beginning with the first column. You may use lower-case or capital letters when typing the sample exercise. When you reach the end of a line, single space and begin typing the next line. If you reach the end of the sample items in the first column, continue with the items in the second column. If you finish both columns, simply begin again with the first column and continue to type until the five minutes have elapsed.

See whether you can copy the entire Sample Test once in a five minute timing. Now count the number of lines you typed correctly and divide this number by five to determine your per minute score. Correctly typing only the items in column 1 is approximately equal to typing 5 correct lines per minute. Correctly typing all of the items in both columns is approximately equal to typing 7 correct lines per minute.

In the exam you will have five minutes in which to type the test material. Keep in mind that in order to pass the test you must type both rapidly and accurately.

(See Data Conversion Operator, page 283.)

The Book of U.S. Postal Exams

SAMPLE TEST COPY

```
  4.90 STEERING DAMPER        18.25 DOWN SPRING
 16.55 REAR DOOR LATCH         3.10 VC GASKET
 23.80 TIMING CHAIN           35.45 ROCKER ARM
 8721 8906                    4973 5261
 2013 2547                    6057 7382
 5972 6841                    2783 4195
 HANOVER RD. 600 - 699        GREENBRIAR DR. 1100 - 1399
 ARKANSAS AVE. 4000 - 4199    MADISON ST. 3700 - 3799
 SO. MAIN ST. 1200 - 1299     BRUNSWICK AVE. 8100 - 8199
 CAPITOL DR. 500 - 599        INDUSTRIAL RD. 2300 - 2499
 L ON MAPLEWOOD PL.
 RETRACE TO 421
 R ON MOHICAN TO TOWER
 4478267 LSM/LSM
 4478271 MPLSM
 4478289 EGR SECONDARY
 KNIGHT, J.R. 04/17/67
 CHARLES, S.M. 11/19/68
 JEFFERSON, W.A. 08/20/69
 SPRINGFIELD 07215
 GREENSBORO 07098
 LEXINGTON 07540
 FOURTH CLASS 363
 INTN. SECTION 27
 200 BOX 10
```

Examination 715

26

Typing Test for Mark-Up Clerks

(Sample Typing Test for Mark-Up Clerk)

Examination 715 is a computer administered and scored exam. Applicants are assisted with the start-up of the exam and with the exam instructions. You do *not* need prior experience on a computer terminal to take this test.

The exam contains a list of seven digit mail codes each consisting of four letters and three numbers just as you see in the sample items below. To pass this test, applicants must show that they can type these codes on the computer terminal at a rate of 14 correct lines per minute. Credit is given only for correctly typed lines. Practice for the exam by typing the sample provided below.

Type each line as shown in the exercise using lower case or capital letters. When you reach the end of a line, single space and begin typing the next line. When you reach the end of the sample items, simply begin again with the first line and continue to type until the five minutes have elapsed.

See whether you can copy it three times in a five-minute timing. Now count the number of lines you typed correctly and divide this number by five to determine your per minute score.

In the examination you will have five minutes in which to type the test material. Keep in mind that in order to pass the test you must type both rapidly and accurately.

Sample Test Copy

KATZ204
CURR907
ADAM101
BONN530
GORD223
OWEN241
SCHN421
HALL375
LOGU779
ROSE995
USHER963
MART895
KATA854
SHAN289
JAME409
CHER103
LINC510
MOSI521
NORM486
SALY541
MCNE326
PATS293
PRIN815
KAPL337
DUNN919

Practice Typing Test

Work—5 Minutes

As the Post Office instructs, type each line as shown in the exercise using lower case or capital letters. It's easier for you to use the upper case because you won't have to hit the "shift" key every time to capitalize any letter. Just set the Caps lock, and that's it. Type the sample material below in five minutes. When you reach the end of the sample items, simply begin again with the first line and continue to type until the five minutes have elapsed. See whether you can copy it three times in a five-minute timing. Afterwards, count the number of lines you typed correctly and divide this number by five to determine your per minute store. In order to pass the test, you must type both quickly and accurately. However, before typing the sample codes below, learn the technique for fast and accurate typing of the items. Also, see why these codes are typed by mark-up clerks.

Typing Techniques. When you type the line, MARC891. vou divide the line into two parts: MAR-891. First, type the letters MARC and then 891. As you type the lines below, you'll notice that you'll gain your own rhythm. That is, you type the lines as if you were hearing music. Or better still, listen to a radio station playing music.

Actually as a mark-up clerk, you'll be typing these codes. The codes as shown below representing the first four letters of a family name or last name and the first three number of a street or a P.O. box address. These codes are used by mark-up clerks to enter names and addresses of people moving to other addresses. Change of address cards are sent by letter carriers within a certain area consisting of several Post Offices to so-called Computerized Forwarding System Units of a Postal Sectional Center, such as the Royal Oak Post Office. In the Royal Oak area, letter carriers from associate Post Offices send their Change-of-address cards and all mail to be forwarded to the CFS Unit of the Royal Oak Post Office which is on the corner of American Way and Minnesota St. in Troy, Michigan. In the Detroit area, letter carriers from the associate Post Offices send their mail and change-of-address cards to the U.S. Postal Service building on Fort Street in Detroit, Michigan. Clerks in CFS units enter these addresses into the systems. Once entered, when a mark-up clerk keys the codes such as HARR541, the computer will generate labels, automatically attached to letters passing by through a mini-conveyor in front of a clerk's typing the codes on the computer terminal. Other mail, with unknown forwarding addresses are returned to senders. The computer also attaches the corresponding label for mail with notes: "Return to Sender." That's why

mark-up clerks should type rapidly and accurately "to process" more mails to be forwarded to new addresses.

Now, type the example test below:

HARR541
BAUT215
REYE041
ALVE915
POOL412
MARC286
CART316
REYE981
PAJA315
BURN886
WOOD451
ASIR199
CLAR773
CRUZ839
DERR321
MARV315
PADI315
NATI384
MARR310
RAVA938
ABDU336
MANG991
CORR327
MARR387
LEON447

As indicated above, you must type the above lines at least three times in five minutes.

Examination 911

Cleaner, Custodian, & Custodial Laborer Test

## 27

The positions of cleaner, custodian, and custodial laborer are exclusively for veterans and present employees. Only individuals entitled to veteran preference are eligible to take this entrance exam.

Cleaner

Grade: L-2

Salary Range: See schedule of salary & rates on pages 412-415.

Persons Eligible to Apply: Open to veterans only

Examination Requirements: All applicants will be required to take Examination M/N 911 to test their ability to interpret and follow instructions. The test and completion of the forms will require approximately 1 1/2 hours. Competitors will be rated on a scale of 100 and must score 70 to be eligible.

Duties: Performs light and heavy manual cleaning and housekeeping at a postal facility.

Custodian

Grade: L-2

Salary Range: See schedule of salary & rates on pages 412-415.

Persons Eligible to Apply: Open to veterans only

Examination Requirements: Applicants will be required to take Examination M/N 911 to test their ability to interpret and follow instructions.

Duties: Performs heavier manual cleaning, housekeeping, and buildings and grounds maintenance tasks at a postal facility.

Custodial Laborer

Grade: L-3

Salary Range: See schedule of salary & rates on pages 412-415.

Persons Eligible to Apply: Open to veterans only

Examination Requirements: Must pass Examination M/N 911 to determine the ability to interpret and follow instructions.

Duties: Performs manual labor in maintaining and cleaning buildings and grounds of a postal facility.

Examination 911

United States Postal Service

Sample Questions

STUDY CAREFULLY BEFORE YOU GO TO THE EXAMINATION ROOM

The purpose of this booklet is to illustrate the types of questions you will use in Examination M/N 911. It also shows you how the questions are to be answered.

The suggested answers to each question are lettered. Select the *best* answer, and make a heavy pencil mark.in the space on the sample answer sheet by darkening the space for the best answer to that question. Each mark must be dense black. Each mark must cover more than half of the area of the space, and must not extend into neighboring spaces. If the answer to sample 1 is B, you would mark the sample answer sheet like this:

Record your answers to each sample question. Then compare your answers with those given in the sample question instructions.

During the test, directions for answering questions will be given orally. You are to listen closely to the directions and follow them. To practice for the test, you might have a friend read the directions to you while you mark your answers on the sample answer sheet on the next page.

You will be told to follow directions by writing in a test booklet and then on an answer sheet. The test booklet will have lines of material like the following four samples:

SAMPLE **1**   5 _____

SAMPLE **2**   I   6   4   3   7

SAMPLE **3**   D   B   A   E   C

SAMPLE **4**   (8__)   (5__)   (2__)   (9__)   (10__)

SAMPLE **5**   (7__)   [6__]   (1__)   [12__]

To practice this test, tear off page 3. Then have somebody read the instructions to you. When you are told to darken a space on the sample answer sheet, use the one on this page.

Sample Answer Sheet

1 Ⓐ Ⓑ Ⓒ Ⓓ Ⓔ	5 Ⓐ Ⓑ Ⓒ Ⓓ Ⓔ	9 Ⓐ Ⓑ Ⓒ Ⓓ Ⓔ
2 Ⓐ Ⓑ Ⓒ Ⓓ Ⓔ	6 Ⓐ Ⓑ Ⓒ Ⓓ Ⓔ	10 Ⓐ Ⓑ Ⓒ Ⓓ Ⓔ
3 Ⓐ Ⓑ Ⓒ Ⓓ Ⓔ	7 Ⓐ Ⓑ Ⓒ Ⓓ Ⓔ	11 Ⓐ Ⓑ Ⓒ Ⓓ Ⓔ
4 Ⓐ Ⓑ Ⓒ Ⓓ Ⓔ	8 Ⓐ Ⓑ Ⓒ Ⓓ Ⓔ	12 Ⓐ Ⓑ Ⓒ Ⓓ Ⓔ

Instructions to be read (the words in parentheses should not be read aloud):

You are to follow the instructions that I shall read to you. I cannot repeat them.

Look at the samples. Sample 1 has a number and a line beside it. On the line write an A. (Pause 2 seconds.) Now on the sample answer sheet, find number 5 (pause 2 seconds) and darken the space for the letter you just wrote on the line. (Pause 2 seconds.)

Look at Sample 2. (Pause slightly.) Draw a line under the third number. (Pause 2 seconds.) Now look on the sample answer sheet, find the number under which you just drew a line, and darken space B, as in "baker" for that number. (Pause 5 seconds.)

Look at Sample 3. (Pause slightly.) Draw a line under the third letter in the line. (Pause 2 seconds.) Now on your answer sheet find number 9 (pause 2 seconds) and darken the space for the letter under which you drew a line. (Pause 5 seconds.)

Look at the five circles in Sample 4. (Pause slightly.) Each circle has a number and a line in it. Write D, as in "dog," on the blank in the last circle. (Pause 2 seconds.) Now on the sample answer sheet, darken the space for the number-letter combination that is in the circle you just wrote in (pause 5 seconds).

Now look at the sample answer sheet. (Pause slightly.) You should have darkened spaces 4B, 5A, 9A, and 10D on the sample answer sheet. (If the person preparing to take the examination made any mistakes, try to help him see why he made wrong marks.)

Postal Test 91   28

Garageman, Motor Vehicle & Tractor-Trailer Operators Exam

Applicants for these positions will take a written test, Examination M/N 91, to measure their ability to understand instructions. The exam will last for approximately two hours, including filling out forms. (See **Who Is Qualified to Apply for Exams?** on pages 5-10 and **Strategies for Standardized Tests,** pages 253-258.)

The job descriptions of the these positions are as follows:

Garageman

Grade: L-5

Salary Range: See schedule of salary & rates on pages 412-415.

Persons Eligible to Apply: Open to the general public

Examination Requirements: Applicants must pass the written test and the road test.

Duties: Lubricates, services, and cleans trucks; drives trucks to and from the garage; assists automotive mechanics; cleans garage and washroom.

Qualifications: Ability to service trucks, to understand written instructions, and to fill out forms; ability to work independently and to help mechanics.

Motor Vehicle Operator

Grade: L-5

Salary Range: See schedule of salary & rates on pages 412-415.

Persons Eligible to Apply: Open to the general public

Examination Requirements: Must pass the written test and road test.

Duties: Operates trucks and performs related work.

Qualifications: At least one year's experience in driving trucks of at least 5-ton capacity or buses of 24-passenger capacity or over. Ability to drive safely and with a satisfactory driving record; to drive under local driving conditions; to follow instructions and to prepare trip and other reports. Experience in driving pickups, vans, jeeps, step-in vans, etc. does not qualify.

Tractor-Trailer Operator

Grade: L-6

Salary Range: See schedule of salary & rates on pages 412-415.

Persons Eligible to Apply: Open to the general public

Examination Requirements: Applicants must pass the written test and road test.

Duties: Operates heavy-duty tractor-trailers and performs related work.

Qualifications: Must have at least one year's experience in driving trucks of at least 5-ton capacity or buses of 24-passenger capacity or over, of which at least 6 months' experience must be in driving tractor-trailers.

U.S. Postal Service
Sample Questions for Test 91

The sample questions in this booklet show the kinds of questions that you will find in the written test. By reading and answering these questions, you will find out how to answer the questions in the test and about how hard the questions will be.

Read the questions carefully. Be sure you know what the questions are about and then answer the questions in the way you are told to do. If you are told the answer to a question, be sure you understand why the answer is right.

Here are the sample questions for you to answer.

Question 1 is about picture 1, below. Look at the picture.

Picture 1

1. How many vehicles are shown in the picture?

(Write your answer for question 1 here.)

GO ON TO THE NEXT PAGE

Question 2 and 3 are about picture 2, below. Look at the picture.

Picture 2

2. Who is sitting on the motorcycle?

(Write your answer for question 2 here.)

3. What is the policeman probably doing?

(Write your answer for question 3 here.)

Questions 4 and 5 are about picture 3 below. Look at the picture.

Picture 3

4. What is happening in this picture?

(Write your answer for question 4 here.)

5. Show the positions of the truck and the passenger car by drawing boxes like those shown below. (Your boxes will not be in the same positions as these.)

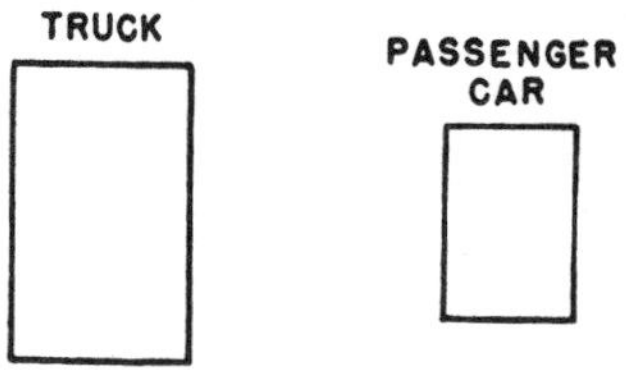

TRUCK

PASSENGER
CAR

Draw your boxes in the space below.

GO ON TO THE NEXT PAGE

Questions 6 and 7 are about pictures of oilcans. Each picture has a letter. You are to tell what each picture shows by writing a short description of the picture on the answer line that goes with the question.

Now look at picture X.

6. What does picture X show?

(Write your answer for question 6 here.)

Picture X shows two oilcans. So you should have written something like "two oilcans" on the line under question 6.

Now look at picture Y.

7. What does picture Y show?

(Write your answer for question 7 here.)

Question 8 is filling in a chart. You are given the following information to put in the chart.

Truck, license number 48-7128, had its oil changed last at speedometer reading 96,005. Truck, license number 858-232, was greased last at speedometer reading 89,564.

Look at the chart below. The information for the first truck has already been filled in. For question 8, fill in the information for the other truck. You are to show in the proper columns the license number of the truck, the kind of service, and the speedometer reading when serviced.

CHART

Truck License Number	Kind of Service	Speedometer Reading When Serviced
48-7128	Oil Change	96,005

(For question 8, write the information for the second truck in the proper columns above.)

GO ON TO THE NEXT PAGE

Question 9 and 10 are about words that might appear on traffic signs.

In questions like 9, there is one numbered line and then, just below that line, four other lines which are lettered A, B, C, and D. Read the first line. Then read the other four lines. Decide which line—A, B, C, or D—means most nearly the same as the first line in the question. Write the letter of the line that means the same as the numbered line in the answer space.

Here is an example.

9. Speed Limit—20 Miles

   A) Do not exceed 20 Miles per Hour

   B) Railroad Crossing

   C) No Turns

   D) Dangerous Intersection   ---
                                    (Write letter of answer here for question 9.)

The first line says "Speed Limit—20 Miles." Line A says "Do Not Exceed 20 Miles per Hour." B says "Railroad Crossing." C says "No Turns." D says "Dangerous Intersection." The line that says almost the same thing as the first line is line A. That is, the one that most nearly means "Speed Limit—20 Miles" is "Do not Exceed 20 Miles per Hour." The answer to question 9 is A. You should have marked A on the answer line for question 9.

Here is another example.

10. Dead End

   A) Merging Traffic

   B) No U-Turns

   C) Turn on Red

   D) No Through Traffic   ---
                               (Write your answer here for question 10.)

GO ON TO THE NEXT PAGE

After you answer questions like the ones you have just finished, you will be asked other questions to see how well you understand what you have written. To answer the next questions, you will use the information that you wrote for the first 10 questions. Mark your answers to the next questions on the sample answer sheet on the next page.

The sample answer sheet has spaces that look like these:

1 Ⓐ Ⓑ Ⓒ Ⓓ Ⓔ

2 Ⓐ Ⓑ Ⓒ Ⓓ Ⓔ

If you wanted to mark D for your answer to question 1, you would mark it like this:

1 Ⓐ Ⓑ Ⓒ ● Ⓔ

If you wanted to mark C for your answer to question 2, you would mark it like this:

2 Ⓐ Ⓑ ● Ⓓ Ⓔ

Each of the questions in the next part is about something you should have written on your answer lines.

In answering the next questions you may look back to what you have already written as often as you wish. You may look back while you are marking the sample answer sheet. In the actual test, the pictures and their questions will be taken away from you before you mark the answer sheet, but you will keep what you wrote about the pictures while marking the answer sheet. So for this practice, try not to look at the pictures but look at what you wrote about them.

Answer each of the following questions by darkening completely space A, B, C, D, or E beside the number that you are told in the question. Mark all your answers on the sample answer sheet.

Question 11 is about question 1. Use what you wrote under question 1 to answer question 11. Mark your answer on the sample answer sheet.

11. For number 1 on the sample answer sheet,
    mark space A if only one vehicle is shown in the picture
    mark space B if only two vehicles are shown in the picture
    mark space C if only three vehicles are shown in the picture
    mark space D if only four vehicles are shown in the picture
    mark space E if only five vehicles are shown in the picture

If you look at the answer you gave for question 1, you will see that you wrote that three vehicles were shown in the picture. The question above tells you to mark space C on the sample answer sheet if only three vehicles are shown. So you should have marked space C for number 11 on the sample answer sheet.

Question 12 below is about question 2, and question 13 below is about question 3.

12. For number 12 on the sample answer sheet, mark space
    A if a policeman is sitting on the motorcycle
    B if a man in overalls is sitting on the motorcycle
    C if a boy in a sport shirt is sitting on the motorcycle
    D if a nurse is sitting on the motorcycle
    E if a man with a white beard is sitting on the motorcycle

    Be sure to mark your answer on the sample answer sheet.

13. For number 13 on the sample answer sheet, mark space
    A if the policeman is probably fixing a tire
    B if the policeman is probably using a telephone
    C if the policeman is probably taking off his cap
    D if the policeman is probably blowing a whistle
    E if the policeman is probably writing a "ticket"

GO ON TO THE NEXT PAGE

Question 14 below is about question 4, and question 15 below is about question 5.

14. For number 14 on the sample answer sheet, mark space
   A if a bus is passing a fire truck
   B if a motorcycle is hitting a fence
   C if a truck is backing up to a platform
   D if a passenger car is getting gas
   E if a passenger car is hitting a truck

15. Look at the boxes you drew for question 5. For number 15 on the sample answer sheet, mark space

   A if a truck is on a ramp and a passenger car is on the street
   B if a truck is to the rear of a passenger car
   C if the front bumpers of a passenger car and a truck are in line
   D if a passenger car is to the rear of a truck
   E if a motorcycle is between a truck and a passenger car

Question 16 below is about question 6 under picture X, and question 17 below is about question 7 under picture Y.

16. For number 16 on the sample answer sheet, mark space

   A if there is only one oilcan in picture X
   B if there are only two oilcans in picture X
   C if there are only three oilcans in picture X
   D if there are only four oilcans in picture X
   E if there are only five oilcans in picture X

17. For number 17 on the sample answer sheet, mark space
   A if there is only one oilcan in picture Y
   B if there are only two oilcans in picture Y
   C if there are only three oilcans in picture Y
   D if there are only four oilcans in picture Y
   E if there are only five oilcans in picture Y

Question 18 below is about the chart you filled in. For this question, mark on the sample answer sheet the letter of the suggested answer—A, B, C, D, or E— that answers the question best.

18. What is the license number of the truck that was greased? (Look at what you wrote on the chart. Don't answer from memory.)
   A) 89,564
   B) 48-7128
   C) 858-232
   D) 96,005

For number 19 on the sample answer sheet, mark the space that has the same letter as the letter you wrote on the answer line for question 9.

For number 20 on the sample answer sheet, mark the space that has the same letter as the letter you wrote on the answer line for question 10.

(See the correct answers on page 175.)

Correct Answers

Sample Questions

11.	C	16.	B
12.	A	17.	D
13.	E	18.	C
14.	E	19.	A
15.	D	20.	D

Examination 924

Maintenance Mechanic Test

29

The test for maintenance mechanic consists of two parts: Part I, a multiple-choice test dealing with basic mechanics, electricity, and electronics and with the use of hand and portable power tools and test equipment; and Part II, a multiple-choice test dealing with basic mathematical computations, reading comprehension, and how to follow verbal instructions. Each part of the exam takes about four hours. (See **Who Can Apply for Exams?,** page 5.)

For the reading comprehension and multiple-choice test, see **Analyzing Examination 710**—*Clerical and Verbal Abilities,* page 293), and **Strategies for Standardized Test**, page 393.)

As an applicant, you must have knowledge of basic mechanics, basic electricity, basic electronics, safety procedures, and equipment; you must know how to perform basic and complex mathematical computations, apply theory, detect patterns, use reference materials, communicate orally and in writing, use hand and power tools, use shop power equipment, and use technical drawings and test equipment.

If you are hired, you'll perform preventive maintenance and repair work at the journeyman level on the mechanical, electrical, electronic, pneumatic, or hydraulic controls and on the operating mechanisms of mail processing equipment.

T0478 00 00 00   **United States Postal Service**   SQ-924

Maintenance Mechanic

STUDY CAREFULLY BEFORE YOU GO TO THE EXAMINATION ROOM

Sample Questions

Part I

The purpose of this booklet is to illustrate the types of questions you will see in Examination M/N 924. It also shows you how the questions are to be answered.

Examination M/N 924 measures the knowledge and ability areas which are described in this booklet. First read the definition to get a general idea of the test content. Then answer the sample questions on the sample answer sheet.

The suggested answers to each question are lettered. Select the *best* answer, and make a heavy pencil mark in the space on the sample answer sheet by darkening the space of the best answer to that question. Each mark must be dense black. Each mark must cover more than half of the area of the space, and must not extend into neighboring spaces. If the answer to sample 1 is B, you would mark the sample answer sheet like this:

Record your answers to each sample question. Then compare your answers with those given in the correct answers to sample questions.

The following categories are covered by Examination M/N 924:

1. **Knowledge of basic mechanics** refers to the theory of operation, terminology, usage, and characteristics of basic mechanical principles as they apply to such things as gears, pulleys, cams, pawls, power transmissions, linkages, fasteners, chains, sprockets, and belts; and including hoisting, rigging, roping, and pneumatic and hydraulic devices.

2. **Knowledge of lubrication materials and procedures** refers to the terminology, characteristics, storage, preparation, disposal, and usage techniques involved with lubrication materials such as oils, greases, and other types of lubricants.

3. **Knowledge of basic electricity** refers to the theory, terminology, usage, and characteristics of basic electrical principles such as Ohm's Law, Kirchoff's Law, and magnetism, as they apply to such things as AC-DC circuitry and hardware, relays, switches, and circuit breakers.

4. **Knowledge of basic electronics** refers to the theory, terminology, usage, and characteristics of basic electronic principles concerning such things as solid-state devices, vacuum tubes, coils, capacitors, resistors, and basic logic circuitry.

5. **Knowledge of safety procedures and equipment** refers to the knowledge of industrial hazards (e.g., mechanical, chemical, electrical, electronic) and procedures and techniques established to avoid injuries to self and others such as lock-out devices, protective clothing, and waste disposal techniques.

6. **Ability to apply theoretical knowledge to practical applications** refers to the ability to recall specific theoretical knowledge and apply it to mechanical, electrical, or electronic maintenance applications such as inspection, troubleshooting, equipment repair and modification, preventive maintenance, and installation of electrical equipment.

7. **Ability to use hand tools** refers to the knowledge of, and proficiency with, various hand tools. This ability involves the safe and efficient use and maintenance of such tools as screwdrivers, wrenches, hammers, pliers, chisels, punches, taps, dies, rules, gauges, and alignment tools.

8. **Ability to use portable power tools** refers to the knowledge of, and proficiency with, various power tools. This ability involves the safe and efficient use and maintenance of power tools such as drills, saws, sanders, and grinders.

9. **Ability to solder** refers to the knowledge of, and the ability to apply safely and effectively, the appropriate soldering techniques.

10. **Ability to use test equipment** refers to the knowledge of, and proficiency with, various types of mechanical, electrical, and electronic test equipment such as VOMS, oscilloscopes, circuit tracers, amprobes, and RPM meters.

(**Author's Note:** See **Strategies for Standardized Tests,** *multiple choice,* pages 393-396 and review any books about basic mechanics, basic electricity, and basic electronics.)

1. The primary function of a take-up pulley in a belt conveyor is to

   A) carry the belt on the return trip
   B) track the belt
   C) maintain proper belt tension
   D) change the direction of the belt
   E) regulate the speed of the belt

2. Which device is used to transfer power and rotary mechanical motion from one shaft to another?

   A) bearing
   B) lever
   C) idler roller
   D) gear
   E) bushing

3. What special care is required in the storage of hard steel roller bearings? They should be

   A) cleaned and spun dry with compressed air
   B) oiled once a month
   C) stored in a humid place
   D) wrapped in oiled paper
   E) stored at temperatures below 90° F

4. Which is the correct method to lubricate a roller chain?

   A) use brush to apply lubricant while chain is in motion
   B) use squirt can to apply lubricant while chain is in motion
   C) use brush to apply lubricant while chain is not in motion
   D) soak chain in pan of lubricant and hang to allow excess to drain
   E) chains do not need lubrication

5. A circuit has two resistors of equal value in series. The voltage and current in the circuit are 20 volts and 2 amps respectively. What is the value of *each* resistor?

   A) 5 ohms
   B) 10 ohms
   C) 15 ohms
   D) 20 ohms
   E) Not enough information given

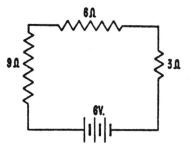

Figure III-A-22

6. Which of the following circuits is shown in Figure III-A-22?

   A) series circuit
   B) parallel circuit
   C) series, parallel circuit
   D) solid state circuit
   E) none of the above

7. What is the total net capacitance of two 60-farad capacitors connected in series?

   A) 30 F
   B) 60 F
   C) 90 F
   D) 120 F
   E) 360 F

8. If two 30-mH inductors are connected in series, what is the total net inductance of the combination?

   A) 15 mH
   B) 20 mH
   C) 30 mH
   D) 45 mH
   E) 60 mH

Figure 75-25-1

9. Crowbars, light bulbs, and vacuum bags are to be stored in the cabinet shown in Figure 75-25-1. Considering the balance of weight, what would be the safest arrangement?

A) top drawer — crowbars
   middle drawer — light bulbs
   bottom drawer — vacuum bag

B) top drawer — crowbars
   middle drawer — vacuum bag
   bottom drawer — light bulbs

C) top drawer — vacuum bag
   middle drawer — crowbars
   bottom drawer — light bulbs

D) top drawer — vacuum bag
   middle drawer — light bulbs
   bottom drawer — crowbars

E) top drawer — light bulbs
   middle drawer — vacuum bag
   bottom drawer — crowbars

10. Contaminants have caused bearings to fail prematurely. Which pair of the items listed below should be kept away from the bearings?

A) dirt and oil
B) grease and water
C) oil and grease
D) dirt and moisture
E) water and oil

11. The electrical circuit term *open circuit* refers to a closed loop being opened. When an ohmmeter is connected into this type of circuit, one can expect the meter to

A) read infinity
B) read infinity and slowly return to *zero*
C) read *zero*
D) read *zero* and slowly return to infinity
E) none of the above

12. Which is most appropriate for pulling a heavy load?

A) electric lift
B) fork lift
C) tow conveyor
D) dolly
E) pallet truck

13. In order to operate a breast drill, in which direction should you turn it?

A) clockwise
B) counterclockwise
C) up and down
D) back and forth
E) right, then left

14. Which is the correct tool for tightening or loosening a water pipe?

A) slip joint pliers
B) household pliers
C) monkey wrench
D) water pump pliers
E) pipe wrench

15. What is one purpose of a chuck key?

A) open doors
B) remove drill bits
C) remove screws
D) remove set screws
E) unlock chucks

16. When smoke is generated as a result of using a portable electric drill for cutting holes into a piece of angle iron, one should

A) use a fire watch
B) cease the drilling operation
C) use an exhaust fan to remove smoke
D) use a prescribed coolant solution to reduce friction
E) call the fire department

17. The primary purpose of soldering is to

A) melt solder to a molten state
B) heat metal parts to the right temperature to be joined
C) join metal parts by melting the parts
D) harden metal
E) join metal parts

18. Which of the following statements is correct of a soldering gun?

A) tip is not replaceable
B) cannot be used in cramped places
C) heats only when trigger is pressed
D) not rated by the number of watts they use
E) has no light

19. What unit of measurement is read on a dial torque wrench?

A) pounds
B) inches
C) centimeters
D) foot-pounds
E) degrees

20. Which instrument is used to test insulation breakdown of a conductor?

A) ohmmeter
B) ammeter
C) megger
D) wheatstone bridge
E) voltmeter

(See the correct answers on the next page.)

Correct Answers

Sample Questions

Part I

1.	C	11.	A
2.	D	12.	E
3.	D	13.	A
4.	D	14.	E
5.	A	15.	B
6.	A	16.	D
7.	A	17.	E
8.	E	18.	C
9.	E	19.	D
10.	D	20.	C

T0472 00 00 00   # United States Postal Service   SQ-912

Maintenance Mechanic

Sample Questions

Part II

STUDY CAREFULLY BEFORE YOU GO TO THE EXAMINATION ROOM

The purpose of this booklet is to illustrate the types of questions you will see in Examination M/N 912. It also shows you how the questions are to be answered.

At the beginning of each set of sample questions you will find the definition of a question category which the test measures. First read the definition to get a general idea of the test content. Then answer the sample questions on the sample answer sheet at the bottom of the page.

The suggested answers to each question are lettered. Select the *best* answer, and make a heavy pencil mark in the space on the sample answer sheet by darkening the space of the best answer to that question. Each mark must be dense black. Each mark must cover more than half of the area of the space, and must not extend into neighboring spaces. If the answer to sample 1 is B, you would mark the sample answer sheet like this:

Record your answers to each sample question. Then compare your answers with those given in the correct answers to sample questions.

During the test, directions for answering questions in the last category will be given orally, either by a cassette tape or by the examiner. You are to listen closely to the directions and follow them. To practice for this part of the test you might have a friend read the directions to you while you mark your answers on the sample answer sheet.

85280

Ability to perform basic mathematical computations refers to the ability to perform basic calculations such as addition, subtraction, multiplication, and division with whole numbers, fractions, and decimals. Perform the computations required by each problem. Decide which answer (A, B, C, D, or E) is correct and mark it on the sample answer sheet. If the correct answer is not provided, mark E (none of the above).

Author's Note: See **Strategies for Standardized Tests,** *solving mathematics problems,* pages 393-396 and review any books about basic mechanics, basic electricity, and basic electronics.

1) 23 + 34 =

A) 46
B) 47
C) 56
D) 57
E) 66

2) 2.6 − .5 =

A) 2.0
B) 2.1
C) 3.1
D) 3.3
E) none of the above

3) ½ of ¼ =

A) $\frac{1}{12}$
B) ⅛
C) ¼
D) ½
E) 8

4) 168 ÷ 8 =

A) 20
B) 22
C) 24
D) 26
E) none of the above

```
+---------------------+        +---------------------+
|      SAMPLE         |        |  CORRECT ANSWERS    |
|   ANSWER SHEET      |        | TO SAMPLE QUESTIONS |
|                     |        |                     |
|   1 Ⓐ Ⓑ Ⓒ Ⓓ Ⓔ     |        |   1 Ⓐ Ⓑ Ⓒ ● Ⓔ     |
|                     |        |                     |
|   2 Ⓐ Ⓑ Ⓒ Ⓓ Ⓔ     |        |   2 Ⓐ ● Ⓒ Ⓓ Ⓔ     |
|                     |        |                     |
|   3 Ⓐ Ⓑ Ⓒ Ⓓ Ⓔ     |        |   3 Ⓐ ● Ⓒ Ⓓ Ⓔ     |
|                     |        |                     |
|   4 Ⓐ Ⓑ Ⓒ Ⓓ Ⓔ     |        |   4 Ⓐ Ⓑ Ⓒ Ⓓ ●     |
+---------------------+        +---------------------+
```

Ability to perform more complex mathematics refers to the ability to perform calculations such as basic algebra, geometry, scientific notation, and number conversions, as applied to mechanical, electrical, and electronic applications. For each problem, decide which is the correct answer (i.e., A, B, C, D, E) and mark it on the sample answer sheet. If the correct answer is not provided mark E (none of the above).

1) Simplify the following expression in terms of amps:

$$563 \times 10^{-6}$$

A) 563,000,000 amps
B) 563,000 amps
C) .563 amps
D) .000563 amps
E) .000000563 amps

2) Solve the power equation

$P = I^2 R$ for R

A) $R = EI$
B) $R = I^2 P$
C) $R = PI$
D) $R = P/I^2$
E) $R = E/I$

3) The product of 3 kilo ohms times 3 micro ohms is

A) 6×10^{-9} ohms
B) 6×10^{-3} ohms
C) 9×10^{3} ohms
D) 9×10^{-6} ohms
E) 9×10^{-3} ohms

```
         SAMPLE
     ANSWER SHEET

     1 Ⓐ Ⓑ Ⓒ Ⓓ Ⓔ

     2 Ⓐ Ⓑ Ⓒ Ⓓ Ⓔ

     3 Ⓐ Ⓑ Ⓒ Ⓓ Ⓔ
```

```
     CORRECT ANSWERS
   TO SAMPLE QUESTIONS

     1 Ⓐ Ⓑ Ⓒ ● Ⓔ

     2 Ⓐ Ⓑ Ⓒ ● Ⓔ

     3 Ⓐ Ⓑ Ⓒ Ⓓ ●
```

Ability to detect patterns refers to the ability to observe and analyze qualitative and quantitative factors such as number progressions, spatial relationships, and auditory and visual patterns. This includes combining information and determining how a given set of numbers, objects, or sounds are related to each other. Solve each problem below and mark the correct answer on the sample answer sheet on the next page.

1) Select from the drawings of objects labeled A, B, C, and D the one that would have the top, front, and right views shown in the drawing at the left.

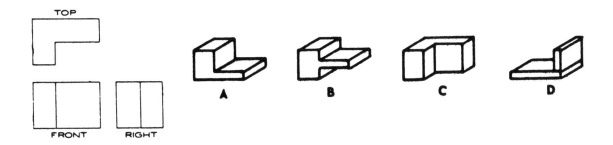

2) In the problem below there is at the left a drawing of a flat piece of paper and at the right four figures labeled A, B, C, and D. When the paper is bent on the dotted lines, it will form one of the figures at the right. Decide which figure can be formed from the flat piece.

In each of the sample questions, look at the symbols in the first two boxes. Something about the three symbols in the first box makes them alike; something about the two symbols in the other box with the question mark makes them alike. Look for some characteristic that is common to all symbols in the same box, yet makes them different from the symbols in the other box. Among the five answer choices, find the symbol that can best be substituted for the question mark, because it is *like* the symbols in the second box, and, *for the same reason,* different from those in the first box.

3.

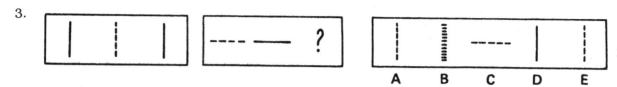

In the sample question 3, all the symbols in the first box are vertical lines. The second box has two lines, one broken and one solid. Their *likeness* to each other consists of their being horizontal; and their being horizontal makes them *different* from the vertical lines in the other box. The answer must be the only one of the five lettered choices that is a horizontal line, either broken or solid. *Note:* There is not supposed to be a *series* or progression in these symbol questions. If you look for a progression in the first box and try to find the missing figure to fill out a similar progression in the second box, you will be wasting time. Remember to look for a *likeness* within each box and a *difference* between the two boxes. Now answer sample questions 4 and 5.

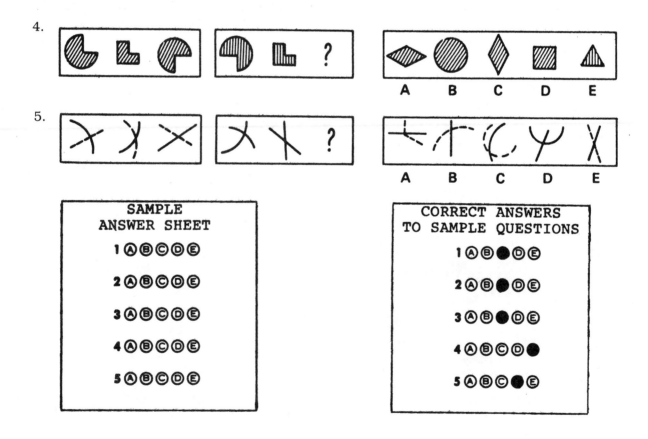

Ability to use written reference materials refers to the ability to locate, read, and comprehend text material such as handbooks, manuals, bulletins, directives, checklists, and route sheets. Read the following paragraph, determine the answer which is most nearly correct (A, B, C, D, or E), and mark it on the sample answer sheet.

1) "Prior to 1870, a conveyor that made use of rollers was developed for transporting clay. This construction substituted rolling friction at the idler bearing points for the sliding friction of the slider bed. A primitive type of troughing belt conveyor was developed about the same time for the handling of grain. This design was improved during the latter part of the century when the troughing idler was developed."

Author s Note: See **Analyzing Examination 710,** *Clerical and Verbal Abilies*, pages 293-302.

According to the above paragraph, which of the following statements is *most* nearly correct?

A) The troughing belt conveyor was developed about 1870 to handle clay and grain.

B) Rolling friction construction was replaced by the sliding friction construction prior to 1870.

C) In the late nineteenth century, conveyors were improved with the development of the troughing idler.

D) The troughing idler, a significant design improvement for the conveyors, was developed in the early nineteenth century.

E) Conveyor belts were invented and developed in the 1800's.

```
+-----------------------------+        +-----------------------------+
|          SAMPLE             |        |      CORRECT ANSWER         |
|       ANSWER SHEET          |        |    TO SAMPLE QUESTION       |
|                             |        |                             |
|                             |        |                             |
|      1 (A)(B)(C)(D)(E)       |        |      1 (A)(B)(●)(D)(E)       |
|                             |        |                             |
+-----------------------------+        +-----------------------------+
```

Ability to use technical drawings refers to the ability to read and comprehend technical materials such as diagrams, schematics, flow charts, and blueprints. For each problem, decide which is the correct answer.

1) In Figure 3-8-6, what is the measurement of dimension F?

A) 1 ¾ inches
B) 2 ¼ inches
C) 2 ½ inches
D) 3 ¾ inches
E) none of the above

2) In Figure 612.160-57, what is the current flow through R_3 when V = 50 volts, R_1 = 25 ohms, R_2 = 25 ohms, R_3, R_4, and R_5 each equal 50 ohms, and the current through the entire circuit totals one amp?

A) 0.5 amp
B) 5.0 amps
C) 5.0 milliamps
D) 50.0 milliamps
E) none of the above

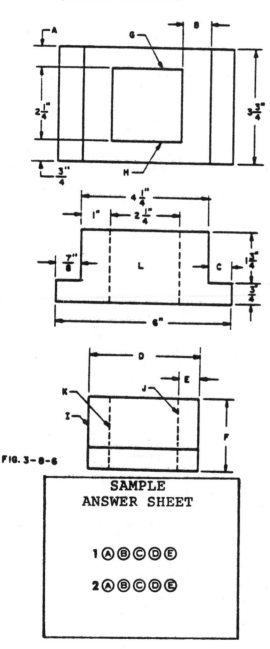

FIG. 3-8-6

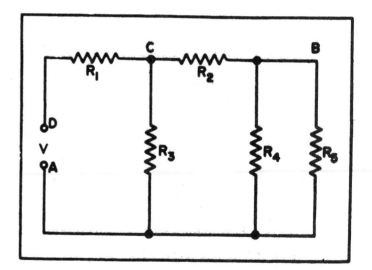

Fig. 612. 160—57

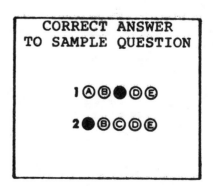

SAMPLE
ANSWER SHEET

1 Ⓐ Ⓑ Ⓒ Ⓓ Ⓔ

2 Ⓐ Ⓑ Ⓒ Ⓓ Ⓔ

CORRECT ANSWER
TO SAMPLE QUESTION

1 Ⓐ Ⓑ ● Ⓓ Ⓔ

2 ● Ⓑ Ⓒ Ⓓ Ⓔ

Ability to follow instructions refers to the ability to comprehend and execute written and oral instructions such as work orders, checklists, route sheets, and verbal directions and instructions. The previous questions tested your ability to follow written instructions. The remaining items test your ability to follow instructions given verbally.

You will be told to follow directions by writing in a test booklet and then on an answer sheet. The test booklet will have lines of material like the five samples:

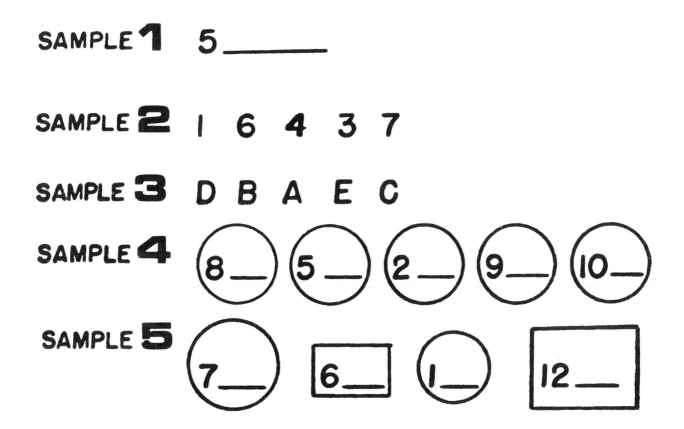

To practice this test, have somebody read the instructions to you and you follow the instructions. When he or she tells you to darken the space on the sample answer sheet, use the one on this page.

```
            SAMPLE ANSWER SHEET
   1 Ⓐ Ⓑ Ⓒ Ⓓ Ⓔ    5 Ⓐ Ⓑ Ⓒ Ⓓ Ⓔ     9 Ⓐ Ⓑ Ⓒ Ⓓ Ⓔ

   2 Ⓐ Ⓑ Ⓒ Ⓓ Ⓔ    6 Ⓐ Ⓑ Ⓒ Ⓓ Ⓔ    10 Ⓐ Ⓑ Ⓒ Ⓓ Ⓔ

   3 Ⓐ Ⓑ Ⓒ Ⓓ Ⓔ    7 Ⓐ Ⓑ Ⓒ Ⓓ Ⓔ    11 Ⓐ Ⓑ Ⓒ Ⓓ Ⓔ

   4 Ⓐ Ⓑ Ⓒ Ⓓ Ⓔ    8 Ⓐ Ⓑ Ⓒ Ⓓ Ⓔ    12 Ⓐ Ⓑ Ⓒ Ⓓ Ⓔ
```

Instructions to be read (the words in parentheses should not be read aloud).

You are to follow the instructions that I shall read to you. I cannot repeat them.

Look at the samples. Sample 1 has a number and a line beside it. On the line write an A. (Pause 2 seconds.) Now on the sample answer sheet, find number 5 (pause 2 seconds) and darken the space for the letter you just wrote on the line. (Pause 2 seconds.)

Look at sample 2. (Pause slightly.) Draw a line under the third number. (Pause 2 seconds.) Now look on the sample answer sheet, find the number under which you just drew a line and darken space B as in baker for that number. (Pause 5 seconds.)

Look at sample 3. (Pause slightly.) Draw a line under the third letter in the line. (Pause 2 seconds). Now on your answer sheet, find number 9 (pause 2 seconds) and darken the space for the letter which you drew a line. (Pause 5 seconds.)

Look at the five circles in sample 4. (Pause slightly.) Each circle has a number and a line in it. Write D as in dog on the blank in the last circle. (Pause 2 seconds.) Now on the sample answer sheet, darken the space for the number-letter combination in the box or circle in which you just wrote. (Pause 5 seconds.)

Look at sample 5. (Pause slightly.) There are two circles and two boxes of different sizes with numbers in them. (Pause slightly.) If 4 is more than 2 and if 5 is less than 3, write A in the smaller circle. (Pause slightly.) Otherwise, write C in the larger box. (Pause 2 seconds.) Now on the sample answer sheet, darken the space for the number-letter combination in the box or circle in which you just wrote. (Pause 5 seconds.)

Now look at the sample answer sheet. (Pause slightly.) You should have darkened spaces 4B, 5A, 9A, 10D, and 12C on the sample answer sheet. (If the person preparing to take the examination made any mistakes, try to help him see why he made the wrong marks.)

Examination 914

Electronics Technician Test

30

The test for electronics technician is broken down into two parts: Part I deals with basic mechanics, basic, electricity, and basic electronics; Part II deals with Mathematical computations and how to follow instructions. (See **Who Can Apply for Exams?,** pages 5-10, and **Strategies for Standardized Tests,** *multiple choice and vocabulary* tests and *solving mathematics problems,* pages 393-396.

If you are hired as an electronics technician, you'll carry out what the post office calls "well-documented phases of maintenance, testing, and troubleshooting and knowledge of solid state electronics." To do this job, you must have the knowledge of basic mechanics, basic electricity, and basic electronics, and you should be familiar with such things as gears, pulleys, linkages, belts, magnetism, switches, circuit breakers, coils, capacitors, and resistors.

As an applicant, you must be able to solve problems in basic algebra and geometry, understand scientific notation, and number conversions as applied to mechanical, electrical, and electronic problems. You must also have knowledge of industrial hazards (mechanical, chemical, electrical, and electronics), and understand devices, protective clothing, and waste disposal techniques.

T0474 00 00 00   SG-914

United States Postal Service

Electronics Technician

STUDY CAREFULLY BEFORE YOU GO TO THE EXAMINATION ROOM

Sample Questions

Part I

The purpose of this booklet is to illustrate the types of questions you will see in Examination M/N 914. It also shows you how the questions are to be answered.

Examination M/N 914 measures the knowledge and ability areas which are described in this booklet. First read the definition to get a general idea of the test content. Then answer the sample questions on the sample answer sheet.

The suggested answers to each question are lettered. Select the *best* answer, and make a heavy pencil mark in the space on the sample answer sheet by darkening the space of the best answer to that question. Each mark must be dense black. Each mark must cover more than half of the area of the space, and must not extend into neighboring spaces. If the answer to sample 1 is B, you would mark the sample answer sheet like this:

Record your answers to each sample question. Then compare your answers with those given in the correct answers to sample questions.

Note: See **Strategies for Standardized Tests,** *multiple-choice test techniques,* pages 393-396, and review any books about basic mechanics, basic electricity, and basic electronics.

1. The primary function of a take-up pulley in a belt conveyor is to

    A) carry the belt on the eturn trip
    B) track the belt
    C) maintain proper belt tension
    D) change the direction of the belt
    E) regulate the speed of the belt

2. Which device is used to transfer power and rotary mechanical motion from one shaft to another?

    A) bearing
    B) lever
    C) idler roller
    D) gear
    E) bushing

3. A circuit has two resistors of equal value in series. The voltage and current in the circuit are 20 volts and 2 amps respectively. What is the value of *each* resistor?

    A) 5 ohms
    B) 10 ohms
    C) 20 ohms
    D) not enough information given

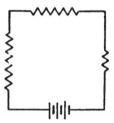

Figure III-A-22

4. Which of the following circuits is shown in Figure III-A-22?

    A) series circuit
    B) parallel circuit
    C) series, parallel circuit
    D) solid state circuit
    E) none of the above

5. What is the total net capacitance of two 60-farad capacitors connected in series?

    A) 30 farads
    B) 60 farads
    C) 90 farads
    D) 120 farads
    E) 360 farads

6. If two 30-mH inductors are connected in series, what is the total net inductance of the combination?

    A) 15 mH
    B) 20 mH
    C) 30 mH
    D) 45 mH
    E) 60 mH

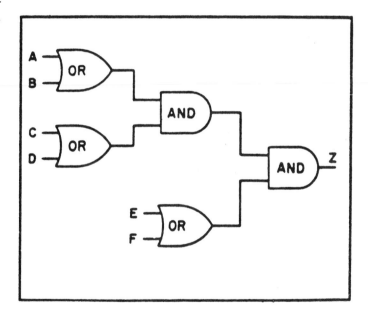

Figure 79-4-17B

7. Select the Boolean equation that matches the circuit diagram in Figure 79-4-17B.

    A) $Z = AB + CD + EF$
    B) $Z = (A+B)(C+D)(E+F)$
    C) $Z = A+B+C+D+EF$
    D) $Z = ABCD(E+F)$

8. In pure binary the decimal number 6
   would be expressed as

   A) 001
   B) 011
   C) 110
   D) 111

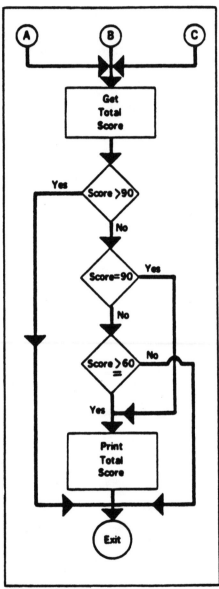

FIGURE 75-8-11

9. In Figure 75-8-11, which of the following
   scores will be printed?

   A) all scores > 90 and < 60
   B) all scores < 90
   C) all scores < 90 and > 60
   D) all scores < 60

Figure 75-25-1

10. Crowbars, light bulbs, and vacuum bags
    are to be stored in the cabinet shown in
    Figure 75-25-1. Considering the balance
    of weight, what would be the safest
    arrangement?

    A) top drawer   — crowbars
       middle drawer   — light bulbs
       bottom drawwer   — vacuum bag

    B) top drawer   — crowbars
       middle drawer   — vacuum bag
       bottom drawer   — light bulbs

    C) top drawer   — vacuum bag
       middle drawer   — crowbars
       bottom drawer   — light bulbs

    D) top drawer   — vacuum bag
       middle drawer   — light bulbs
       bottom drawer   — crowbars

    E) top drawer   — light bulbs
       middle drawer   — vacuum bag
       bottom drawer   — crowbars

11. Which is most appropriate for pulling a heavy load?

    A) electric lift
    B) fork lift
    C) tow conveyor
    D) dolly
    E) pallet truck

12. The electrical circuit term *open circuit* refers to a closed loop being opened. When an ohmmeter is connected into this type of circuit, one can expect the meter to

    A) read infinity
    B) read infinity and a slowly return to *zero*
    C) read *zero*
    D) read *zero* and slowly return to infinity
    E) none of the above

13. Contaminants have caused bearings to fail prematurely. Which pair of the items listed below should be kept away from bearings?

    A) dirt and oil
    B) grease and water
    C) oil and grease
    D) dirt and moisture
    E) water and oil

14. In order to operate a breast drill, in which direction should you turn it?

    A) clockwise
    B) counterclockwise
    C) up and down
    D) back and forth
    E) right, then left

15. Which is the correct tool for tightening or loosening a water pipe?

    A) slip joint pliers
    B) household pliers
    C) monkey wrench
    D) water pump pliers
    E) pipe wrench

16. What is the purpose of a chuck key?

    A) open doors
    B) remove drill bits
    C) remove screws
    D) remove chucks
    E) remove set screws

17. When smoke is generated as a result of cutting holes into a piece of angle iron using a portable electric drill, one should

    A) use a fire watch
    B) cease the drilling operation
    C) use an exhaust fan to remove smoke
    D) use a prescribed coolant solution to reduce friction
    E) call the fire department

18. The primary purpose of soldering is to

    A) melt solder to a molten state
    B) heat metal parts to the right temperature to be joined
    C) join metal parts by melting the parts
    D) to harden the metal
    E) join metal parts

19. Which of the following statements is correct about a soldering gun?

    A) tip is not replaceable
    B) cannot be used in cramped places
    C) heats only when trigger is pressed
    D) not rated by the number of watts they use
    E) has no light

20. What unit of measurement is read on a dial torque wrench?

    A) pounds
    B) inches
    C) centimeters
    D) foot-pounds
    E) degrees

21. Which instrument is used to test insulation breakdown of a conductor?

    A) ohmmeter
    B) ammeter
    C) megger
    D) wheatstone bridge
    E) voltmeter

(See the correct answers on the next page.)

Correct Answers

Sample Questions

Part I

1.	C	11.	E
2.	D	12.	A
3.	A	13.	D
4.	A	14.	A
5.	A	15.	E
6.	E	16.	B
7.	B	17.	D
8.	C	18.	E
9.	C	19.	C
10.	E	20.	D
		21.	C

Sample Questions

Part II

Note: Part II of the electronics exam is the same as Part II of the maintenance mechanic exam. See **Maintenance Mechanic Exam,** pages 323-338. For the reading comprehension part of the test (Part II), see **Analyzing Examination 710** - *Clerical and Verbal Abilities,* pages 293-296.

Examination 940

## 31

Automotive Mechanic Test

Automotive Mechanic

Grade: L-6

Salary Range: $27,619 - $37,827

Persons Eligible to Apply: Open to the general public

Examination Requirement: Applicants must pass Examination V/N 940. The test and completion of forms will require approximately 1 1/2 hours. Competitions must score 70, exclusive of veteran preference points, to be eligible. (See **Who Is Qualified to Apply for Exams?** on pages 5-10 and **Veterans in the U.S. Postal Service,** pages 29-32.)

To make a high score on this test, read books on tools and shop equipment, brakes, steering and suspension systems, automatic transmissions and torque converters, manual transmissions, and rear axles.

To qualify as an automotive mechanic in the U.S. Postal Service you must know how to diagnose mechanical and operating difficulties of vehicles; adjust and tune engines and clean fuel pumps, carburetors, and radiators.

You must also know how to regulate timing and make other necessary adjustments to maintain trucks that are in service in proper operating condition. In addition, you must know how to repair and replace automotive electrical equipment such as generators, starters, ignition systems, distributors, and wiring; install new spark plugs; conduct road tests of vehicles after repairs, noting performance of engine, clutch, transmission, brakes, and other parts.

As an automotive mechanic, you may also perform any of the following duties: remove, disassemble, and install entire engines; overhaul transmissions, rear end assemblies, and braking systems; straighten frames and axles; make road calls to obtain emergency repairs; and make required truck inspections.

Note: See **Strategies for Standardized Tests,** *multiple-choice test techniques,* pages 393-396, and review any books about basic mechanics, basic electricity, and basic electronics.

U.S. Postal Service

Automotive Mechanic Exam

Sample Questions for Examination V/N 940

The following samples show the types of questions that will be used in the written automotive mechanic examination. They will show how the questions are to be answered by those who take the test and the approximate difficulty of the test. Read the directions below; then look over these questions carefully and try to answer them. Record your answers on the sample answer sheet. Then check your answers with the correct answers.

Each sample question has a number of suggested answers, lettered A, B, C, etc. Decide which one is the *best* answer to the question. Then on the sample answer sheet, find the answer space numbered to correspond with the number of the question and *blacken* the space lettered the same as the suggested answer you consider best.

Here are the sample questions for you to answer on the sample answer sheet.

1. During a cylinder leakage test, what is indicated when air escapes through the radiator from two adjacent cylinders?

   A) Leaking intake valves
   B) Worn piston rings
   C) Burnt exhaust valves
   D) Defective cylinder head gasket
   E) Worn cylinder walls

2. Which of the following would cause a soft, spongy brake pedal?

   A) Master cylinder not returning to proper stop
   B) A brake disc with excessive runout
   C) Out-of-round brake drums
   D) Air in the hydraulic system
   E) Bent brake shoe hold-down pins

3. What is wrong during a compression test, if a low compression reading goes up after a small amount of oil is squirted into a spark plug hole?

   A) Cracked cylinder head
   B) A burnt valve
   C) Worn rings
   D) A blown cylinder head gasket
   E) Valves adjusted too tightly

4. For which of the following should a torque wrench be used?

   A) Measuring engine torque at a specific engine r.p.m.
   B) Tightening automatic transmission valve body bolts
   C) Checking a hydraulic lifter clearance in its bore
   D) Measuring distributor point gap to check swell
   E) Correctly identifying threads per inch on large-diameter bolts

5. Which of the following conditions will result when a brake drum is out of round?

   A) A spongy pedal
   B) A pulsating pedal
   C) A hard pedal
   D) A high pedal
   E) A low pedal

6. A vacuum gauge connected to a well-tuned engine should show a steady reading between which of the following during engine idle?

   A) 5" - 9"
   B) 10" - 13"
   C) 14" - 22"
   D) 23" - 27"
   E) 28" - 30"

7. Which one of the following emission control systems is common to all automobiles and light trucks manufactured at the present time in the United States?

A) CAS — Cleaner Air System
B) CCS — Controlled Combustion System
C) ImCo — Improved Combustion
D) PCV — Positive Crankcase Ventilation
E) AIR — Air Injection Reaction

8. A PCV valve is controlled by which of the following?

A) Throttle linkage
B) Engine temperature
C) Exhaust pressure or flow
D) Engine vacuum
E) Valve lifter or rocker arm

9. Which of the following is used to adjust the up-and-down clearance between an I-beam or solid front axle and the steering knuckle?

A) King pin bushings
B) King pin
C) Draw key
D) Thrust bearing
E) Spacer shims

Gear	Normal Application
Neutral	No Clutches - No Bands
First	Front Clutch - One-way Clutch
Second	Front Clutch - Front Band
Third	Front Clutch - Rear Clutch
Low	Front Clutch - Rear Band
Reverse	Rear Clutch - Rear Band

Fig. 613.180-10

10. Using Figure 613.180-10, determine which unit is defective when the vehicle will not move in *Drive* or *Low* but moves in *Reverse.*

A) Rear band
B) Front clutch
C) Front band
D) One-way clutch
E) Rear clutch

11. In an automatic transmission, which of the following is part of a planetary gear set?

A) Pinion
B) Stator support
C) Modulator
D) Impeller
E) Rotor support

12. The front band of an automatic transmission is applied through which of the following?

A) Front clutch
B) One-way clutch
C) Input shaft bushing
D) Servo lever
E) Sun gear

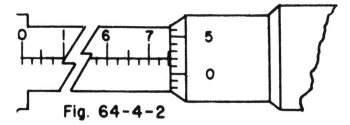

Fig. 64-4-2

13. The reading shown in Fig. 64-4-2 is

A) 0.722
B) 0.742
C) 0.752
D) 0.7112
E) 1.6722

Correct Answers

1. D
2. D
3. C
4. B
5. B
6. C
7. D
8. D
9. E
10. B
11. A
12. D
13. C

Examination 931

Test for 26 Postal Job Categories

United States Postal Service
Sample Questions

The following positions use Test M/N 931:

Area Maintenance Specialist	Letter Box Mechanic
Area Maintenance Technician	Machinist
Assistant Engineman	Maintenance Electrician
Blacksmith-Welder	Mason
Building Equipment Mechanic	Mechanic Helper
Building Maintenance Custodian	Oiler, MPE
Carpenter	Painter
Elevator Mechanic	Painter/Finisher
Engineman	Plumber
Fireman	Postal Machines Mechanic
Fireman-Laborer	Postal Maintenance Trainee
General Mechanic	Scale Mechanic
Industrial Equipment Mechanic	Stationary Engineer

The examination, which is known as Examination 931, is given to applicants for the above positions. The exam consists of Part I, Following Oral Instructions; and Part II, which involves basic mechanics, basic electricity, and basic electronics. See **Who Can Apply for Exams?**, pages 5-10; **Analyzing Examination 710**, pages 293-304; and **Strategies for Standardized Tests,** *multiple choice, vocabulary,* and *solving mathematics problems,* pages 293-296. The total qualifications of an applicant will be evaluated based on the results of the written test and the review panel evaluation.

Sample Answer Sheet

Test M/N 931 measures 16 Knowledge, Skills, and Abilities (KSAs) used by a variety of maintenance positions. Exhibit A lists the actual KSAs that are measured. However, not all KSAS that are
measured in this test are scored for every position listed. The qualification standard for each
position lists the KSAs required for the position. Only those questions that measure KSAs required
for the position(s) for which you are applying will be scored for the position(s).

The suggested answers to each question are lettered A, B, C, etc. Select the *best* answer and make a
heavy pencil mark in the corresponding space on the sample answer sheet. Each mark must be
dense black. Each mark must cover more than half the space and must not extend into neighboring
spaces. If the answer to Sample 1 is B, you would make the sample answer sheet like this:

After recording your answers, compare them with those in the correct answers to sample questions. If they do not agree, carefully reread the questions that were missed to get a clear understanding of what each question is asking.

During the test, directions for answering questions in Part I will be given orally, either by a cassette
tape or by the examiner. You are to listen closely to the directions and follow them. To practice for this
part of the test you might have a friend read the direction to you while you mark your answers on the
sample answer sheet. Directions for answering questions in Part II will be completely described in
the test booklet.

STUDY CAREFULLY BEFORE YOU GO TO THE EXAMINATION ROOM

PART I

In Part I of the test, you will be told to follow directions by writing in a test booklet and then on an
answer sheet. The test booklet will have lines of material like the following five samples.

SAMPLE 1.   5 _____

SAMPLE 2.   1 6 4 3 7

SAMPLE 3.   D B A E C

SAMPLE 4.   (8__) (5__) (2__) (9__) (10__)

SAMPLE 5.   (7__) [6__] (1__) [12__]

To practice this test, have someone read the instructions on the next page to you and you follow the instructions. When they tell you to darken the space on the sample answer sheet, use the one on this page.

Instructions to be read (the words in parentheses should not be read aloud).

You are to follow the instructions that I shall read to you. I cannot repeat them.

Look at the samples. Sample 1 has a number and a line beside it. On the line write an A. (Pause 2 seconds.) Now on the sample answer sheet, find numbers 5 (pause 2 seconds) and darken the space for the letter you just wrote on the line. (Pause 2 seconds.)

Look at Sample 2. (Pause slightly.) Draw a line under the third number. (Pause 2 seconds.) Now look on the sample answer sheet, find the number under which you just drew a line and darken space B as in baker for that number. (Pause 5 seconds.)

Look at Sample 3. (Pause slightly.) Draw a line under the third letter in the line. (Pause 2 seconds.) Now on your sample answer sheet, find number 9 (pause 2 seconds) and darken the space for the letter under which you drew a line. (Pause 5 seconds.)

Look at the five circles in Sample 4. (Pause slightly.) Each circle has a number and a line in it. Write D as in dog on the blank in the last circle. (Pause 2 seconds.) Now on the sample answer sheet, darken the space for the number-letter combination that is in the circle you just wrote in. (Pause 5 seconds.)

Look at Sample 5. (Pause slightly.) There are two circles and two boxes of different sizes with numbers in them. (Pause slightly.) If 4 is more than 2 and if 5 is less than 3, write A in the smaller circle. (Pause slightly.) Otherwise write C in the larger box. (Pause 2 seconds.) Now on the sample answer sheet, darken the space for the number-letter combination in the circle or box in which you just wrote. (Pause 5 seconds.)

Now look at the sample answer sheet. (Pause slightly.) You should have darkened spaces 4B, 5A, 9A, 10D, and 12C on the sample answer sheet. (If the person preparing to take the examination made any mistakes, try to help him or her understand why the answers are wrong.)

Note: See **Strategies for Standardized Tests,** *multiple-choice test techniques,* pages 393-396, and review any books about basic mechanics, basic electricity, and basic electronics.

Part II

1. Which device is used to transfer power and rotary mechanical motion from one shaft to another?

   A) bearing
   B) lever
   C) idler roller
   D) gear
   E) bushing

2. Lead anchors are usually mounted in

   A) steel paneling
   B) drywall construction
   C) masonry construction
   D) wood construction
   E) gypsum board

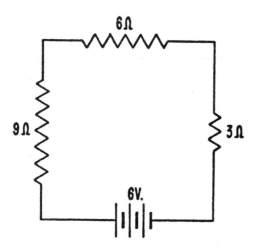

Figure III-A-22

3. Which of the following circuits is shown in Figure III-A-22?

   A) series circuit
   B) parallel circuit
   C) series, parallel circuit
   D) solid state circuit
   E) none of the above

4. Which component would *best* simulate the actions of the photocell in Figure 24-3-1?

   A) variable resistor
   B) variable capacitor
   C) variable inductor
   D) autotransformer
   E) battery

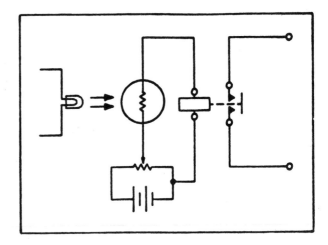

Figure 24-3-1

5. The semi-conductor materials contained in a transistor are designated by the letter(s)

   A) Q
   B) N, P
   C) CR
   D) M, P, M
   E) none of the above

6. Which of the following circuits or devices always has inductance?

   A) rectifier
   B) coil
   C) current limiter
   D) condenser
   E) filter

7. Crowbars, light bulbs, and vacuum bags are to be stored in the cabinet shown in Figure 75-25-1. Considering the balance of weight, what would be the safest arrangement?

A) top drawer   — crowbars
    middle drawer   — light bulbs
    bottom drawer   — vacuum bags

B) top drawer   — crowbars
    middle drawer   — vacuum bags
    bottom drawer   — light bulbs

C) top drawer   — vacuum bags
    middle drawer   — crowbars
    bottom drawer   — light bulbs

D) top drawer   — vacuum bags
    middle drawer   — light bulbs
    bottom drawer   — crowbars

E) top drawer   — light bulbs
    middle drawer   — vacuum bags
    bottom drawer   — crowbars

Figure 75-25-1

8. Which is most appropriate for pulling a heavy load?

A) electric lift
B) fork lift
C) tow conveyor
D) dolly
E) pallet truck

9. What measuring device is illustrated in Figure 75-26-1?

A) screw pitch gage
B) vernier calipers
C) inside calipers
D) outside calipers
E) outside micrometer

Figure 75-26-1

10. A screw pitch gage can be used for

  A) determining the pitch and number of internal threads
  B) measuring the number of gages available for use
  C) measuring the depth of a screw hole
  D) checking the thread angle
  E) cleaning the external threads

11. What measuring device is illustrated in Figure 75-20-17?

  A) screw pitch gage
  B) vernier caliper
  C) inside calipers
  D) outside calipers
  E) outside micrometer

12. One characteristic of the breast drill is that it

  A) is gearless
  B) is hand operated
  C) has a 3 ¼ hp motor
  D) has 4 speeds
  E) is steam powered

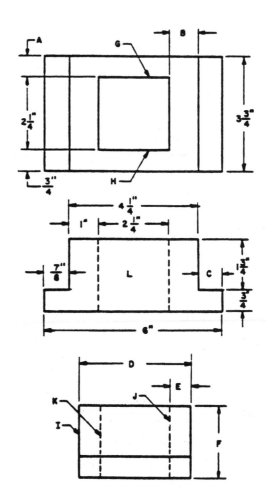

Figure 3-8-6

Figure 75-20-17

13. In Figure 3-8-6, what is the measurement of dimension F?

  A) 1 ¾ inches
  B) 2 ¼ inches
  C) 2 ½ inches
  D) 3 ¾ inches
  E) none of the above

14. The device pictured in Figure 36 is in a rest position. Which position, if any, is the normal closed?

    A) A
    B) B
    C) C
    D) devices of this sort have no normal closed position
    E) the normal closed is not shown in this diagram

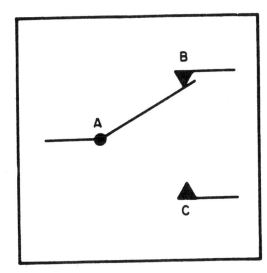

Figure 36

15. Which of the following test equipment would most likely be used in determining amplifier band width?

    A) clamp-on ammeter
    B) tube tester
    C) watt meter
    D) frequency analyzer
    E) sweep frequency generator

16. Which instrument is used to test insulation breakdown of a conductor?

    A) ohmmeter
    B) ammeter
    C) megger
    D) wheatstone bridge
    E) voltmeter

17. The primary purpose of soldering is to

    A) melt solder to a molten state
    B) heat metal parts to the right temperature to be joined
    C) join metal parts by melting the parts
    D) harden metal
    E) join metal parts

18. Which of the following statements is correct of a soldering gun?

    A) tip is not replaceable
    B) cannot be used in cramped places
    C) heats only when trigger is pressed
    D) not rated by the number of watts they use
    E) has no light

19. Contaminants have caused bearings to fail prematurely. Which pair of the items listed below should be kept away from bearings?

    A) dirt and oil
    B) grease and water
    C) oil and grease
    D) dirt and moisture
    E) water and oil

20. The electrical circuit term *open circuit* refers to a closed loop being opened. When an ohmmeter is connected into this type of circuit, one can expect the meter to

    A) read infinity
    B) read infinity and slowly return to *zero*
    C) read *zero*
    D) read *zero* and slowly return to infinity
    E) none of the above

21. A change from refrigerant vapor to liquid while the temperature stays constant results in a

    A) latent pressure loss
    B) sensible heat loss
    C) sensible pressure loss
    D) latent heat loss
    E) super heat loss

22. The mediums normally used in condensing refrigerants are

    A) air and water
    B) air and vapor
    C) water and gas
    D) liquid and vapor
    E) vapor and gas

23. Most condenser problems are caused by

   A) high head pressure
   B) high suction pressure
   C) low head pressure
   D) low suction pressure
   E) line leaks

24. Most air conditioners with motors of 1 horsepower, or less, operate on which type of source?

   A) 110-volt, single-phase
   B) 110-volt, three-phase
   C) 220-volt, single-phase
   D) 220-volt, three-phase
   E) 220-440-volt, three-phase

25. $2.6 - .5 =$

   A) 2.0
   B) 2.1
   C) 3.1
   D) 3.3
   E) None of the above

26. ½ of ¼ is

   A) $\frac{1}{12}$
   B) ⅛
   C) ¼
   D) ½
   E) 8

27. A drawing of a certain large building is 10 inches by 15 inches. On this drawing, 1 inch represents 5 feet. If the same drawing had been made 20 inches by 30 inches, 1 inch on the drawing would represent

   A) 2 1/2 feet
   B) 3 ⅓ feet
   C) 5 feet
   D) 7 1/2 feet
   E) 10 feet

28. In a shipment of bearings, 51 were defective. This is 30 percent of the total number of bearings ordered. What was the total number of bearings ordered?

   A) 125
   B) 130
   C) 153
   D) 171
   E) None of the above

Note: To answer the question that follow, see **Analyzing Examination 710,** *Reading Comprehension,* pages 301-302.

In sample questions 29 below, select the statement which is most nearly correct according to the paragraph.

"Without accurate position descriptions, it is difficult to have proper understanding of who is to do what and when. As the organization obtains newer and different equipment and as more and more data are accumulated to help establish proper preventive maintenance routines, the organization will change. When changes occur, it is important that the organization charts and the position descriptions are updated to reflect them."

29. According to the above paragraph, which of the following statements is most nearly correct?

   A) Job descriptions should be general in nature to encourage job flexibility.
   B) The organizational structure is not dependent upon changes in preventive maintenance routines.
   C) As long as supervisory personnel are aware of organizational changes, there is no need to constantly update the organization chart.
   D) Organizational changes can result from procurement of new, advanced equipment.
   E) Formal job descriptions are not needed for an office to function on a day-to-day basis. The supervisor knows who is to do what and when.

30. A small crane was used to raise the heavy part. Raise *most* nearly means

    A) lift   D) deliver
    B) drag   E) guide
    C) drop

31. Short *most* nearly means

    A) tall   D) heavy
    B) wide   E) dark
    C) brief

In each of the sample questions below, look at the symbols in the first two boxes. Something about the three symbols in the first box makes them alike; something about the two symbols in the other box with the question mark makes them alike. Look for some characteristics that is common to all symbols in the same box, yet makes them different from the symbols in the other box. Among the five answer choices, find the symbol that can best be substituted for the question mark, because it is *like* the symbols in the second box, and, *for the same reason,* different from those in the first box.

32.

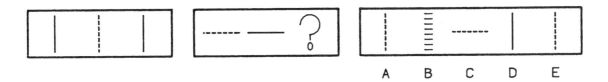

In the sample question above, all the symbols in the first box are vertical lines. The second box has two lines, one broken and one solid. Their *likeness* to each other consists in their being horizontal; and their being horizontal makes them *different* from the vertical lines in the other box. The answer must be the only one of the five lettered choices that is a horizontal line, either broken or solid. NOTE: There is not supposed to be a series of progression in these symbol questions. If you look for a progression in the first box and the second box, you will be wasting time. Remember, look for a *likeness* within each box and a *difference* between the two boxes. Now do sample question 33.

33.

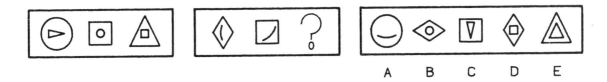

In sample question 34 below, there is at the left a drawing of a flat piece of paper and at the right, four figures labeled A, B, C, and D. When the paper is rolled, it will form one of the figures at its right. Decide which figure can be formed from the flat piece. Then on the answer sheet darken the space which has the same letter as your answer.

34.

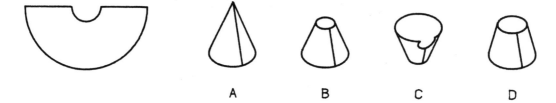

A   B   C   D

Correct Answers

Sample Questions

Part I

1. D	18. C
2. C	19. D
3. A	20. A
4. A	21. D
5. B	22. A
6. B	23. A
7. E	24. A
8. E	25. B
9. C	26. B
10. A	27. A
11. E	28. E
12. B	29. D
13. C	30. A
14. B	31. C
15. D	32. C
16. C	33. A
17. E	34. B

Test 916

Custodial Maintenance Exam

The purpose of this section is to illustrate the types of questions that will be used in Test 916. The samples will also show how the questions in the test are to be answered.

The test questions are designed to evaluate the following subject areas:

VOCABULARY AND READING: These questions test your ability to read and understand written materials as used in reading product label instructions and warnings, material safety data sheets (MSDS), equipment operating instructions, and cleaning route sheets.

BASIC SAFETY: These questions test your knowledge of basic safety principles and practices such as proper lifting techniques, use of personal protective equipment, and awareness of electrical, chemical, and other health hazards in the area of cleaning and building maintenance.

GENERAL CLEANING: These questions test your knowledge of general cleaning and disinfecting materials, techniques, equipment, and tools commonly used by custodians.

FOLLOWING WRITTEN INSTRUCTIONS: These questions test your ability to understand and carry out instructions similar to those you might receive on the job.

The suggested answers to each question are lettered A, B, C, D, and E. Select the BEST answer and make a heavy pencil mark in the corresponding space on the Sample Answer Sheet. Each mark must be dense black. Each mark must cover more than half the space and must not extend into neighboring spaces. If the answer to Sample 1 is B, you would mark the Sample Answers Sheet like this:

After recording your answers below, compare them with those in the Correct Answers to Sample Questions on Page 11. If they do not agree, carefully re-read the questions that were missed to get a clear understanding of what each question is asking.

Sample Answer Sheet

1 Ⓐ Ⓑ Ⓒ Ⓓ Ⓔ	5 Ⓐ Ⓑ Ⓒ Ⓓ Ⓔ	9 Ⓐ Ⓑ Ⓒ Ⓓ Ⓔ	13 Ⓐ Ⓑ Ⓒ Ⓓ Ⓔ
2 Ⓐ Ⓑ Ⓒ Ⓓ Ⓔ	6 Ⓐ Ⓑ Ⓒ Ⓓ Ⓔ	10 Ⓐ Ⓑ Ⓒ Ⓓ Ⓔ	14 Ⓐ Ⓑ Ⓒ Ⓓ Ⓔ
3 Ⓐ Ⓑ Ⓒ Ⓓ Ⓔ	7 Ⓐ Ⓑ Ⓒ Ⓓ Ⓔ	11 Ⓐ Ⓑ Ⓒ Ⓓ Ⓔ	15 Ⓐ Ⓑ Ⓒ Ⓓ Ⓔ
4 Ⓐ Ⓑ Ⓒ Ⓓ Ⓔ	8 Ⓐ Ⓑ Ⓒ Ⓓ Ⓔ	12 Ⓐ Ⓑ Ⓒ Ⓓ Ⓔ	16 Ⓐ Ⓑ Ⓒ Ⓓ Ⓔ

DIRECTIONS AND SAMPLE QUESTIONS

Study sample questions 1 through 12 carefully. Each question has several alternative responses. Decide from among the alternatives which is the best response. Find the question number on the Sample Answer Sheet on Page 7 and mark your answer to the question by completely darkening the space corresponding to the letter you have chosen.

VOCABULARY AND READING

1. Avoid **inhaling** the fumes from this product. Inhaling most nearly means:

A) Diluting
B) Expelling
C) Breathing
D) Vaporizing
E) Ventilating

2. The contents of this load are **fragile** and require special handling. Fragile most nearly means:

A) Durable
B) Delicate
C) Valuable
D) Jagged
E) Greasy

3. Safety goggles are **mandatory** when handling corrosive chemicals. Mandatory most nearly means:

A) Essential
B) Awkward
C) Optional
D) Useless
E) Foolproof

4. "Although mixing cleaners can be risky, there are many products that can be harmful on their own. They range from window cleaners to all-purpose scrubs. Even liquid soap containing ammonia can be toxic. Ammonia can cause dizziness, and mixed with certain types of bleach, can create deadly fumes."

The quotation best supports the statement that:

A) Gases can be detected by their color
B) All-purpose cleaners are rarely effective
C) Chemicals should never be mixed with water
D) Cleaners can be toxic even when used alone
E) Combining products will improve air quality

BASIC SAFETY

5. Which of the following lists information on the health hazards of cleaning products?

    A) Lockout/tagout fact sheet
    B) National Electrical Code (NEC)
    C) National Building Code (NBC)
    D) Better Business Bureau (BBB)
    E) Material Safety Data Sheet (MSDS)

6. What should be done if an electrical cord is defective, damaged, or frayed?

    A) Splice to a one-pronged plug
    B) Apply finish to maintain appearance
    C) Use only when working near water
    D) Have the cord replaced at once
    E) Run the electrical cord under a rug

7. Which of the following is a general rule of safe manual lifting?

    A) Use the back to bear the entire load
    B) Bend the back with knees straight
    C) Keep the load close to one's body
    D) Lift alone, no matter how heavy the load
    E) Twist at the waist while carrying loads

8. Which of the following makes it unsafe to stand directly under ladders, lifts, and scaffolds?

    A) Radiant energy
    B) Falling tools or debris
    C) Dog and insect bites
    D) Cross-breeze venting
    E) Stiff neck syndrome

9. Which of the following is used to apply cleaning solution to a painted wall?

    A) Sponge
    B) Spatula
    C) Scraper
    D) Wire brush
    E) Drop cloth

10. Which of the following is used to clean inside a toilet?

    A) Treated dust cloth
    B) Bowl brush
    C) Chamois cloth
    D) Feather duster
    E) HEPA vacuum

11. What is the primary purpose of a disinfectant?

    A) Freshen air
    B) Prevent fires
    C) Flavor foods
    D) Stain fabrics
    E) Destroy germs

12. Which of the following is used to sweep dust and dirt from smooth floors?

    A) Push broom
    B) Sponge cloth
    C) Floor stripper
    D) Counter brush
    E) Pressure washer

GENERAL CLEANING

FOLLOWING INSTRUCTIONS

Sample items 13 through 16 below test your ability to follow instructions.

Read each item carefully. Following the instructions in each item will lead you to identify or create a letter-number combination (e.g., P1, S4, Q10, T6). Next, go to the "Look-Up Table" to find the specific letter ("P" through "T") and number (1 through 10) from the combination you identified or created. Locate the intersection of this letter-number combination on the table to find your answer of A, B, C, D, or E. After you have found an answer, darken the corresponding space on your Sample Answer Sheet on Page 7.

For example, if you came up with P1 for Item 1, then your answer from the Look-Up Table would be "A", and you would darken "A" for question 1 on your Sample Answer Sheet. If you came up with T4 as the letter-number combination, then your answer would be "C" and you would darken "C" on your answer sheet, and so on. Apply these instructions when answering sample items 13 through 16.

LOOK-UP TABLE

	P	Q	R	S	T
1	A	B	C	D	E
2	B	C	D	E	A
3	C	D	E	A	B
4	D	E	A	B	C
5	E	A	B	C	D
6	A	B	C	D	E
7	B	C	D	E	A
8	C	D	E	A	B
9	D	E	A	B	C
10	E	A	B	C	D

13. Look at the letter-number combinations below. Draw a line under the second letter-number combination from the left. Write the letter-number combination you drew a line under here: __ __.

        Q4   P3   R4   S9   T5

14. Draw a line under each letter in the line below that is not a "P" or "S". Write the letter under which you drew the lines and the number of lines you drew here: __ __.

        P S Q P S S P Q P S P Q

15. Look at the circles below. The number inside each circle represents the number of light bulbs in a container. Write the letter "Q" below the container with the most bulbs.

    ⑤   ⑧   ④   ⑥   ⑦
    __   __   __   __   __

16. Look at the list of hand tools below. Circle the tool with the fewest letters. Count the number of letters in that word. Now write that number and the first letter of that tool here: __ __.

    SHOVEL   EDGER   RAKE   SCRAPER   SHEARS

Examination 410

34

Postal Center Technician Test

The following samples show the types of questions you will see in the written test. They also show how the questions in the test are to be answered. Test 410 contains questions which test the ability to read and understand technical information, questions on mechanical and electrical principals and applications, and questions on arithmetic. The sample questions illustrate these types of questions.

The suggested answers to each question are lettered A, B, C, D, and E. Select the BEST answer and make a heavy pencil mark in the corresponding space on the Sample Question Answer Sheet. Each mark must be dense black. Each mark must cover more than half the space and must not extend into neighboring spaces. If the answer to Sample 1 is B, you would mark the Sample Question Answer Sheet like this:

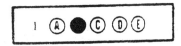

After recording your answers compare them with those in the Correct Answers to sample questions.

SAMPLE QUESTIONS

USE THE FOLLOWING PASSAGE TO ANSWER QUESTION 1.

Coins inserted into the machine are registered by the recorder and are in the escrow area of the coin unit. When the coin return lever (scavenger bar) is depressed, the upper cancel switch is moved to the N.O. position, thereby removing the selector switch series from the circuit. This prevents simultaneous vend and coin return.

1. When a customer wants his money back, he pushes the coin return lever. What protection is there against his also getting merchandise as well as return of his money?

   A) The scavenger bar is also depressed
   B) The escrow area prevents vending
   C) The coin return is registered by the recorder
   D) The selector switches are cut out of the circuit
   E) All of the above

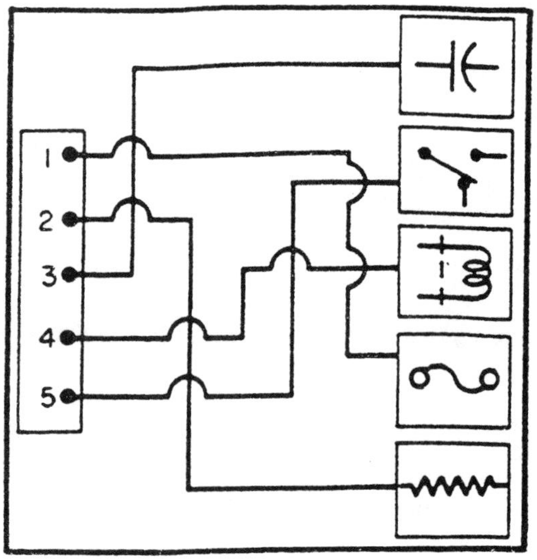

Figure 1

2. Wire 1 connects to which of the following in the diagram shown in Figure 1?

   A) Transformer
   B) Fuse
   C) Switch
   D Battery
   E) Resistor

3. What is the total cost of a coil of 29-cent stamps, a coil of 8-cent stamps, and a coil of 1-cent stamps, if there are 500 stamps to a coil?

   A) $ 59.50
   B) $180.00
   C) $190.00
   D) $595.00
   E) None of these

4. A Technician paid $25.50 for 3 boxes of envelopes. Each box contained 25 envelopes. What was the cost for each envelope?

   A) $ .34
   B) $ .35
   C) $1.02
   D) $3.40
   E) None of these

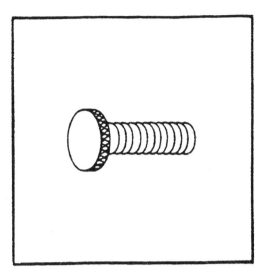

Figure 2

5. The proper method to tighten the item shown in Figure 2 is to use

    A) slip-joint pliers
    B) spanner wrench
    C. thumb and forefinger
    D) spin-type socket
    E) mechanical finger

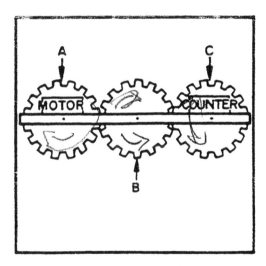

Figure 3

6. In Figure 3, gears A, B, and C are the same size. If gear A is moving in a clockwise direction, which of the following describes the action of gear C?

    A) Turns counterclockwise slower than gear A
    B) Turns clockwise slower than gear A
    C) Turns counterclockwise at the same speed as gear A
    D) Turns clockwise faster than gear A
    E) Turns clockwise at the same speed as gear A

Examination 932

Test For Electronics Group

35

United States Postal Service
Sample Questions

The following positions use Examination 932:

Electronics Technician 8 (Register Number M26)
Electronics Technician 9 (Register Number M27)
Electronics Technician 10 (Register Number M28)

This examination, which is known as Examination 932, is given to applicants for the above positions. This exam consists of Part I, *Following Oral Instructions;* and Part II - *Multiple Choice Test,* which involves basic mechanics, basic electricity, and basic electronics and with the use of hand and portable power tools and test equipment. Study books on basic mechanics, basic electricity, and basic electronics in your local library. (See **Who Can Apply for Exams?**, pages 5-10; **Analyzing Examination 710,** pages 293-304; and **Strategies for Standardized Tests**, *multiple choice, vocabulary* and *solving mathematics problems,* pages 393-396. The total qualifications for an application will be evaluated based on the results of the written test and the review panel evaluation.

Test M/N 932 measures 16 Knowledge, Skills, and Abilities
(KSAs) used by a variety of maintenance positions. Exhibit A
lists the actual KSAs that are measured, and Exhibit B lists
the positions that use this examination. However, not all
KSAs that are measured in this test are scored for every
position listed.   The qualification standard for each
position lists the KSAs required for the position. Only
those questions that measure KSAs required for the
position(s) for which you are applying will be scored for the
position(s).

The suggested answers to each question are lettered A, B, C,
etc. Select the BEST answer and make a heavy pencil mark in
the corresponding space on the Sample Answer Sheet. Each
mark must be dense black. Each mark must cover more than
half the space and must not extend into neighboring spaces.
If the answer to Sample 1 is B, you would mark the Sample
Answer Sheet like this:

After recording your answers, compare them with those in the
Correct Answers to Sample Questions. If they do not agree,
carefully re-read the questions that were missed to get a
clear understanding of what each question is asking.

During the test, directions for answering questions in Part I
will be given orally, either by a cassette tape or by the
examiner. You are to listen closely to the directions and
follow them. To practice for this part of the test you might
have a friend read the direction to you while you mark your
answers on the Sample Answer Sheet. Directions for answering
questions in Part II will be completely described in the test
booklet.

   STUDY CAREFULLY BEFORE YOU GO TO THE EXAMINATION ROOM

PART I

In Part I of the test, you will be told to follow directions by writing in a test booklet and then on an answer sheet. The test booklet will have lines of material like the following five samples:

SAMPLE QUESTIONS

SAMPLE 1.   5 _____

SAMPLE 2.   1 6 4 3 7

SAMPLE 3.   D B A E C

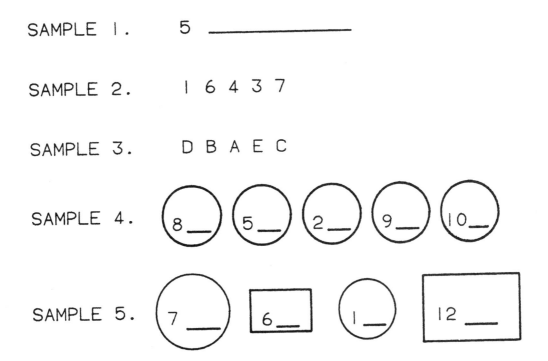

To practice this test, have someone read the instructions on the next page to you and you follow the instructions. When they tell you to darken the space on the Sample Answer Sheet, use the one on this page.

SAMPLE ANSWER SHEET

1 Ⓐ Ⓑ Ⓒ Ⓓ Ⓔ   5 Ⓐ Ⓑ Ⓒ Ⓓ Ⓔ   9 Ⓐ Ⓑ Ⓒ Ⓓ Ⓔ

2 Ⓐ Ⓑ Ⓒ Ⓓ Ⓔ   6 Ⓐ Ⓑ Ⓒ Ⓓ Ⓔ   10 Ⓐ Ⓑ Ⓒ Ⓓ Ⓔ

3 Ⓐ Ⓑ Ⓒ Ⓓ Ⓔ   7 Ⓐ Ⓑ Ⓒ Ⓓ Ⓔ   11 Ⓐ Ⓑ Ⓒ Ⓓ Ⓔ

4 Ⓐ Ⓑ Ⓒ Ⓓ Ⓔ   8 Ⓐ Ⓑ Ⓒ Ⓓ Ⓔ   12 Ⓐ Ⓑ Ⓒ Ⓓ Ⓔ

<u>Instructions to be read</u> (the words in parentheses should not be read aloud).

You are to follow the instructions that I shall read to you. I cannot repeat them.

Look at the samples. Sample 1 has a number and a line beside it. On the line write an A. (Pause 2 seconds.) Now on the Sample Answer Sheet, find number 5 (pause 2 seconds) and darken the space for the letter you just wrote on the line. (Pause 2 seconds.)

Look at Sample 2. (Pause slightly.) Draw a line under the third number. (Pause 2 seconds.) Now look on the Sample Answer Sheet, find the number under which you just drew a line and darken space B as in baker for that number. (Pause 5 seconds.)

Look at Sample 3. (Pause slightly.) Draw a line under the third letter in the line. (Pause 2 seconds.) Now on your Sample Answer Sheet, find number 9 (pause 2 seconds) and darken the space for the letter under which you drew a line. (Pause 5 seconds.)

Look at the five circles in Sample 4. (Pause slightly.) Each circle has a number and a line in it. Write D as in dog on the blank in the last circle. (Pause 2 seconds.) Now on the Sample Answer Sheet, darken the space for the number-letter combination that is in the circle you just wrote in. (Pause 5 seconds.)

Look at Sample 5. (Pause slightly.) There are two circles and two boxes of different sizes with numbers in them. (Pause slightly.) If 4 is more than 2 and if 5 is less than 3, write A in the smaller circle. (Pause slightly.) Otherwise write C in the larger box. (Pause 2 seconds.) Now on the Sample Answer Sheet, darken the space for the number-letter combination in the circle or box in which you just wrote. (Pause 5 seconds.)

Now look at the Sample Answer Sheet. (Pause slightly.) You should have darkened spaces 4B, 5A, 9A, 10D, and 12C on the Sample Answer Sheet. (If the person preparing to take the examination made any mistakes, try to help him or her understand why the mistakes are wrong.)

SAMPLE ANSWER QUESTIONS

1 Ⓐ Ⓑ Ⓒ Ⓓ Ⓔ

2 Ⓐ Ⓑ Ⓒ Ⓓ Ⓔ

3 Ⓐ Ⓑ Ⓒ Ⓓ Ⓔ

4 Ⓐ Ⓑ Ⓒ Ⓓ Ⓔ

5 Ⓐ Ⓑ Ⓒ Ⓓ Ⓔ

6 Ⓐ Ⓑ Ⓒ Ⓓ Ⓔ

7 Ⓐ Ⓑ Ⓒ Ⓓ Ⓔ

8 Ⓐ Ⓑ Ⓒ Ⓓ Ⓔ

9 Ⓐ Ⓑ Ⓒ Ⓓ Ⓔ

10 Ⓐ Ⓑ Ⓒ Ⓓ Ⓔ

11 Ⓐ Ⓑ Ⓒ Ⓓ Ⓔ

12 Ⓐ Ⓑ Ⓒ Ⓓ Ⓔ

13 Ⓐ Ⓑ Ⓒ Ⓓ Ⓔ

14 Ⓐ Ⓑ Ⓒ Ⓓ Ⓔ

15 Ⓐ Ⓑ Ⓒ Ⓓ Ⓔ

16 Ⓐ Ⓑ Ⓒ Ⓓ Ⓔ

17 Ⓐ Ⓑ Ⓒ Ⓓ Ⓔ

18 Ⓐ Ⓑ Ⓒ Ⓓ Ⓔ

19 Ⓐ Ⓑ Ⓒ Ⓓ Ⓔ

20 Ⓐ Ⓑ Ⓒ Ⓓ Ⓔ

21 Ⓐ Ⓑ Ⓒ Ⓓ Ⓔ

22 Ⓐ Ⓑ Ⓒ Ⓓ Ⓔ

23 Ⓐ Ⓑ Ⓒ Ⓓ Ⓔ

24 Ⓐ Ⓑ Ⓒ Ⓓ Ⓔ

25 Ⓐ Ⓑ Ⓒ Ⓓ Ⓔ

26 Ⓐ Ⓑ Ⓒ Ⓓ Ⓔ

27 Ⓐ Ⓑ Ⓒ Ⓓ Ⓔ

28 Ⓐ Ⓑ Ⓒ Ⓓ Ⓔ

29 Ⓐ Ⓑ Ⓒ Ⓓ Ⓔ

30 Ⓐ Ⓑ Ⓒ Ⓓ Ⓔ

31 Ⓐ Ⓑ Ⓒ Ⓓ Ⓔ

32 Ⓐ Ⓑ Ⓒ Ⓓ Ⓔ

33 Ⓐ Ⓑ Ⓒ Ⓓ Ⓔ

34 Ⓐ Ⓑ Ⓒ Ⓓ Ⓔ

1. The primary function of a take-up pulley in a belt conveyor is to

   A) carry the belt on the return trip.
   B) track the belt.
   C) maintain proper belt tension
   D) change the direction of the belt

2. Which device is used to transfer power and rotary mechanical motion from one shaft to another?

   A) Bearing
   B) Lever
   C) Idler roller
   D) Gear
   E) Bushing

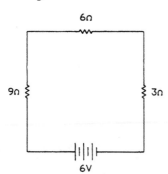

Figure III-A-22

3. Which of the following circuits is shown in Figure III-A-22?

   A) Series circuit
   B) Parallel circuit
   C) Series, parallel circuit
   D) Solid state circuit
   E) None of the above

4. A circuit has two resistors of equal value in series. The voltage and current in the circuit are 20 volts and 2 amps respectively. What is the value of EACH resistor?

   A) 5 ohms
   B) 10 ohms
   C) 20 ohms
   D) Not enough information given

PART II

5. What is the total net capacitance of two 60-farad capacitors connected in series?

   A) 30 farads
   B) 60 farads
   C) 90 farads
   D) 120 farads
   E) 360 farads

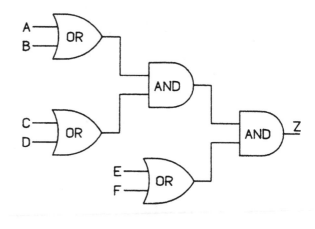

FIGURE 79-4-17B

6. Select the Boolean equation that matches the circuit diagram in Figure 79-4-17B.

   A) Z = AB+CD+EF
   B) Z = (A+B) (C+D) (E+F)
   C) Z = A+B+C+D+EF
   D) Z = ABCD(E+F)

7. If two 30-mH inductors are connected in series, what is the total net inductance of the combination?

   A) 15 mH
   B) 20 mH
   C) 30 mH
   D) 45 mH
   E) 60 mH

8. In pure binary the decimal number 6 would be expressed as

A) 001
B) 011
C) 110
D) 111

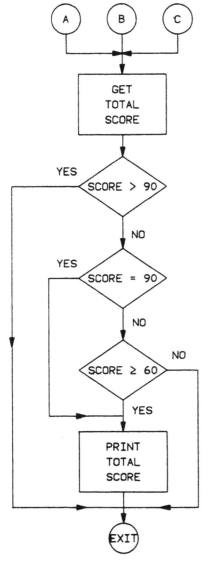

FIGURE 75-8-11

9. In Figure 75-8-11, which of the following scores will be printed?

A) All scores > 90 and < 60

B) All scores < 90

C) All scores ≤ 90 and ≥ 60

D) All scores < 60

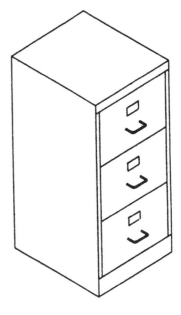

Figure 75-25-1

10. Crowbars, light bulbs and vacuum bags are to be stored in the cabinet shown in Figure 75-25-1. Considering the balance of weight, what would be the safest arrangement?

A) Top Drawer - Crowbars
   Middle Drawer - Light Bulbs
   Bottom Drawer - Vacuum bags
B) Top Drawer - Crowbars
   Middle Drawer - Vacuum bags
   Bottom Drawer - Light Bulbs
C) Top Drawer - Vacuum Bags
   Middle Drawer - Crowbars
   Bottom Drawer - Light Bulbs
D) Top Drawer - Vacuum Bags
   Middle Drawer - Light Bulbs
   Bottom Drawer - Crowbars
E) Top Drawer - Light Bulbs
   Middle Drawer - Vacuum Bags
   Bottom Drawer - Crowbars

11. Which is most appropriate for pulling a heavy load?

A) Electric lift
B) Fork lift
C) Tow Conveyor
D) Dolly
E) Pallet truck

12. The electrical circuit term "open circuit" refers to a closed loop being opened. When an ohmmeter is connected into this type of circuit, one can expect the meter to

A) Read infinity
B) Read infinity and slowly return to ZERO
C) Read ZERO
D) Read ZERO and slowly return to infinity
E) None of the above

13. Contaminants have caused bearings to fail prematurely. Which pair of the items listed below should be kept away from bearings?

A) Dirt and oil
B) Grease and water
C) Oil and grease
D) Dirt and moisture
E) Water and oil

14. In order to operate a breast drill, which direction should you turn it?

A) Clockwise
B) Counterclockwise
C) Up and down
D) Back and forth
E) Right, then left

15. Which is the correct tool for tightening or loosening a water pipe?

A) Slip joint pliers
B) Household pliers
C) Monkey wrench
D) Water pump pliers
E) Pipe wrench

16. What is one purpose of a chuck key?

A) Open doors
B) Remove drill bits
C) Remove screws
D) Remove set screws
E) Unlock chucks

17. When smoke is generated as a result of using a portable electric drill for cutting holes into a piece of angle iron, one should

A) use a fire watch.
B) cease the drilling operation.
C) use an exhaust fan to remove smoke.
D) use a prescribed coolant solution to reduce friction.
E) call the Fire Department.

18. The primary purpose of soldering is to

A) melt solder to a molten state.
B) heat metal parts to the right temperature to be joined.
C) join metal parts by melting the parts.
D) harden metal.
E) join metal parts.

19. Which of the following statements is correct of a soldering gun?

A) Tip is not replaceable
B) Cannot be used in cramped places
C) Heats only when trigger is pressed
D) Not rated by the number of watts they use
E) Has no light

20. What unit of measurement is read on a dial torque wrench?
A) Pounds
B) Inches
C) Centimeters
D) Foot-pounds
E) Degrees

21. Which instrument is used to test insulation breakdown of a conductor?

A) Ohmmeter
B) Ammeter
C) Megger
D) Wheatstone bridge
E) Voltmeter

22. 1/2 of 1/4 =

    A) 1/12
    B) 1/8
    C) 1/4
    D) 1/2
    E) 8

23. 2.6 - .5 =

    A) 2.0
    B) 2.1
    C) 3.1
    D) 3.3
    E) None of the above

24. Simplify the following
    expression in terms of amps:

    563×10^{-6}

    A)   563,000,000 amps
    B)   563,000 amps
    C)   .563 amps
    D)   .000563 amps
    E)   .000000563 amps

25. Solve the power equation

    $P = I^2R$ for R

    A) R = EI

    B) $R = I^2P$

    C) R = PI

    D) $R = P/I^2$

    E) R = E/I

26. The product of 3 kilo ohms
    times 3 micro ohms is

    A) 6×10^{-9} ohms

    B) 6×10^{-3} ohms

    C) 9×10^3 ohms

    D) 9×10^{-6} ohms

    E) 9×10^{-3} ohms

In sample question 25 below, select the statement which is most nearly correct according to the paragraph.

"Prior to 1870, a conveyor that made use of rollers was developed for transporting clay. This construction substituted rolling friction at the idler bearing points for the sliding friction of the slider bed. A primitive type of troughing belt conveyor was developed about the same time for the handling of grain. This design was improved during the latter part of the century when the troughing idler was developed."

27. According to the above paragraph, which of the following statements is most nearly correct?

    A) The troughing belt conveyor was developed about 1870 to handle clay and grain.

    B) Rolling friction construction was replaced by sliding friction construction prior to 1870.

    C) In the late nineteenth century, conveyors were improved with the development of the troughing idler.

    D) The troughing idler, a significant design improvement for conveyors, was developed in the early nineteenth century.

    E) Conveyor belts were invented and developed in the 1800's.

For sample question 28 below, select from the drawings of objects on the right labeled A, B, C, and D, the one that would have the TOP, FRONT, and RIGHT views shown in the drawing at the left

28.

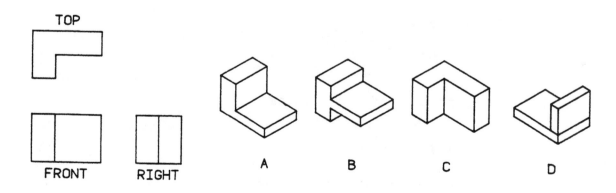

TOP

FRONT   RIGHT

A   B   C   D

In sample question 29 below, there is, on the left, a drawing of a flat piece of paper and, on the right, four figures labeled A, B, C, and D. When the paper is bent on the dotted lines it will form one of the figures on the right. Decide which alternative can be formed from the flat piece.

29.
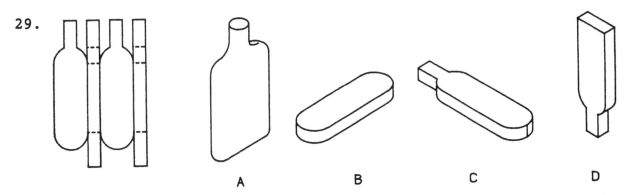

A   B   C   D

In each of the sample questions below, look at the symbols in the first two boxes. Something about the three symbols in the first box makes them alike; something about the two symbols in the other box with the question mark makes them alike. Look for some characteristic that is common to all symbols in the same box, yet makes them different from the symbols in the other box. Among dthe five answer choices, find the symbol that can best be substituted for the question mark, because it is <u>like</u> the symbols in the second box, and, <u>for the same reason</u>, different from those in the first box.

30.
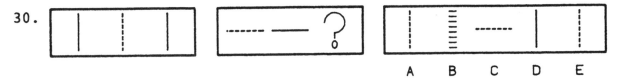

A   B   C   D   E

In sample question 30 above, all the symbols in the first box are vertical lines. The second box has two lines, one broken and one solid. Their <u>likeness</u> to each other consists in their being horizontal; and their being horizontal makes them <u>different</u> from the vertical lines in the other box. The answer must be the only one of the five lettered choices that is a horizontal line, either broken or solid. NOTE: There is not supposed to be a series or progression in these symbol questions. If you look for a progression in the first box and the second box, you will be wasting time. Remember, look for a <u>likeness</u> within each box and a <u>difference</u> between the two boxes.

Now do sample questions 31 and 32.

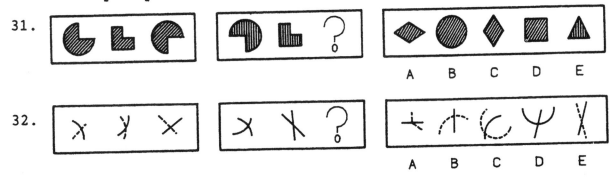

31.

A   B   C   D   E

32.

A   B   C   D   E

33. In Figure 3-8-6 below, what is the measurement of Dimension F? Drawing is not actual size.

A) 1 3/4 inches
B) 2 1/4 inches
C) 2 1/2 inches
D) 3 3/4 inches
E) None of the above

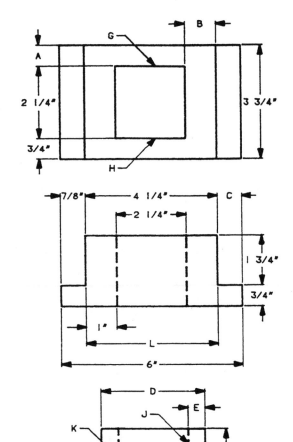

Figure 3-8-6

34. In Figure 160-57 below, what is the current flow through R_3 when:

$$V = 50 \text{ volts}$$

$$R_1 = 25 \text{ ohms}$$

$$R_2 = 25 \text{ ohms}$$

$$R3 = 50 \text{ ohms}$$

$$R_4 = 50 \text{ ohms}$$

$$R_5 = 50 \text{ ohms}$$

and the current through the entire circuit totals one amp?

A) 0.5 amp
B) 5.0 amps
C) 5.0 milliamps
D) 50.0 milliamps
E) None of the above

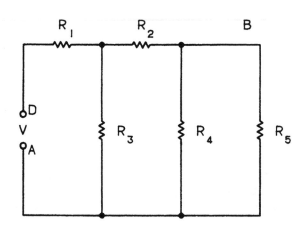

Figure 160-57

CORRECT ANSWERS TO
SAMPLE QUESTIONS

1 Ⓐ Ⓑ ● Ⓓ Ⓔ
2 Ⓐ Ⓑ Ⓒ ● Ⓔ
3 ● Ⓑ Ⓒ Ⓓ Ⓔ
4 ● Ⓑ Ⓒ Ⓓ Ⓔ
5 ● Ⓑ Ⓒ Ⓓ Ⓔ
6 Ⓐ ● Ⓒ Ⓓ Ⓔ
7 Ⓐ Ⓑ Ⓒ Ⓓ ●
8 Ⓐ Ⓑ ● Ⓓ Ⓔ
9 Ⓐ Ⓑ ● Ⓓ Ⓔ
10 Ⓐ Ⓑ Ⓒ Ⓓ ●
11 Ⓐ Ⓑ Ⓒ Ⓓ ●
12 ● Ⓑ Ⓒ Ⓓ Ⓔ
13 Ⓐ Ⓑ Ⓒ ● Ⓔ
14 ● Ⓑ Ⓒ Ⓓ Ⓔ
15 Ⓐ Ⓑ Ⓒ Ⓓ ●
16 Ⓐ ● Ⓒ Ⓓ Ⓔ
17 Ⓐ Ⓑ Ⓒ ● Ⓔ

18 Ⓐ Ⓑ Ⓒ Ⓓ ●
19 Ⓐ Ⓑ ● Ⓓ Ⓔ
20 Ⓐ Ⓑ Ⓒ ● Ⓔ
21 Ⓐ Ⓑ ● Ⓓ Ⓔ
22 Ⓐ ● Ⓒ Ⓓ Ⓔ
23 Ⓐ ● Ⓒ Ⓓ Ⓔ
24 Ⓐ Ⓑ Ⓒ ● Ⓔ
25 Ⓐ Ⓑ Ⓒ ● Ⓔ
26 Ⓐ Ⓑ Ⓒ Ⓓ ●
27 Ⓐ Ⓑ ● Ⓓ Ⓔ
28 Ⓐ Ⓑ ● Ⓓ Ⓔ
29 Ⓐ Ⓑ ● Ⓓ Ⓔ
30 Ⓐ Ⓑ ● Ⓓ Ⓔ
31 Ⓐ Ⓑ Ⓒ Ⓓ ●
32 Ⓐ Ⓑ Ⓒ ● Ⓔ
33 Ⓐ Ⓑ ● Ⓓ Ⓔ
34 ● Ⓑ Ⓒ Ⓓ Ⓔ

Examination 933

Test for Mail Processing Equipment Group

## 36

United States Postal Service
Sample Questions

The following positions use Examination 933:

Maintenance Mechanic, MPE 06 (Register Number 32)
Maintenance Mechanic, MPE/07 (Register Number M33))
Overhaul Specialist (Register Number M34)

This examination, which is known as Examination 933, is given to applicants for the above positions. This exam consists of Part I, *Following Oral Instructions;* and Part II - *Multiple Choice Test,* which involves basic mechanics, basic electricity, and basic electronics and with the use of hand and portable power tools and test equipment. Study books on basic mechanics, basic electricity, and basic electronics in your local library. (See **Who Can Apply for Exams?**, pages 5-10; **Analyzing Examination 710,** pages 293-304; and **Strategies for Standardized Tests**, *multiple choice, vocabulary* and *solving mathematics problems,* pages 393-396. The total qualifications for an application will be evaluated based on the results of the written test and the review panel evaluation.

PART I

In Part I of the test, you will be told to follow directions by writing in a test booklet and then on an answer sheet. The test booklet will have lines of material like the following five samples:

SAMPLE QUESTIONS

SAMPLE 1.   5 _____

SAMPLE 2.   1 6 4 3 7

SAMPLE 3.   D B A E C

SAMPLE 4.   (8__) (5__) (2__) (9__) (10__)

SAMPLE 5.   (7__) [6__] (1__) [12 __]

To practice this test, have someone read the instructions on the next page to you and you follow the instructions. When they tell you to darken the space on the Sample Answer Sheet, use the one on this page.

SAMPLE ANSWER SHEET		
1 Ⓐ Ⓑ Ⓒ Ⓓ Ⓔ	5 Ⓐ Ⓑ Ⓒ Ⓓ Ⓔ	9 Ⓐ Ⓑ Ⓒ Ⓓ Ⓔ
2 Ⓐ Ⓑ Ⓒ Ⓓ Ⓔ	6 Ⓐ Ⓑ Ⓒ Ⓓ Ⓔ	10 Ⓐ Ⓑ Ⓒ Ⓓ Ⓔ
3 Ⓐ Ⓑ Ⓒ Ⓓ Ⓔ	7 Ⓐ Ⓑ Ⓒ Ⓓ Ⓔ	11 Ⓐ Ⓑ Ⓒ Ⓓ Ⓔ
4 Ⓐ Ⓑ Ⓒ Ⓓ Ⓔ	8 Ⓐ Ⓑ Ⓒ Ⓓ Ⓔ	12 Ⓐ Ⓑ Ⓒ Ⓓ Ⓔ

Instructions to be read (the words in parentheses should not be read aloud).

You are to follow the instructions that I shall read to you. I cannot repeat them.

Look at the samples. Sample 1 has a number and a line beside it. On the line write an A. (Pause 2 seconds.) Now on the Sample Answer Sheet, find number 5 (pause 2 seconds) and darken the space for the letter you just wrote on the line. (Pause 2 seconds.)

Look at Sample 2. (Pause slightly.) Draw a line under the third number. (Pause 2 seconds.) Now look on the Sample Answer Sheet, find the number under which you just drew a line and darken space B as in baker for that number. (Pause 5 seconds.)

Look at Sample 3. (Pause slightly.) Draw a line under the third letter in the line. (Pause 2 seconds.) Now on your Sample Answer Sheet, find number 9 (pause 2 seconds) and darken the space for the letter under which you drew a line. (Pause 5 seconds.)

Look at the five circles in Sample 4. (Pause slightly.) Each circle has a number and a line in it. Write D as in dog on the blank in the last circle. (Pause 2 seconds.) Now on the Sample Answer Sheet, darken the space for the number-letter combination that is in the circle you just wrote in. (Pause 5 seconds.)

Look at Sample 5. (Pause slightly.) There are two circles and two boxes of different sizes with numbers in them. (Pause slightly.) If 4 is more than 2 and if 5 is less than 3, write A in the smaller circle. (Pause slightly.) Otherwise write C in the larger box. (Pause 2 seconds.) Now on the Sample Answer Sheet, darken the space for the number-letter combination in the circle or box in which you just wrote. (Pause 5 seconds.)

Now look at the Sample Answer Sheet. (Pause slightly.) You should have darkened spaces 4B, 5A, 9A, 10D, and 12C on the Sample Answer Sheet. (If the person preparing to take the examination made any mistakes, try to help him or her understand why the mistakes are wrong.)

SAMPLE ANSWER QUESTIONS

1 Ⓐ Ⓑ Ⓒ Ⓓ Ⓔ	18 Ⓐ Ⓑ Ⓒ Ⓓ Ⓔ
2 Ⓐ Ⓑ Ⓒ Ⓓ Ⓔ	19 Ⓐ Ⓑ Ⓒ Ⓓ Ⓔ
3 Ⓐ Ⓑ Ⓒ Ⓓ Ⓔ	20 Ⓐ Ⓑ Ⓒ Ⓓ Ⓔ
4 Ⓐ Ⓑ Ⓒ Ⓓ Ⓔ	21 Ⓐ Ⓑ Ⓒ Ⓓ Ⓔ
5 Ⓐ Ⓑ Ⓒ Ⓓ Ⓔ	22 Ⓐ Ⓑ Ⓒ Ⓓ Ⓔ
6 Ⓐ Ⓑ Ⓒ Ⓓ Ⓔ	23 Ⓐ Ⓑ Ⓒ Ⓓ Ⓔ
7 Ⓐ Ⓑ Ⓒ Ⓓ Ⓔ	24 Ⓐ Ⓑ Ⓒ Ⓓ Ⓔ
8 Ⓐ Ⓑ Ⓒ Ⓓ Ⓔ	25 Ⓐ Ⓑ Ⓒ Ⓓ Ⓔ
9 Ⓐ Ⓑ Ⓒ Ⓓ Ⓔ	26 Ⓐ Ⓑ Ⓒ Ⓓ Ⓔ
10 Ⓐ Ⓑ Ⓒ Ⓓ Ⓔ	27 Ⓐ Ⓑ Ⓒ Ⓓ Ⓔ
11 Ⓐ Ⓑ Ⓒ Ⓓ Ⓔ	28 Ⓐ Ⓑ Ⓒ Ⓓ Ⓔ
12 Ⓐ Ⓑ Ⓒ Ⓓ Ⓔ	29 Ⓐ Ⓑ Ⓒ Ⓓ Ⓔ
13 Ⓐ Ⓑ Ⓒ Ⓓ Ⓔ	30 Ⓐ Ⓑ Ⓒ Ⓓ Ⓔ
14 Ⓐ Ⓑ Ⓒ Ⓓ Ⓔ	31 Ⓐ Ⓑ Ⓒ Ⓓ Ⓔ
15 Ⓐ Ⓑ Ⓒ Ⓓ Ⓔ	32 Ⓐ Ⓑ Ⓒ Ⓓ Ⓔ
16 Ⓐ Ⓑ Ⓒ Ⓓ Ⓔ	33 Ⓐ Ⓑ Ⓒ Ⓓ Ⓔ
17 Ⓐ Ⓑ Ⓒ Ⓓ Ⓔ	34 Ⓐ Ⓑ Ⓒ Ⓓ Ⓔ

PART II

1. The primary function of a take-up pulley in a belt conveyor is to

   A) carry the belt on the return trip.
   B) track the belt.
   C) maintain proper belt tension.
   D) change the direction of the belt.
   E) regulate the speed of the belt.

2. Which device is used to transfer power and rotary mechanical motion from one shaft to another?
   A) Bearing
   B) Lever
   C) Idler roller
   D) Gear
   E) Bushing

3. What special care is required in the storage of hard steel roller bearings? They should be
   A) cleaned and spun dry with compressed air.
   B) oiled once a month.
   C) stored in a humid place.
   D) wrapped in oiled paper.
   E) stored at temperatures below 90 degrees Fahrenheit.

4. Which is the correct method to lubricate a roller chain?

   A) Use brush to apply lubricant while chain is in motion
   B) Use squirt can to apply lubricant while chain is in motion
   C) Use brush to apply lubricant while chain is not in motion
   D) Soak chain in pan of lubricant and hang to allow excess to drain
   E) Chains do not need lubrication

5. A circuit has two resistors of equal value in series. The voltage and current in the circuit are 20 volts and 2 amps respectively. What is the value of EACH resistor?

   A) 5 ohms
   B) 10 ohms
   C) 15 ohms
   D) 20 ohms
   E) Not enough information given

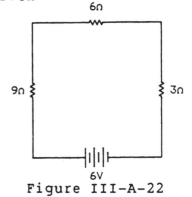

Figure III-A-22

6. Which of the following circuits is shown in Figure III-A-22?
   A) Series circuit
   B) Parallel circuit
   C) Series, parallel circuit
   D) Solid state circuit
   E) None of the above

7. What is the total net capacitance of two 60 farad capacitors connected in series?

   A) 30 F
   B) 60 F
   C) 90 F
   D) 120 F
   E) 360 F

8. If two 30 mH inductors are connected in series, what is the total net inductance of the combination?

   A) 15 mH
   B) 20 mH
   C) 30 mH
   D) 45 mH
   E) 60 mH

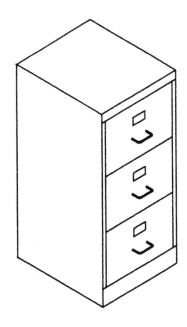

Figure 75-25-1

9. Crowbars, light bulbs and vacuum bags are to be stored in the cabinet shown in Figure 75-25-1. Considering the balance of weight, what would be the safest arrangement?

A) Top drawer – Crowbars
   Middle drawer – Light bulbs
   Bottom drawer – Vacuum bags
B) Top drawer – Crowbars
   Middle drawer – Vacuum bags
   Bottom drawer – Light bulbs
C) Top drawer – Vacuum bags
   Middle drawer – Crowbars
   Bottom drawer – Light bulbs
D) Top drawer – Vacuum bags
   Middle drawer – Light bulbs
   Bottom drawer – Crowbars
E) Top drawer – Light bulbs
   Middle drawer – Vacuum bags
   Bottom drawer – Crowbars

10. Contaminants have caused bearings to fail prematurely. Which pair of the items listed below should be kept away from bearings?

A) Dirt and oil
B) Grease and water
C) Oil and grease
D) Dirt and moisture
E) Water and oil

11. The electrical circuit term "open circuit" refers to a closed loop being opened. When an ohmmeter is connected into this type of circuit, one can expect the meter to

A) read infinity.
B) read infinity and slowly return to ZERO.
C) read ZERO.
D) read ZERO and slowly return to infinity.
E) None of the above

12. Which is most appropriate for pulling a heavy load?

A) Electric lift
B) Fork lift
C) Tow conveyor
D) Dolly
E) Pallet truck

13. In order to operate a breast drill, which direction should you turn it?

A) Clockwise
B) Counterclockwise
C) Up and down
D) Back and forth
E) Right, then left

14. Which is the correct tool for tightening or loosening a water pipe?

A) Slip joint pliers
B) Household pliers
C) Monkey wrench
D) Water pump pliers
E) Pipe wrench

15. What is one purpose of a chuck key?

A) Open doors
B) Remove drill bits
C) Remove screws
D) Remove set screws
E) Unlock chucks

16. When smoke is generated as a result of using a portable electric drill for cutting holes into a piece of angle iron, one should

A) use a fire watch.
B) cease the drilling operation.
C) use an exhaust fan to remove smoke.
D) use a prescribed coolant solution to reduce friction.
E) call the Fire Department.

17. The primary purpose of soldering is to
A) melt solder to a molten state.
B) heat metal parts to the right temperature be be joined.
C) join metal parts by melting the parts.
D) harden metal.
E) join metal parts.

18. Which of the following statements is correct concerning a soldering gun?
A) Tip is not replaceable
B) Cannot be used in cramped places
C) heats only when trigger is pressed
D) Not rated by the number of watts it uses
E) Has no light

19. What unit of measurement is read on a dial torque wrench?
A) Pounds
B) Inches
C) Centimeters
D) Foot-pounds
E) Degrees

20. Which instrument is used to test insulation breakdown of a conductor?.

A) Ohmmeter
B) Ammeter
C) Megger
D) Wheatstone bridge
E) Voltmeter

21. 1/2 of 1/4 =

A) 1/12
B) 1/8
C) 1/4
D) 1/2
E) 8

22. 2.6 - .5 =

A) 2.0
B) 2.1
C) 3.1
D) 3.3
E) None of the above

23. Solve the power equation

$P = I^2R$ for R

A) $R = EI$

B) $R = I^2P$

C) $R = PI$

D) $R = P/I^2$

E) $R = E/I$

24. The product of 3 kilo ohms times 3 micro ohms is

A) 6×10^{-9} ohms

B) 6×10^{-3} ohms

C) 9×10^{3} ohms

D) 9×10^{-6} ohms

E) 9×10^{-3} ohms

In sample question 25 below, select the statement which is most nearly correct according to the paragraph.

"Prior to 1870, a conveyor that made use of rollers was developed for transporting clay. This construction substituted rolling friction at the idler bearing points for the sliding friction of the slider bed. A primitive type of troughing belt conveyor was developed about the same time for the handling of grain. This design was improved during the latter part of the century when the troughing idler was developed."

25.   According to the above paragraph, which of the following statements is most nearly correct?

   A)   The troughing belt conveyor was developed about 1870 to handle clay and grain.

   B)   Rolling friction construction was replaced by sliding friction construction prior to 1870.

   C)   In the late nineteenth century, conveyors were improved with the development of the troughing idler.

   D)   The troughing idler, a significant design improvement for conveyors, was developed in the early nineteenth century.

   E)   Conveyor belts were invented and developed in the 1800's.

26. A small crane was used to raise the heavy part. Raise MOST nearly means

   A)   lift
   B)   drag
   C)   drop
   D)   deliver
   E)   guide

27. Short MOST nearly means

   A)   tall
   B)   wide
   C)   brief
   D)   heavy
   E)   dark

For sample question 28 below, select from the drawings of objects on the right labeled A, B, C, and D, the one that would have the TOP, FRONT, and RIGHT views shown in the drawing at the left

28.

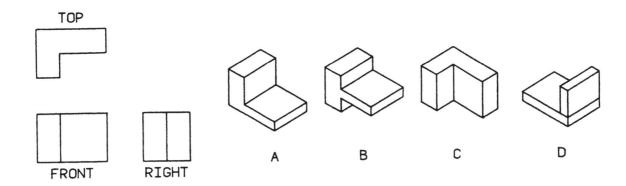

In sample question 29 below, there is, on the left, a drawing of a flat piece of paper and, on the right, four figures labeled A, B, C, and D. When the paper is bent on the dotted lines it will form one of the figures on the right. Decide which alternative can be formed from the flat piece.

29.

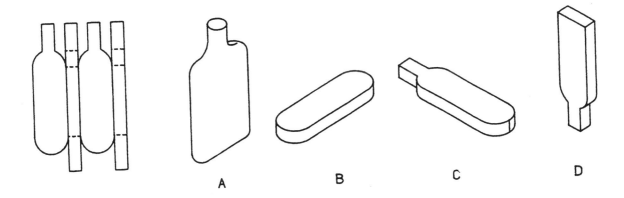

In each of the sample questions below, look at the symbols in the first two boxes. Something about the three symbols in the first box makes them alike; something about the two symbols in the other box with the question mark makes them alike. Look for some characteristic that is common to all symbols in the same box, yet makes them different from the symbols in the other box. Among dthe five answer choices, find the symbol that can best be substituted for the question mark, because it is <u>like</u> the symbols in the second box, and, <u>for the same reason</u>, different from those in the first box.

30.

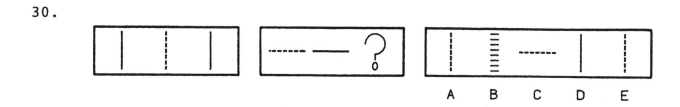

In sample question 30 above, all the symbols in the first box are vertical lines. The second box has two lines, one broken and one solid. Their <u>likeness</u> to each other consists in their being horizontal; and their being horizontal makes them <u>different</u> from the vertical lines in the other box. The answer must be the only one of the five lettered choices that is a horizontal line, either broken or solid. NOTE: There is not supposed to be a series or progression in these symbol questions. If you look for a progression in the first box and the second box, you will be wasting time. Remember, look for a <u>likeness</u> within each box and a <u>difference</u> between the two boxes.

Now do sample questions 31 and 32.

31.

32.

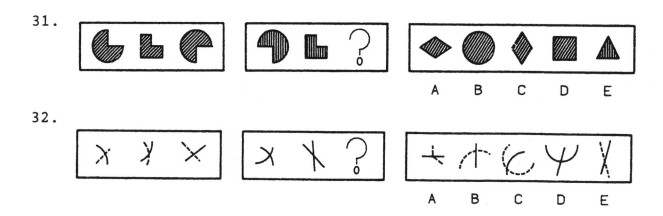

33. In Figure 160-57 below, what is the current flow through R₃ when:

$$V = 50 \text{ volts}$$

$$R_1 = 25 \text{ ohms}$$

$$R_2 = 25 \text{ ohms}$$

$$R3 = 50 \text{ ohms}$$

$$R_4 = 50 \text{ ohms}$$

$$R_5 = 50 \text{ ohms}$$

and the current through the entire circuit totals one amp?

A)   0.5 amp
B)   5.0 amps
C)   5.0 milliamps
D)   50.0 milliamps
E)   None of the above

34. In Figure 3-8-6 below, what is the measurement of Dimension F? Drawing is not actual size.

A)   1 3/4 inches
B)   2 1/4 inches
C)   2 1/2 inches
D)   3 3/4 inches
E)   None of the above

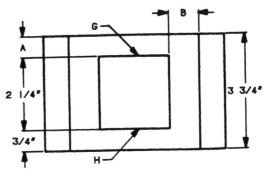

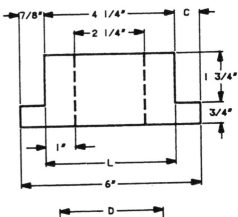

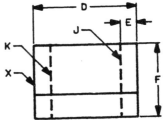

Figure 3-8-6

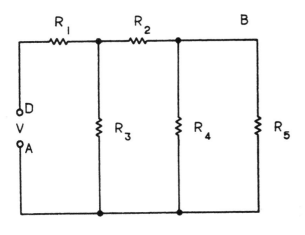

Figure 160-57

CORRECT ANSWERS TO
SAMPLE QUESTIONS

1 Ⓐ Ⓑ ● Ⓓ Ⓔ	18 Ⓐ Ⓑ ● Ⓓ Ⓔ
2 Ⓐ Ⓑ Ⓒ ● Ⓔ	19 Ⓐ Ⓑ Ⓒ ● Ⓔ
3 Ⓐ Ⓑ Ⓒ ● Ⓔ	20 Ⓐ Ⓑ ● Ⓓ Ⓔ
4 Ⓐ Ⓑ Ⓒ ● Ⓔ	21 Ⓐ ● Ⓒ Ⓓ Ⓔ
5 ● Ⓑ Ⓒ Ⓓ Ⓔ	22 Ⓐ ● Ⓒ Ⓓ Ⓔ
6 ● Ⓑ Ⓒ Ⓓ Ⓔ	23 Ⓐ Ⓑ Ⓒ ● Ⓔ
7 ● Ⓑ Ⓒ Ⓓ Ⓔ	24 Ⓐ Ⓑ Ⓒ Ⓓ ●
8 Ⓐ Ⓑ Ⓒ Ⓓ ●	25 Ⓐ Ⓑ ● Ⓓ Ⓔ
9 Ⓐ Ⓑ Ⓒ Ⓓ ●	26 ● Ⓑ Ⓒ Ⓓ Ⓔ
10 Ⓐ Ⓑ Ⓒ ● Ⓔ	27 Ⓐ Ⓑ ● Ⓓ Ⓔ
11 ● Ⓑ Ⓒ Ⓓ Ⓔ	28 Ⓐ Ⓑ ● Ⓓ Ⓔ
12 Ⓐ Ⓑ Ⓒ Ⓓ ●	29 Ⓐ Ⓑ ● Ⓓ Ⓔ
13 ● Ⓑ Ⓒ Ⓓ Ⓔ	30 Ⓐ Ⓑ ● Ⓓ Ⓔ
14 Ⓐ Ⓑ Ⓒ Ⓓ ●	31 Ⓐ Ⓑ Ⓒ Ⓓ ●
15 Ⓐ ● Ⓒ Ⓓ Ⓔ	32 Ⓐ Ⓑ Ⓒ ● Ⓔ
16 Ⓐ Ⓑ Ⓒ ● Ⓔ	33 Ⓐ Ⓑ ● Ⓓ Ⓔ
17 Ⓐ Ⓑ Ⓒ Ⓓ ●	34 ● Ⓑ Ⓒ Ⓓ Ⓔ

Standardized Test

Tips, Techniques, & Strategies

37

Standardized tests, prepared in standard patterns and ways, are time tested. That is, a time limit is set for each test. For example, Part A should be finished in five minutes and Part B should be finished in six.

There are strategies you can use to attack the questions. A test is a game; if you take a standardized test, you are a football quarterback and the testmaker is the opposing team: you read the defense, anticipating what kind of defense the opponent has formed and deciding what to do, whether to throw the ball to a wide receiver or give it to a fullback for a touchdown. If you aren't sure, at least make a guess.

Since postal tests are standardized, you can become an exam expert and make a high score on any test once you master the types of questions which have been asked in past years.

I. Multiple-Choice Test Strategies

One of the most common types of examination is the multiple-choice test, in which you select one correct answer from four or five choices. Some questions contain more than one correct answer.

Here are some strategies you can use in answering multiple-choice tests.

■ **Tactic 1:** Answer the sample questions for practice.

■ **Tactic 2:** Answer the easy questions first and the tough questions last.

■ **Tactic 3:** Evaluate the questions and see how they are designed. For example, questions within each test usually progress in difficulty from easy to hard.

■ **Tactic 4:** Search for hints. Some clues will help you find the right answer. Testmakers, for instance, usually use correct grammar in the correct answers and sometimes use incorrect grammar in the wrong answers without knowing it, because of their speed in preparing the other answers.

■ **Tactic 5:** If you're sure of a correct answer, select it and don't look for any traps.

■ **Tactic 6:** If you can't figure out the correct answer to a question, pick one. Make a little mark alongside the number with your pencil, and tell yourself, "I shall return!" (That is, if you have the time to do so.)

■ **Tactic 7:** Be on the lookout for choices like "all of the above" and "none of the above"; usually they are not the right answers. If the first three choices are right, for instance, and if the fourth is wrong, and if the fifth is "all of the above," don't select number 4 or 5. Choose among 1, 2, and 3.

■ **Tactic 8:** Watch out for sentences that contain words such as *all, only, none, never, always, usually, generally.* Often these words are traps; they do not belong to the correct answers. Unless you're sure that it's the right answer. don't select it.

■ **Tactic 9:** Most often, two out of the four or five choices are obvious wrong answers; so eliminate them first. In other words, eliminate the answers which are clearly wrong until you come to a point where you are to choose between the two best choices.

■ **Tactic 10.** Follow your first hunch on a particular answer; don't change it unless you're certain that you're making the right move.

■ **Tactic 11:** When two answers have opposite meanings, usually one of them is the right answer; when two answers express the same thing, usually one of the pair is the right answer.

■ **Tactic 12:** Guess if you don't know the answer, but be careful when the test score is calculated by subtracting the wrong answers from the right answers.

II. Vocabulary Test Strategies

■ **Tactic 1:** Watch out for traps. For example, if the question and one of the answers sound alike or look alike, it may be a trap, and most often it's not the right answer.

■ **Tactic 2:** Eliminate wrong parts of speech. If the word you are to define is a noun, the correct answer will be a noun; if it's a verb, the answer will be a verb. If you aren't sure whether a word is a noun or a verb, place "the" before the word. If it looks or sounds right, it's a noun. Place "to" before a word that may be a verb. If it sounds okay, it's a verb.

■ **Tactic 3:** Read a lot and look up every unfamiliar word in the dictionary. Learning vocabulary is a continuing education.

III. Solving Mathematics Problems

You can find the answers to math problems, no matter how complicated they are, by addition, subtraction, multiplication, and division, or by conversion of millimeters into centimeters, ounces into pounds, and so on. First, though, you must know whether you're going east or west. If you don't know, you're lost.

■ **Tactic 1:** The first time you're faced with a math problem, figure out how you're going to solve it. You must know the following:

- What you are supposed to find out.
- The given numbers.
- The principles or formulas needed to solve the problems.

■ **Tactic 2:** Write the numbers carefully. Be extra careful in writing 0 so that it doesn't look like a 6 or 8, and vice versa. Don't write a 3 that looks like a 5 or a 1 that looks like a 7, or vice versa. The columns should be in straight lines so that you don't make mistakes in addition or subtraction.

■ **Tactic 3:** Be sure to check the units of measurement. If they are not in the proper units, convert them into the correct units, such as millimeters into centimeters, ounces into pounds, or kilometers into miles. Don't try to add pounds to ounces, for example.

■ **Tactic 4:** Use diagrams such as squares, triangles and other shapes as much as possible. Label all the given numbers if such diagrams are needed to simplify solving.

■ **Tactic 5:** In solving any problem, particularly in a multiple-choice math test, don't glance at the choices (A, B, C, D, E) before you work on the problem. Work on the problem first, and when you have an answer, see if it matches any of the given numbers. It's like comparing your numbers with the numbers in a lottery; if your numbers don't match the winning numbers, you didn't win and you must try another time. So if your answer is not among the choices, it's not the correct answer.

■ **Tactic 6:** If you don't really know how to solve the problem, you'd better guess; that's better than leaving the question unanswered. Use the following elimination system:

- First eliminate the least probable answers.
- Eliminate the lowest and highest values among the remaining answers.
- Then select the most likely answer from the answers that remain.

Math Test techniques

Thomas F. Ewald, a former college instructor, gives the following advice on multiplication problems:

Solve the following multiplication problem:

$$3453 \times 4376 =$$

A) 15,112,432   C) 15,110,328
B) 15,121,324   D) 15,432,222

How long did it take you? If it took more than five seconds, you need this technique!

Take the last digit of each of the numbers to be multiplied against each other; now find the product of these two digits (that is, multiply them against each other): $3 \times 6 = 18$. Now notice the last digit of the correct answer above, Answer C. (You did get the right answer, didn't you?) It's 8. What was the last digit of the simple problem we just did (3×6)? That was also 8. It's not a coincidence. It will happen every time! As long as only one answer is given with the correct last digit, it's easy to pick the right answer!

If more than one answer ends in the correct digit, you'll have to do the actual multiplication. Also, my advice won't work if "none of the above" is given as an option. But it will help some of the time and can save precious seconds, or even minutes.

On some tests, such as the SAT, speed is extra important. Tactics like the one above helped me achieve a perfect score on the math portion of the SAT! It can be done!

## 38

Wanted: U.S. Postal Inspectors

Only the Exceptional May Apply

Postal inspectors are federal law enforcement officers with investigative jurisdiction in all criminal matters involving the integrity of the mail and the security of the U.S. Postal Service.

U.S. Postal Inspectors

Postal inspectors, among others, investigate criminal and civil violations of postal laws and protect the revenue and assets of the U.S. Postal Service. They are authorized to carry firearms, make arrests, and they testify in court, serve subpoenas, and write comprehensive reports.

It was only January 8, 2003, that the U.S. Postal Inspection Service began recruiting college graduates who don't have previous work experience. Just in case you don't meet one of the special requirements listed in the Application for U.S. Inspectors, but have either a conferred, four-year college degree with a minimum GPA of 3.0 or an advance degree, you may apply for a Postal Inspector job, by submitting the *Application for U.S. Postal Inspector,* with a copy of your college transcript. Or write to: **U.S. Postal Inspection Service,** Office of Recruitment, 9600 Newbridge Drive, Potomac, MD 20854-4436. Or call the office at 301-983-7400.

Other U.S. Postal Inspection Service Jobs

From time to time, the U.S. Postal Inspection Service also recruits for other positions such as:

- Postal Police Officers
- Forensic Scientists
- Information Technology Specialists
- Security Electronic Technicians
- Administration Support Specialists

Excerpted from the U.S. Postal Inspection Service Website:
http://usps.com/postalinspectors/employmt.htm

Requirements for U.S. Postal Inspectors

U.S. Postal Inspectors are federal law enforcement officers. They investigate criminal, civil, and administrative violations of postal laws and are responsible for protecting the revenue and assets of the Postal Service. Inspectors are required to carry firearms, make arrests, testify in court, serve subpoenas, and write comprehensive reports. They must operate motor vehicles and may undergo moderate to arduous physical exertion under unusual environmental conditions. It is essential that Inspectors be in sound physical condition and be capable of performing vigorous physical activities on a sustained basis. The activities may require Inspectors to perform the following: climb ladders; work long and irregular hours; occupy cramped or crowded spaces for extended periods of time; exert physical force in the arrest, search, pursuit, and restraint of another person; and protect themselves and others from imminent danger.

The duties of the position require the ability to communicate with people from all walks of life, be proficient with firearms, have skills in self-defense, and have the ability to exercise good judgment. Inspectors may be relocated according to the needs of the Service.

The recruitment process is extremely thorough, and there is intense competition for relatively few positions. The recruitment and selection process must be completed prior to the applicant's 37th birthday.

This position is exempt from the Fair Labor Standards Act (FLSA) and does not qualify for overtime compensation. Postal Inspector salaries are based on the Inspection Service Law Enforcement (ISLE) pay system. The ISLE pay grades and steps correspond to the General Schedule (GS) pay scale for law enforcement officers.

Selection procedures include the following:

- Completion of this application.
- Written examination, including a business writing test and the 620 Entry Examination (cognitive abilities).
- Language proficiency test, if applicable.
- Completion of the *Comprehensive Application Packet*.
- Assessment Center evaluation of knowledge, skills, and abilities.
- Medical examination
- Polygraph examination.
- Background suitability investigation.
- Management interview.
- Drug screening.
- Residential basic training program at Potomac, Maryland.
- Six-month probation period for nonpostal and nonfederal law enforcement applicants.

Recruiting Standards

Applicants must be U.S. citizen between 21 and 36 years of age and meet all the General Requirements to apply for the position of U.S. Postal Inspector. The Postal Inspection Service is currently seeking individuals who meet the General Requirements, as well as at least one of the Special Requirements, listed below. Applications that do not contain one of the Special Requirements will be kept on file for two years and then purged. If an applicant's skills change during the two-year period, the applicant should contact the Postal Inspection Service.

General Requirements

Applicants must meet the requirements below and undergo a full medical suitability exam to determine fitness to perform the duties of a Postal Inspector, including, but not limited to, the following:

- A conferred-four-year degree from an accredited college or university.
- Binocular vision must test 20/40 (Snellen) without corrective lens. Unconnected vision must test at least 20/100 in each eye. Each eye must be corrected to 20/20, with good color identification and discrimination, depth perception, and normal peripheral vision. Radial keratotomy or orthokeratology are not acceptable.
- Hearing loss, as measured by an audiometer, must not exceed 30 decibels (A.S.A. or equivalent I.S.O.) in either ear in the 500, 1,000, and 2,000 Hz ranges. The applicant must have the ability to perceive normal speech discrimination.
- In good physical condition (weight proportional to height) and possessing emotional and mental stability. Manual dexterity with comparatively free motion of fingers, wrists, elbows, shoulders, hips, and knee joints. Arms, hands, legs, and feet must be sufficiently intact and functioning in order to perform duties satisfactorily.
- No felony convictions (felony charges may also render applicant ineligible.)
- No misdemeanor conviction of domestic violence (other misdemeanor charges or convictions may also render applicant ineligible).
- A current, valid state driver's license, held for at least two years.
- Ability to demonstrate these attributes, as measured by the Assessment Center:

  - Write and speak English clearly.

  - Schedule and complete activities in a logical, timely sequence.
  - Comprehend and execute instructions written and spoken in English.
  - Think clearly and comprehend verbal and nonverbal information.
  - Interact with others to obtain or exchange information or services.
  - Perceive or identify relevant details and associate them with other facts.

Special Requirements

Language Skills

Applicants seeking to enter the recruitment process under the language skills track must have advanced competency in a foreign language deemed as needed by the Postal Inspection Service to meet its investigative mission. The current list is as follows:

Arabic
Czech
French Creole

Hebrew
Italian
Mandarin
Punjabi
Spanish
Thai
Vietnamese
Armenian
Dutch
German
Hindi
Japanese
Norwegian
Russian
Swahili
Turkish
Cambodian
Egyptian
Greek (Modern)
Hmong
Korean
Polish
Serbo-Croatian
Swedish
Ukranian
Cantonese
Farsi (Persian)
Haitian
Indonesian
Lao
Portuguese
Slovak
Tagalog
Urdu

Applicants must pass a formal proficiency test administered by a contractor of the Postal Inspection Service. In addition to the language requirement, applicants in this track must have one year of full-time work experience with the same company or firm within two years of the date of their application.

Specialized Postal Experience

Applicants entering through the specialized postal experience track must be currently employed by the U.S. Postal Service and have at least one year of full-time work experience in one of the postal functional areas designated as critical to the needs of the Postal Inspection Service. Currently, critical needs exist in the following areas:

- Business Mail Entry
- Computer Analysis

- EEO Investigation
- Finance/Budget/Revenue Assurance
- Industrial Engineering
- Information/Computer/LAN Systems
- In-Plant Support
- Labor Relations/Workplace Intervention
- Media Relations
- Operations Support
- Safety/Health/Security/Injury Compensation

In addition, Postal Service supervisors in any functional area (including acting supervisors) with at least one year of supervisory experience will also be eligible under this entry track. A letter from he applicant's immediate supervisor must verify that the applicant has been a supervisor for at least one year. Also, Postal Inspection Service employees and/or contract employees with one year of full-time work experience with the Postal Inspection Service would qualify under this skill track.

Specialized Nonpostal Experience

Applicants seeking consideration under the specialized nonpostal skill track must have experience in one of the areas of expertise designated as critical to the needs of the Postal Inspection Service. The areas are as follows:

Law Degree. Candidates must have a Juris Doctorate degree and one year of full-time work experience with the same company or firm within two years of the date of their application.

Certification in auditing or investigations. Candidates with certifications in accounting, such as Certified Public Accountant (CPA), Certified Management Accountant (CMA), Certified Internal Auditor (CIA), and Certified Information Systems examination, such as Certified Protection Professional (CPP) and Certified Fraud Examiner (CFE), are accepted under this skills track. Applicants in this track must have a one year of full-time work experience with the same company or firm within two years of the date of their application. Applicants must also provide proof of certification.

Specialized computer education. Candidates with a four-year degree in one of the following fields: computer science, computer engineering, telecommunications, management information systems, electronic commerce, decision and information science, or computer information systems. Applicants in this track must have one year of full-time work experience with the same company or firm within two years of the date of their application.

Specialized computer expertise. Candidates who are currently employed (and have been employed for at least one year) in a position(s) specialized in one of the following computer forensics, internet investigations, internet security, network security, or information systems security. Applicants in this track must have one year of full-time work experience with the same company or firm within two years of the date of their application.

Certification in computer systems. Candidates with one of the following certifications and one year of work experience with the same firm within two years of the date of their application: Microsoft Certified Systems Engineer (MCSE), Microsoft Certified Professional +_ Internet (MCP+I), Cisco Certified Network Professional (CCNP), Certified Novell Engineer (CNE), A+ Certified Computer Technician, Certified Information Systems Security Professional (CISSP), Linux certification, or Sun Systems Certified Administrator.

Law enforcement. Candidates with at least one year of full-time work experience, within the last two years, in the law enforcement field. This includes detectives, criminalists, and polygraph examiners, and patrol, probation, correction, and parole officers. This track excludes clerical or other technical support personnel. Applicants must provide examples of the type of work conducted.

Diversified Experience

To increase competitiveness and acquire a more diversified candidate pool, applicants may enter the recruitment process along a fourth track, which combines higher education and work experience, including:

■ Bachelor's degree (B.A. or B.S. in any field) plus two years of full-time work experience.

■ Advanced degree (M.A., or Ph.D. in any field) plus one year of full-time work experience.

Applicants entering the recruitment process under the diversified experience entry track must have completed at least one year of full-time work experience with the same company or firm within two years of the date of their application. This includes U.S. Postal Service employees who have a four-year degree and meet the required minimum work experience.

Excerpted from the U.S. Postal Inspection Service Website:
http://usps.com/postalinspectors/employmt.htm

For information on other postal jobs, go to:
tp://usps.com/employment/welcome.htm?from=global&page=employment

Supplement A

National Directory of U.S. Postal Service Examination Centers

Copyright 2006 by Veltisezar B. Bautista. The following testing centers are main offices generally known as District Offices, General Mail facilities (GMF), Sectional Center Facilities (SCF), and Management Sectional Centers (MSC). Needless to say, this directory is very valuable for finding a Post Office Job. If you want a postal job, call all the testing centers in your state, especially those in your area, at least once a week to find out if there are any examinations coming up. If you are thinking of moving to another state, call the testing centers in that state at least once a week. Always reach out and touch someone! If there are openings in another city, fly there and apply for examinations. Go where the action is! Here are the addresses and telephone numbers of the USPS testing centers.

ALABAMA

U.S. Postal Service
351 24th Street N
Birmingham, AL 35203-9998
(205) 521-0251
Job Hotline
(205) 521-0214

ALASKA

U.S. Postal Service
4141 Postmark Drive
Anchorage, AK 99599-9998
(Job Hotline
(907) 564-2962

ARIZONA

U.S. Postal Service
1441 East Buckeye Road
Phoenix, AZ 85026-9998
(602) 223-3631
Job Hotline
(602) 223-3624

ARKANSAS

U.S. Postal Service
4700 E McCain Boulevard
Little Rock, AR 72231-9998
(501) 945-6665

CALIFORNIA

U.S. Postal Service
300 Long Beach Boulevard
Long Beach, CA 90809-9998
(562) 983-3072
Job Hotline
(562) 435-4529

U.S. Postal Service
7001 S Central Avenue
Los Angeles, CA 90052-9998
(323) 586-1340
Job Hotline
(323) 586-1351

U.S. Postal Service
1675 7th Street
Oakland, CA 94615-9998
(510) 874-8344
Job Hotline
(510) 251-3040

U.S. Postal Service
11251 Rancho Carmel Drive
San Diego, CA 92199-9998
(619) 674-0430
Job Hotline
(619) 674-0577
(619) 674-2690

U.S. Postal Service
1300 Evans Avenue
San Francisco, CA 94188-9998
Job Hotline
(415) 550-5534

U.S. Postal Service
1750 Lunday Avenue
San Jose, CA 95101-0086
(408) 437-6925

Job Hotline
(408) 437-6986

U.S. Postal Service
3101 W Sunflower Avenue
Santa Ana, CA 92799-9998
Job Hotline
(714) 662-6375
U.S. Postal Service
28201 Franklin Parkway
Santa Clarita, CA 91383-9461
(661) 775-7040
Job Hotline
(661) 294-7680

U.S. Postal Service
3775 Industrial Boulevard
West Sacramento, CA 95799-0062
(916) 373-8686
Job Hotline
(916) 373-8448

COLORADO

U.S. Postal Service
7500 E 53rd Place Rm 2204
Denver, CO 80266-2204
(303) 853-6132
Job Hotline
(303) 853-6060

CONNECTICUT

U.S. Postal Service
141 Weston Street
Hartford, CT 06101-9998
(860) 524-6110

FLORIDA

U.S. Postal Service
1100 Kings Road
Jacksonville, FL 32203-9998
(904) 359-2921
Job Hotline
(904) 359-2737

U.S. Postal Service
800 Rinehart Road
Lake Mary, FL 32799-9421
(407) 444-2012
Job Hotline
1-888-771-9056
(407) 444-2029

U.S. Postal Service
2200 NW 72nd Avenue
Pembroke Pines, FL 33082-9990
(305) 470-0705
Job Hotline
(305) 470-0412
1-888-725-7295

U.S. Postal Service
5201 W Spruce Street
Tampa, FL 33630-9998
(813) 877-0318
Job Hotline
(813) 877-0381

GEORGIA

U.S. Postal Service
3900 Crown Road Rm. 272
Atlanta, GA 30304-9998
(404) 765-7200

U.S. Postal Service
451 College Street, -9998
(912) 752-8467
Job Hotline
(912) 752-8465

HAWAII

U.S. Postal Service
3600 Aolele Street
Honolulu, HI 96820-9998
Job Hotline
(808) 423-3690

ILLINOIS

U.S. Postal Service
6801 W 73rd Street
Bedford Park, IL 60499-9998
(708) 563-7493

U.S. Postal Service
500 E Fullerton Avenue
Carol Stream, IL 60099-9998
(630) 260-5153
Job Hotline
(630) 260-5200

U.S. Postal Service
433 W Harrison
Chicago, IL 60607-3905
(312) 983-8542

INDIANA

U.S. Postal Service
3939 Bincennes Rd
Indianapolis, IN 46298-9998
(317) 870-8551
Job Hotline

(317) 870-8500

IOWA

U.S. Postal Service
1165 2nd Avenue
Des Moines, IA 50318-7900
(515) 251-2201
Job Hotline
(515) 251-2061

KENTUCKY

U.S. Postal Service
1420 Gardiner Lane, Rm 320
Louisville, KY 40231-9998
(502) 454-1817
Job Hotline
(502) 454-1625

LOUISIANA

U.S. Postal Service
701 Loyola Avenue Rm. T2009
New Orleans, LA 70113-9998
(504) 589-1171
Job Hotline
(504) 589-1660

MAINE

380 Riverside Street
Portland, ME 041013-9998
Job Hotline
(207) 828-8520

MARYLAND

U.S. Postal Service
900 E Fayette Street
Baltimore, MD 21233-9998

(410) 347-4278
Job Hotline
(410) 347-4320

MASACHUSSETTE

U.S. Postal Service
25 Dorchester Avenue
Boston, MA 02205-9998
(617) 654-5500
Job Hotline
 (617) 654-5569

U.S. Postal Service
74 Main Street
North Reading, MA 01889
(978) 664-7079
Job Hotline
(978) 664-7665

U.S. Postal Service
1883 Main St
Springfield, MA 01101
(413) 785-6263
Job Hotline
(413) 731-0425

MICHIGAN

U.S. Postal Service
1401 W Fort Street, Rm 201
Detroit, MI 48233-9998
(313) 226-8259
(313) 226-8490
Job Hotline
1-888-442-5361

U.S. Postal Service
222 Michigan Street, NW
Grand Rapids, MI 49599-9998

(616) 776-1426
Job Hotline
(616) 776-1835

U.S. Postal Service
200 West 2nd Street
Royal Oak, MI 48068-9998
(810) 546-7106
Job Hotline
(810) 546-7104

MINNESOTA

U.S. Postal Service
180 E Kellog Boulevard
St Paul, MN 55101-9997
(651) 293-3036
Job Hotline
(651) 293-3364

U.S. Postal Service
315 W Pershing Road, Rm 572
Kansas City, MO 64108-9998
(816) 374-9310
Job Hotline
(816) 374-9346

MISSOURI

U.S. Postal Service
1720 Market Street, Rm 3027
St Louis, MO 63155-9998
(314) 436-3852
Job Hotline
(314) 436-3855

MISSISSIPPI

U.S. Postal Service
401 E South Street
Jackson, MS 39201-9998

(601) 351-7270
Job Hotline
(601) 351-7099

MONTANA

U.S. Postal Service
841 S 26th Street
Billings, MT 59101-9998
(406) 255-6427
Job Hotline
(406) 657-5763

NEBRASKA

U.S. Postal Service
1124 Pacific Street, Rm 325
Omaha NE 68108-0421
(402) 348-2506
Job Hotline
(402) 348-2523

NEW HAMPSHIRE

U.S. Postal Service
955 Goffs Falls Road
Manchester, NH 03103-9998
Job Hotline
(603) 644-4065

NEW JERSEY

U.S. Postal Service
501 Benigno Boulevard
Bellmawr, NJ 08099-9998
Job Hotline
(609) 933-4314

U.S. Postal Service
21 Kilmer Road

Edison, NJ 08901-9998
(732) 819-3272

U.S. Postal Service
2 Federal Square
Newark, NJ 07102-9998
(973) 693-5200

NEW MEXICO

U.S. Postal Service
1135 Broadway Boulevard, NE, Rm 230
Albuquerque, NM 87101-9998
(505) 245-9518
Job Hotline
(505) 245-9517

NEVADA

U.S. Postal Service
1001 E Sunset Road
Las Vegas, NV 89199-9998
(702) 361-9375
Job Hotline
(702) 361-9564

NEW YORK

U.S. Postal Service
30 Old Karmer Road
Albany, NY 12288-9998
Job Hotline
(518) 452-2445

U.S. Postal Service
1200 William Street
Buffalo, NY 14240-9998
(716) 846-2470
Job Hotline
(716) 846-2478

U.S. Postal Service
142-02 20th Avenue
Flushing, NY 11351-9998
(718) 321-5170
Job Hotline
(718) 529-7000

U.S. Postal Service
1377 Motor Parkway
Hauppauge, NY 11760-9998
(516) 582-7416
Job Hotline
(516) 582-7530

U.S. Postal Service
421 8th Avenue, Rm 3018
New York, NY 10199-9998
(212) 330-3600
(212) 330-2907

U.S. Postal Service
1000 Westchester Avenue
White Plains, NY 10610-9800
(914) 697-7190
(914) 967-8585

NORTH CAROLINA

U.S. Postal Service
2901 S Interstate 85 Service Road
Charlotte, NC 28228-9962
(704) 393-4495
Job Hotline
(704) 393-4490

U.S. Postal Service
900 Market Street, Rm 232
Greensboro, NC 27498-0001
(336) 669-1214
Job Hotline

(336) 271-5573

NORTH DAKOTA

(Same as South Dakota)

OHIO

U.S. Postal Service
675 Wolfledges Parkway
Akron, OH 44309-9998
(330) 996-9501
Job Hotline
(330) 996-9530

U.S. Postal Service
1591 Dalton Avenue, 2nd Floor
Cincinnati, OH 45234-9998
(513) 684-5451
(513) 684-5449

U.S. Postal Service
2200 Orange Avenue
Cleveland, OH 44104-9998
(216) 443-4339

U.S. Postal Service
850 Twin Rivers Drive
Columbus, OH 43216-9998
(614) 469-4357
Job Hotline
(614) 469-4356

OKLAHOMA

U.S. Postal Service
3030 NW Expressway Street, Ste 1042
Oklahoma City, OK 73198-9420
(405) 553-6172

OREGON
U.S. Postal Service
715 NW Hoyt Street
Portland, OR 97208-9999
(503) 294-2277
1-800-275-8777
Job Hotline
(503) 294-2270

PENNSYLVANIA

U.S. Postal Service
2108 E 38th Street
Erie, PA 16515-9998
(814) 898-7031
Job Hotline
(814) 899-0354

U.S. Postal Service
1425 Crooked Hill Road
Harrisburg, PA 17107-9998
(717) 257-2250
Job Hotline
(717) 390-7400

U.S. Postal Service
1400 Harrisburg Pike
Lancaster, PA 17602-9998
(717) 390-7460
Job Hotline
(717) 390-7400

U.S. Postal Service
2970 Market Street
Philadelphia, PA 19104-9422
Job Hotline
(800) 276-5627

U.S. Postal Service
1001 California Avenue
Pittsburgh, PA 15290-9998
(412) 359-7688
Job Hotline
(412) 359-7516
PUERTO RICO

U.S. Postal Service
P O. Box 363367
San Juan, PR 00936-9998
787-767-3351

RHODE ISLAND

U.S. Postal Service
24 Corliss Street
Providence, RI 02904
(401) 276-6845
Job Hotline
(401) 276-6844

SOUTH CAROLINA

U.S. Postal Service
P O. Box 29292
Columbia, SC 29292
(803) 926-6437
Job Hotline
(803) 926-6400

SOUTH DAKOTA

320 S Second Avenue
Sioux Falls, SD 57104-7554
(605) 357-5032

TENNESSEE

U.S. Postal Service
525 Royal Parkway, Rm 207
Nashville, TN 37229-9998
(615) 885-9962
Job Hotline
(615) 885-9190

TEXAS

U.S. Postal Service
951 W Bethel Road
Chappell, TX 75099-9998
Job Hotline
(214) 760-4531

U.S. Postal Service
4600 Mark IV Parkway
Fort Worth, TX 7616-9998
(817) 317-3350
Job Hotline
(817) 317-3366

U.S. Postal Service
1002 Washington Avenue
Houston, TX 77201 -9701
Job Hotline
(713) 226-3872

U.S. Postal Service
10410 Perin Beitel Road
San Antonio, TX 78284-9998
Job Hotline
(210) 368-8400

UTAH
U.S. Postal Service
1760 West 2100, S
Salt Lake City, UT 84199-9998
(801) 974-2210
Job Hotline
(801) 974-2209

VIRGINIA

U.S. Postal Service
8409 Lee Highway
Merrifield, VA 22081-9998
(703) 698-6438
Job Hotline
(703) 698-6561

U.S. Postal Service
1801 Brook Road
Richmond, VA 23232-9998
(804) 775-6196

WASHINGTON

U.S. Postal Service
415 1st Avenue N
Seattle, WA 98109-9998
(206) 442-6236
Job Hotline
(206) 442-6240

U.S. Postal Service
707 W Main Avenue
Spokane, WA 99202-9998
(509) 626-6824
Job Hotline
(509) 626-6896

WASHINGTON, DC

U.S. Postal Service
3300 V Street, NE
Washington, DC 20018-1527
Job Hotline
(202) 636-1537

WEST VIRGINIA

U.S. Postal Service
10002 Lee Street, E
Charleston, WV 25301-9998
Job Hotline
(304) 357-0648

WISCONSIN

U.S. Postal Service
245 W Saint Paul Avenue, 5th Floor
Milwaukee, WI 53203-9998
(414) 287-1834
Job Hotline
(414) 287-1835

APWU National Agreement
Schedule One — Salary and Rates
Effective March 19, 2005

Grade and Step	Full-time Regular Rates				BIWEEKLY DEDUCTIONS										
					CSRS			FERS		FERS — THRIFT SAVINGS PLAN					
	Annual Salary	Biweekly Pay	Straight Time	Night Differential	7% CSRS	1.45% Medicare	Maximum 10% TSP	0.8% FERS	7.65% FICA	1% USPS Minimum	3% Employee	3% USPS	5% Employee	5% USPS	15% Employee Maximum
2 D	39,733	1,528.19	19.1024	1.37	106.97	22.16	152.82	12.23	116.91	15.28	45.85	61.13	76.41	76.41	229.23
2 E	39,987	1,537.96	19.2245	1.38	107.66	22.30	153.80	12.30	117.65	15.38	46.14	61.52	76.90	76.90	230.69
2 F	40,242	1,547.77	19.3471	1.39	108.34	22.44	154.78	12.38	118.40	15.48	46.43	61.91	77.39	77.39	232.17
2 G	40,496	1,557.54	19.4692	1.40	109.03	22.58	155.75	12.46	119.15	15.58	46.73	62.30	77.88	77.88	233.63
2 H	40,755	1,567.50	19.5938	1.41	109.73	22.73	156.75	12.54	119.91	15.68	47.03	62.70	78.38	78.38	235.13
3 D	40,349	1,551.89	19.3986	1.39	108.63	22.50	155.19	12.42	118.72	15.52	46.56	62.08	77.59	77.59	232.78
3 E	40,624	1,562.46	19.5308	1.40	109.37	22.66	156.25	12.50	119.53	15.62	46.87	62.50	78.12	78.12	234.37
3 F	40,903	1,573.19	19.6649	1.41	110.12	22.81	157.32	12.59	120.35	15.73	47.20	62.93	78.66	78.66	235.98
3 G	41,175	1,583.66	19.7957	1.42	110.86	22.96	158.37	12.67	121.15	15.84	47.51	63.35	79.18	79.18	237.55
3 H	41,451	1,594.27	19.9284	1.43	111.60	23.12	159.43	12.75	121.96	15.94	47.83	63.77	79.71	79.71	239.14
4 D	41,018	1,577.62	19.7202	1.42	110.43	22.88	157.76	12.62	120.69	15.78	47.33	63.10	78.88	78.88	236.64
4 E	41,313	1,588.96	19.8620	1.43	111.23	23.04	158.90	12.71	121.56	15.89	47.67	63.56	79.45	79.45	238.34
4 F	41,615	1,600.58	20.0072	1.44	112.04	23.21	160.06	12.80	122.44	16.01	48.02	64.02	80.03	80.03	240.09
4 G	41,912	1,612.00	20.1500	1.45	112.84	23.37	161.20	12.90	123.32	16.12	48.36	64.48	80.60	80.60	241.80
4 H	42,207	1,623.34	20.2918	1.46	113.63	23.54	162.33	12.99	124.19	16.23	48.70	64.93	81.17	81.17	243.50
5 D	41,742	1,605.46	20.0683	1.45	112.38	23.28	160.55	12.84	122.82	16.05	48.16	64.22	80.27	80.27	240.82
5 E	42,062	1,617.77	20.2221	1.46	113.24	23.46	161.78	12.94	123.76	16.18	48.53	64.71	80.89	80.89	242.67
5 F	42,383	1,630.11	20.3764	1.47	114.11	23.64	163.01	13.04	124.70	16.30	48.90	65.20	81.51	81.51	244.52
5 G	42,700	1,642.30	20.5288	1.48	114.96	23.81	164.23	13.14	125.64	16.42	49.27	65.69	82.12	82.12	246.35
5 H	43,023	1,654.73	20.6841	1.50	115.83	23.99	165.47	13.24	126.59	16.55	49.64	66.19	82.74	82.74	248.21
6 D	42,522	1,635.46	20.4433	1.48	114.48	23.71	163.55	13.08	125.11	16.35	49.06	65.42	81.77	81.77	245.32
6 E	42,869	1,648.81	20.6101	1.49	115.42	23.91	164.88	13.19	126.13	16.49	49.46	65.95	82.44	82.44	247.32
6 F	43,219	1,662.27	20.7784	1.50	116.36	24.10	166.23	13.30	127.16	16.62	49.87	66.49	83.11	83.11	249.34
6 G	43,564	1,675.54	20.9442	1.52	117.29	24.30	167.55	13.40	128.18	16.76	50.27	67.02	83.78	83.78	251.33
6 H	43,914	1,689.00	21.1125	1.53	118.23	24.49	168.90	13.51	129.21	16.89	50.67	67.56	84.45	84.45	253.35
7 D	43,367	1,667.96	20.8495	1.51	116.76	24.19	166.80	13.34	127.60	16.68	50.04	66.72	83.40	83.40	250.19
7 E	43,742	1,682.38	21.0298	1.52	117.77	24.39	168.24	13.46	128.70	16.82	50.47	67.30	84.12	84.12	252.36
7 F	44,116	1,696.77	21.2096	1.54	118.77	24.60	169.68	13.57	129.80	16.97	50.90	67.87	84.84	84.84	254.52
7 G	44,491	1,711.19	21.3899	1.55	119.78	24.81	171.12	13.69	130.91	17.11	51.34	68.45	85.56	85.56	256.68
7 H	44,867	1,725.66	21.5707	1.57	120.80	25.02	172.57	13.81	132.01	17.26	51.77	69.03	86.28	86.28	258.85

PART-TIME FLEXIBLE RATES

Grade	Pay Steps				
	D	E	F	G	H
2	19.87	19.99	20.12	20.25	20.38
3	20.17	20.31	20.45	20.59	20.73
4	20.51	20.66	20.81	20.96	21.10
5	20.87	21.03	21.19	21.35	21.51
6	21.26	21.43	21.61	21.78	21.96
7	21.68	21.87	22.06	22.25	22.43

PART-TIME REGULAR RATES

Grade	Pay Steps				
	D	E	F	G	H
2	19.10	19.22	19.35	19.47	19.59
3	19.40	19.53	19.66	19.80	19.93
4	19.72	19.86	20.01	20.15	20.29
5	20.07	20.22	20.38	20.53	20.68
6	20.44	20.61	20.78	20.94	21.11
7	20.85	21.03	21.21	21.39	21.57

APWU
SALARY AND RATES
Schedule 1 and 2

AMERICAN POSTAL WORKERS UNION, AFL-CIO
1300 L STREET, NW, WASHINGTON, DC 20005

APWU National Agreement
Schedule Two — Salary and Rates
Effective March 19, 2005

Grade and Step	Annual Salary	Biweekly Pay	Straight Time	Night Differential	7% CSRS	1.45% Medicare	Maximum 10% TSP	0.80% FERS	7.65% FICA	1% USPS Minimum	3% Employee	3% USPS	5% Employee	5% USPS	15% Employee Maximum
1 BB	26,079	1,003.04	12.5380	0.84	70.21	14.54	100.30	8.02	76.73	10.03	30.09	40.12	50.15	50.15	150.46
AA	27,041	1,040.04	13.0005	0.88	72.80	15.08	104.00	8.32	79.56	10.40	31.20	41.60	52.00	52.00	156.01
A	28,003	1,077.04	13.4630	0.92	75.39	15.62	107.70	8.62	82.39	10.77	32.31	43.08	53.85	53.85	161.56
B	28,965	1,114.04	13.9255	0.95	77.98	16.15	111.40	8.91	85.22	11.14	33.42	44.56	55.70	55.70	167.11
C	29,927	1,151.04	14.3880	0.99	80.57	16.69	115.10	9.21	88.05	11.51	34.53	46.04	57.55	57.55	172.66
D	30,889	1,188.04	14.8505	1.03	83.16	17.23	118.80	9.50	90.89	11.88	35.64	47.52	59.40	59.40	178.21
E	31,851	1,225.04	15.3130	1.07	85.75	17.76	122.50	9.80	93.72	12.25	36.75	49.00	61.25	61.25	183.76
F	32,813	1,262.04	15.7755	1.11	88.34	18.30	126.20	10.10	96.55	12.62	37.86	50.48	63.10	63.10	189.31
G	33,775	1,299.04	16.2380	1.15	90.93	18.84	129.90	10.39	99.38	12.99	38.97	51.96	64.95	64.95	194.86
H	34,737	1,336.04	16.7005	1.18	93.52	19.37	133.60	10.69	102.21	13.36	40.08	53.44	66.80	66.80	200.41
I	35,699	1,373.04	17.1630	1.22	96.11	19.91	137.30	10.98	105.04	13.73	41.19	54.92	68.65	68.65	205.96
J	36,661	1,410.04	17.6255	1.26	98.70	20.45	141.00	11.28	107.87	14.10	42.30	56.40	70.50	70.50	211.51
K	37,623	1,447.04	18.0880	1.30	101.29	20.98	144.70	11.58	110.70	14.47	43.41	57.88	72.35	72.35	217.06
L	38,585	1,484.04	18.5505	1.34	103.88	21.52	148.40	11.87	113.53	14.84	44.52	59.36	74.20	74.20	222.61
M	39,547	1,521.04	19.0130	1.37	106.47	22.06	152.10	12.17	116.36	15.21	45.63	60.84	76.05	76.05	228.16
N	40,509	1,558.04	19.4755	1.41	109.06	22.59	155.80	12.46	119.19	15.58	46.74	62.32	77.90	77.90	233.71
O	41,754	1,605.92	20.0740	1.45	112.41	23.29	160.59	12.85	122.85	16.06	48.18	64.24	80.30	80.30	240.89
RC	42,716	1,642.92	20.5365	1.46	115.00	23.82	164.29	13.14	125.68	16.43	49.29	65.72	82.15	82.15	246.44
2 BB	27,191	1,045.81	13.0726	0.88	73.21	15.16	104.58	8.37	80.00	10.46	31.37	41.83	52.29	52.29	156.87
AA	28,143	1,082.42	13.5303	0.92	75.77	15.70	108.24	8.66	82.81	10.82	32.47	43.30	54.12	54.12	162.36
A	29,095	1,119.04	13.9880	0.95	78.33	16.23	111.90	8.95	85.61	11.19	33.57	44.76	55.95	55.95	167.86
B	30,047	1,155.66	14.4457	0.99	80.90	16.76	115.57	9.25	88.41	11.56	34.67	46.23	57.78	57.78	173.35
C	30,999	1,192.27	14.9034	1.03	83.46	17.29	119.23	9.54	91.21	11.92	35.77	47.69	59.61	59.61	178.84
D	31,951	1,228.89	15.3611	1.07	86.02	17.82	122.89	9.83	94.01	12.29	36.87	49.16	61.44	61.44	184.33
E	32,903	1,265.50	15.8188	1.11	88.59	18.35	126.55	10.12	96.81	12.66	37.97	50.62	63.28	63.28	189.83
F	33,855	1,302.11	16.2764	1.14	91.15	18.88	130.21	10.42	99.61	13.02	39.06	52.08	65.11	65.11	195.32
G	34,807	1,338.73	16.7341	1.18	93.71	19.41	133.87	10.71	102.41	13.39	40.16	53.55	66.94	66.94	200.81
H	35,759	1,375.34	17.1918	1.22	96.27	19.94	137.53	11.00	105.21	13.75	41.26	55.01	68.77	68.77	206.30
I	36,711	1,411.96	17.6495	1.26	98.84	20.47	141.20	11.30	108.01	14.12	42.36	56.48	70.60	70.60	211.79
J	37,663	1,448.58	18.1072	1.29	101.40	21.00	144.86	11.59	110.82	14.49	43.46	57.94	72.43	72.43	217.29
K	38,615	1,485.19	18.5649	1.33	103.96	21.54	148.52	11.88	113.62	14.85	44.56	59.41	74.26	74.26	222.78
L	39,567	1,521.81	19.0226	1.37	106.53	22.07	152.18	12.17	116.42	15.22	45.65	60.87	76.09	76.09	228.27
M	40,519	1,558.42	19.4803	1.41	109.09	22.60	155.84	12.47	119.22	15.58	46.75	62.34	77.92	77.92	233.76
N	41,471	1,595.04	19.9380	1.44	111.65	23.13	159.50	12.76	122.02	15.95	47.85	63.80	79.75	79.75	239.26
O	42,538	1,636.08	20.4510	1.48	114.53	23.72	163.61	13.09	125.16	16.36	49.08	65.44	81.80	81.80	245.41
RC	43,490	1,672.70	20.9087	1.49	117.09	24.25	167.27	13.38	127.96	16.73	50.18	66.91	83.63	83.63	250.90
3 BB	28,297	1,088.34	13.6043	0.93	76.18	15.78	108.83	8.71	83.26	10.88	32.65	43.53	54.42	54.42	163.25
AA	29,240	1,124.62	14.0577	0.97	78.72	16.31	112.46	9.00	86.03	11.25	33.74	44.98	56.23	56.23	168.69
A	30,183	1,160.89	14.5111	1.00	81.26	16.83	116.09	9.29	88.81	11.61	34.83	46.44	58.04	58.04	174.13
B	31,126	1,197.15	14.9644	1.04	83.80	17.36	119.72	9.58	91.58	11.97	35.91	47.89	59.86	59.86	179.57
C	32,069	1,233.42	15.4178	1.08	86.34	17.88	123.34	9.87	94.36	12.33	37.00	49.34	61.67	61.67	185.01
D	33,012	1,269.70	15.8712	1.11	88.88	18.41	126.97	10.16	97.13	12.70	38.09	50.79	63.48	63.48	190.45
E	33,955	1,305.96	16.3245	1.15	91.42	18.94	130.60	10.45	99.91	13.06	39.18	52.24	65.30	65.30	195.89
F	34,898	1,342.23	16.7779	1.18	93.96	19.46	134.22	10.74	102.68	13.42	40.27	53.69	67.11	67.11	201.33
G	35,841	1,378.50	17.2313	1.22	96.50	19.99	137.85	11.03	105.46	13.79	41.36	55.14	68.93	68.93	206.78
H	36,784	1,414.77	17.6846	1.26	99.03	20.51	141.48	11.32	108.23	14.15	42.44	56.59	70.74	70.74	212.22
I	37,727	1,451.04	18.1380	1.29	101.57	21.04	145.10	11.61	111.00	14.51	43.53	58.04	72.55	72.55	217.66
J	38,670	1,487.30	18.5913	1.33	104.11	21.57	148.73	11.90	113.78	14.87	44.62	59.49	74.37	74.37	223.10
K	39,613	1,523.58	19.0447	1.37	106.65	22.09	152.36	12.19	116.55	15.24	45.71	60.94	76.18	76.18	228.54
L	40,556	1,559.85	19.4981	1.40	109.19	22.62	155.98	12.48	119.33	15.60	46.80	62.39	77.99	77.99	233.98
M	41,499	1,596.11	19.9514	1.44	111.73	23.14	159.61	12.77	122.10	15.96	47.88	63.84	79.81	79.81	239.42
N	42,442	1,632.38	20.4048	1.47	114.27	23.67	163.24	13.06	124.88	16.32	48.97	65.30	81.62	81.62	244.86
O	43,385	1,668.66	20.8582	1.51	116.81	24.20	166.87	13.35	127.65	16.69	50.06	66.75	83.43	83.43	250.30
RC	44,328	1,704.92	21.3115	1.52	119.34	24.72	170.49	13.64	130.43	17.05	51.15	68.20	85.25	85.25	255.74
4 A	31,871	1,225.81	15.3226	1.06	85.81	17.77	122.58	9.81	93.77	12.26	36.77	49.03	61.29	61.29	183.87
B	32,758	1,259.92	15.7490	1.10	88.19	18.27	125.99	10.08	96.38	12.60	37.80	50.40	63.00	63.00	188.99
C	33,645	1,294.04	16.1755	1.13	90.58	18.76	129.40	10.35	98.99	12.94	38.82	51.76	64.70	64.70	194.11
D	34,532	1,328.15	16.6019	1.17	92.97	19.26	132.82	10.63	101.60	13.28	39.84	53.13	66.41	66.41	199.22
E	35,419	1,362.27	17.0284	1.20	95.36	19.75	136.23	10.90	104.21	13.62	40.87	54.49	68.11	68.11	204.34
F	36,306	1,396.38	17.4548	1.24	97.75	20.25	139.64	11.17	106.82	13.96	41.89	55.86	69.82	69.82	209.46
G	37,193	1,430.50	17.8813	1.27	100.14	20.74	143.05	11.44	109.43	14.31	42.92	57.22	71.53	71.53	214.58
H	38,080	1,464.62	18.3077	1.31	102.52	21.24	146.46	11.72	112.04	14.65	43.94	58.58	73.23	73.23	219.69
I	38,967	1,498.73	18.7341	1.34	104.91	21.73	149.87	11.99	114.65	14.99	44.96	59.95	74.94	74.94	224.81
J	39,854	1,532.85	19.1606	1.38	107.30	22.23	153.28	12.26	117.26	15.33	45.99	61.31	76.64	76.64	229.93
K	40,741	1,566.96	19.5870	1.41	109.69	22.72	156.70	12.54	119.87	15.67	47.01	62.68	78.35	78.35	235.04
L	41,628	1,601.08	20.0135	1.45	112.08	23.22	160.11	12.81	122.48	16.01	48.03	64.04	80.05	80.05	240.16
M	42,515	1,635.19	20.4399	1.48	114.46	23.71	163.52	13.08	125.09	16.35	49.06	65.41	81.76	81.76	245.28
N	43,402	1,669.30	20.8663	1.52	116.85	24.20	166.93	13.35	127.70	16.69	50.08	66.77	83.47	83.47	250.40
O	44,289	1,703.42	21.2928	1.55	119.24	24.70	170.34	13.63	130.31	17.03	51.10	68.14	85.17	85.17	255.51
RC	45,176	1,737.54	21.7192	1.56	121.63	25.19	173.75	13.90	132.92	17.38	52.13	69.50	86.88	86.88	260.63
5 A	33,509	1,288.81	16.1101	1.12	90.22	18.69	128.88	10.31	98.59	12.89	38.66	51.55	64.44	64.44	193.32
B	34,349	1,321.11	16.5139	1.15	92.48	19.16	132.11	10.57	101.07	13.21	39.63	52.84	66.06	66.06	198.17
C	35,189	1,353.42	16.9178	1.19	94.74	19.62	135.34	10.83	103.54	13.53	40.60	54.14	67.67	67.67	203.01
D	36,029	1,385.73	17.3216	1.22	97.00	20.09	138.57	11.09	106.01	13.86	41.57	55.43	69.29	69.29	207.86
E	36,869	1,418.04	17.7255	1.25	99.26	20.56	141.80	11.34	108.48	14.18	42.54	56.72	70.90	70.90	212.71
F	37,709	1,450.34	18.1293	1.28	101.52	21.03	145.03	11.60	110.95	14.50	43.51	58.01	72.52	72.52	217.55
G	38,549	1,482.66	18.5332	1.32	103.79	21.50	148.27	11.86	113.42	14.83	44.48	59.31	74.13	74.13	222.40
H	39,389	1,514.96	18.9370	1.35	106.05	21.97	151.50	12.12	115.89	15.15	45.45	60.60	75.75	75.75	227.24
I	40,229	1,547.27	19.3409	1.38	108.31	22.44	154.73	12.38	118.37	15.47	46.42	61.89	77.36	77.36	232.09
J	41,069	1,579.58	19.7447	1.42	110.57	22.90	157.96	12.64	120.84	15.80	47.39	63.18	78.98	78.98	236.94
K	41,909	1,611.89	20.1486	1.45	112.83	23.37	161.19	12.90	123.31	16.12	48.36	64.48	80.59	80.59	241.78
L	42,749	1,644.19	20.5524	1.48	115.09	23.84	164.42	13.15	125.78	16.44	49.33	65.77	82.21	82.21	246.63
M	43,589	1,676.50	20.9563	1.51	117.36	24.31	167.65	13.41	128.25	16.77	50.30	67.06	83.83	83.83	251.48
N	44,429	1,708.81	21.3601	1.55	119.62	24.78	170.88	13.67	130.72	17.09	51.26	68.35	85.44	85.44	256.32
O	45,269	1,741.11	21.7639	1.58	121.88	25.25	174.11	13.93	133.20	17.41	52.23	69.64	87.06	87.06	261.17
RC	46,109	1,773.42	22.1678	1.60	124.14	25.71	177.34	14.19	135.67	17.73	53.20	70.94	88.67	88.67	266.01

APWU National Agreement
Schedule Two — Salary and Rates
Effective March 19, 2005

| Grade and Step | Full-time Regular Rates | | | | BIWEEKLY DEDUCTIONS | | | | | | | | | | |
	Annual Salary	Biweekly Pay	Straight Time	Night Differential	CSRS 7%	Medicare 1.45%	Maximum 10% TSP	FERS 0.80%	FICA 7.65%	1% USPS Minimum	3% Employee	3% USPS	5% Employee	5% USPS	15% Employee Maximum
6 A	35,252	1,355.85	16.9481	1.19	94.91	19.66	135.58	10.85	103.72	13.56	40.68	54.23	67.79	67.79	203.38
B	36,044	1,386.30	17.3288	1.22	97.04	20.10	138.63	11.09	106.05	13.86	41.59	55.45	69.32	69.32	207.95
C	36,836	1,416.77	17.7096	1.25	99.17	20.54	141.68	11.33	108.38	14.17	42.50	56.67	70.84	70.84	212.52
D	37,628	1,447.23	18.0904	1.28	101.31	20.98	144.72	11.58	110.71	14.47	43.42	57.89	72.36	72.36	217.08
E	38,420	1,477.70	18.4712	1.32	103.44	21.43	147.77	11.82	113.04	14.78	44.33	59.11	73.88	73.88	221.65
F	39,212	1,508.15	18.8519	1.35	105.57	21.87	150.82	12.07	115.37	15.08	45.24	60.33	75.41	75.41	226.22
G	40,004	1,538.62	19.2327	1.38	107.70	22.31	153.86	12.31	117.70	15.39	46.16	61.54	76.93	76.93	230.79
H	40,796	1,569.08	19.6135	1.41	109.84	22.75	156.91	12.55	120.03	15.69	47.07	62.76	78.45	78.45	235.36
I	41,588	1,599.54	19.9942	1.44	111.97	23.19	159.95	12.80	122.36	16.00	47.99	63.98	79.98	79.98	239.93
J	42,380	1,630.00	20.3750	1.47	114.10	23.64	163.00	13.04	124.70	16.30	48.90	65.20	81.50	81.50	244.50
K	43,172	1,660.46	20.7558	1.50	116.23	24.08	166.05	13.28	127.03	16.60	49.81	66.42	83.02	83.02	249.07
L	43,964	1,690.92	21.1365	1.54	118.36	24.52	169.09	13.53	129.36	16.91	50.73	67.64	84.55	84.55	253.64
M	44,756	1,721.38	21.5173	1.57	120.50	24.96	172.14	13.77	131.69	17.21	51.64	68.86	86.07	86.07	258.21
N	45,548	1,751.85	21.8981	1.60	122.63	25.40	175.18	14.01	134.02	17.52	52.56	70.07	87.59	87.59	262.78
O	46,340	1,782.30	22.2788	1.63	124.76	25.84	178.23	14.26	136.35	17.82	53.47	71.29	89.12	89.12	267.35
RC	47,132	1,812.77	22.6596	1.64	126.89	26.29	181.28	14.50	138.68	18.13	54.38	72.51	90.64	90.64	271.92
7 A	36,059	1,386.89	17.3361	1.22	97.08	20.11	138.69	11.10	106.10	13.87	41.61	55.48	69.34	69.34	208.03
B	36,875	1,418.27	17.7284	1.25	99.28	20.56	141.83	11.35	108.50	14.18	42.55	56.73	70.91	70.91	212.74
C	37,691	1,449.66	18.1207	1.28	101.48	21.02	144.97	11.60	110.90	14.50	43.49	57.99	72.48	72.48	217.45
D	38,507	1,481.04	18.5130	1.32	103.67	21.48	148.10	11.85	113.30	14.81	44.43	59.24	74.05	74.05	222.16
E	39,323	1,512.42	18.9053	1.35	105.87	21.93	151.24	12.10	115.70	15.12	45.37	60.50	75.62	75.62	226.86
F	40,139	1,543.81	19.2976	1.38	108.07	22.39	154.38	12.35	118.10	15.44	46.31	61.75	77.19	77.19	231.57
G	40,955	1,575.19	19.6899	1.41	110.26	22.84	157.52	12.60	120.50	15.75	47.26	63.01	78.76	78.76	236.28
H	41,771	1,606.58	20.0822	1.45	112.46	23.30	160.66	12.85	122.90	16.07	48.20	64.26	80.33	80.33	240.99
I	42,587	1,637.96	20.4745	1.48	114.66	23.75	163.80	13.10	125.30	16.38	49.14	65.52	81.90	81.90	245.69
J	43,403	1,669.34	20.8668	1.51	116.85	24.21	166.93	13.35	127.70	16.69	50.08	66.77	83.47	83.47	250.40
K	44,219	1,700.73	21.2591	1.54	119.05	24.66	170.07	13.61	130.11	17.01	51.02	68.03	85.04	85.04	255.11
L	45,035	1,732.11	21.6514	1.57	121.25	25.12	173.21	13.86	132.51	17.32	51.96	69.28	86.61	86.61	259.82
M	45,851	1,763.50	22.0438	1.61	123.45	25.57	176.35	14.11	134.91	17.64	52.91	70.54	88.18	88.18	264.53
N	46,667	1,794.89	22.4361	1.64	125.64	26.03	179.49	14.36	137.31	17.95	53.85	71.80	89.74	89.74	269.23
O	47,483	1,826.27	22.8284	1.67	127.84	26.48	182.63	14.61	139.71	18.26	54.79	73.05	91.31	91.31	273.94
RC	48,299	1,857.66	23.2207	1.69	130.04	26.94	185.77	14.86	142.11	18.58	55.73	74.31	92.88	92.88	278.65
8 D	42,033	1,616.66	20.2082	1.45	113.17	23.44	161.67	12.93	123.67	16.17	48.50	64.67	80.83	80.83	242.50
E	42,644	1,640.15	20.5019	1.48	114.81	23.78	164.02	13.12	125.47	16.40	49.20	65.61	82.01	82.01	246.02
F	43,255	1,663.66	20.7957	1.50	116.46	24.12	166.37	13.31	127.27	16.64	49.91	66.55	83.18	83.18	249.55
G	43,866	1,687.15	21.0894	1.53	118.10	24.46	168.72	13.50	129.07	16.87	50.61	67.49	84.36	84.36	253.07
H	44,477	1,710.66	21.3832	1.55	119.75	24.80	171.07	13.69	130.87	17.11	51.32	68.43	85.53	85.53	256.60
I	45,088	1,734.15	21.6769	1.58	121.39	25.15	173.42	13.87	132.66	17.34	52.02	69.37	86.71	86.71	260.12
J	45,699	1,757.66	21.9707	1.60	123.04	25.49	175.77	14.06	134.46	17.58	52.73	70.31	87.88	87.88	263.65
K	46,310	1,781.15	22.2644	1.62	124.68	25.83	178.12	14.25	136.26	17.81	53.43	71.25	89.06	89.06	267.17
L	46,921	1,804.66	22.5582	1.65	126.33	26.17	180.47	14.44	138.06	18.05	54.14	72.19	90.23	90.23	270.70
M	47,532	1,828.15	22.8519	1.67	127.97	26.51	182.82	14.63	139.85	18.28	54.84	73.13	91.41	91.41	274.22
N	48,143	1,851.66	23.1457	1.70	129.62	26.85	185.17	14.81	141.65	18.52	55.55	74.07	92.58	92.58	277.75
O	48,754	1,875.15	23.4394	1.72	131.26	27.19	187.52	15.00	143.45	18.75	56.25	75.01	93.76	93.76	281.27
P	49,365	1,898.66	23.7332	1.74	132.91	27.53	189.87	15.19	145.25	18.99	56.96	75.95	94.93	94.93	284.80
RC	49,976	1,922.15	24.0269	1.76	134.55	27.87	192.22	15.38	147.04	19.22	57.66	76.89	96.11	96.11	288.32
9 D	42,985	1,653.27	20.6659	1.50	115.73	23.97	165.33	13.23	126.48	16.53	49.60	66.13	82.66	82.66	247.99
E	43,630	1,678.08	20.9760	1.52	117.47	24.33	167.81	13.42	128.37	16.78	50.34	67.12	83.90	83.90	251.71
F	44,275	1,702.89	21.2861	1.55	119.20	24.69	170.29	13.62	130.27	17.03	51.09	68.12	85.14	85.14	255.43
G	44,920	1,727.70	21.5962	1.57	120.94	25.05	172.77	13.82	132.17	17.28	51.83	69.11	86.38	86.38	259.15
H	45,565	1,752.50	21.9063	1.60	122.68	25.41	175.25	14.02	134.07	17.53	52.58	70.10	87.63	87.63	262.88
I	46,210	1,777.30	22.2163	1.62	124.41	25.77	177.73	14.22	135.96	17.77	53.32	71.09	88.87	88.87	266.60
J	46,855	1,802.11	22.5264	1.65	126.15	26.13	180.21	14.42	137.86	18.02	54.06	72.08	90.11	90.11	270.32
K	47,500	1,826.92	22.8365	1.67	127.88	26.49	182.69	14.62	139.76	18.27	54.81	73.08	91.35	91.35	274.04
L	48,145	1,851.73	23.1466	1.70	129.62	26.85	185.17	14.81	141.66	18.52	55.55	74.07	92.59	92.59	277.76
M	48,790	1,876.54	23.4567	1.72	131.36	27.21	187.65	15.01	143.56	18.77	56.30	75.06	93.83	93.83	281.48
N	49,435	1,901.34	23.7668	1.75	133.09	27.57	190.13	15.21	145.45	19.01	57.04	76.05	95.07	95.07	285.20
O	50,080	1,926.15	24.0769	1.77	134.83	27.93	192.62	15.41	147.35	19.26	57.78	77.05	96.31	96.31	288.92
P	50,725	1,950.96	24.3870	1.80	136.57	28.29	195.10	15.61	149.25	19.51	58.53	78.04	97.55	97.55	292.64
RC	51,370	1,975.77	24.6971	1.82	138.30	28.65	197.58	15.81	151.15	19.76	59.27	79.03	98.79	98.79	296.37

1. CSRS. The Civil Service Retirement System requires a 7% deduction from biweekly basic pay. In addition, there is a 1.45% deduction for Medicare. Total deductions are then 8.45%. Basic pay includes COLAs. The CSRS deduction is based on straight-time wages which includes COLAs, but does not include overtime, night differential, etc. The Medicare deduction is based on gross pay and may be higher than reported here. CSRS employees can contribute up to 10% to the Thrift Savings Plan. As of April 15, 2005, postal workers will be allowed to make changes to their TSP accounts at any time. **2. FERS.** The Federal Employees Retirement System requires a 0.8% deduction from biweekly straight-time pay. In addition there is a 7.65% deduction for Social Security including Medicare. Total deduction is then 8.45%. The FICA deduction is based on gross pay and may be higher than reported here. **3. TSP.** CSRS employee may contribute up to 10% to the Thrift Savings Plan without a USPS match. FERS employees can contribute up to 15% to TSP. Employees over 49 may make "catch-up" contributions of up to $4,000 in 2005. The Postal Service automatically contributes 1% for all FERS employees and matches employee contributions up to 5%. The Service matches every dollar up to 3% plus the 1% USPS minimum. So the 3% USPS match shown here is 4%. A FERS employee who contributes 3% actually banks 7% with the USPS contribution. The Service contributes 50¢ on every employee dollar between 3% and 5%.

APWU National Agreement
Schedule Two — Salary and Rates
Effective March 19, 2005

Grade and Step	Annual Salary	Biweekly Pay	Straight Time	Night Differential	7% CSRS	1.45% Medicare	Maximum 10% TSP	0.80% FERS	7.65% FICA	1% USPS Minimum	3% Employee	3% USPS	5% Employee	5% USPS	15% Employee Maximum
10 D	43,988	1,691.85	21.1481	1.54	118.43	24.53	169.18	13.53	129.43	16.92	50.76	67.67	84.59	84.59	253.78
E	44,674	1,718.23	21.4779	1.56	120.28	24.91	171.82	13.75	131.44	17.18	51.55	68.73	85.91	85.91	257.73
F	45,360	1,744.62	21.8077	1.59	122.12	25.30	174.46	13.96	133.46	17.45	52.34	69.78	87.23	87.23	261.69
G	46,046	1,771.00	22.1375	1.62	123.97	25.68	177.10	14.17	135.48	17.71	53.13	70.84	88.55	88.55	265.65
H	46,732	1,797.38	22.4673	1.64	125.82	26.06	179.74	14.38	137.50	17.97	53.92	71.90	89.87	89.87	269.61
I	47,418	1,823.77	22.7971	1.67	127.66	26.44	182.38	14.59	139.52	18.24	54.71	72.95	91.19	91.19	273.57
J	48,104	1,850.15	23.1269	1.70	129.51	26.83	185.02	14.80	141.54	18.50	55.50	74.01	92.51	92.51	277.52
K	48,790	1,876.54	23.4567	1.72	131.36	27.21	187.65	15.01	143.56	18.77	56.30	75.06	93.83	93.83	281.48
L	49,476	1,902.92	23.7865	1.75	133.20	27.59	190.29	15.22	145.57	19.03	57.09	76.12	95.15	95.15	285.44
M	50,162	1,929.30	24.1163	1.78	135.05	27.97	192.93	15.43	147.59	19.29	57.88	77.17	96.47	96.47	289.40
N	50,848	1,955.70	24.4462	1.80	136.90	28.36	195.57	15.65	149.61	19.56	58.67	78.23	97.78	97.78	293.35
O	51,534	1,982.08	24.7760	1.83	138.75	28.74	198.21	15.86	151.63	19.82	59.46	79.28	99.10	99.10	297.31
P	52,220	2,008.46	25.1058	1.86	140.59	29.12	200.85	16.07	153.65	20.08	60.25	80.34	100.42	100.42	301.27
RC	52,906	2,034.85	25.4356	1.88	142.44	29.51	203.48	16.28	155.67	20.35	61.05	81.39	101.74	101.74	305.23
11 D	45,047	1,732.58	21.6572	1.58	121.28	25.12	173.26	13.86	132.54	17.33	51.98	69.30	86.63	86.63	259.89
E	45,773	1,760.50	22.0063	1.61	123.24	25.53	176.05	14.08	134.68	17.61	52.82	70.42	88.03	88.03	264.08
F	46,499	1,788.42	22.3553	1.64	125.19	25.93	178.84	14.31	136.81	17.88	53.65	71.54	89.42	89.42	268.26
G	47,225	1,816.34	22.7043	1.66	127.14	26.34	181.63	14.53	138.95	18.16	54.49	72.65	90.82	90.82	272.45
H	47,951	1,844.27	23.0534	1.69	129.10	26.74	184.43	14.75	141.09	18.44	55.33	73.77	92.21	92.21	276.64
I	48,677	1,872.19	23.4024	1.72	131.05	27.15	187.22	14.98	143.22	18.72	56.17	74.89	93.61	93.61	280.83
J	49,403	1,900.11	23.7514	1.75	133.01	27.55	190.01	15.20	145.36	19.00	57.00	76.00	95.01	95.01	285.02
K	50,129	1,928.04	24.1005	1.78	134.96	27.96	192.80	15.42	147.50	19.28	57.84	77.12	96.40	96.40	289.21
L	50,855	1,955.96	24.4495	1.81	136.92	28.36	195.60	15.65	149.63	19.56	58.68	78.24	97.80	97.80	293.39
M	51,581	1,983.89	24.7986	1.83	138.87	28.77	198.39	15.87	151.77	19.84	59.52	79.36	99.19	99.19	297.58
N	52,307	2,011.81	25.1476	1.86	140.83	29.17	201.18	16.09	153.90	20.12	60.35	80.47	100.59	100.59	301.77
O	53,033	2,039.73	25.4966	1.89	142.78	29.58	203.97	16.32	156.04	20.40	61.19	81.59	101.99	101.99	305.96
P	53,759	2,067.66	25.8457	1.92	144.74	29.98	206.77	16.54	158.18	20.68	62.03	82.71	103.38	103.38	310.15
RC	54,485	2,095.58	26.1947	1.94	146.69	30.39	209.56	16.76	160.31	20.96	62.87	83.82	104.78	104.78	314.34
12 D	46,162	1,775.46	22.1933	1.62	124.28	25.74	177.55	14.20	135.82	17.75	53.26	71.02	88.77	88.77	266.32
E	46,933	1,805.11	22.5639	1.65	126.36	26.17	180.51	14.44	138.09	18.05	54.15	72.20	90.26	90.26	270.77
F	47,704	1,834.77	22.9346	1.68	128.43	26.60	183.48	14.68	140.36	18.35	55.04	73.39	91.74	91.74	275.22
G	48,475	1,864.42	23.3053	1.71	130.51	27.03	186.44	14.92	142.63	18.64	55.93	74.58	93.22	93.22	279.66
H	49,246	1,894.08	23.6760	1.74	132.59	27.46	189.41	15.15	144.90	18.94	56.82	75.76	94.70	94.70	284.11
I	50,017	1,923.73	24.0466	1.77	134.66	27.89	192.37	15.39	147.17	19.24	57.71	76.95	96.19	96.19	288.56
J	50,788	1,953.38	24.4173	1.80	136.74	28.32	195.34	15.63	149.43	19.53	58.60	78.14	97.67	97.67	293.01
K	51,559	1,983.04	24.7880	1.83	138.81	28.75	198.30	15.86	151.70	19.83	59.49	79.32	99.15	99.15	297.46
L	52,330	2,012.70	25.1587	1.86	140.89	29.18	201.27	16.10	153.97	20.13	60.38	80.51	100.63	100.63	301.90
M	53,101	2,042.34	25.5293	1.89	142.96	29.61	204.23	16.34	156.24	20.42	61.27	81.69	102.12	102.12	306.35
N	53,872	2,072.00	25.9000	1.92	145.04	30.04	207.20	16.58	158.51	20.72	62.16	82.88	103.60	103.60	310.80
O	54,643	2,101.66	26.2707	1.95	147.12	30.47	210.17	16.81	160.78	21.02	63.05	84.07	105.08	105.08	315.25
P	55,414	2,131.30	26.6413	1.98	149.19	30.90	213.13	17.05	163.04	21.31	63.94	85.25	106.57	106.57	319.70
RC	56,185	2,160.96	27.0120	2.01	151.27	31.33	216.10	17.29	165.31	21.61	64.83	86.44	108.05	108.05	324.14

BIWEEKLY DEDUCTIONS: CSRS (7% CSRS, 1.45% Medicare, Maximum 10% TSP); FERS (0.80% FERS, 7.65% FICA); FERS — THRIFT SAVINGS PLAN (1% USPS Minimum, 3% Employee, 3% USPS, 5% Employee, 5% USPS, 15% Employee Maximum). Full-time Regular Rates: Annual Salary, Biweekly Pay, Straight Time, Night Differential.

PART-TIME FLEXIBLE RATES

Grade	BB	AA	A	B	C	D	E	F	G	H	I	J	K	L	M	N	O	P	RC
1	13.04	13.52	14.00	14.48	14.96	15.44	15.93	16.41	16.89	17.37	17.85	18.33	18.81	19.29	19.77	20.25	20.88		21.36
2	13.60	14.07	14.55	15.02	15.50	15.98	16.45	16.93	17.40	17.88	18.36	18.83	19.31	19.78	20.26	20.74	21.27		21.75
3	14.15	14.62	15.09	15.56	16.03	16.51	16.98	17.45	17.92	18.39	18.86	19.34	19.81	20.28	20.75	21.22	21.69		22.16
4			15.94	16.38	16.82	17.27	17.71	18.15	18.60	19.04	19.48	19.93	20.37	20.81	21.26	21.70	22.14		22.59
5			16.75	17.17	17.59	18.01	18.43	18.85	19.27	19.69	20.11	20.53	20.95	21.37	21.79	22.21	22.63		23.05
6			17.63	18.02	18.42	18.81	19.21	19.61	20.00	20.40	20.79	21.19	21.59	21.98	22.38	22.77	23.17		23.57
7			18.03	18.44	18.85	19.25	19.66	20.07	20.48	20.89	21.29	21.70	22.11	22.52	22.93	23.33	23.74		24.15
8							21.02	21.32	21.63	21.93	22.24	22.54	22.85	23.16	23.46	23.77	24.07	24.38 24.68	24.99
9							21.49	21.82	22.14	22.46	22.78	23.11	23.43	23.75	24.07	24.40	24.72	25.04 25.36	25.69
10							21.99	22.34	22.68	23.02	23.37	23.71	24.05	24.40	24.74	25.08	25.42	25.77 26.11	26.45
11							22.52	22.89	23.25	23.61	23.98	24.34	24.70	25.06	25.43	25.79	26.15	26.52 26.88	27.24
12							23.08	23.47	23.85	24.24	24.62	25.01	25.39	25.78	26.17	26.55	26.94	27.32 27.71	28.09

Transitional Employee Rates — Effective 11/27/2004

Grade	Rate
1	10.85
2	11.01
3	11.19
4	12.43
5	13.21
6	14.03

PART-TIME REGULAR RATES

Grade	BB	AA	A	B	C	D	E	F	G	H	I	J	K	L	M	N	O	P	RC
1	12.54	13.00	13.46	13.93	14.39	14.85	15.31	15.78	16.24	16.70	17.16	17.63	18.09	18.55	19.01	19.48	20.07		20.54
2	13.07	13.53	13.99	14.45	14.90	15.36	15.82	16.28	16.73	17.19	17.65	18.11	18.56	19.02	19.48	19.94	20.45		20.91
3	13.60	14.06	14.51	14.96	15.42	15.87	16.32	16.78	17.23	17.68	18.14	18.59	19.04	19.50	19.95	20.40	20.86		21.31
4			15.32	15.75	16.18	16.60	17.03	17.45	17.88	18.31	18.73	19.16	19.59	20.01	20.44	20.87	21.29		21.72
5			16.11	16.51	16.92	17.32	17.73	18.13	18.53	18.94	19.34	19.74	20.15	20.55	20.96	21.36	21.76		22.17
6			16.95	17.33	17.71	18.09	18.47	18.85	19.23	19.61	19.99	20.38	20.76	21.14	21.52	21.90	22.28		22.66
7			17.34	17.73	18.12	18.51	18.91	19.30	19.69	20.08	20.47	20.87	21.26	21.65	22.04	22.44	22.83		23.22
8							20.21	20.50	20.80	21.09	21.38	21.68	21.97	22.26	22.56	22.85	23.15	23.44 23.73	24.03
9							20.67	20.98	21.29	21.60	21.91	22.22	22.53	22.84	23.15	23.46	23.77	24.08 24.39	24.70
10							21.15	21.48	21.81	22.14	22.47	22.80	23.13	23.46	23.79	24.12	24.45	24.78 25.11	25.44
11							21.66	22.01	22.36	22.70	23.05	23.40	23.75	24.10	24.45	24.80	25.15	25.50 25.85	26.19
12							22.19	22.56	22.93	23.31	23.68	24.05	24.42	24.79	25.16	25.53	25.90	26.27 26.64	27.01

AMERICAN POSTAL WORKERS UNION, AFL-CIO
William Burrus, President
1300 L Street, NW
Washington, DC 20005